HABERMAS

HABERMAS

Introduction and Analysis

DAVID INGRAM

Cornell University Press
Ithaca and London

Cornell University Press gratefully acknowledges support from the
Office of Research Services, Loyola University, which aided in the
publication of this book.

First published 2010 by Cornell University Press
First printing, Cornell Paperbacks, 2010

Printed in the United States of America

Library of Congress Cataloging-in-Publication Data

Ingram, David, 1952–
    Habermas : introduction and analysis / David Ingram.
        p. cm.
    Includes bibliographical references and index.
    ISBN 978-0-8014-4879-9 (cloth : alk. paper) —
    ISBN 978-0-8014-7601-3 (pbk. : alk. paper)
    1. Habermas, Jürgen.   2. Social sciences—
Philosophy.   I. Title.
    B3258.H234I55   2010
    193—dc22   2010004404

Cloth printing   10 9 8 7 6 5 4 3 2 1
Paperback printing   10 9 8 7 6 5 4 3 2 1

There is a place where Contrarieties are equally true

This place is called Beulah. It is a pleasant lovely Shadow

Where no dispute can come, because of those who sleep.

WILLIAM BLAKE, *Milton: Book the Second*

In Memory of

HANS SEIGFRIED and IRIS MARION YOUNG

Contents

List of Tables   xi
Preface   xiii
Abbreviations for Titles of Works by Habermas   xv

1: A Public Intellectual Committed to Reason   1
Habermas's Life   2
From the Critique of Ideology to the Dialectic
   of Enlightenment   12
Outline of Chapters   25

2: Habermas's Defense of Psychoanalytic Social Science   33
The Positivism Debate in German Social Science   34
Modern Nihilism: The Crisis of Science and the
   Theory/Practice Problem   40
Knowledge and Human Interests   44
A Critique of *Knowledge and Human Interests*   57

3: The Linguistic Turn   67
TCA and the Dialectic of Enlightenment   68
Situating Habermas's Philosophy of Language   72

Transcendental Philosophy of Language
   as Rational Reconstruction   74
Universal Pragmatics and Formal Semantics   77
Formal Pragmatics and Speech Act Theory   79
Discourse   81
Communicative and Strategic Speech Acts   83
A Critique of Universal Pragmatics   87

4: Knowledge and Truth Revisited   95
Subject-Object Paradigms of Knowledge   99
Internal Realism   101
Reference and Meaning   103
Knowledge and Evolution   109
Moral Realism   109
Is Formal Pragmatism a Defensible Alternative to
   Realism and Contextualism?   111

5: Discourse Ethics   115
Practical Reason: Delimiting the Domain of the Moral   116
The Priority of the Right over the Good   117
Modernity and Moral Development   118
Deontological Moral Theory and Universalizability:
   Kant and Rawls   122
Moral Cognitivism versus Moral Skepticism   127
Moral Argumentation as Discourse   129
Neo-Aristotelian Objections and the Abortion Controversy   138
Justification and Application   140
Discourse Ethics Applied: Genetic Testing and the
   Future of Human Nature   142
Problems and Paradoxes   144
Habermas's Ideal of Argumentation: A Final Assessment   146

6: Law and Democracy: Part I: The Foundational Rights   153
Modern Law and Morality: A Paradoxical Wedding
   of Facts and Norms   154
Situating Habermas's Theory of Law and Democracy:
   Some Contemporary Debates   155

The Sociological Genesis of Modern Law   161
The System of Rights   166
Negative and Positive Rights (Duties)   170
Constitutional Foundations   173
Human Rights: Subsistence as a Test Case for a Juridical
    Conception of Rights   175
Final Thoughts on the Procedural Ideal
    of Deliberative Democracy   189

7: Law and Democracy: Part II: Power and the Clash of Paradigms   193
Democracy and the Powers of Government   193
The Separation of Powers   197
The Transmission of Communicative Power: From Public
    Sphere to Government Administration   201
Discourse and Adjudication   206
The Proceduralist Paradigm of Law and Democracy   211
A Concluding Assessment   215

8: Law and Democracy: Part III: Applying the Proceduralist
    Paradigm   221
Separation of Church and State: The Public/Private Distinction   221
Gender Difference and the Law   229
Multiculturalism   234
Immigration   244

9: Law and Democracy: Part IV: Social Complexity and
    a Critical Assessment   253
Questioning the Proceduralist Paradigm   258
Substantive Economic Justice and Workplace Democracy   260
The Technological Dimension of Democracy   262
Revolution and Democracy   264

10: Crisis and Pathology: The Future of Democracy
    in a Global Age   267
Capitalism and the Crisis of Democracy   268
Social Pathologies and the Colonization of the Lifeworld   271
Globalization: The New Challenge   283

Cosmopolitan Democracy and Global Politics as a Response
to Global Crisis   285
Politics and the Rule of Law in International Relations   286
The Constitutionalization of International Relations   294
The Limits of Democratization: A Critical Assessment   301

11: Postsecular Postscript: Modernity and Its Discontents   307
Marx on the Evolution of Modern Society   310
Weber on Modernization and the Problem of Meaning   316
Secularization and the Rationalization of the Lifeworld   320
Between Past and Future: Art, Religion, and the Dialectic
of Enlightenment Revisited   323

Appendix A: Explaining Action   329
Appendix B: Understanding Action   331
Appendix C: Habermas and Brandom   335
Appendix D: Developmental Psychology   339
Appendix E: Rational Choice Theory   341
Appendix F: Systems Theory   345

Index   351

Tables

1. Transcendental constitution of experience   53

2. Taxonomy of knowledge   59

3. Components of speech acts   81

4. The formal pragmatic taxonomy of validity claims   82

5. Types of rationality   84

6. Types of social action   88

7. Levels of democracy: The flow of communicative, administrative, and social forms of power   202

8. Social evolutionary stages and their corresponding principles of organization   313

9. Marx's functionalist explanation of social crisis in capitalist society   348

Preface

This book was written with the express purpose of clarifying the philosophical arguments underlying the social theory of Jürgen Habermas. The biographical details and intellectual history presented in the first chapter lead directly to the second chapter's retrospective synopsis of Habermas's early writings on social science, psychoanalytic ideology critique, and knowledge-constitutive interests before turning, in chapters 3 and 4, to his writings from the first decade of the twenty-first century on philosophy of language and theory of knowledge. I then take up Habermas's moral and legal theories. Because of the intense interest that Habermas's discourse theory of rights and democracy has generated among philosophers, political scientists, and legal theorists, I have thought it prudent to devote five chapters to this topic alone. Particularly noteworthy is the discussion in chapter 10 of global democracy. The book concludes with a brief examination of Habermas's theory of modernity and his diagnosis of contemporary social pathologies. Here I return to the opening theme of chapter 1, the dialectic of enlightenment, and show how Habermas's views on religion and art bring him closer to his predecessors in the Frankfurt school than most commentators realize.

A few comments about the approach and content of the book are in order. Habermas's writings impose severe demands on even the most seasoned scholar. He writes on virtually every topic that has been taken up by philosophers and social scientists and does so in a systematic way. He writes dense prose and presumes that the reader has more than just passing familiarity with the many figures and theories he engages as counterpoints to his own thought. This book, however, does not presuppose any such familiarity. It aims to present

Habermas's ideas in the clearest way possible, without relying on technical language. It is unique in illustrating the practical implications of Habermas's abstract theory across a range of applications, extending from abortion and genetic engineering to human rights, multiculturalism, religion and politics, feminist theory, immigration, workplace democracy, and technology.

Parts of chapters 6 and 8 were published, respectively, under the following titles: "Of Sweatshops and Subsistence: Habermas on Human Rights" in *Ethics and Global Justice* 2/3 (Fall 2009): 193–217 and "Exceptional Justice? A Discourse Ethical Contribution to the Immigrant Question" in *Critical Horizons* 10/1 (April 2009): 1–30.

I thank the Michigan State University Department of Philosophy for generously funding a one-year research appointment as a Distinguished Visiting Professor in 2005–6, which enabled me to write the first draft of this book. I am especially grateful to MSU and Loyola University Chicago graduate students for their invaluable feedback in my Habermas seminars, and to Daniel Lorca, Drew Pierce, and Nathan Hopkins for their insightful advanced research on Habermas. Special thanks are owed to Bill Rehg, Cristina Lafont, J. D. Trout, Diana Meyers, David Schweickart, Asaf Bar-Tura, and Paul Leisen for their helpful comments, which I incorporated into revisions of this book. I am particularly grateful to my editor at Cornell University Press, Roger Haydon, for his strong advocacy of the book, and to Katy Meigs for her excellent copyediting. Last but not least, I thank Jennifer Parks, for her loving support in our philosophical and parental collaboration, and Sabina, Max, and Sam, for bringing joy to our lives.

Abbreviations for Titles of Works by Habermas

BFN   *Between Facts and Norms: Contributions to a Discourse Theory of Law and Democracy.* Trans. W. Rehg. Cambridge: MIT Press, 1996.

BNR   *Between Naturalism and Religion: Philosophical Essays.* Trans. C. Cronin. Cambridge: Polity Press, 2008.

BR   *A Berlin Republic: Writings on Germany.* Trans. S. Rendell. Lincoln: University of Nebraska Press, 1997.

CD   *Habermas: Critical Debates.* Ed. D. Held and J. Thompson. Cambridge: MIT Press, 1982.

CES   *Communication and the Evolution of Society.* Trans. T. McCarthy. Boston: Beacon Press, 1979.

DS   *The Dialectics of Secularization: On Reason and Religion,* with Joseph Cardinal Ratzinger (Pope Benedict XVI). Trans. B. McNeil. San Francisco: Ignatius Press, 2006.

DW   *The Divided West.* Trans. C. Cronan. Cambridge: Polity Press, 2006.

EFP   *Europe: The Faltering Project.* Trans. C. Cronin. Cambridge: Polity Press, 2009.

FHN   *The Future of Human Nature.* Trans. W. Rehg et al. Cambridge: Polity Press, 2003.

HAS   *Habermas: Autonomy and Solidarity: Interviews with Jürgen Habermas.* Trans. and ed. P. Dews. London: Verso, 1986.

HCU   "The Hermeneutic Claim to Universality." In *Contemporary Herme-neutics*. Ed. J. Bleicher. London: Routledge and Kegan Paul, 1980.

IO   *The Inclusion of the Other: Studies in Political Theory*. Trans. and ed. C. Cronin and P. De Greiff. Cambridge: MIT Press, 1998.

JA   *Justification and Application: Remarks on Discourse Ethics*. Trans. C. Cronin. Cambridge: MIT Press, 1993.

KHI   *Knowledge and Human Interests*. Trans. J. Shapiro. Boston: Beacon Press, 1971.

LC   *Legitimation Crisis*. Trans. T. McCarthy. Boston: Beacon Press, 1975.

LPS   *The Liberating Power of Symbols: Philosophical Essays*. Trans. P. Dews. Cambridge: MIT Press, 2001.

MCCA *Moral Consciousness and Communicative Action*. Trans. C. Lenhardt and S. W. Nicholsen. Cambridge: MIT Press, 1990.

MUP   "Modernity: An Unfinished Project." In *Critical Theory: The Essential Readings*. Ed. D. Ingram and J. Simon. Trans. S. W. Nicholsen. New York: Paragon House, 1991.

OLSS *On the Logic of the Social Sciences*. Trans. S. W. Nicholsen and J. Stark. Cambridge: MIT Press, 1988.

OPC   *On the Pragmatics of Communication*. Ed. M. Cooke. Cambridge: MIT Press, 1998.

PC   *The Postnational Constellation: Political Essays*. Trans. M. Pensky. Cambridge: MIT Press, 2001.

PDGS *The Positivist Dispute in German Sociology*, with T. Adorno et al. Trans. G. Adey and D. Frisby. New York: Harper and Row, 1976.

PDM   *The Philosophical Discourse of Modernity: Twelve Lectures*. Trans. F. Lawrence. Cambridge: MIT Press, 1987.

PKHI "A Postscript to Knowledge and Human Interests." *Philosophy of the Social Sciences* 3 (1973): 157–89.

PP   *Philosophical-Political Profiles*. Trans. F. Lawrence. Cambridge: MIT Press, 1983.

PSI   *On the Pragmatics of Social Interaction: Preliminary Studies in the Theory of Communicative Action*. Trans. and ed. B. Fultner. Cambridge: MIT Press, 2001.

PT   *Postmetaphysical Thinking*. Trans. W. M. Hohengarten. Cambridge: MIT Press, 1992.

QC   "Questions and Counter-Questions," *Praxis International* 4/3 (1984).

RC   "A Reply to My Critics." In *Habermas: Critical Debates* (see *CD* above).

REPLY "A Reply." In *Communicative Action: Essays on Jürgen Habermas's "The Theory of Communicative Action."* Ed. A. Honneth and H. Joas. Cambridge: MIT Press, 1991.

RR   *Religion and Rationality: Essays on Reason, God, and Modernity,* Ed. E. Mendietta. Cambridge: MIT Press, 2002.

STPS   *The Structural Transformation of the Public Sphere: An Inquiry into a Category of Bourgeois Society.* Trans. T. Burger. Cambridge: MIT Press, 1989.

TCA 1   *The Theory of Communicative Action.* Volume 1: *Reason and the Rationalization of Society.* Trans. T. McCarthy. Boston: Beacon Press, 1984.

TCA 2   *The Theory of Communicative Action.* Volume 2: *Lifeworld and System: A Critique of Functionalist Reason.* Trans. T. McCarthy. Boston: Beacon Press, 1987.

TJ   *Truth and Justification.* Trans. and ed. B. Fultner. Cambridge: MIT Press, 2003.

TP   *Theory and Practice.* Trans. and ed. J. Viertel. Boston: Beacon Press, 1973.

TRS   *Toward a Rational Society.* Trans. and ed. J. Shapiro. Boston: Beacon Press, 1970.

TT   *Time of Transitions.* Trans. and ed. C. Cronin and M. Pensky. Cambridge: Polity Press, 2006.

HABERMAS

1

A Public Intellectual Committed to Reason

Philosophers are often dismissed for having their heads in the clouds—in a word, for being irrelevant to the ways of the world. But history tells a different story. Ideas *can* have world-transforming consequences. This was true of the eighteenth-century period known as the Enlightenment—a period that witnessed the American and French revolutions. And it is true today. The philosopher whose ideas are examined in this book—whose entire life has been devoted to showing how freedom, equality, and rational enlightenment are embedded in our everyday speech—has not only revolutionized the academy. He has revolutionized the politics of his native Germany and continues to affect the politics of Europe and Asia.

Jürgen Habermas is indisputably an international star in the pantheon of living thinkers, but he is also a public intellectual who has engaged political and religious leaders.[1] Few have measured the breadth of academic learning as deeply as he has; science, religion, history, politics, literature, and art are but a few of the intellectual pathways along which he has journeyed. His contributions to philosophy are of special note. In addition to his original interpretation of the history of modern philosophy since Descartes, he has developed a new system of ideas encompassing language and communication, knowledge and reason, ethics and law, science and technology, economics and democracy,

---

1. On January 19, 2004, Habermas met Cardinal Joseph Ratzinger (now Pope Benedict XVI) at the Catholic Academy of Bavaria to discuss the topic "Pre-Political Foundations of the Democratic State" (published in *DS*). On June 5–6, 1998, he met with Gerhard Schroeder, German chancellor from 1998 to 2005, at the Willy Brandt Haus in Berlin to discuss "the inclusion of the other."

as well as individual cognitive development and social evolution. This systematic grasp of the human condition in all its facets has gained him the reputation for being a formidable spokesperson on behalf of public policies that advance equal rights and the common good, at home and abroad.

These ideals are now under attack. In an age racked by the extremes of religious fundamentalism and scientific skepticism, Habermas has emerged as the leading defender of the Enlightenment's faith in reason as a guide to morality and politics. While many academics have embraced the postmodern view that reason designates only a subculture within Western civilization and one, moreover, that perpetuates the destruction of traditional community and the rise of capitalist exploitation and bureaucratic domination,[2] Habermas has staunchly maintained that reason resides at the very heart of human communication, which he believes is the great engine for human emancipation.

For some, like American philosopher Richard Rorty, Habermas's obsession with defending reason amounts to "scratching where it doesn't itch," since "reason" is mainly just the name of a philosophical parlor game whose importance to civilization is overrated and whose validity is largely relative to Western culture.[3] Others, taking an opposite tack, maintain that reason is indeed centrally embodied in such institutions as science, human rights, and democracy but that the need to defend these institutions philosophically is unnecessary since their ultimate global dominance in the future is assured.[4] The upsurge of religious fundamentalism and the politics of "might makes right" during the first decade of the twenty-first century now suggests that these dismissals of philosophical enlightenment are premature.

Habermas's Life

Habermas's enlightenment project has a long history, dating back to his experiences growing up in Nazi Germany. Hitler presented his fascist dictatorship as the exact antithesis of the liberal, democratic humanism heralded by the Enlightenment. For Hitler, universal humanity was a myth of reason that was at odds with the world historical destiny of the German people as the

2. The term "postmodernism" designates a criticism of reason, conceived as a universal and certain foundation for knowledge and morality, and of modern culture, understood as a progressive unfolding of knowledge and morality. Postmodern themes regarding the fragmentation (or deconstruction) of reason bear on sociological dislocations associated with multiculturalism, the destruction of tradition, the dissolution of autonomous moral agency, and the delegitimation of scientific and political forms of authority. See J.-F. Lyotard, *The Postmodern Condition: A Report on Knowledge* (Minneapolis: University of Minnesota Press, 1984).

3. R. Rorty, "Habermas and Lyotard on Postmodernism," in *Essays on Heidegger and Others: Philosophical Papers*, vol. 2 (Cambridge: Cambridge University Press, 1991). I discuss Habermas's differences with Rorty in chapter 3 of this book.

4. F. Fukuyama, *The End of History and the Last Man* (New York: Free Press, 1992).

"master race." Most Germans embraced this vision, including the citizens of Gummersbach, where Habermas (b. 1929, Düsseldorf) grew up. His father, who directed the Bureau of Trade and Industry in the town, followed most Germans in adapting to the Nazi regime that came to power in 1933. Although young Habermas suffered from a debilitating speech impediment that stigmatized him as something of an outsider,[5] he himself appears to have accepted the "normalcy" of a regime that was premised on racist ideals of biological perfection. In any case, he was deemed fit enough to be drafted into the Hitler Youth in 1939 and to serve as a first-aid instructor after this indoctrination movement was converted over to a military reserve for homeland defense in 1944.

Habermas tells us that he was shocked out of his intellectual slumber shortly after the war when he watched documentary footage of the Nuremberg trials and concentration camp atrocities. With his country devastated by war and divided into mutually hostile Soviet and pro-Western governments, his people cast into material deprivation and spiritual chaos, he yearned for a radical political break with the past. Seeking to confirm this impulse intellectually, he turned to the antirationalist existential thought of two philosophers. The first was Jean-Paul Sartre (1905–80), a former activist in the French Resistance whose *Being and Nothingness* was all the rage of postwar Europe. The second was Martin Heidegger (1889–1976), a former Nazi who, as rector of the University of Freiburg, had overseen the purge of Jewish academics and students. Eventually, Habermas's pacifism in the face of the nuclear threat unleashed by the cold war and his growing commitment to social democracy collided with these earlier existential leanings. For, while Sartre may have interpreted existential choice in a humanistic way that required active commitment to the Enlightenment ideal of individual freedom and responsibility, Heidegger understood it to imply resolutely harnessing one's will to the nation's destiny.

Heidegger's radical critique of rationalist philosophy that dated back to Plato (428–347 BCE)—not his elitist and authoritarian understanding of authentic existence—was what drew Habermas to his philosophy. This fascination could not have endured long given Heidegger's refusal to apologize for his involvement in the Nazi Party—something that most German academics, including Habermas's own dissertation advisers, had done. The final break was precipitated by a new edition of Heidegger's *An Introduction to Metaphysics* (1935/1953), which retained the original reference to the greatness of the Nazi vision.[6]

---

5. Habermas traces his "heightened sensitivity to the social nature of human beings [and] the intersubjective constitution of the human mind" to feelings of dependence and vulnerability he experienced from being born with a cleft palate. He remarks that his reluctance to speak "without a script" led him to appreciate the "theoretically important distinction" between ordinary, unproblematic communication and rational discourse, which is characterized by precision and deliberate reflection (*BNR* 14–16).

6. Habermas was attracted to a Kierkegaardian reading of Heidegger that drew from aspects of Heidegger's pre-Nazi thought (chiefly from *Being and Time* [1927]) that emphasized the appeal to

Only Habermas's deep appreciation of Sartre and the ethical writings of the nineteenth-century Christian existentialist Søren Kierkegaard (1813–55) prevented him from rejecting existentialism outright.[7] From this point on, his growing appreciation of philosophical rationalism began to converge with his political sympathies. But these sympathies once again pulled him toward conflicting philosophies: Marxism and liberalism. After he completed his dissertation on the German philosopher Friedrich Wilhelm Joseph von Schelling (1775–1854) in 1954 (at Bonn, under the directorship of Erich Rothacker),[8] Habermas went to Frankfurt to study humanistic Marxism at the Frankfurt Institute for Social Research (founded in 1923), whose leading members had recently returned from their long exile in the United States. During the cold war, Marxism was commonly identified with the totalitarian Communism associated with the Soviet Union, whose leaders claimed Karl Marx (1818–83) as their ideological founder.[9] In fact, Marx was critical of the modern state and

---

"individual conscience, to the individual's existential sincerity." Habermas responded to the publication of Heidegger's 1935 lectures with a newspaper article, "Thinking with Heidegger against Heidegger," in which he took issue with Heidegger's linking of "creative violence" with a "cult of sacrifice"; his dismissal of publicly accessible analysis in favor of esoteric, philosophical revelation; his rejection of the "egalitarian universalism of the Enlightenment"; and his "denial of moral and political responsibility for the consequences of the mass criminality" associated with a "destiny of Being" that culminated in Nazism (BNR 20).

7. As of 2000, Habermas was still favorably contrasting Kierkegaard's intersubjective account of authentically becoming one's own individual self through the despairing recognition of one's inadequacy (sinfulness) and dependency on the redeeming aid of another (God) to Sartre's radically voluntaristic, subject-centered choice of oneself as a "project" and Heidegger's fatalistic submission to the "call" of one's primal cultural identity (EFP 25–28, 31–34). Habermas's critique of Heidegger's existentialism also stands in marked contrast to his appreciation of the existential philosophies of communication developed by Karl Jaspers and his (and Heidegger's) former student, Hannah Arendt (LPS 30–45; PP 45–52, 171–88).

8. J. Habermas, Das Absolute und die Geschichte: Von der Zwiespältigkeit in Schellings Denken [The Absolute and History: About the Schismatic Nature of Schelling's Thought]. In Schelling, Habermas found a philosopher, inspired by Romanticism and Jewish philosophy, who denied that nature was a pure mechanism capable of being known and dominated by analytical technological reason. Like Heidegger, Schelling appealed to aesthetic experience in understanding the primal identity of subject and object, unconsciousness and consciousness, necessity and freedom. Unlike Heidegger, he saw nature as striving to realize itself as conscious life. In later life, Schelling condemned the intellectual will for its detachment from divine nature and moral conscience (the impersonal soul)—a sin that Schelling ascribed to humanity's hubris and that Habermas later implicated in the Holocaust—and urged relief from subjective striving through self-renunciation. (Note the parallel between this critique of instrumental reason and Adorno and Horkheimer's Dialectic of Enlightenment.) Habermas would later argue that redemption of a fallen (objectified) nature provided a naturalistic humanism that was far superior to Heidegger's volkisch-conservative "call to Being." See Habermas's writings: "Schelling und die 'Submission unter das Höhere,'" Frankfurter Allgemeine Zeitung (August 21, 1954); "Karl Jaspers über Schelling," Frankfurter Allgemeine Zeitung (January 14, 1956); "Ernst Bloch: A Marxist Schelling" (PP 61–77); as well as A. D. Moses, Germans and the Nazi Past (Cambridge: Cambridge University, 2007), esp. 115–30.

9. Marx wrote as a philosopher, journalist, political propagandist, historian, social scientist, and economist. He and his lifelong friend and collaborator, Friedrich Engels, wrote The Communist Manifesto in 1847 for the Communist League, and its popularity may have influenced the Revolution of 1848. Following the failure of the revolution, Marx and Engels moved to England where Marx

its complicity in dominating and oppressing individuals. Marx was also critical of liberal political philosophy, because he believed that its defense of individual rights served to justify the domination and exploitation of the working class by the capitalist class.[10] But the leading members of the Frankfurt school—Herbert Marcuse (1898–1979); Max Horkheimer (1895–1973); and Theodor Adorno (1903–69), whom Habermas assisted until 1959—noted that Marx's critique of liberal freedom and equality was really a critique of the capitalist state's failure to realize freedom and equality in a way that would be meaningful and effective for all persons, and not just wealthy capitalists. So their humanistic Marxism conflicted not with liberal ideals but with the social and political reality in which those ideals were embedded. More precisely, their use of the so-called dialectical method—first developed by Johann Gottlieb Fichte (1762–1814) and Schelling and perfected by Marx's chief inspiration, Georg Wilhelm Friedrich Hegel (1770–1831)—involved showing how liberal ideals simultaneously legitimate and contradict modern capitalism.

In essence, the kind of humanistic Marxism endorsed by the Frankfurt school, which Horkheimer euphemistically dubbed "critical theory" so as to avoid confusion with Soviet Marxism,[11] involved synthesizing philosophical idealism,

---

became deeply involved in the leadership of the International Workingmen's Association (also known as the First International), which was founded in 1864. There Marx argued that a market system based on wage labor was inherently exploitative, since the profits garnered by capitalists consisted in value added by living labor that was not remunerated to the laborers. Besides criticizing the injustice built into the system of wage labor, Marx provided ample statistical and narrative documentation of the brutal conditions endured by women, children, and men in England's factories. His historical account of the emergence of capitalism and the importance of technological innovation in lowering labor costs in price competition between capitalists led him to predict that capitalism would eventually collapse under its own weight. In short, as more workers were replaced by machines and the value-adding component of labor was reduced, the overall rate of profit throughout the economy would eventually decline and consumption would lag behind production, thereby leading to chronic and increasingly worsening business cycles. Eventually, Marx predicted, the mass of impoverished, overworked (or underemployed) workers would organize themselves politically (in part thanks to capitalism's efficient organization of the working class) and replace the system with a "dictatorship of the proletariat" in which productive property would be owned in common, wage labor would be abolished, and the entire history of economic class domination—from ancient slavery on—would come to an end.

10. Marx never denied that rights represented an important advance beyond feudal privileges. He maintained, however, that they were compatible with capitalist exploitation and economic coercion of the working class and so could not be the final form of human emancipation. However, he conceded that during the transition from capitalism to communism rights guaranteeing formal equality would still play an important role. K. Marx, "On the Jewish Question" (1843) and "Critique of the Gotha Programme" (1875), in *Karl Marx: Selected Writings,* ed. L. Simon (Indianapolis: Hackett, 1994), 2–26, 316–32.

11. Soviet Marxism is an outgrowth of the orthodox Marxist appropriation of Marx's later writings—chiefly *Capital*—by Karl Kautsky, Georgi Plekhanov, and other thinkers associated with the Second and Third Internationals. Reading *Capital* as an exemplar of "scientific socialism" (as Engels referred to it) that eschewed utopian moral exhortation in favor of a cold description of the "iron laws" of economic development, orthodox Marxists were inclined to accept the inevitable collapse of capitalism. At the same time, many of them observed that conditions in some

mainly that of Immanuel Kant and Hegel, and social scientific realism, mainly that of Marx and Max Weber (1864–1920).[12] Accordingly, Habermas, whose education had heretofore centered on philosophy, was forced to reeducate himself one more time. His immersion in sociology and economics during his residence at the institute made him a master philosopher of social science. As for other formative influences, the institute was especially famous for integrating the insights of Freudian psychotherapy into its method of social criticism. Marcuse's 1956 lectures on Sigmund Freud (1856–1939) proved especially seminal for Habermas in this regard.[13] Indeed, many scholars consider Habermas's first major book, *Knowledge and Human Interests* (1968), which I discuss in

countries (notably Russia) were not ripe enough for revolution due to the undeveloped state of industry, while others observed that the capitalist welfare state that was beginning to emerge in Germany would simply evolve into socialism as a matter of course. Given the backward state of Russian industry in comparison to that of western Europe, the Russian Bolsheviks headed by Lenin adopted the view that only a vanguard party of intellectual elites could compel a hesitant working class and a backward peasant class to seize the revolutionary moment. By contrast, the Austrian neo-Marxism of Max Adler, Otto Bauer, Rudolf Hilferding, and Carl Grünberg (who was to serve as the first director of the Frankfurt Institute for Social Research, whose views are known as the Frankfurt school) affirmed the importance of democratic political struggle and the role of culture and ideology in advancing or hindering the working class. Paradoxically, this renewed interest in the importance of ideology and moral idealism conspired with a less-than-revolutionary social reality to consign neo-Marxism to the academy where, in contrast to the overtly political nature of Bolshevik Marxism, it preoccupied itself with philosophical questions concerning the social nature of knowledge and the rational grounds of social critique. The development of a more Hegelian interpretation of Marxism by Karl Korsch and Georg Lukács, which emphasized the importance of a nonscientific form of practical reason in penetrating the veil of ideology and passive self-understanding, coupled with the discovery and eventual publication (1932) of Marx's youthful humanistic writings, such as the fragments from *Economic and Philosophic Manuscripts* (1844) and *The German Ideology* (1845–46), lent further impetus to this redirection of Marxism. The *Manuscripts* sketch a philosophical anthropology, largely influenced by the radical Hegelian philosopher and theologian Ludwig Feuerbach, which examines the alienation of workers in capitalist society. In it Marx finds all modern industrial forms alienating, including varieties of crude communism that impose totalitarian leveling. By contrast, authentic communism affirms the strivings of individuals for freedom and fulfillment. Hence, it stands opposed to the simple "redistribution" of property and "leveling" of distinctions championed by Soviet-style Communism. Although Habermas, like most his predecessors in the Frankfurt school, is deeply influenced by this humanistic strand of Marxism (see chapter 11 of this book) he nonetheless criticizes Marx's own misunderstanding of his critical theory as a predictive science. See chapter 2 of this book and D. Ingram, *Critical Theory and Philosophy* (New York: Paragon House, 1990).

12. Weber is considered to be one of the founding fathers of modern social science. A member of the committee that submitted the first draft of Germany's first republican government (the Weimar Republic of 1919–33), he was a liberal who supported democracy for pragmatic reasons and remained highly distrustful of bureaucratic socialism. Weber assimilated much of Marx's critique of capitalism and empathized with the plight of the working class. However, he jettisoned Marx's economic explanations of social behavior in favor of explanations that took into account the complex mutual interweaving of economic interests and cultural ideas (see chapters 2 and 9 of this book).

13. See S. Freud, *Group Psychology and the Analysis of the Ego,* trans. J. Strachey (New York: Bantam Books, 1960); H. Marcuse, *Five Lectures* (Boston: Beacon Press, 1970); T. Adorno, "Freudian Theory and the Pattern of Fascist Propaganda," in *Critical Theory: The Essential Readings,* ed. D. Ingram and J. Simon (New York: Paragon House, 1992), 84–102; and E. Fromm,

chapter 2, as culminating the institute's development of psychoanalytic social critique. According to this critique, mass social delusion (ideology) and unthinking conformity to rigid patterns of authority are social neuroses grounded in societal repression of basic instincts that aim at individual and social fulfillment.[14]

As Habermas became more convinced of the importance of unlimited and "undistorted" communication in furthering emancipation from ideological delusions, he also became more committed to the idea of an open and democratic society. Forced to leave Frankfurt due to clashes with his former mentors (particularly Horkheimer, who had become increasingly hostile to his left-wing brand of social democracy),[15] Habermas was invited by two former Heidegger students, Hans-Georg Gadamer (1900–2002) and Karl Löwith (1897–1973), to take up the Extraordinary Professorship of Philosophy at Heidelberg. That same year (1961) he applied for a second doctorate in political science (at Marburg, under the direction of Wolfgang Abendroth),[16] and within the short span of just three years, in a stunning turn

---

"The Method and Function of an Analytic Social Psychology," *The Essential Frankfurt School Reader*, ed. A. Arato and E. Gebhardt (New York: Continuum, 1982), 477–97.

14. By "ideology" Marx meant any idea that justifies the nondominating nature of class hierarchies. *The German Ideology* describes ideologies as abstract ideas that falsely deny the inequality and unfreedom of society as it exists. Marx had in mind modern philosophical views about human nature that proclaim—in the name of universal reason or universal humanity—the equal status of all humans, thereby insinuating that the factory worker is just as free and equal as his or her employer when it comes to owning and exchanging property. Marx also gave a genetic account of ideology as any view created by a dominant class in order to advance its interests. Although Marx appears to commit a "genetic fallacy" (which assumes that the genesis of a belief determines its truth or falsity), there is a sense in which the genesis of a belief determines our assessment of its reliability. Any belief that emerges from partial experiences, irrational thought processes, or indoctrination must be considered inherently suspect. However, since no belief about society is acquired independently of social constraint, we are left with the troubling notion that all such beliefs are ideologically suspect. To delimit ideological beliefs from other social beliefs we must appeal to their function in maintaining social domination. The Frankfurt school's emphasis on psychic repression and other pathological processes of belief (de)formation and neurotic reaction formation deploys both genetic and functional conceptions of ideology. The result was a powerful psychoanalytic form of ideology critique. See Ingram, *Critical Theory and Philosophy;* and R. Geuss, *The Idea of Critical Theory* (Cambridge: Cambridge University Press, 1981).

15. In a long letter to Adorno (September 27, 1958), Horkheimer expressed his dislike of Habermas, whom he feared was "setting the tone in the institute" with a recent publication in which he cited the early Marx in defense of what seemed to Horkheimer to be a revolutionary politics. While predicting that "Habermas has a good, and probably brilliant, career ahead of him," Horkheimer maintained that Habermas was damaging the pro-Western reputation of the institute (and thereby threatening its capacity to attract funding) by presenting a simplistic Marxist interpretation of Horkheimer's and Adorno's ideas that overlooked their skepticism about drawing practical consequences from philosophical theory and the liberating potential of modern revolutionary movements that endanger constitutional limits on state power. See J. Habermas, "Zur philosophischen Diskussion um Marx und Marxismus," *Philosophical Rundschau* 5/3–4 (1957); and "Max Horkheimer to Theodor Adorno," quoted in Detlev Claussen, *Theodor W. Adorno: One Last Genius,* trans. R. Livingston (Cambridge: Harvard University Press, 2008), 343–53.

16. German academics are required to write a second dissertation in order to be eligible for a full-time teaching post. Habermas's *Habilitationschrift,* later published in translation under the

of events, he was appointed chair of Philosophy and Sociology at the Institute for Social Research in Frankfurt (1964). By now he was well positioned to take a leading role, along with Marcuse, as chief faculty spokesperson for the prodemocracy student movement that had arisen in response to a conservative German bureaucracy and its support for the American-led cold war strategy that included U.S. military installations and missile sites in Germany, a hostile policy toward socialist movements in the Third World, and a war in Vietnam. A fervent critic of the Vietnam War and the German government's attempts to curtail freedom of speech, he was more sympathetic to radical students' demands for greater participation in running the university than either Horkheimer or Adorno were (although he was not as sympathetic as Marcuse was to their revolutionary political aims and their use of disruptive tactics in obtaining them).[17]

By 1970 Habermas's belief that unlimited and undistorted communication was basic to both political action and knowledge led him to reconsider his former knowledge-centered conception of critical theory in favor of one founded on a theory of communicative action. From this point on he increasingly focused his attention on linguistics, philosophy of language, and the relationship between moral development and the acquisition of rational communicative competence. In 1971 he left Frankfurt to become codirector with Carl Friedrich von Weizsäcker of the Max Planck Institute in Starnberg, where he deepened this line of inquiry. In 1981, two years before his return to Frankfurt, he compiled this research in his two-volume magnum opus, *Theorie des kommunikativen Handelns* [*The Theory of Communicative Action*. Volume One. *Reason and the Rationalization of Society* (1984) and Volume Two. *Lifeworld*

---

title *The Structural Transformation of the Public Sphere* (1962), had earlier been rejected by both Horkheimer and Adorno for being too Marxist. Ironically, the original inspiration for the book may have been an idea developed by the archconservative legal theorist and former Nazi, Carl Schmitt (1888–1985). In his *The Crisis of Parliamentary Democracy* (1923–26) Schmitt had argued that the principle of parliamentary liberalism, which required that a general consensus on common interests be reached through rational, disinterested, and open discussion, had been undermined by the partisan, propagandistic politics of modern mass democracy based on strategic compromises favoring the powerful. *The Crisis of Parliamentary Democracy,* trans. E. Kennedy (Cambridge: MIT Press, 1988), 3, 5–6. Habermas accepted this indictment of mass democracy (*STPS* 81, 205) while rejecting Schmitt's Rousseauian thesis that democracy implies the undivided rule of a sovereign (even dictatorial) will in opposition to liberalism's "will-less" dialogue of dissonant voices.

17. Habermas's invocation of the term "Left Fascism" at a conference on democracy and the university held in Hanover on June 9, 1967, arose with reference to student leader Rudi Dutschke's call for "direct action" in response to the police killing of activist Benno Ohnesorg. Habermas thought Dutschke's call might stir up unconstrained mass revolt using violent tactics that resembled those used by Italian Fascists in the 1920s—a misapprehension that was repudiated by Dutschke and implicitly by Marcuse as a sign of how far Habermas had fallen out of touch with the student movement. Habermas later retracted his characterization as an "overreaction" in a 1977 *Der Spiegel* interview. For a full account of this episode, see M. Matustik, *Jürgen Habermas: A Philosophical-Political Profile* (Lanham, MD: Rowman and Littlefield, 2001), 49–54.

and System. A Critique of Functionalist Reason (1987)]. A work of breathtaking scope, it shows how the emergence of communicative action is central to the evolution of modern society. It also explains how economic and administrative tendencies within modern society undermine the democratic ideals implicit in communicative interaction. For Habermas, these tendencies endanger the social and natural environments so essential to promoting and preserving vibrant families and communities. This concern about maintaining the integrity of our "lifeworld"—the implicit background of shared understanding and communication that gives our lives meaning, purpose, and cohesion—explains why he has long been a supporter of profeminist, anti-nuke, and limited economic growth positions associated with the German Green Party.

The 1980s marked a period in which Habermas developed his theory with an eye toward practical applications in the area of theoretical ethics. While he and his colleague Karl-Otto Apel (b. 1922) were developing their new "discourse ethic" in Frankfurt,[18] Habermas set about vigorously defending what he called the "project of modernity" and its rational foundations against a wide assortment of antimodernist critics: traditionalists, conservatives, and so-called postmodernists. The latter group, following the thought of nineteenth-century philosopher Friedrich Nietzsche (1844–1900), saw reason as but one among many particular perspectives an isolated subject might choose or reject, and one whose promise of enlightenment, emancipation, and progress was belied by cold economic calculus and amoral social engineering.

Habermas shares the conservatives' and postmodernists' concerns about a scientific and technological culture set adrift from morality. His recent attack on human cloning and genetic enhancement is one in a long succession of critiques of social engineering that attests to this. Yet, unlike conservatives and postmodernists, he maintains that the substitution of self-interested calculation for moral thinking is not definitive of the Enlightenment but only of its one-sided "scientistic" articulation, which neglects the foundation of reason in "communicative *intersubjectivity.*"

Habermas's attempts to trace this "dialectic of enlightenment" (as Adorno and Horkheimer dubbed it) back to its origins in Kant's transcendental philosophy of "subject-centered" reason (see below) coincided with a real-life debate about modern subjectivity that brought him face-to-face with an old nemesis: German nationalism.[19] This debate, which was covered in all of Germany's

---

18. See Habermas's tribute to Apel's pioneering research on the ideal speech situation and discourse ethics in *LPS* 66–77.

19. J. Habermas, *The New Conservatism: Cultural Criticism and the Historians' Debate*, ed. and trans. S. W. Nicholsen (Cambridge: MIT Press, 1989). The debate centered on whether (and how) Germans should cultivate a sense of patriotism in the wake of the catastrophe of World War II. Chancellor Helmut Kohl had urged Germans to put the past behind them and join the community of nations with Germany as a leading economic and geopolitical power. The crowning moment was staged when he and President Ronald Reagan honored Germany's soldiers at the Kolmeshohe military cemetery in Bitburg on May 5, 1985. The staging of this event had already been prepared

leading newspapers and journals, concerned nothing less than the fate of German identity at the dawn of German reunification. With the emergence of Germany as the leading economic power in Europe, revisionist historians in the 1980s were arguing that Germans should cease feeling guilty about their nation's Nazi past and adopt a more forgiving and balanced attitude toward Hitler's expansionist policies. Coinciding with the resurgence of nationalism and neo-Nazi activism, a strong (and at times racist) reaction arose against Germany's foreign guest workers, who were mainly Turkish and Yugoslavian. Later, during the Yugoslav civil war of the early 1990s, public opinion turned against Germany's postwar Basic Law that required the admission of political refugees and asylum seekers.

In opposition to this reactionary nationalism, Habermas urged his compatriots to question the exclusionary racial prejudices underlying their patriotism. In place of the old patriotism he sought to substitute a "constitutional patriotism" that would acknowledge the rational ideals of democratic inclusion implicit in Germany's postwar constitution. Such patriotism, he hoped, might incline Germans to extend the privileges of citizenship to guest workers and permanent refugees as well as including all Germans in the process of deciding the terms under which East and West Germany might be reunified as "equal partners" in a new social contract.[20]

Habermas's contribution to these debates reflected his own philosophy that personal and social identity—indeed, all socialization and transmission of tradition—are products of communicative interaction in which the "other" person (or culture) necessarily informs how we understand ourselves. The standpoint

---

by the whitewashing of Germany's war of aggression in revisionary historical writings by Joachim Fest, Klaus Hildebrand, Andreas Hillgruber, Ernst Nolte, and Michael Stürmer, who attempted to recast Germany's soldiers as heroes who defended not only Germans but Western Europeans from the onslaught of Stalin's Red Army. Habermas was appalled by both their manipulation of historical research for apologist political ends and their appeal to a regressive ethnocentric form of patriotism. For Habermas, ethnic pride, by contrast, should give way to pride in Germany's provisional Basic Law, which was imposed on Germans by the victorious Allies at the conclusion of World War II. Matustik, *Philosophical-Political Profile*, 131–39.

20. Following the collapse of the Berlin Wall on November 9, 1989, intense debate raged over how to reunify East and West Germany. Kohl invoked Article 23 of the Basic Law, which contains a provision for incorporating new states into the German Federal Republic, but Habermas thought that this expedient—chosen by Kohl to lift his popularity—represented a missed opportunity by Germans to discuss and create an entirely new liberal, social democratic order. Furthermore, Habermas believed that the Kohl government's imposition of economic and political reforms on a hesitant East Germany would create new resentments, as older ways of life were simply swept aside. Finally, Habermas feared that the costs of forced economic integration and development on both sides of the East-West divide might unleash new social unrest and new forms of ethnocentric nationalism—a fear that was later confirmed when disgruntled unemployed Germans attacked foreign guest workers in Rostock and Hoyerswerda in the former East Germany shortly after reunification. See J. Habermas, "Yet Again German National Identity—A Nation of Angry DM-Burghers?" in *When the Wall Came Down: Reactions to German Unification*, ed. H. James and M. Stone (New York: Routledge, 1992); Matustik, *Philosophical-Political Profile*, 170–74; J. G. Finlayson, *Habermas: A Very Short Introduction* (Oxford: Oxford University Press, 2005), 128–31.

of the other, and ultimately of a generalized other—humanity—is always one that each of us brings to bear when questioning who we are.

The renewed interest in a humanism that is as universal and cosmopolitan as it is particular and multicultural inaugurated a new phase in Habermas's philosophy that continues to inform his thinking. One aspect of his thinking concerns the relationship between constitutional law and democratic institutions, the two pillars legitimating the modern state. Habermas argues that the universal ideals of rational discourse he had earlier thought essential to ethics also apply to legal and political institutions, albeit in a different and more complicated way. Above all, these ideals suggest that individual rights and democracy are more intimately linked than political philosophers have hitherto conceded.

The second aspect concerns his belief that the concept of the nation-state that had once been so central to the formation of European constitutional democracy in the nineteenth and early twentieth centuries is no longer tenable in its original form. Not only do constitutions imply universal rights that transcend national boundaries, but global economic and political realities—not to mention global communication networks—increasingly limit the internal sovereignty of the state from the outside. In particular, Habermas believes that disparities in wealth and power within and between countries generated by neoliberal economic policies reflecting the American consensus—policies that promote free trade, deregulation and privatization of industries and utilities, and downsizing of government bureaucracies—threaten to undermine the health, education, welfare, and social solidarity requisite for maintaining stable and legitimate democracies. Habermas's proposal to limit these and other unwanted side effects of globalization revolve around the development of supranational governing bodies (as exemplified by the European Union and the United Nations) and the promotion of transnational social movements and nongovernmental organizations.

By the 1990s Habermas was advocating that the UN change its original mandate from that of peacekeeper to defender of human rights. This idea found expression in a number of controversial positions he adopted with respect to the use of military force in stanching human rights violations. On the one hand, grievous human rights violations led him to support the 1991 UN-sanctioned Persian Gulf War, which was provoked by Iraq's invasion of Kuwait, as well as the 1999 NATO-led intervention against Yugoslavia over its violent military escapade in Kosovo. On the other hand, he objected—again on human rights grounds—to the conduct of these interventions, which caused heavy civilian casualties. In 2003 he criticized the U.S. invasion of Iraq for bypassing UN approval and violating international conventions governing warfare (*DW* 26–36, 85–112, 179–82). Reflecting further on the "war against terror" has also led him to reconsider the so-called clash of civilizations (as Samuel Huntington famously phrased it) dividing West and East. (Habermas's culture-bridging ventures include a trip to Iran in 2002, where his work has been widely read by leading intellectuals and liberal-democratic reformers, including former Iranian president Mohammad Khatami.) Criticizing all forms of ideological fundamentalism—Western as well as Eastern, religious as well as secular—he has returned once more to examining the dialectical relationship between reason and religion, a relationship, he insists, that rightly favors reason in all matters affecting basic rights and policies (*DW* 3–25).

From the Critique of Ideology to the Dialectic of Enlightenment

Now that we have some idea about Habermas's career as a public intellectual, I would like to conclude by briefly examining the two philosophical issues that have dominated his thought since the 1960s: the concept of social critique (or more precisely, ideology critique) and the dialectic of enlightenment. Habermas's predecessors at the Frankfurt Institute responded to these issues in different ways, but by and large they agreed that social critique had to be *immanent* critique, drawing its standards of critique from the very society it was criticizing rather than from some transcendent or external source, such as pure (universal) reason. During World War II, their view on the proper grounding of social critique was all the more confirmed (in their minds) by what they perceived to be the sinister effects of reason (or enlightenment) on modern society. In their opinion, the diffusion of rational methods of thinking throughout society ends up undermining the very values of freedom, equality, and universal human solidarity that the diffusion of reason is supposed to promote.

Habermas takes issue with both of these assessments. First, let us begin with the issue of social critique. First-generation critical theorists argued that social critique—by which they meant exposing the injustice and unhappiness of society—was the chief responsibility of the critical theorist. To carry out this enterprise the critical theorist needed to be guided by theoretical norms of justice and happiness. But unless these norms resonated with the real historical needs and aspirations of social agents whose society was being criticized as unjust and unhappy, they would not be able to persuade these agents to change their society for the better. The whole point of social critique—to get social agents to see that their society is unjust and unhappy by criteria that they themselves would endorse upon reflection—would be undermined. So first-generation critical theorists—who saw themselves as theoretical agents of social change—accepted Marx's own advise and sought to ground their critical norms in the existing needs and aspirations of the social agents whose society they were criticizing. Their critique was therefore *internal* to that society and amounted to showing how that society failed to live up to its own ideals. However, if society were to live up to its ideals, then the ideals themselves would change. This is because such ideals simultaneously reflect and transcend the imperfect justice and imperfect happiness of the reality in which they are embedded.[21]

Habermas finds several things wrong with this way of conducting social critique. First, it implies a kind of moral relativism. Are we to judge Nazi society by its own standards of justice and happiness or by more universal standards of justice and happiness that transcend it and, by definition, every existing society? Second (and related), this kind of immanent critique appears to lack the critical distance (transcendence) from its own subject matter that would be necessary in order for it to be radically critical. In fact, it appears to move within a kind of vicious circle in which the cultural beliefs and attitudes that ground critique are the very ones it is trying to critically distinguish itself from.

First-generation critical theorists were not oblivious to these problems. Turning to Marx, they maintained that human history manifests a pattern that points in a definite direction: history is propelled by a struggle between dominant and oppressed economic classes over the form that society should take, in such a way that each succeeding form of society emancipates more classes of oppressed people than its predecessor. Modern capitalist societies claim to have emancipated everyone by giving everyone equal rights to own and exchange property (free from the bonds of feudal serfdom and the strictly controlled guild system of craft production). But, Marx argued, this claim and the idea of universal humanity on which it is premised remains at least partly false and *ideological,* serving as but a justification for a new form of class domination: that of capitalist over wage worker.

By arguing that the norms of universal equality, freedom, and community implicit within capitalism were the necessary outcome of a long process of historical development, first-generation critical theorists could avoid the charge of moral relativism. These norms were the norms of the historically most advanced society. Of course, because these norms were abstract and ideal—and were, for that very reason, false reflections of that society—they functioned ideologically to persuade people to accept their oppression. But this vice, critical theorists argued, concealed a hidden virtue. For their very abstractness enabled them to accommodate concrete hopes for a freer, happier, and more just society. Pointing beyond the oppressive society they served to justify, they were truer than the reality they reflected.

Habermas agrees with his predecessors that there must be a way to classify and rank forms of society along a unidirectional axis of progress, for otherwise critical theory would lack justification for its own distinctly modern and forward-looking norms. Likewise, he accepts their view that these norms

---

21. Horkheimer observed that "if we take seriously the ideas by which the bourgeoisie explains its own order—free exchange, free competition, harmony of interests, and so on—and if we follow them to their logical conclusion, they manifest their inner contradiction and therewith their real opposition to the bourgeois order." M. Horkheimer, "Traditional and Critical Theory" (1937) in Ingram and Simon, *Critical Theory: The Essential Readings,* 247.

function as partly empty vessels whose meaning and purpose remains to be filled by historically situated social agents rather than by the critical theorists. However, while agreeing with them on these general points, he disagrees with their particular understanding of them. Specifically, he believes that they lacked the theoretical apparatus and analytic tools that would have enabled them to make good these theoretical claims.

To begin with, first-generation critical theorists appealed to a speculative philosophy of history in which a particular interpretation of historical changes in Western civilization, and more specifically during the period that began with the emergence of capitalism out of feudalism, would provide them (or so they hoped) with a relatively clear understanding of the concrete shape the next stage society would take. Following Marx, they simply assumed that the next stage of society would "resolve" the class contradictions of capitalism by replacing the whole capitalist system—private property in the means of production, wage labor, the market system, and ultimately the coercive administration of law and order—by a socialist system in which private property in productive assets would be abolished, scarcity would be overcome through technological advances in efficiency, economic production and distribution would come under common "democratic" supervision, and people's needs would become more social and less competitive and acquisitive.

Habermas contests both the method by which this "prediction" was reached as well as its conclusion. Philosophy of history, he avers, is too speculative—too much grounded in philosophical imagination and too little supported by empirical science—to sustain this prediction. A more scientifically responsible method for classifying and ranking societies along a continuum of progress must begin by reconstructing the irreversible and progressive stages of learning that transpire in childhood development, and it must conclude by showing how this developmental "logic" also explains social evolution. The logical progression of social forms that results from this transposition of childhood development is not only very difficult to confirm empirically (as Habermas himself concedes, it functions as a kind of regulative idea, or philosophical presupposition, of critical theory whose confirmation requires further investigation), but it tells us much less than a full-blown philosophy of history. It cannot predict the actual course of social change, which may not be progressive, or at least not uniformly progressive, and it cannot provide much in the way of concrete normative guidance in helping us to *theoretically* "project" what a more progressive society would look like beyond the current and most advanced form of liberal, social democratic capitalism. However, what it does tell us, Habermas observes, is that social progress is a complex process of institutionalizing rational thinking at all levels of cultural learning and societal coordination. These processes proceed along different paths—normative (oriented toward maximizing individual freedom, universal moral equality, and social justice) and functional (oriented toward maximizing efficiency and success)—that stand in a complex, dialectical relationship to each other, being at once complementary and opposed. Following Habermas's characterization of the progressive endpoint of these distinctive processes (and contrary to the prediction set forth by his predecessors), even the most advanced society would necessarily retain many of the features of today's capitalist, social democratic societies—economic markets, bureaucratic administrations, and the like.

Habermas's second objection to the use of philosophy of history in deriving standards for social critique—that it succumbs to the *fallacy of false concreteness* in claiming to project a model of a more just society from its interpretation of the past—is essentially connected to the first, methodological, objection. In Habermas's opinion, the social critic must not succumb to the temptation of Plato's fictive philosopher-king in *The Republic* who appeals to his superior wisdom as justification for imposing his model of a just society on the rest of society. First-generation critical theorists had no qualms about prescribing the true path toward emancipation from on high. In the words of Horkheimer, "This truth [regarding the unity and conflict of social forces that promise liberation] becomes clearly evident in the person of the theoretician; he exercises an aggressive critique not only against the conscious defenders of the status quo but also against distracting, conformist, or utopian tendencies within his own household."[22] Against this line of reasoning, Habermas denies that the normative guidelines called for by a logic of social evolution contain enough concrete specificity to enable a critical theorist to exercise an aggressive critique. Horkheimer held that "the viewpoints which the [critical theorist] derives from historical analysis as the goals of human activity, especially the idea of a reasonable organization of society that will meet the needs of the whole community, are immanent in human work, but are not correctly grasped by individuals or by the common mind."[23] Habermas rejects both of the assumptions asserted in this claim; not only are the concrete goals of a reasonable society that will meet the needs of the whole community not theoretically determined by a theory of social evolution, but the goal (or telos) of a free society resides in free communication, not in unalienated work. Because the critical theorist lacks the kind of philosophy of history requisite for deciding what people's "true" needs are and making concrete recommendations for revolutionizing society, he must adopt a more circumspect attitude. The convergent preferences of the "common mind" are the only preferences that should count in specifying the concrete goal of bringing about a "reasonable society"—at least as long as they are the product of public discussions that meet minimum standards of rationality. All the critical theorist as *philosopher* can do is enlighten people about the norms implicit in these standards, which requires that all affected interlocutors be allowed to discuss their preferences free from self-interest and prejudice and with equal opportunity and capacity. And all the critical theorist as *social critic* can do is

22. Horkheimer, "Traditional and Critical Theory," 248–49.
23. Ibid., 246.

uncover the various powers in society that threaten to undermine and distort these norms. Beyond that, the social critic can only speculate about whether actual agreements between citizens falsely claim to advance policies that are genuinely in the equal interest of everyone or whether they prematurely terminate in a compromise in which the more powerful impose their will on the less powerful.[24]

Habermas thus denies that the standards of social critique are immanent in the historical dynamics of particular societies. A more scientifically responsible reconstruction of social evolution, he hopes, might establish (if successfully carried out) very abstract norms that transcend their concrete embodiment by any factual society. This presumes, Habermas believes, that they can be grounded in the very process that underlies social evolution, namely, in the process of reasoning that propels learning within institutions that are responsible for cultural and social rationalization. That means that standards of critique possess a necessary and universal (or a priori) validity that is no less certain and indubitable than the validity possessed by our own reason. The *transcendent* validity of these standards across time and place is at one with their *transcendental* necessity for all forms of knowledge.

In the next chapter I examine Habermas's first attempt at making good this claim, and with it a purely rational grounding of ideology critique. But this

24. According to Habermas, the social critic can offer therapeutic diagnoses regarding the relationship between a social system and the unhappiness of its members, who experience its contradictions as an identity crisis. The social critic can also criticize the injustice of its institutions. The first kind of injustice occurs whenever a legal compromise is reached that favors the interests of the more powerful party and is accepted by the weaker party on the false belief that this is the best it (the weaker party) can reasonably hope for. In cases like this, failure to pursue rational dialogue enabling the transformation of partisan interests conducive to generating a common interest leads to a "suppression of [potentially] generalizable interests," or what Habermas calls "pseudo compromise." For example: the "class compromise" permits capitalists to exploit laborers within limits determined by collective bargaining but never calls into question the right of capitalists to own productive assets and the consequences such ownership has for achieving an environmentally healthy democratic society. The second kind of injustice occurs whenever a policy is advanced as if it were in the interest of everyone when it is not. In cases like this, failure to pursue rational dialogue leads to ideological self-delusion. Tax cuts for the rich that supposedly encourage investment and job creation, for instance, arguably do not benefit the poor since they strengthen the power of the rich and promote destructive, unregulated forms of economic growth. In *Legitimation Crisis* (1973) Habermas observes that criticizing ideology and pseudo compromise requires hypothetically imagining how members of a social system "would...at a given stage in the development of productive forces, have collectively and bindingly interpreted their needs (and which norms [they would] have accepted as justified) if they could and would have decided on an organization of social intercourse through discursive will formation, with adequate knowledge of the limiting conditions and functional imperatives of their society" (*LC* 113). This thought experiment, however, appears to be a rather uncertain undertaking in light of the limits and paradoxes associated with utilitarian and collective choice calculations (see chapter 6 of this book). The reference to "functional imperatives of their society" is problematic as well because it is difficult to determine which imperatives are truly necessary, and even necessary imperatives impose constraints on the scope and freedom—and thus rationality—of social members in deliberating about their needs.

ambitious project confronts an obstacle that was raised by his predecessors in the Frankfurt Institute: the dialectic of enlightenment. As I have remarked, conservatives and postmodernists who are skeptical of reason's capacity to ground our faith in morality argue that it is reason itself that is to blame for this state of affairs. This skeptical viewpoint was even defended by such stalwart critical theorists as Adorno and Horkheimer in their masterpiece, *Dialectic of Enlightenment* (1947).

Their skepticism was understandable. The twentieth century had witnessed two world wars, the rise of fascism and communism, and the rationally coordinated genocide of millions of Jews and other "undesirables" using modern science and technology. How could Germany of all places—the birthplace of Immanuel Kant (1724–1804), who inspired one the most enlightened forms of morality ever conceived—become the focal point for the century's worst moral disaster?

The answer to this question, they believed, extended beyond German or European history. Far from being relics of a precivilized and unenlightened age, virulent racism and aggression were inherent within modern society as such. Modern society, in turn, could be understood as the culmination of a process of *rationalization,* in the peculiar sense of the term deployed by Weber. This concept, which I will examine in greater detail later on, resists summary definition. For now, it suffices to note that Weber closely linked rationalization to secularization, or the gradual substitution of rational attitudes oriented toward calculated success in the material world for spiritual attitudes oriented toward salvation in the beyond. Rationalization entails the "disenchantment of the world" and paves the way for capitalism and its individualist ethic of work and responsibility. Although Weber had argued that the roots of rationalization extended back to Protestant Christianity, which developed certain ethical possibilities peculiar to Judeo-Christian culture, Adorno and Horkheimer argued that its origins were archaic. In their opinion, the earliest forms of myth and magic already reveal a rational tendency in their categorization of nature as something whose "behavior" can be predicted and controlled. Still, they agreed with Weber that the full blossoming of rationalization as a cultural phenomenon did not occur until the European Enlightenment, which was first and foremost marked by the emergence of modern philosophy.

The scientific drive to predict and control nature was celebrated by early modern philosophers for its utility (usefulness), a virtue that Adam Smith famously extolled in observing the workings of a market economy. For Adorno and Horkheimer, however, the calculated pursuit of self-interest did not yield the general happiness that Smith thought it would. On the contrary, they believed that the rational pursuit of profit underpinned a logic of competition, exploitation, and domination whose ugliest manifestation could be documented in wars of imperial expansion, the genocidal extermination of indigenous peoples and Jews, and the enslavement of Africans. They also observed that the increasing coincidence of rational domination with aggressive self-preservation (self-assertion) and capitalist exploitation also marked the distortion, if not decline, of a universal ethic that values persons intrinsically as sovereign subjects. In their opinion, the rational idea underlying this ethic—that each person embodies something divine called "humanity"—owed its very existence to prerational religious sentiments that now stood discredited by rational enlightenment itself. Thus, concealed within rational society was a deadly countercurrent that offered not universal humanitarian emancipation from the constraints of tradition and prejudice but rather the reduction of all persons and things to calculable means to an end under the auspices of top-down scientific management.

To Adorno and Horkheimer the irrationality of modern "rational" society appeared to be rooted in an archaic drive to reduce all phenomena to objects possessing stable properties (preferably ones reducible to calculable quantities) for purposes of satisfying a subject's need to be in control of itself and its environment.[25] Because this drive first came to full expression in modern philosophy, it was important for Habermas to examine modern philosophy's major figures in order to see how their point of departure—the subject's knowledge of external objects—led Adorno and Horkheimer to their depressing conclusion. This is precisely what he set out to do in one of his most important books, *The Philosophical Discourse of Modernity* (1985).

According to Habermas, the dialectic of enlightenment first became a dilemma for Kant and his successors as they were grappling with problems first posed by René Descartes (1596–1649), who many consider to be the founder of modern philosophy. These problems revolved around a central concern of the Enlightenment as a harbinger of modernity: conceptualizing reason as an instrument of knowledge and conceptualizing knowledge as an instrument of scientific progress and technological control.

25. Adorno and Horkheimer radically extend Lukács's thesis about the equivalence of objectifying analytic reason and the capitalist commodity form, which reduces everything to measurable exchange value (equivalence or identity), back to mythic thought and its classification of particular things into distinct general categories. Habermas criticizes this demonizing of instrumental reason along with its corresponding neglect of a nondomineering form of communicative reason. This neglect prevents them from defending the democratic rationality of their own social criticism except by way of appealing to an aesthetic reason wherein conceptual distinctions between subject and object, fact and value, etc., no longer hold sway (PDM 119–22, 126–30). These objections, however, may not be entirely justified. In "Society," in *Critical Theory: The Essential Readings*, Adorno insisted that totalitarianism "is not the fault of technical development or industrialization," since "a genuinely rational society could do without administration as little as it could do without the division of labor itself." In "Subject and Object," in The *Essential Frankfurt School Reader*, he even anticipates Habermas's notion of communicative reason in arguing that reconciling subject and object would entail not mimetic identification so much as "communication of what is distinguished." Cf. G. Lukács, *History and Class Consciousness: Studies in Marxist Dialectics* (1923; repr., Cambridge: MIT Press, 1971); Adorno, "Society," 66–67; "Subject and Object," 499–500. See D. Cook, *Adorno, Habermas, and the Search for a Rational Society* (New York: Routledge, 2004); and Ingram, *Critical Theory and Philosophy.*

Descartes is famous for formulating the problem of knowledge that animates this modern vision: If religious dogma and tradition are unreliable sources of truth, how can we (i.e., each one of us) be certain that we really know what we *think* we know? Descartes' famous solution to this problem in his *Meditations on First Philosophy* (1641) appeals to what we can know immediately and directly through rational introspection of the contents of our mental life. Descartes argued as follows: First, each of us can be certain that he or she exists, if not as a corporeal being in space and time (which might conceivably be a figment of our imagination), then as a pure mental substance, or *subject*. Second, using this subjective self-certainty as a standard of knowledge, we can prove that our idea of God as a perfect Being—where existence is understood to be a part of the meaning of "perfect Being"—is as certain as our own existence, thereby proving that a perfect God really exists. Finally, because a perfect God would not deceive us with regard to our most certain, reason-based beliefs about mathematics and geometry, there really must exist a mind-independent, mathematically ordered world that corresponds to these beliefs.

When examined carefully, Descartes' proof of the existence of a mind-independent world of objects reveals a profound irony: it presupposes the primacy of the subject. As Habermas puts it, "subject-centered" philosophy now becomes the paradigm of all rationally justifiable knowledge, extending down to the present day. This subject centeredness, as we shall now see, proves to be modern philosophy's Achilles' heel.

By the mid-eighteenth century, English philosopher David Hume (1711–76) had shown in his *Treatise of Human Nature* (1739–40) that subject-centered philosophy leads to radical skepticism. Within the interiority of my own subjective experience I know with certainty only that there are sensory impressions of sights, smells, sounds, and the like. I do not perceive anything—neither a "self" nor an object—that continuously underlies and unites these logically irreducible and discrete sensory qualities. As for truths known by pure reason, such as "All bachelors are unmarried men," their certainty is indeed indisputable, as Descartes rightly noted, since their denial issues in a logical contradiction. But pure reason provides us with scant consolation. As Hume observed, because such truths are merely about the meanings of concepts and do not extend our knowledge about what exists in the material world, they cannot provide us with the metaphysical knowledge Descartes seeks. Descartes' attempt to show that God's actual existence follows from our (subjective) idea of his essence fails, for he has only shown (at best) that the *idea* of God's existence follows from the *idea* of his essence.

The most devastating implications of Hume's critique of reason were reserved for science and morality. Scientific knowledge depends on the validity of causal laws, or *necessary* and *invariant* connections between things we experience. Moral knowledge depends on prescriptions about what we *ought* to do. Neither causal laws nor moral prescriptions, Hume noted, can be rationally inferred from sensory experience. Just because something happens (or has happened) a certain way does not mean that it *must* or *ought* to happen that way. Our belief that the future must conform to the past or that an ideal expectation must conform to present reality is without reason, since unpredictable events have been known to occur and ideals are by definition aims that must be striven for because they do not yet fully exist (i.e., are not yet realized). Hence, Hume concluded that our faith in science and morality has no other basis than unthinking habit (or custom).

This is where Kant makes his entry. He accepts Hume's skepticism about *pure* reason as a source of *metaphysical* knowledge but not his skepticism about *applied* reason as a source of scientific and moral knowledge. Let us begin with Kant's skepticism about pure reason, which is developed in the second part of his great masterpiece, *Critique of Pure Reason* (1781). As rational beings we are compelled to ask why things are the way they are. When directed toward ultimate beginnings, ends, and limits that concern the totality of the universe, this questioning becomes *metaphysical*. The problem, for Kant, is not in the questioning itself, but in the answering, for any answer we give in response to a metaphysical question entails a kind of contradiction (antinomy).

Suppose I ask whether there is a first cause (God) of the universe. If I reason that there must be a first cause because everything that exists has a cause—this is known as the principle of sufficient reason—then I refute my thesis; for the first cause would also require a cause to explain its existence, and so on to infinity. If I now answer that there cannot be a first cause, but only an infinite series of causes, I refute my thesis that the universe exists, because an infinite (incomplete) causal series cannot suffice as a complete (sufficient) explanation for the existence of anything. The lesson Kant draws from this contradiction (transcendental dialectic) is this: we must limit our knowledge inquiries to natural phenomena in space and time whose existence can be ascertained through sense experience.

But how can we be certain that such knowledge is possible, if (as Hume noted) we can never get outside of our subjective experience to see whether it corresponds to the real world "out there"? Kant's response to this question is revolutionary: we can be assured of a correspondence between subjective experience and objective reality only if we can show that (a) objective reality and its necessary conditions—space, time, substantiality, and causality—are necessary for having *coherent* subjective experience, without which I would not be able to experience myself as an "I"; and (b) having coherent subjective experience is a necessary condition for experiencing space, time, substantiality, and causality as objective, nonpsychological (necessary) unities or relationships thereof. Kant's arguments in support of this biconditional relationship (no "I" without a subject-transcending world; no subject-transcending world without an "I") are too complicated to be given a fair treatment here, but we can at least get some idea of their overall structure and conclusion, namely, that the prior logical ground for both objective exteriority and subjective interiority must reside in the unifying (synthetic), rule-governed activity of reason. Stated more precisely, it is the logical function of inference (i.e., of connecting ideas) applied to organizing coherent experience that constitutes a known self and a known world.

Who or what applies these logical functions to my experience? According to Kant, what applies them must be a subject of some kind. It cannot be a personal and familiar (psychological) "I" understood as a contingent flow of private and discrete sensations—a "subject" so fleeting in its impressions that Hume doubted its existence. So, Kant reasoned, it must be an impersonal and rational (transcendental) "I" understood as a synthetic activity *prior to experience.*

A crude paraphrase of Kant's argument might go something like this: Each of us has subjective experience only on condition that we can think of all of our disparate mental representations as belonging to a single "I." But I could not experience such a unitary self if my experience were only of these representations. In order to have an experience of selfhood—the unitary focal point to which I refer my representations as belonging to me—my representations must also refer to a unitary focal point that is *not* me (without a world "out there" no contrast could be made of a mind "in here"). That is, I must be able to refer my discrete (nonidentical) sensations of taste, sound, sight, and tactile feeling to an *object.* Such an object is simply a substance (or substrate of sensory qualities) that I identify as "the same thing" despite changes in its spatiotemporal sensory states. What enables me to so identify it is its regularity, or necessary and immutable (causally predetermined) "behavior." My identification of its sameness is thus predicated on my anticipation of its future behavior; I *infer* how it will behave based on a causal rule.

According to Kant, such necessary associations of possible sensory states are in turn possible only if reason itself—the power of inferring logical relations of identity between ideas or concepts—has another, nonlogical application. Only if reason's logical operations are applied to sensory experiences (and not merely to concepts) can I infer the existence of an object (and therewith, of a subject). In this *transcendental* use of reason, sensory states are unified according to a rule that elsewhere finds deployment in logic: just as I infer the idea of "unmarried man" from the idea of "bachelor" so I infer the sensory state "hard" from the nontactile sensory states that make up "diamond." The only difference between these two kinds of necessary inference is that the former is based on logical *analysis,* as when I infer that "unmarried man" is part of the meaning of "bachelor," while the latter is based on *synthesis,* as when I infer that "hard sensation" must accompany the nontactile sensations states that are associated with "diamond experience." (To visualize what Kant is getting at here, think of the synthesizing mind as a computer that receives and logically processes raw sense data into three-dimensional images.)

Kant's refutation of both metaphysical dogmatism—which claims to deduce grandiose truths about the existence and nature of God, the universe, and the immaterial soul through the irrefutable analysis of ideas—and psychological skepticism—which claims to debunk all knowledge save the mute certainty of sensation—is unquestionably brilliant. It is also deeply problematic. First, by limiting the range of possible knowledge to the knowledge of material objects (observable facts), it places in doubt the possibility of other kinds of knowledge. To begin with, it places in doubt the kind of philosophical knowledge that Kant himself purports to be offering in the *Critique*. This knowledge is not about material objects and observable facts; it is not physical science. Philosophical knowledge is knowledge about knowledge; its method is critical reflection, not observation. Furthermore, Kant's philosophy places in doubt the idea of moral knowledge, at least insofar as we conceive of the latter as a body of fact-transcending beliefs about what is good and right.

Second, if Kant is right about the necessary link between objective experience and causal regularity, then we are compelled to experience our physically embodied selves as causally determined. That would mean that I cannot choose (act) otherwise than the way I in fact choose (act). If this were so, none of us could be held morally responsible for what we do, because we would not be free.

It is here where we first encounter the dialectic of enlightenment that would later be taken up by postmodernists.[26] In order to reconcile the causal necessity of the world as experienced (known) with the freedom demanded of us by morality, Kant had to *divide* reason itself into two *opposed* deployments: theoretical (experiential) and practical (moral). As in the case of logical and theoretical deployments of reason, the practical deployment of reason demands consistency—not to laws of logic or of causation but to lawfulness as such, or *universalizability*. According to Kant's formulation of practical reason (the categorical imperative), which he developed in his *Groundwork of the Metaphysics of Morals* (1785), I am morally permitted to do Y only if I can command that everyone else do it as well without contradiction.

The key words here are "without contradiction." For Kant, whenever I act I am implicitly following a maxim: In situation S I will do Y. My practical reason commands me to formulate this maxim as if it were a *universal* rule that permitted no exception: Everyone in situation S will do Y. Suppose that S = "securing a loan by promising to repay it" and Y = "break a promise." Can I consistently will that everyone in S do Y? The answer, Kant says, is no. If everyone refused to repay their loans then a necessary condition underlying

26. Kant observed that reason recognizes no limits in questioning the ultimate grounds underlying reality but answering such metaphysical questioning entails contradiction. Kant's understanding of the limits of reason thus anticipates postmodern skepticism regarding the completeness of our knowledge of things in their totality, which in turn implies the fragmentation of reason into antithetical context-specific applications. As Hegel noted, Kant's philosophy undermines its own claim to absolutely certain and complete knowledge of the limits of knowledge even as it denigrates natural science to the realm of partial knowledge.

the maxim—engaging the trust of lenders—would be violated; doing Y will have contradicted S.

I will have more to say in chapter 5 about the cogency of Kant's moral theory. Let us accept it for now and ask a more fundamental question: How can I be held responsible for immoral behavior if I am not free to act otherwise? Kant says that even if we must physically *experience* ourselves as causally determined, we might not *be* causally determined. Although we can only experience ourselves through our own mental apparatus, which processes sensory experience according to the logical rule of causal succession, we can imagine a Being who might know us differently. God's infinite knowledge (assuming he might exist) would not be constrained by space, time, causal necessity, and materiality. Therefore he would not know us as material, causally predetermined beings.

Kant rescues moral freedom by dividing reason and the self into two opposed aspects; corresponding to the distinction between moral and scientific reason is a parallel distinction between supernatural (noumenal and unknowable) and natural (phenomenal and knowable) selves. But this dualistic model of reason and selfhood creates a new problem: How do we explain the interaction between these opposed supernatural and natural aspects? How can free immaterial (moral) selves cause anything to happen in the physical world? And how can they, in turn, be causally affected by this same world?

Kant's followers in the German idealist tradition—Fichte, Schelling, and Hegel—thought they had an answer to these questions, albeit one that required abandoning formal logic and the law of noncontradiction as the highest and most consistent meaning of reason. In his *Phenomenology of Spirit* (1807) Hegel argued against Kant that reasoning about reality as a coherent unity implied metaphysical knowledge of the absolute grounds and limits of reality in its totality. Hegel conceded Kant's point that such reasoning results in contradiction (or dialectic), but he thought that this was but a step toward establishing a closed system of complementary oppositions in which, for example, freedom is shown to be an essential condition for necessity and vice versa.

Hegel thought that his system resolved the opposition between subject and object, spirit and nature, individual and society, society and humanity, and morality and science. He no longer conceived reason the way Kant did, as a logical faculty innately embedded within each of our minds. Instead, he elevated reason to the godlike status of a supersubject—the human spirit—that progressively realizes (objectifies) itself in the nonmental physical world of culture and nature. As we shall see, the essence of this spirit—freedom in thought and action—dictated to his followers the logical endpoint of human history: the overcoming of all natural and spiritual resistances and the harmonization of all forces.

Marx, who was perhaps Hegel's most important successor, retained this Promethean view of reason, albeit in an "inverted" materialistic form. For Marx, it is the technological rationale built into economic laboring activity that propels the historical evolution of society toward its predestined goal of universal freedom for all. Only a technological society that has conquered material scarcity and liberated humanity from the need to toil can accomplish the full reconciliation of humanity with itself and with nature. Such a society is implicit in the social essence of technology itself, the historical development of which demands the revolutionary overthrow of capitalist property relations that restrict its fullest application.

Marx was perhaps the last great prophet of progress who still believed that a humane scientific reason, as the great driving force behind an emancipated communist society, could resolve the contradictions of the Enlightenment in its moral and economic aspects. A younger generation of existential philosophers, led by Nietzsche, was not so optimistic. Indeed, Nietzsche's pessimism about the emancipatory effects of reason, expressed in works such as *On the Genealogy of Morals* (1887), later inspired Adorno and Horkheimer's best work, *Dialectic of Enlightenment,* and provided a powerful stimulus to postmodern thought.[27]

Nietzsche argued that reason is but an instrument of deeper irrational drives and instincts, foremost among them being a "will to power."[28] The will to power propels the human organism to rationally identify and control its natural psychological passions for the sake of gaining mastery over inner and outer nature. So understood, the subject (or "I") is a product of the will's own

27. According to postmodernists, Hegel's system marks the last great attempt to resolve the crisis of reason bequeathed by Kantian philosophy. It does so by affirming what Kant denies: reason's unyielding demand to know the infinite totality even at the cost of contradiction. But Hegel thought that philosophical reflection could demonstrate that seemingly opposed categories mutually implied each other in a closed system of resolved complementarities. Postmodernists deny this. For example, in *The Postmodern Condition* Lyotard cites Kurt Gödel and Werner Heisenberg in defending the logical indeterminacy, incompleteness, and uncertainty of any "metanarrative" that proclaims to be all-encompassing. He insists, however, that the loss of identity that comes with the postmodern demise of rationalist idealism is not inherently inhospitable to liberal values of justice. On the contrary, insisting on impossible norms of certainty, clarity, and identity devalues the imaginative source of values and encourages a totalitarian "will to power" that eliminates or marginalizes whatever and whoever cannot be made rational.

28. Nietzsche here follows Arthur Schopenhauer, who maintained that reason and all worldly representations of objects and subjects constituted by reason were plural manifestations of a single metaphysical Will. The impossibility of the Will's satisfying its insatiable desire led Schopenhauer to seek in artistic contemplation a release from the Will's unhappiness—a stance that Nietzsche repudiated as life denying. Among critical theorists, it was Horkheimer who most identified with Schopenhauer's pessimism. Renouncing melioristic political struggle and redemptive reconciliation with nature and society as futile, he took solace in the religious solidarity of a suffering humanity. Adorno, however, rejected this pessimistic metaphysics. See A. Schopenhauer, *The World as Will and Representation,* 2 vols. (New York: Dover, 1969); M. Horkheimer, *Die Sehnsucht nach dem ganz Anderen* [The Longing for the Totally Other] (Hamburg: Furche, 1971), and the notes on conversations between Adorno and Horkheimer in October 1946 regarding the writing of a second volume of the *Dialectic of Enlightenment* that were taken by Adorno's wife, Gretel Karplus Adorno, in *Gesammelte Schriften, Band 12: Nachgelassene Schriften 1931–1949.* I thank Stefano Giacchetti for this reference.

inward-directed objectification and repression, just as the object of knowledge (nature) is a product of the will's subjugation of matter, that is, its reduction of the rich variety of concrete sensory qualities to the lawful calculus of abstract mathematic identity.

For Adorno and Horkheimer, the upshot of Nietzsche's diagnosis is that reason, far from being a moral factor propelling the progressive emancipation of human nature, is rather an instrumental (or technological) factor involved in its domination. Taking Kant's philosophy as an accurate description of the modern moral subject, Nietzsche showed that freedom from natural passion demands submission to rigid, rational consistency and conformity to law. The fact that this law is allegedly one to which we rationally consent, so that our obligation is ostensibly self-imposed and voluntary—as in a contract—merely underscores the affinity between Kant's moral law and the law of the market, which also consists in the mutual imposition of constraints through contractual exchange. Breaking the contract (law) introduces a disequilibrium in what is otherwise an equal exchange of promises; hence the inevitable punitive reaction that it calls forth: the debt must be repaid, the books balanced. But here Adorno and Horkheimer extend Nietzsche's genealogical history of morality further. As an elaboration of what must be done in order to realize morality, Kant's social contractarian political theory undoubtedly demands a coercive legal order in which our "external" freedom from arbitrary constraint is protected. Yet this order, they observed, is meaningless apart from conceptions of private property and commodity exchange that manifest a more sinister, freedom-denying social determinism: the laws of the market. Moreover, because the market is anything but regular in its anarchic operation, it needs the additional discipline imposed on it by a scientifically trained cadre of economic planners, social engineers, and managerial elites, who seek to constrain the behavior of individual economic agents in ways that are less unpredictable and less antagonistic to the aims of production.

To sum up: Reason was the foundation on which Adorno and Horkheimer erected their critique of modern society. That foundation now stood unmasked by them as brute domination. Critical reason—the Kantian philosophy of reflection—ends up by enthroning a technological tyrant. It does so, moreover, at the expense of abdicating its own authority and, along with it, that of morality. Such is the dialectic of enlightenment that critical philosophy itself must dissolve if it is to restore our faith in moral idealism and social critique.

Outline of Chapters

The reader will have to await the conclusion of this book to decide whether Habermas has an answer to this dialectic. From what little has been revealed so far, it should come as no surprise that Habermas has devoted the greater part of his career to redeeming the *integrity* of reason as a rationally well-founded (universal) source of both cognitive (scientific) *and* moral enlightenment. This project, he insists, depends on abandoning the subject-centered (or self-reflective) paradigm of knowledge bequeathed to philosophy by Descartes.

In the remainder of this book I chart the path Habermas has followed—from his earliest to his latest writings—in trying to invent a *new* paradigm that will accomplish two related goals: the Kantian grounding of social critique in transcendental (necessary and universal) presuppositions of practical reason, and the defense of practical reason against the objection that reason contradicts itself. In charting this path I focus on the various research programs Habermas has developed in pursuing these aims. These programs address:

1. the nature of social action (focusing on communicative action)
2. the nature of meaningful speech (focusing on the relationship between validity and language)
3. the nature of reason (focusing on practical, or communicative, reason)
4. the nature of knowledge and truth (focusing on the relationship between language and reality)
5. the nature of society (focusing on the dual nature of society as lifeworld and system)
6. the logic of child development and the logic of social evolution (focusing on the psychological "decentering" of the ego and the correlative modernization of society)
7. a discourse ethical account of morality (focusing on the use of real and simulated dialogue in resolving conflicts justly)
8. a discourse theoretic account of law and democracy (focusing on the use of a proceduralist paradigm in resolving tensions between liberal and welfare paradigms)
9. a diagnosis of social pathologies and ideological delusions (focusing on the contradictions of advanced capitalism and the dialectic of enlightenment)[29]

Although I list these nine research programs separately because they address different areas of knowledge, they are all intimately interrelated in the social theory developed by Habermas. Generally speaking, programs listed under higher numbers presuppose those listed under lower numbers. Thus, understanding Habermas's theory of knowledge and truth presupposes understanding his theories about action, meaning, and reason, although it does not presupposes an understanding of his theories about society, developmental logic, discourse ethics, law and democracy, or social pathology. That said, the sequence I have adopted is not absolute, since (for instance) Habermas's defense of discourse ethics partly depends on accepting his theory about moral

29. This nine-point summary extends James Gordon Finlayson's five-point scheme based on "relatively self-standing" programs that address separate areas of knowledge. *Habermas: A Very Short Introduction*, xviii.

development and social evolution; and his account of social action partly depends on his theories of meaning and rationality.

The chapters of this book are arranged with the above nine-program sequence in mind. In chapter 2 I examine the philosophical issues that occupied Habermas during the 1960s, which mainly revolved around the first five programs mentioned above as well as the last program.[30] Habermas's programmatic research during this period culminated in *Knowledge and Human Interests* (1968) and *On the Logic of the Social Sciences* (1967/1970), but the seminal ideas of these works took root during the "positivist debate" with Karl Popper and his school in the early 1960s over the proper function of social science. Defending the theoretical possibility of a nonexplanatory science devoted to social criticism, Habermas drew from four research programs: a theory of action inspired by Max Weber, a theory of meaning inspired by Ludwig Wittgenstein, a theory of interpretation modeled on Hans-Georg Gadamer's philosophical hermeneutics, and a theory of critical reflection beholden to Freudian psychoanalysis.

Knowledge and Human Interests defends the knowledge status of psychoanalytic ideology critique by appropriating the thought of two late-nineteenth century thinkers, Charles Sanders Peirce (1839–1914) and Wilhelm Dilthey (1833–1911), each of whom contributed to understanding the transcendental grounds of scientific knowledge in their respective fields: natural science and the humanities. These grounds refer to different kinds of action—instrumental and communicative. However, with the advent of social science a third medium of knowledge besides work and language comes into focus: social power (or social domination). Because power constrains and distorts the communicative medium in which knowledge across all disciplines is authoritatively justified, it must be critically unmasked and neutralized before we can claim with any assurance that we truly know. Once we have transparent, nonideological understanding of our needs, we can then build a society that maximally satisfies them.

Knowledge and Human Interests represented an ambitious attempt to ground a standard against which ideological false consciousness could be measured— "undistorted communication." However, Habermas soon abandoned this program because of its defects. For one thing, it presupposed a speculative philosophy of history (the "natural evolution of the species," as Habermas put it), which, as I noted earlier, he came to reject as unscientific. Second, it sought to ground critical theory in the necessary presuppositions underlying knowledge rather than in those underlying social interaction. In that respect it remained bound to the subject-object paradigm of philosophy that fueled the dialectic of enlightenment. Third, the use of psychoanalysis as a model for critical theory proved to be practically, if not theoretically, untenable, for it placed the critical theorist as

---

30. The single exception is Habermas's first major work, *The Structural Transformation of the Public Sphere*, which addressed changes in the structure of public debate during the rise of mass democracy in the nineteenth and twentieth centuries.

social therapist in an unequal relationship to his fellow citizens—an "analytical" relationship to which they would never willingly submit.

These failings were rectified in Habermas's mature social theory. The theory of communicative action, which I take up in chapter 3, asserts that reason is always operant—if not dominant—in everyday social interaction. Habermas bases social interaction on the communicative competence to criticize and reject offers to engage in meaningful cooperation. Explaining linguistic meaning in terms of acceptability conditions and normative validity claims, this program—which Habermas refers to as "formal pragmatics"—deploys a weak method of transcendental argumentation that enables him to ground universal norms of critical reason. Whether it actually succeeds in doing so is a question I raise in the conclusion, since linguistic meaning appears to be contextual and referential in ways that threaten his account of critical reason as a distinctive type of practical discourse.

These themes are again addressed in chapter 4, where I take up Habermas's theory of knowledge and truth. Unlike his earlier account of knowledge in *Knowledge and Human Interests,* his later account, which he mainly develops in *Truth and Justification* (1999), builds on the "linguistic turn"—or philosophical paradigm shift to language and communication—articulated in his universal pragmatics. This work marks two advances in Habermas's thought: it rejects the *consensus theory of truth* that he favored in the early 1970s, and it articulates a theory of reference that explains how different scientific "paradigms" can be compared and ranked. A question remains, however, as to whether Habermas's epistemic realism does not also imply moral realism.

Habermas's views on morality are taken up in chapter 5, where I compare and contrast his discourse theoretical account of moral reasoning, as developed in "Discourse Ethics: Notes on a Program of Philosophical Justification" (1983), to similar rights-based accounts of moral reasoning proposed by Kant and John Rawls. Unlike these theories, which appeal to procedures of moral universalization that individuals apply on their own, Habermas's discourse ethic requires that moral universalization be the outcome of mutual questioning and mutual consent (discourse) guided by norms of rational dialogue. I also discuss Habermas's theory of moral development, which is indebted to the genetic structuralism of Jean Piaget and Lawrence Kohlberg, on the one hand, and the account of moral socialization and individuation developed by George Herbert Mead, on the other. Although this chapter is mainly devoted to analyzing Habermas's refutation of moral skepticism, it also scrutinizes discourse ethics from the standpoint of an ethics of care. The chapter then applies discourse ethics to contemporary debates on genetic engineering. Habermas here appeals to a kind of moral realism—revolving around a universal conception of human nature—that appears to conflict with his earlier positions. He also proposes—again defying earlier assertions he has made to the contrary—the use of a hypothetical (simulated) dialogue in deciding between acceptable and unacceptable forms of genetic intervention. I conclude that Habermas's formal understanding of moral dialogue cannot capture contextual features of argumentative cogency that emerge in institutional settings.

Habermas partly addresses my objection when he shows how his formal model captures some important dimensions of our understanding of the legitimacy of democratic law making, the topic of the next four chapters. Chapter 6 focuses on Habermas's linkage of individual rights and democracy—terms that are often thought to be mutually opposed. He sharply distinguishes this democratic use of discourse ethics, which he develops in *Between Facts and Norms* (1992), from its moral use. He then proceeds to deduce five main categories of right whose prescriptive content must be filled in by democratically elected lawmakers. This deduction, I argue, privileges civil and political rights over welfare and subsistence rights in ways that are problematic, even from the standpoint of Habermas's own theory. However, rescuing the theory by supplementing it with a substantive account of human capabilities of the sort appealed to in his discussion of genetic engineering undermines the strong deontological status of his conception of deliberative democracy.

In chapter 7 I examine Habermas's theory of democratic legitimation. According to Habermas, a legitimate circulation of power must be grounded in communicative power, or the power of public opinion as it is generated in the public sphere and taken up for debate by legislators. But his use of systems theory in describing how public opinion is selectively filtered by administrative elites suggests that the administrative power we get at the end of the power circuit might not sufficiently resemble the communicative power that supposedly justifies it. Furthermore, the predominance of bargaining, compromise, and preference aggregation suggests that democratic dialogue is really a strategic game in which social power eclipses the achievement of unconstrained consensus. Habermas's defense of judicial review as a check on social and administrative power does not solve the problem, since judicial review—a counter-democratic device—cannot be exercised in a politically neutral way. Accepting his view that competing paradigms of law need to be balanced and harmonized by a democratic (proceduralist) paradigm only raises deeper questions about the salience of this synthesis, diachronically and synchronically understood.

Chapter 8 answers these questions by examining Habermas's application of the proceduralist paradigm to four areas of conflict: the separation of church and state, the private/public distinction as seen from the standpoint of women's rights, the multicultural defense of group rights, and the conflict between democratic sovereignty and the right to immigrate. These applications, I argue, do not successfully mediate competing liberal and welfare paradigms and appear to be driven by substantive rather than procedural factors.

Chapter 9 addresses Habermas's attempt to reconcile deliberative democracy with capitalism. The contradiction between class domination and democratic solidarity would appear to require considerations of substantive distributive justice that take us beyond proceduralism. Workplace democracy and market socialism are just some of the institutions briefly mentioned by Habermas that relieve his theory of deliberative democracy of some of its procedural sterility. However, I argue that these "reforms" cannot succeed without also changing technological paradigms.

The contradictions between capitalism and democracy also inform the theme of chapter 10: the legitimation crisis besetting the modern welfare state in an age of globalization. After critically examining Habermas's diagnosis of the crisis tendencies of the welfare state as articulated in *Legitimation Crisis* (1973) and *Lifeworld and System: A Critique of Functionalist Reason,* volume 2 of *The Theory of Communicative Action,* I take up his treatment of globalization and its impact on the nation-state. Habermas recommends the establishment of cosmopolitan law and supranational forms of democracy of the sort that have been institutionalized in the European Union as necessary steps toward securing human rights, eliminating poverty, and regulating the environment. His multilayered model of a global "constitutional" order defends a division of labor between a global human rights regime centered on the International Criminal Court and a reformed UN, on one side, and regional and national regimes, which are delegated responsibility for implementing "world domestic policy" affecting economic redistribution, environmental control, and the like, on the other. Added to this mix are the "weak" publics and their corresponding institutions within global civil society that are responsible for generating world public opinion, as well as midlevel regulatory institutions, such as the World Trade Organization, the World Bank, and the International Monetary Fund. I conclude this chapter by asking whether his proposals go far enough in dealing with the challenges of globalization.

The final chapter returns to the themes raised in the first chapter: the foundations of social critique and the dialectic of enlightenment. According to Habermas, social pathologies emanate from imbalances between system and lifeworld and between different rationalization complexes that are driven by capitalism's growth imperative, not by social rationalization (modernization) per se, as first-generation critical theorists maintained. Yet other pathologies revolving around a loss of meaning do appear to stem from social rationalization, thereby once again recalling the dialectic of enlightenment.

Habermas's discussion of these social pathologies raises two questions about his social theory. The first is whether the theory of communicative action can ground a critique of alienation without appealing to standards of criticism that lie outside the transcendental conditions for rational speech. Habermas expressly says that it cannot, but he then leaves us with little guidance as to how—if at all—such standards might be grounded. A second (and related) question concerns the capacity of rational speech to preserve the prerational sources of meaning and motivation that find expression in religion and ethical worldviews. Do we not need to have faith in a better world if we are to engage in progressive political reform? And do we not need to have a vivid imagination to guide us in this endeavor?

I answer these questions in the affirmative by returning to some of Habermas's lesser-known writings on aesthetics and religion that recall his youthful fascination with Schelling and Heidegger. Just as the transcendent norms implicit in communicative reason represent secularized translations of religious motifs, so, too, do religious motifs represent a "postsecular" acknowledgment of what cannot be known and controlled by reason: nature and the lifeworld that simultaneously grounds and exceeds our conscious experience. Despite the rational differentiation of lived experience into opposing cognitive, moral-practical, and erotic-expressive dimensions, we nonetheless aspire to a sense of wholeness in which these dimensions are reconciled with one another and re-integrated into a single identity. We aspire to this not through abstract thought but rather through a distinctly aesthetic kind of reason. Aesthetic reason holds open the possibility, Habermas believes, for a secular illumination of our lifeworld in its totality—a utopian disclosure of a balanced life in reason that just might aid us in perceiving the depths of our alienation and rekindling hope for genuine happiness.

2

Habermas's Defense of Psychoanalytic Social Science

Habermas's first effort at developing a system of philosophy was motivated by the problems bequeathed to him by modern philosophy. These problems concern the capacity of reason to justify our knowledge claims. On one side, we find rationalists such as Descartes claiming that pure reason can justify grandiose metaphysical claims in a manner that is beyond dispute. On the other side, we find empiricists such as Hume insisting that reason can provide no certainty for even our most mundane beliefs. We thus seem torn between two unacceptable alternatives: an uncritical use of reason (dogmatism) versus an excessively critical rejection of the same (skepticism). Kant's appeal to a transcendental use of reason attempts to steer a middle course between these extremes: it critically limits the employment of reason to experience in a way that shows how reason can constitute real knowledge of world and self.

Unfortunately, Kant's solution to these problems left philosophers with new ones. Perhaps the most serious was his limitation of valid knowledge to the world of physical objects. Accepting this limitation, neither understanding of moral duties nor reflection on transcendental (necessary and universal) conditions appears to count as knowledge. The unintended result of Kant's philosophy was therefore a new kind of skepticism as well as a new kind of dogmatism. On the one hand, empirical science and its methods of causal explanation and value-free observation are uncritically put forth as the only valid kind of knowledge. On the other hand, the elevation of mechanistic science as the sole source of legitimate knowledge—what Habermas calls *scientism*—entails moral skepticism and *objectivism,* or the idea that experience consists in passively mirroring and adapting to the objects around us. Left out of this equation are *reflective* experiences about ourselves as *free* moral agents guided by our own chosen interests, values, and norms.

The Positivism Debate in German Social Science

In the 1960s Habermas was especially keen on refuting one variant of scientism and objectivism that had captivated philosophers for over a century: *positivism*. Positivism owes its fame to the nineteenth-century French social theorist and inventor of the modern concept of sociology, August Comte (1798–1857). Comte's main idea—that positive science culminates social evolution, surpassing theological and metaphysical stages of thinking—later inspired the twentieth-century *logical positivism* of the Vienna Circle, who were equally skeptical of religion and metaphysics. More important, logical positivism's embrace of scientism left no room for morality as it is normally understood. Indeed, the only way logical positivists could make sense of moral judgments was to reduce them to expressions of personal preferences coupled with commands mandating their acceptance by others.

I will have more to say about this *emotivist* reduction of moral language in chapter 5. Suffice it to say, some of the earliest and most influential critics of logical positivism, such as Karl Popper (1902–94), convincingly argued that emotivism eliminated the most essential part of moral language, namely our belief that moral judgments raise claims to rational validity that can be criticized and defended, if need be, by appeal to shared norms. However, Popper's critical rationalism still retained a trace of positivist skepticism in at least one sense. Accepting a deductive model of logical argumentation, he held that the highest and most universal moral norms from which we derive our particular moral judgments cannot themselves be rationally deduced and hence must be accepted on faith.

Habermas and Adorno, however, disagreed with Popper and positivism on just this score. They sought to defend the legitimate nonmetaphysical status of universal moral insight—or, more broadly speaking, critical evaluative knowledge—which they believed was emblematic of the so-called sciences of critical reflection, such as psychoanalysis and Marxian ideology critique. Although Popper himself embraced critical rationalism as compatible with science—evaluative judgments like those found in morality, law, and politics could be tested in terms of their consistency with higher-order principles, and these, in turn, could be ranked and qualified in terms of their capacity to advance commonly accepted ends—he denied that there was any other science besides empirical social science for testing these ends. In other words, empirical science can tell us whether our ends are "rational" given available technologies and resources, but there is no science that can tell us that these ends are intrinsically "false," "inauthentic," or "delusional" according to metaphysical notions of human nature or of history. Indeed, any attempt to think of social science as a kind of philosophical reflection on human nature and human history was, in his opinion, insufficiently critical, insofar as it strayed from what could be known through the scientific method.

Habermas and Adorno challenged this view with Popper and his followers in the so-called positivism debate of the early 1960s. They argued that critical rationalism—with its demand that values and norms be logically consistent, rank ordered in terms of maximizing overall long-term well-being, and capable of being technologically implemented—was not critical enough. In order to understand why they believed this, we must first briefly discuss the "methodology debate" in Germany that had coalesced around the human sciences, such as sociology, psychology, political science, and historical science, since their inception in the latter half of the nineteenth century. By the turn of the twentieth century this debate had come to dominate German philosophy. Neo-Kantians such as Heinrich Rickert, Wilhelm Dilthey, and Max Weber argued that the human sciences were methodologically distinct from the natural (physical) sciences. The human sciences, they insisted, were not oriented toward the discovery and confirmation of timeless causal laws but toward the understanding and interpretation of unique historical events. These events ostensibly were made up of human actions that were thought to be intrinsically meaningful. Explaining an action (see appendix A), they noted, involves understanding the actor's intentions and his or her own understanding of what he or she is up to.[1] This understanding implicitly refers to values, norms, ends, interests, and other beliefs about society and world that the actor shares with others. Indeed, in Dilthey's opinion, the entire web of social meaningfulness that defines a historical event must be interpreted as if it were a text (or narrative), and this must be done in order to explain why it occurred at all. Although there was considerable debate among historians and sociologists regarding how this was to be done—Weber developed an *action-theoretical* approach that Habermas would later adopt, while others, such as Dilthey, developed more *contextualist* approaches (see appendix B)—there was general agreement that only a unique web of concrete meanings—not a general law applicable to similar kinds of events—must at some point be referred to in explaining why just *this* action happened and not some other action.

As the next three chapters reveal, the methodology debate has ramifications that extend beyond social science to include epistemology, ethics, and the philosophy of language. Should (can) language, knowledge, and morality be characterized from an *internal* point of view (from the *participant* standpoint of a social agent who *experiences* linguistic, epistemic, and moral life from the inside, as a lived phenomenon of which we can become reflectively, or phenomenologically, aware) or from an *external* point of view (from the *observer* standpoint of a scientist who explains this life in terms of a theory

1. For this reason Habermas denies that brute physical movements are actions (*TCA 1* 97).

whose description of that life the participating social agents might not recognize), or from some combination of the above? For the time being, I will
bracket this broader question and focus on the narrower sociological question
by noting that what is true about history—with its obvious connection to
literary narrative—might not be true about social science. Unlike history, social sciences seek general knowledge about the laws of social behavior. Weber
thus concluded that understanding the concrete meaning of a social action
was at best preparatory to explaining action as an instance of a more general
law.[2] So, despite the fact that cultural anthropology appears to be predomi-
nately interpretative (involving the decoding of otherwise incomprehensible
languages and practices), other important branches of social science, including behavioral science and experimental psychology (not to mention economics), appear to be explanatory in the law-subsuming manner characteristic of
natural science.

The emergence of logical positivism during the 1920s and 1930s also favored this reductive understanding of social science. Logical positivists were
strongly motivated by the Cartesian quest for logical clarity and epistemic certainty. These logical and empirical concerns where brought together under a
single theory—the "verificationist" theory of meaning that had been advanced
by Ludwig Wittgenstein (1889–1951) in his *Tractatus Logico-Philosophicus*
(1921). Wittgenstein intended his theory as a criticism of any philosophy
that deviates from the narrow logical task of "showing" how our language
means, or "pictures," a world of "atomic facts," but its immediate effect was
to impugn as meaninglessness all nonfactual propositions (propositions whose
truth or falsity could not in principle be verifiable by observation). The results
were deeply disturbing and paradoxical: not only were the evaluative and expressive statements of ethics, religion, metaphysics, and aesthetics suddenly
consigned to practical irrelevance, but (as Wittgenstein ironically noted) so
were the propositions of philosophy that asserted the verificationist theory of
meaning.

According to logical positivists, interpretation was not a method of knowing whose results (interpretations) could be decisively verified by empirical observation. Two or more opposed interpretations might explain the meaning of
a person's behavior equally well. This possibility increases to the extent that
other categories of meaning beyond the agent's intended purposes—functional
purposes vis-à-vis the maintenance of society, unconscious purposes vis-à-vis

---

2. Sometimes, however, Weber suggests that behavioral laws are themselves requisite for understanding an intentional action. According to this *positivistic* view of understanding, the sociologist
imputes an intention to the agent on the basis of an analogy between the agent's behavior and a
behavioral law that the sociologist generalizes from his or her own behavior, whose motive (cause)
he or she directly intuits. Habermas's most recent criticism of this behaviorist notion of understanding is directed against Donald Davidson's theory of radical interpretation, which I discuss in
chapter 3. See M. Truzzi, ed. *Subjective Understanding and the Social Sciences* (London: Addison-
Wesley, 1974).

societal repressions, and so on—assume greater explanatory importance (see appendix B). Interpreting this deeper layer of unintended meaning struck positivists as a bit like reading tea leaves. Hence, they concluded that the only epistemologically certain (and, following the doctrine of verificationism, meaningful) form of social science was the noninterpretative, observation-based variety.

Popper also defended scientism—the idea that science embodies a unified method of causal explanation—but rejected the positivistic version of it. To begin with, he rejected the positivistic commitment to a kind of objectivism in his belief that scientific theories are general conjectures—inventive hypotheses—that cannot be inductively inferred from observations of particular events. From this rejection of objectivism he concluded that no scientific theories—indeed, no *theory*—could ever be justified. The essence of scientific rationality is therefore not to prove or justify any truth but to criticize.[3] General laws, he observed, refer to an indefinite number of possible experiments and so can never be completely verified. They can, however, be falsified by a single disconfirming instance (which can be more or less verified). Hence the meaningfulness of a scientific theory is proportional to its capacity to generate potentially falsifiable hypotheses.

Aside from this major disagreement with positivism, Popper upheld the scientistic dogma that any meaningful social science must reject interpretation in favor of causal explanation. In *The Poverty of Historicism* (1957) he argued that such explanation must appeal to behavioral laws that can be observationally tested and serve piecemeal social reform. By contrast, the so-called laws of historical development and social evolution that defenders of total revolution such as Marx and his followers advocated—what Popper referred to as "historicism"—are largely meaningless, since they do not yield falsifiable hypotheses.[4]

Although they accepted much of Popper's critique of Marx's historicism, Habermas and Adorno rejected Popper's critical rationalism as fundamentally uncritical and reactionary.[5] Popper's insistence on defining a meaningful

3. Popper's most mature defense of this view is contained in his *Conjectures and Refutations* (1962).

4. Popper's notion of historicism must not be confused with the concept of historicism that was used by Edmund Husserl, Wilhelm Dilthey, and other (mainly neo-Kantian) thinkers at the turn of the century, for whom the term referred to a kind of historical relativity in the understanding of distinctive historical epochs and cultural worldviews.

5. Habermas (*KHI* 46), for instance, expressly repudiates Marx's own assessment of the natural scientific nature of his critique of political economy, as contained in Marx's approval of a Russian reviewer's methodological description of volume 1 of *Capital*. The assessment occurs in the epilogue to the second edition: "Marx considers the movement of society as a process of natural history, governed by laws that are not only independent of the will, consciousness, and intention of men but instead, and conversely, determine their will, consciousness, and intentions." According to Habermas, Marx misidentified the reflective nature of critical social science by taking as the paradigm of reflection the objectifying (or self-expressive and self-mirroring) activity

social theory in terms of its potential falsification by what they (not necessarily Popper) regarded as a value-free observation of facts—in total abstraction from the broader historical, economic, political, and sociocultural context conditioning perception, thought, and language—struck them as a false and ideological affirmation of the status quo (*PDGS* 157–58, 216–18). While they did not deny the epistemic value of predictive and technically useful knowledge within the natural sciences, they regarded such knowledge as but a subordinate aspect within social science taken as a whole. Critically evaluating norms and values in terms of their consistency and consequences for furthering our chosen ends is only one of the functions of critical reason. The other function is to test these ends against the ideal and unprejudiced understanding of our genuine universal interests. They therefore concluded that the proper aim of social science was not instrumental prediction and control of human behavior for the sake of socially engineering piecemeal reform but radical criticism—and revolutionary transformation—of society as a whole. In their opinion, the "false" desires of the masses, in thrall to work and consumption and mindless of the meaning of true freedom and sociality, were of a piece with the "false" totality of society. Indeed, part of the falseness of this society was its very outward appearance—which Popper, in their minds, unquestionably accepted—of being a "natural" realm of unchanging mechanistic laws, resistant to the genuine emancipatory interests of fully free and rational subjects. By rigidly distinguishing observable facts (the critical touchstone of scientific falsification) from nonobservable values, Popper had consigned any critical evaluation of humanity's true interests to the subjective status of a prescientific personal preference, or rationally unmotivated "decision" (*PDGS* 137–42)

Ironically, it was none other than Wittgenstein himself whom Habermas sought to enlist in his cause against Popperian decisionism. Wittgenstein's late philosophy of language, the most mature expression of which is expounded in his posthumous work, *Philosophical Investigations* (1953), develops a normative account of meaning that is completely antithetical to the positivist view he had earlier developed in the *Tractatus*. In the mature work, Wittgenstein argues that the meaning of language is holistic and contextual (syncategorematic) and linked to public use rather than to ostensive reference. Language, Wittgenstein tells us, is structured as if it were a rule-governed game. Such *language games* comprise speech acts that coordinate social interaction around shared norms of social understanding, or "ways of life" (*OLSS* 130–35).

---

of labor, or instrumental action: "Marx deludes himself about the nature of reflection when he reduces it to labor" and when he "reduces the process of reflection to the level of instrumental action" (*KHI* 43–44). In Marx's defense, it should be noted that he himself appeared to speak of labor in ways that encompassed expressive language and communication. After pointing out that "cooperation is itself a 'productive force'" he notes that this "conscious" activity is essentially mediated by language. See K. Marx, *The German Ideology: Part I*, excerpted in *Karl Marx: Selected Writings*, ed. L. Simon (Indianapolis: Hackett, 1994), 116–17.

Habermas cited Peter Winch's pioneering manifesto, *The Idea of a Social Science* (1958), to show how Wittgenstein's theory of speech action could be used to defend an interpretative social science. Winch argued that meaningful action is distinguished from brute behavior in being structured, identified, and constituted by the intentions of the actor. Such intentions are therefore not discrete psychic causes that precede physical action as Popper, Carl Hempel, and other advocates of the so-called covering law model of social and historical explanation had maintained.[6] Furthermore, Winch insisted that intentional actions can be understood and interpreted only within the context of a way of life. More precisely, the conscious intention of the actor—what it is he or she explicitly intends to do—implicitly refers to unconscious norms of speaking and acting. To explain an action is therefore to understand it as a meaningful instance of a norm that could, in principle, be creatively applied or even violated (*OLSS* 127–30).

Wittgenstein's philosophy of language proved pivotal for Habermas's refutation of Popper's "moral decisionism." According to Wittgenstein's philosophy, language and action are constituted as meaningful because they express social norms and interests that possess a publicly demonstrable force capable of limiting and regulating private moral decision. This normative meaning is implicitly understood by speakers and actors, if not expressly intended by them.

This common sense theory of meaning as something shared and public would be utterly convincing except for one fact, which Habermas and Adorno readily seized on: psychoanalysis has taught us that persons can deceive themselves about the real meaning of *this* meaning. In other words, the language and behavior into which we are socialized may seem meaningful and rational to us, but on deeper reflection it appears to be less so. If it is the product of habitual conditioning and prejudice, it may not speak to our deeper interests as human beings. Instead, it may advance the partial interests of a dominant class or function to stabilize an oppressive and unjust society. Thus, just because we are conditioned to believe that we are free simply because we can choose this or that option does not mean that we are actually free, for our choices may be manipulated by advertising and propaganda. Equally important, choice alone may not capture other dimensions of freedom, such as thoughtful reflection on core values and beliefs. Moreover, it excludes any reference to the conditions underlying its own robust exercise, such as education and knowledge, resource and opportunity, which may be restricted by social circumstances.

Habermas summarized this psychoanalytic line of argument in his second major work, *The Logic of the Social Sciences* (1967/1970). In order to explain social behavior, the social scientist must first understand it as meaningful,

---

6. The covering law model refers to the logical form of a causal explanation. This form subsumes (or covers) two distinct types of events—a cause C and an effect E—under a general causal law possessing a conditional form: 'If C then E' or a counterfactual form 'If not-C then not-E'.

norm- or rule-governed intentional action. But the social scientist cannot simply presume that such action is fully meaningful and coherent as intended by the actor, since the actor might be deluded about what he or she is *really* doing. The conventional ways of understanding and acting might function to frustrate what the actor really wants: freedom, happiness, solidarity, and self-respect based on equal recognition by peers. To expose this lack of coherence and meaningfulness—and unmask the conventional ways of understanding and acting as false, irrational, and supportive of oppression and domination, in short, as *ideological*—we need a critical social science modeled on psychoanalysis (*OLSS* 180–88). But how is such a social science possible?

Modern Nihilism: The Crisis of Science and the Theory/Practice Problem

The possibility of a critical social science recalls one of the most venerable problems of philosophy: the theory/practice problem. This problem can be formulated accordingly: If theory refers to knowledge of a mind-independent reality—objective facts, or what is (or must be) the case independent of our willing—then how can theory possibly alter our mind-dependent volitions, ends, and actions, that is, our practice? To recall Hume's formulation of the problem in chapter 1, how does one's sense of what one *ought* to do follow from one's knowledge of what *is* the case?

This is a distinctly modern problem. From antiquity to the Middle Ages reality was understood as inherently purposive, or guided by divine ends. According to this view, the good is what being (Nature) strives to realize, with "being" designating what is relatively permanent, unitary, and unchanging, in contrast to the flux of shifting appearances. If we define knowledge as a correspondence between knower and known, knowing reality conceived in this moral fashion correspondingly brings about within the knower a state of timeless harmony and repose, or self-sufficiency, the ultimate end of which is well-being (or happiness). Knowledge understood in this objectivistic sense therapeutically purges the passions and interests that would otherwise submerge the soul in a state of restless, unfilled desire and *unfreedom*. Indeed, as Habermas himself astutely observes, "theory" comes from the Greek *theoria,* which, according to Aristotle (384–322 BCE), originally referred to the cathartic purgation of passions that onlookers experienced in passively observing the fateful, ever-recurring, universal constants of the natural-mythic human condition manifested in the plot of a theatrical tragedy (*KHI* 301).

Once reality loses its moral character and becomes a purposeless movement of bodies responding to mechanical cause and effect—a secularizing change in our understanding of the world that corresponds to the rise of modernity—scientific theory (knowledge) ceases to effect moral change in the knower. It is cut off from practice, and practice, in turn, is cut off from it. From now on, knowledge will retain its "traditional" meaning of interest- and desire-free correspondence with the facts but without these having any moral significance.

Positivism is undoubtedly the most extreme manifestation of traditional theory wrapped in modern garb.[7] Its adherence to scientism and objectivism ruthlessly excises both morality and philosophy from the domain of meaningful knowledge. Theoretically (if not practically) speaking, this exclusion is paradoxical.[8] For positivism itself is a philosophy of science, and, as distinguished from science, it appears to be meaningless and without truth according to its own criterion of meaning and truth (PKHI 161). Furthermore, when presented as the only philosophical legitimation of meaning and knowledge, positivism—as meaningless philosophy—fails to justify science.

This theoretical "crisis"—the incapacity of science to philosophically legitimate its own faith in reason, logic, meaningfulness, and methodical value-free inquiry—also has a practical (moral) dark side: *nihilism.* As used by Nietzsche,[9] *nihilism* (from the Latin *nihil* or *nothing*) refers to two interrelated phenomena: On the one hand, it refers to the apparent meaninglessness and nullity of our mundane experiences and beliefs in contrast with the highest and most transcendent philosophical realities—God and Reason. This contrast, however, is susceptible to a dialectical reversal once it is understood that the highest metaphysical realities are themselves utterly empty and meaningless. A similar understanding, as we have seen, is advanced by positivism. On the other hand, nihilism refers to the positive elevation of the will to the highest reality and supreme nihilating force of being. Here Nietzsche rejects positivism: all being is illusory; nothing that presents itself in experience—not even "atomic facts"—possesses intrinsic meaning. In short, meanings and values are tools that the will creates and imposes on reality in its struggle to gain power over it. The positive affirmation of nihilism is therefore therapeutic: it liberates the will from all "presumed" determinations and conditions; even the past is reduced to an illusion. So conceived, the supreme overcoming of

7. Habermas's reference to traditional theory expressly recalls Horkheimer's "Traditional and Critical Theory" (1937), in which traditional theory is understood as any theory that defines knowledge objectivistically, as a passive mirroring of and adaptation to a reality that is given to us independently of our interested action.

8. Habermas concedes Thomas Kuhn's point in *The Structure of Scientific Revolutions* (1962) that normal scientific problem solving is impossible when researchers are absorbed in reflecting on the underlying cognitive interests, paradigmatic foundations, and methodological assumptions underlying their activity. Indeed, failure to be *practically* positivistic (value neutral) poses the risk that one's science will degenerate into political ideology (as evidenced in Nazi race theory and Soviet genetic science) (*KHI* 315). Conversely, positivism does not completely describe scientists' own attitudes, insofar as scientists concede that their practice shapes their understanding of nature and is motivated by a technical interest. Habermas's argument, therefore, is directed against those who, like Ernst Mach and logical positivists Moritz Schlick and Rudolf Carnap, tried to reduce theoretical statements to first-person observation reports of sense data.

9. See Nietzsche's *The Gay Science* (1882–87), *Thus Spoke Zarathustra* (1883–85), and *Beyond Good and Evil* (1886) and Habermas's critique of the positivistic assumptions underlying Nietzsche's perspectival account of knowledge (*KHI* 290–300).

limits—moral, cognitive, objective, and subjective—allows the will to embrace life as a never-ending work of art.

As I remarked in chapter 1, critical theorists saw Nietzsche's celebration of the "will to power" as a sinister harbinger for a new, all-encompassing affirmation of scientific and technological social engineering. Fascism and communism, they observed, were but the most extreme manifestations of a general totalitarian attempt to remake society "as a work of art." As in Nietzsche's philosophy, there exists a categorical distinction between the artistic "over-men," who have overcome conventional moral limits, and their subaltern subjects. The revolutionary recreation of society is a top-down affair. The administrative regimentation of modern life demands passive conformism and authoritarian deference to technological and scientific elites. Indeed, as Habermas himself has remarked on more than one occasion, in an age in which we increasingly turn to the state for securing our welfare, science and technology themselves become ideological. Seeking leeway to manage a complex capitalist economy without aggravating class conflicts, the welfare state cannot afford to risk a divisive debate on the moral justice of its redistribution of wealth. Accordingly, the positivist elimination of morality and the accompanying reduction of practical problems to technological problems become, in their own way, the functional ideologies by which the masses are maintained in their passivity.[10]

How did philosophers respond to the totalitarian threat posed by scientific nihilism? Edmund Husserl (1859–1938) famously urged in *The Crisis of European Sciences and Transcendental Phenomenology* (1934) that modern science should rediscover its original theoretical motivation: to liberate agents from the passions and prejudices that prevent them from becoming responsible moral agents. Accordingly, he insisted on the necessity of philosophical reflection—animated by the scientific spirit—for uncovering the common transcendental condition underlying both science and modern morality. For his part, Heidegger alluded to the possibility of philosophically recovering the original meaning of being that Greek philosophers since Plato had obscured. The original Greek meaning of the technical (*technē*), he claimed, referred to a disclosure of being that resisted any impulse to objectify and dominate nature.[11] Marcuse, who had been a student of both Husserl and Heidegger, also appealed to the Greek understanding of *technē* in appropriating a form of scientific-technological rationality that he hoped would bridge the postmetaphysical positivist divide separating facts and values. Oriented toward the "art of life," this new science and technology, Marcuse believed, could "liberate" nature from its own destructive tendencies even as it realized nature's potentials.

10. See chapter 10 of this book and J. Habermas, "Technology and Science as 'Ideology'," in *Critical Theory: The Essential Readings,* ed. D. Ingram and J. Simon (New York: Paragon House, 1992), 117–45. (It is also reprinted in *TRS.*)

11. M. Heidegger, *The Question Concerning Technology* (New York: Harper and Row, 1977).

The full realization of human capacities, in tandem with the full "pacification" of nature, would restore a vital link of communication between humans and their environment that had been sundered by destructive and exploitative uses of technology in capitalism and bureaucratic socialism.[12]

Marcuse's optimism reflects the Marxist view—proclaimed by Horkheimer in his early manifesto, "Traditional and Critical Theory" (1937)—that science and technology vary historically in their methods and aims. Habermas, however, rejected this position, at least in part. With Marcuse, he conceded that science and technology could serve different political aims depending on what kind of society developed them. The close connection between management technologies and the intense division of labor—including the separation of mental and physical labor that one finds on assembly lines—is a case in point. As Marcuse noted, this technical design is not neutral in its function because built into its conception of efficiency is the maintenance of a top-down system of coordinating and controlling otherwise disconnected laboring activities.[13] More precisely, this technical design is functional for a capitalist class system premised on the maximal technological exploitation of wage labor for purposes of creating profit. Its disempowerment of assembly-line workers perfectly reinforces the undemocratic scientistic ideology that solving problems and coordinating activities are tasks that are best left to technical experts who are in positions of knowledge and power. A different system aimed at producing and developing well-rounded human beings would specify a different conception of efficiency, and would therefore call forth different—in Marx's vocabulary, less dehumanizing and alienating—technologies.[14]

Despite his acceptance of Marcuse's critique of the totalitarian domination implicit in capitalist technology, Habermas denied that the basic methods and underlying "anthropological" interests of science and technology were as historically and politically variable as Marcuse and Horkheimer had suggested. In particular, he rejected Marcuse's vague notion of a "new science" that (on Habermas's reading) would require replacing objectifying methods. As Habermas remarked, the only alternative to a less-objectifying relationship with nature is a communicative one, and no one—least of all Marcuse—would want to replace quantitative experimental methods with magical supplications (*TRS* 81–89).[15] But if natural and behavioral science cannot accommodate our

12. H. Marcuse, *One Dimensional Man: Studies in the Ideology of Advanced Industrial Society* (Boston: Beacon Press, 1964), esp. chap. 9. Also see, A. Feenberg, *Heidegger and Marcuse: The Catastrophe and Redemption of Technology* (New York: Routledge, 2004).

13. H. Marcuse, "Some Social Implications of Modern Technology" (1941), in *The Essential Frankfurt School Reader*, ed. A. Arato and E. Gebhardt (New York: Continuum, 1982), 138–62.

14. Habermas, "Technology and Science as 'Ideology'," 115–19.

15. Andrew Feenberg defends Marcuse against Habermas on precisely this point. Marcuse's claim that we can develop a different technological rationality that would enable us to relate to nature "as a subject" is not to be understood as prescribing a return to premodern teleological or anthropomorphic conceptions of nature. Rather, Marcuse's point is that the dominant mode of

moral yearnings for community and happiness, then what science can? And how can we justify it? In short, how is a critical theory with practical intent possible?

Knowledge and Human Interests

Habermas's first major philosophical work, *Knowledge and Human Interests* (hereafter *KHI*), can be understand as answering just this question. In the course of explaining how a critical theory is possible, Habermas also explains how knowledge in general is possible. But Habermas also has a more ambitious agenda. Following Marx, he wants to show that a purely philosophical critique of knowledge cannot be realized unless (paradoxically) it transcends itself and becomes something other than pure philosophy: a social and natural history of the human species. At stake in this philosophical anthropology is a most startling—indeed, revolutionary—claim: genuine knowledge can be realized only as a communal project in which humans have emancipated themselves from the distorting effects of social and political domination. Even more striking, *KHI* proposes a radical solution to the theory/practice problem: if knowledge implies social freedom, then the critical philosopher's task—to show under what conditions legitimate knowledge is possible—would appear to point beyond itself. From this vantage point, knowledge and philosophy (theory) can no longer be taken for granted as "given" but must instead be seen as ideals that bring about—through the practice of reflection—their very own possibility. So construed, philosophy could no longer continue as a contemplative theory of knowledge but would have to become a practical force for emancipation: a social science that criticizes ideology.

To review these points: I have noted that explaining how critical theory is possible requires answering the more general question, How is knowledge possible? You will recall that this was Kant's question. Like Kant's *Critique of Pure Reason, KHI* combats the dogmatism associated with uncritically extending one kind of knowledge—or one kind of metaphysical objectivism—and its skeptical implications for morality. In *KHI,* the dogmatism pertains not to speculative metaphysics but to positivism's equation of reason with a narrow

---

technological rationality—which favors precisely that quantitative abstraction from qualitative ethical and aesthetic values and norms that Habermas identifies with "a 'project' of the human species *as a whole*"—belies its concrete realization in value-laden designs. Marcuse's reference to nature as subject thus refers to nature as repository of value and meaning revealed by technology (in the way, Heidegger notes, that a bridge defines location and gathers together persons, meanings, values, etc.). As Feenberg remarks, technical design should reverse the abstraction and differentiation ("primary instrumentalization") fetishized by industrial capitalism in furtherance of hierarchical control by embodying democratic, multivalent purposes and meanings ("secondary instrumentalization") analogous to premodern craft production. A. Feenberg, *Questioning Technology* (London: Routledge, 1999), 156–80, 201–25.

logic of experimental inquiry and causal explanation. So, one of the purposes of *KHI* is to show that any attempt to extend this logic beyond its legitimate field of application in the natural and behavioral sciences to the subject matter proper to historical and interpretative science is invalid.

Kant's refutation of skepticism also finds a parallel in Habermas. The logic of inquiry and explanation inherent in the natural scientific method implies a strict separation of values and facts. According to this logic, knowledge is value free—experimental observations and causal explanations are "controlled" in such a way as to eliminate any reference to subjective factors that cannot be empirically confirmed. That means that moral (and critical) knowledge regarding good and bad, right and wrong, is a contradiction in terms. So another purpose of *KHI* is to refute this skeptical conclusion and show how moral and ethical knowledge concerning norms and values is possible. As one might expect, it does this by showing how the interpretative and historical sciences are possible.

Kant failed to show how his own transcendental philosophy could be justified as a legitimate form of knowledge. *KHI* attempts to avoid this error. Besides showing how empirical-analytic and historical-interpretative sciences are possible relative to their respective subject matters, *KHI* also shows how—as a form of philosophical reflection—its own synthesis of theory and practice, knowledge and critique is possible. Philosophical reflection is knowledge about knowledge. But reflection is more than just knowledge (theory); it is also practice. According to a tradition dating back to Fichte and Hegel and continuing down to Freud, reflection changes the nature of its object. To take an obvious example, an unconscious desire has the force of a compulsion; that same desire, brought to reflective consciousness, has the potency of a possibility, or free option. Reflection emancipates. By dissolving compulsions it also eliminates the very prejudices that distort knowledge. So, *KHI* shows how its own peculiar form of critical reflection—qua therapeutic moral knowledge aimed at dispelling dogmatic prejudices such as positivism—is possible, or transcendentally justified from the perspective of our anthropological interest in freedom and happiness and, more important, it shows why such critical reflection is necessary as a political form of revolutionary social praxis that makes possible the only kind of domination-free, emancipated society in which genuine knowledge can emerge.

Now that we have some general idea about what *KHI* is about, I will examine its argument more closely. At issue are two interconnected theses advanced by positivism:

> Thesis 1: All knowledge must be about observed facts.
> Thesis 2: All knowledge must be value free.

Thesis 1 commits us to scientism—the notion that the method of experimental inquiry and causal explanation is the only proper scientific method and must be extended to the historical and social sciences if these are to be considered genuine sciences. Thesis 2 commits us to the view that evaluative judgments are not knowledge, which is to say that they are mere expressions of subjective feeling.

KHI rejects these theses by arguing that there are three types of knowledge, each of which is oriented by deeper, nonsubjective values, or "transcendental interests." Recall Husserl's concern about the crisis of modern science. Value-neutral science, he observed, is incapable of justifying itself. Theorists of science from Weber to Popper had argued that values such as truth and justice could not be grounded in reason but were chosen in an act of faith. For them, no philosophically satisfactory answer exists to the question, Why are science (true belief) and morality (right belief) good and worth pursuing? Failure to answer this question relegates science and morality to preferential options based on mere subjective taste.

KHI answers this question by pointing out that each of the three kinds of science is necessary for the survival of the human species. More precisely, each science possesses a unique logic of inquiry (method) that refines a basic kind of human action. Each basic action, in turn, is oriented by a deep-seated anthropological interest whose satisfaction is necessary for the survival of the human species.

The distinctive thing about this project is its reliance on two kinds of arguments. The first argument consists of a natural scientific account of natural and social evolution. The second argument consists of a transcendental argument about the necessary and universal conditions for experiencing (knowing) phenomena of a certain type. The first argument, from *natural selection* (or natural evolution), explains how three specific types of survival challenges—natural scarcity, absence of social coordination, and social domination—call forth certain deep-seated interests in gaining technical control over a recalcitrant environment, uniting with others around common values and norms, and achieving freedom. These interests are realized in the course of pursuing three kinds of action: instrumental (experimental) action based on behavioral feedback; communicative action based on mutual understanding and consensus; and critical reflection based on examining the causes of one's core beliefs.

The second, *transcendental* argument shows that specific types of action constitute or make possible specific kinds of phenomena; that is, it shows that these types of action are both *necessary* for having knowledge of a certain sort and *universal* to all human beings. Instrumental action enables us to experience a sensory world in the form of material objects that possess measurable properties connected by causal relations. Communicative action enables us to understand a social world composed of persons, norms, values, meanings, and identities connected by narrative relations. Reflection, by contrast, does not constitute a domain of reality as such. However, it does constitute a process whereby impediments to knowledge are discovered and removed.

Habermas elaborates on each of these points by adverting to the arguments of the American philosopher of natural science and founder of pragmatism, Charles Peirce, and the German philosopher of history and founder of hermeneutic philosophy, Wilhelm Dilthey. Both of these philosophers challenged the positivist view that knowledge (truth) involves a passive correspondence with a pregiven object.

Peirce challenged the positivist view that our knowledge of things and the meanings of the words we use to refer to their properties are reducible to our passive experience of sensation. Hume, you will recall, had already shown that *necessary* cause-and-effect relationships could not be derived from our experience of past associations of sensory states, even when these associations have been invariant. Just because the rising of the sun (S) is always preceded by the crowing of the rooster (R) does not mean that the crowing causes the sun to rise. 'Whenever R then S' may be true so far as our passive observation is concerned; indeed the presence of R may be sufficient reason to infer S. But we would not be entitled to infer that R stood in some necessary connection to S, so that absent S, R would not happen.

A cause C must also be *nonaccidentally* or *necessarily* related to its effect E.[16] Therefore, the proper form of a causal law must also include a *counterfactual conditional* of the form: Had event-type C not occurred, then event-type E would not have occurred (where C is "necessary" for E). Notice that this claim is not discovered by passive observation of what has occurred (factual associations of C and E). It is only discovered by experimental action: actively intervening to suppress or remove certain conditions in order to isolate those whose removal or suppression also removes or suppresses a given effect.

---

16. For Peirce, all causal inferences, except *deductive* ones in which we infer an effect E from a cause C and a fully confirmed conditional hypothesis 'If C then E,' are at best probable. *Inductive* inferences—by which Peirce means the experimental testing of hypotheses—are the means by which this probability is established. What Peirce calls *hypothesis* (or *abductive* inference), by contrast, refers to a process of inferring a cause from a result and a given hypothesis. Peirce seems to have conceived this inference in two ways. First, if we formulate our hypothesis as a biconditional ('E if and only if C') we can infer C from E in explaining the cause of E. However, by abduction Peirce also had in mind a process by which we "stretch an induction beyond the limits of observation" in order to produce unexpected results and thus to hypothesize the existence of a cause different from the one contained in our initial hypothesis. In this instance, we infer a new cause and generate a new hypothesis. Abductive inference such as this forms the very heart and soul of the logic of scientific discovery and accordingly conceives experimental activity as a process of what Popper calls "falsification." The generation of anomalous results and their explanation by fruitful hypotheses that cannot yet be experimentally confirmed appears to play a decisive role in motivating scientific revolutions (or major shifts in scientific paradigms and theories, as Kuhn argued). The main point is that the use of experimentation in discovering anomalies involves not the simple replication of old experiments for purposes of (re)confirmation but the design of new experiments to eliminate conditions that were formerly taken to be causes (*KHI* 113–16, 333–34n1–4). C. Peirce, "Lectures on Pragmatism," in *The Collected Papers of Charles Sanders Peirce*, vol. 5 (Cambridge: Harvard University Press, 1934), 161, 171; and Peirce, "Deduction, Induction, and Hypothesis," in *Collected Papers*, vol. 2 (Cambridge: Harvard University Press, 1932), 619–44.

Instrumental action is thus necessary (if not indeed sufficient) for discovering causal relations.[17] Following Peirce, we might say that such action defines (or in Habermas's language, transcendentally constitutes) what it means to be a material object with properties. As noted in chapter 1, one's capacity to identify a material object as the same object despite changes in its properties depends on the fact that these properties interact with other properties in invariant (causal) relationships. Because these properties are defined by causal relationships, and causal relationships are defined counterfactually—in terms of possible instrumental actions—the meanings of properties are also defined in terms of possible instrumental actions. Thus, on Peirce's account, the meaning of any objective property (e.g., "diamond hard") is equivalent to a counterfactual hypothesis of the form: 'If one *were* to perform certain tests (scratching with a knife, biting with one's mouth, etc.) on diamondlike substances under variable conditions, then definite consequences (such as failure to scratch, bite through, etc.) *would* occur' (*KHI* 129–32).[18]

Especially important for Habermas is the way in which Peirce connects this account of meaning to a *consensus* theory of truth. As we have seen, instrumental action establishes which observable regularities make up the noncontingent, causally necessary powers and properties of things. To say they are causally necessary, however, is somewhat misleading. Hume was right to this extent; what distinguishes causal knowledge from random association is a kind of habit or fixity of belief. And it is the fixity of belief that determines the fixity of meaning. But how do we acquire fixity of belief? Peirce's answer—in terms of probability—led him to introduce a new consensus theory of truth.

Beliefs we call "true" are acquired and tested in experimental situations in which the outcomes are at best statistically probable but not absolutely certain. Our knowledge that an experiment will produce a result at a certain frequency becomes more certain in proportion to the number of times we perform the experiment. Fewer experimental trials will decrease the reliability of our

17. According to Habermas (*KHI* 336n30), Peirce is mistaken in his view that instrumental action alone suffices to explain the abductive discovery of causal relations. Falsification does not specify what aspect of the theory needs to be revised (if any, since the anomalous result may be a function of faulty equipment). The process of *interpreting* the result so as to generate a new causal hypothesis is essentially a collective enterprise, largely hashed out in journal articles, that occurs within the framework of communicative interaction. Pierce himself could have appreciated this fact given his belief—very much antagonistic to positivism's postulation of linguistically unmediated sense experience as the criterion of objectivity—that "there is no element in man's consciousness which has not something corresponding to the word." Despite Peirce's appreciation of the essentially symbolic form of thinking, Habermas also takes note of his tendency to lapse into a dichotomy between symbolically uninterpreted sensory experience and symbolically mediated thought (*KHI* 95–112). See C. Peirce, "Some Consequences of Four Incapacities," in *Collected Papers*, vol. 5, esp. 283, 287, 289, 290–91, 307, 311, 313–14.

18. C. Peirce, "The Logic of 1873," in *Collected Papers*, vol. 7 (Cambridge: Harvard University Press, 1958), 340. Habermas, however, notes (*KHI* 132) that Peirce tends to treat the properties of things as if they really adhered in things independently of the instrumental and communicative action frames in which experience is meaningfully organized and interpreted.

prediction that a certain result is likely to obtain. For instance, if I throw a die just six times, the side with six dots might appear thrice, yielding a frequency of 1:2 instead of 1:6, the true probability that would obtain if I threw the die an indefinite number of times.[19]

What Peirce calls "truth" is simply the property of a belief to withstand experimental tests over the long run.[20] It is the experimental method—not tenacity, authority, or a priori reasoning—that allows the truth to emerge. But this occurs only when the experimental method is applied by an *indefinite community* of inquirers over an *indefinite period of time*. True is any belief that an ideal community of experimental inquirers would accept, or consent to, over time (*KHI* 91–95).[21] This communal application of the experimental method presupposes that experimental situations can be replicated under varying conditions, which would be impossible if such situations could not be made standard and uniform by means of precisely calibrated controls. Only by correlating qualitative properties (e.g., heat) with numerical values (volumetric increase in mercury) can inquirers be assured they are studying the same phenomena.

In sum, the reduction of qualitative properties to quantitative properties—the inductive reduction of particular experiences to regular (identical) causal generalizations by means of regular and repeatable experimental interventions—is the hallmark of scientific objectivity.[22] Experimental measurement refines a primitive mode of feedback (trial and error) learning aimed at "stabilizing belief." This is just another way of saying that instrumental action makes possible habitual expectations that things in the world respond in predictable ways to what we do to them. It is on the basis of this causal knowledge that we procure our material well-being. But *work,* in this sense, has also had a technical dimension ever since hominids evolved bipedal motility and opposable thumbs. Indeed, as Habermas notes (citing Arnold Gehlen), one can understand the various technological revolutions as phases in which the human species progressively unburdened itself of its own organic functions "by projecting them one after another onto the plane of technical instruments," beginning with motor functions (hands and legs), followed by energy producing functions (of the human body), and concluding with the calculating and controlling functions (of the brain) (*TRS* 85–86).

---

19. C. Peirce, "The Doctrine of Chances," in *Collected Papers,* vol. 2, 645–60.

20. See C. Peirce, "How to Make Our Ideas Clear," in *Collected Papers,* vol. 5, 406–7.

21. Although Habermas here accepts Peirce's equation of truth with a final ideal consensus, he rejected this view thirty years later (see chapter 3).

22. In the relevant passages of *KHI* where measuring activity is discussed, Habermas comes dangerously close to confusing experiential objectivity and scientific objectivity. Scientific objectivity—the reduction of qualitative experience to quantitative experience—involves imposing a *secondary objectification* on our otherwise prescientific experience of qualitatively meaningful objects. Whereas scientific objectivity involves a deliberate *abstraction* from qualitative experience (or, as Habermas elsewhere argues, a *discursive translation* of experience into testable data), prescientific objectivity involves a transcendentally necessitated instrumental achievement (PKHI 181).

Behind this natural and social evolutionary logic, whose culmination is modern science and cybernetic technology, lies a deep-seated anthropological "technical" interest in operationally reducing the world to causally uniform, predictable, and therefore controllable objects. This interest "evolved" at the moment when hominids had to work in order to survive. But, as I noted above, the logic of technology could not have progressed very far if technical interventions had been random and isolated events. If technical *progress* requires a *community* of investigators as Peirce argued, then we must explain how human community is possible as well.

To do that Habermas enlists the support of Dilthey in articulating the logic of a different kind of interest-action-knowledge syndrome. Communities are held together by communication, a form of action that enables individuals to reach mutual understanding and agreement on the meanings, values, and norms that unite them and that constitute their identities. This latter point—about the importance of communication in constituting oneself as a self with a distinctive identity—recalls our earlier discussion of Kant in chapter 1. Kant had argued that one could not experience one's experiences as belonging to a self unless one could also experience one's experiences as referring to an object (something remaining *identical,* outside of one's stream of disparate sensory impressions). Hegel later developed this insight about identity in an interesting way. In the *Phenomenology of Spirit* he argues that a person cannot experience himself as free and unique person (i.e., he cannot possess "self-certainty") unless others confirm (recognize or acknowledge) him in this belief.

Hegel's insight about personal identity provides Dilthey with a point of departure for examining the transcendental basis for the interpretative and historical sciences. One's identity—literally, who one is—consists of a story: an autobiography. This autobiography is all about growing up: taking on roles, values, and purposes that have *meaning* for (are *recognized* by) others.

How is meaning constituted? Dilthey endorses the view, later developed by Wittgenstein, that meaning is holistic. Gestures, actions, and utterances possess meaning only with reference to one another and the broader context in which they occur. The waving of a hand is a greeting or a warning depending on what gets said and done; "Save this person" means "Save Sally" or "Save Brian" depending on the direction my finger points; striking a ship with a bottle of champagne by the ship's captain is either a christening or a display of macho depending on whether it is accompanied by the words "I hereby christen thee..." or the words "Let's have a swig of this, mates!" This circularity is the hallmark of textual interpretation, where our understanding of meaning fragments (words, sentences, paragraphs, chapters, etc.) enhances our understanding of the whole and vice versa. The part-whole (hermeneutic) circle that underlies the constitution of the self as an (auto)biography grounds the part-whole circle of everyday understanding, and both in turn form the primitive root of the interpretative methods deployed by historians, cultural anthropologists, sociologists, clinical psychologists, and other practitioners of human science (*KHI* 145–60).[23]

Meaning is (con)textual and holistic. However, as I noted above, it is also inherently social. Here Dilthey endorsed another view later defended by Wittgenstein: the impossibility of a private language. I know the meaning of a word if I know how to use it correctly (the same way on different occasions), and I know *that* only if "correctly" can be specified in terms of a publicly recognized rule. The notion of a publicly recognized rule in turn implies agreement and mutual understanding, which in turn implies the ability to share (or communicate) one's perspective to another.

Dilthey inconsistently conceived this act of identifying with another as either entailing a kind of mental transposition into the other's mind or as a genuine act of communicating with the other (*KHI* 180–86). Habermas believes that this latter communicative dimension of understanding is better explicated by the philosophical hermeneutics of Hans-Georg Gadamer (*OLSS* 162–66). According to Gadamer,[24] it is mistaken to think of understanding a person or a text as an act of mysteriously divining the speaker/author's psychological intentions. True understanding (correctly understanding what is said or written) cannot involve this kind of "correspondence" because we are not always in a position to know what the speaker/author's intentions are, and when we do know them it is not because we have entered inside the speaker/author's mind but because we have communicated with her or him.

The accent on communication shows that understanding is a two-way street. Take the example of an anthropologist trying to understand the rituals of a newly discovered tribe. It might seem that objective and unbiased understanding requires suspending one's own cultural presuppositions, as if these were impediments to getting inside the head of one's subject. But, of course, getting inside the head of others—by getting outside one's own head—is impossible. On the contrary, understanding is always a process of making something new familiar in a way that resonates with what one already understands. Understanding is therefore guided by expectations that open up in advance a horizon of possible meaningfulness. What a computer means (and can mean) to an insurance agent is different than what it means to an aborigine who has never seen one; what the *Iliad* means to a seasoned scholar of Homeric epics is different than what it means to a college freshman.

Because we bring our own concerns, interests, and understandings to bear on what we seek to understand, we must conceive of understanding as a process of questioning that seeks a response. Understanding is dialogical. Like any dialogue, it involves dialectic—a process of reaching agreement or synthesis

23. W. Dilthey, *Selected Works*, vol. 4, *The Formation of the Historical World in the Human Sciences*, ed. R. Makkreel and F. Rodi (Princeton: Princeton University Press, 2000).
24. H.-G. Gadamer, *Truth and Method*, 2nd rev. ed. (New York: Continuum, 1992).

(or as Gadamer puts it, fusion) of meaning horizons whereby one horizon alters and expands another.

The meaning of the text unfolds as an event in which both the reader and the text mutually question and inform each other. Gadamer calls this the *ontological* circle, in order to distinguish it from the hermeneutical circle discussed above. My identity and being, as reader/interpreter, is altered by the "truth" conveyed by the text (i.e., I learn something from it). Conversely, by making sense of the text in terms of my own contemporary reference points, I extend its validity, application, meaning, and truth beyond what its author envisaged.

If the reader's prejudices always mediate the text's meaning, how can we avoid biased understanding? Gadamer responds by mentioning two factors. First, although my reading is guided by prejudices over which I have no control (my native language, for instance), there is no reason to think that they are so parochial and time bound as to prevent my understanding the potentially timeless truth of the text. Some of these prejudices—the ones on which we confer the honorific title "tradition"—have withstood the test of time. For this reason, they are a reliable authority for filtering out parochial elements of textual meaning that no longer speak truthfully to us. Second, this process is reciprocal. In resisting easy understanding, the text forces me to question, in turn, parochial and time-bound elements in my own understanding.

The circular part/whole method of interpretation that defines the historical sciences thus models a question-answer dialogue that finds its original analog in everyday self-understanding and communication. Because this process is guided by presuppositions over which one has no control, it cannot strictly be methodically or consciously applied. However, that does not mean it is unscientific or lacking in critical rigor. According to Gadamer, its critical rigor consists in the expansion, deepening, and checking of one's presuppositions over time.

In sum, understanding always takes place within a process of communication. The communication in question may be internal—between "me" and my biography—or external—between "me" and another person (or text). Communication of this sort makes identification and identity possible. It makes possible meaning, understood as something that can be identical for different people. It makes possible values and norms, understood as something that can be agreed on by different people. It thus makes possible the continuous identity of a culture that can be handed down and renewed generation after generation; the socialization and individuation of persons; and the coordination of social actions around shared norms and aims. In short, communicative action makes possible community. All of this can be seen as serving a practical (broadly speaking, moral) interest in achieving unconstrained agreement with others.

Table 1 below summarizes the different contributions that instrumental and communicative types of action make to the transcendental constitution, respectively, of material objects and meaningful entities. Note that the transcendental constitution of material objects requires both instrumental and

Table 1
Transcendental constitution of experience

Experience of	Constituted by
Individual personal identities	Communicative action
Social (group) identities, meanings, values, norms	
Meaningful events, actions, symbols	
Material objects	*Instrumental action*
	Spatiotemporal relations
	Communicative action
	Conceptual categories for identifying (classifying) particular things
	Instrumental and communicative action
	Causal relations and substantive permanence (identity) of things through changes in their properties

communicative action, because, as Kant taught, all experience is mediated by concepts, or general meaningful norms of identification and discrimination by which we distinguish (identify) our experience of this perception as, for instance, that of a chair rather than a short table. I shall have more to say about how communication contributes to our experience of (reference to) the material world of natural scientific objects in chapter 4.

Indeed, looking ahead to his later philosophy, Habermas observed in his 1965 inaugural address to the faculty at the Johann Wolfgang Goethe University of Frankfurt (on taking over Horkheimer's chair at the Institute for Social Research) that the dialogical structure of language itself anticipates ideals of truth, freedom, justice, and happiness.

> What raises us out of nature is the only thing whose nature we can know: *language*. Through its structure, autonomy and responsibility are posited for us. Our first sentence expresses unequivocally the intention of universal and unconstrained consensus. Taken together, autonomy and responsibility constitute the only Idea that we possess a priori in the sense of a philosophical tradition.... However, only in an emancipated society, whose members' autonomy and responsibility had been realized, would communication have developed into the non-authoritarian and universally practiced dialogue from which both our model of reciprocally constituted ego identity and our idea of true consensus are always implicitly derived. To this extent the truth of statements is based on anticipating the realization of the good life. (*KHI* 314)

Dialogue anticipates truth, insofar as interlocutors are oriented toward reaching a final consensus on what is or should be; it anticipates freedom, insofar as they remain open to each other's truth claims, unconstrained by prejudice;

it anticipates justice, insofar as they question one another as equals; and it anticipates happiness, insofar as they seek reconciliation with self and other in fulfilling community.

But, as I have noted, the consensus that we in fact achieve is far from unconstrained. Once the human species evolved to the point where it could only procure its self-preservation in the form of state-administered civilizations, vertical distinctions had to be made between ruling and subaltern classes. The power of the former to compel the latter to work for them could not be sustained through violence alone, but required legitimating ideologies. From this moment, production of the cultural medium of self-understanding and social coordination would no longer be a spontaneous event of egalitarian dialogue. It would be constrained and distorted by power, with the result that the very tradition inculcated through socialization would serve to conceal from people the actual extent to which their everyday lives deviated from the ideals implicit in their communication.

It is here where Habermas pinpoints the need for a new science. The emergence of capitalism substitutes the older religious and metaphysical ideologies justifying the naturalness of hierarchy and domination with a new secular ideology of universal equality. According to this ideology, the wage contract is a model of communication in which equal values are freely exchanged for mutual benefit. The surpassing of the free market with the rise of the welfare state does not abolish this ideology as much as transfer it to the state. Democracy now wears the cloak of free, egalitarian bargaining for mutual advantage. In fact, however, democratic discussion is severely constrained by the imperatives of the economic-political system. The leeway needed to administer the contradictions of the welfare state (in trying to maintain stable growth, low inflation, high employment, and balance of trade) requires that citizens not perceive policy debates in terms of fundamental issues of justice (concerning who gets what). This is accomplished by suppressing any discussion about whether policies serve the general interest, as when it is assumed that the general interest is equivalent to maintaining stable economic growth, or by insisting that there is no general interest to pursue, only particular interests that can be balanced according to their respective weights.

Given these distortions in democratic dialogue, we have every reason to believe that what is really in our general interest is being suppressed behind the facade of ideology and pseudo compromise. The emancipatory interest built into communication—the presumption in favor of a domination-free understanding of self and other—compels us to question the conventional ways of thinking and behaving that have been inculcated in us. Unfortunately, the interpretative sciences cannot help us in this regard, because they seek only to preserve our conventional understanding by rendering it more coherent.

What is needed instead, Habermas contends, is a social science that will reveal our conventional understanding for what it truly is: a form of false consciousness. Psychoanalysis, he notes, has already drawn our attention to the way in which another form of false consciousness—neurosis—manifests a syndrome combining compulsive behavior and systematically distorted understanding.[25] The compulsive hand washer, for instance, does not understand that he is symbolically trying to expiate his guilt for masturbating against his father's wishes. He tries to suppress this memory, but it continues to resurface. To defend against it, he unconsciously reenacts it in a symbolic expiatory form. This is like the behavior of someone who feels guilty about betraying her deepest interest in achieving freedom, justice, and happiness in unconstrained communication with others. To defend against her feelings of emptiness and guilt, she convinces herself that her actual life is truly free and fulfilling, even though she works long hours for a tyrannical boss and compensates for it with compulsive shopping sprees.

Psychoanalysis frees the neurotic from his compulsion by encouraging him to reflect on the hidden meaning of his behavior. Making him conscious of the suppressed (unconscious) motive behind his behavior enables him to freely own up to it instead of being blindly compelled by it. The psychoanalyst helps the patient interpret the deeper (symbolic) meaning of his behavior by presenting him with a general theory of psychosexual development. Sexual maturation and moral growth proceed through stages of conflict, such as the Oedipal conflict, that must be happily resolved in order for sexual health and moral autonomy to develop.[26] Regressions and fixations—the material of neurotic

---

25. Freud had already noted in *The Psychopathology of Everyday Life* that "psychopathological symptoms" often take a linguistic form, with censorship, word substitution (slips of the tongue), irrational word combinations, and word association being typical examples. Although these deviations from language can also provide a sublimated (rechanneled) expression of repressed contents when manifested in jokes, they take a less sublimated form in more extreme psychopathologies (as witnessed by the "word salad" characteristic of delusional and schizophrenic behavior). Habermas himself (*KHI* 256) relies on Alfred Lorenzer's reconstruction of Freud's metatheory in terms of linguistic pathology. Viewing neurotic episodes as evidence of the neurotic's "censored" and "mutilated" autobiographical text, in which repressed meaningful motives are allowed to return in a meaningless paleosymbolic form that simultaneously condenses and fragments meaning contents, Lorenzer argues that psychoanalytic depth interpretation should draw on the findings of linguistics (especially child language development) as well as standard Freudian theories of psychosexual development in deciphering the symbolism of neurosis.

26. The five stages of development identified by Freud are the oral, anal, Oedipal, latency, and genital. Failure to resolve conflicts can result in regression to and fixation at earlier stages (repetition compulsion), which typically find expression in sexual perversions and neuroses. Significantly, normal psychosexual development for Freud involves increasing self-control, or domination, over instinctual drives. At the oral stage of "primary narcissism" libidinal drives (the id) are allowed immediate "polymorphous" gratification in which the entire body becomes a zone of unrestricted pleasure, unlimited by any conscious awareness of self and external reality. Denial of pleasure (the removal of the mother's breast) leads to the projection of otherness outside the body and the birth of consciousness. The need to adapt to this new reality—the source of pain—by delaying gratification culminates in the anal phase, in which the ego learns to control its bowel functions and limit its erogenous zone further. Incestuous desire for the mother produces ambivalent feelings of love and hate (fear of castration) directed toward the father. Healthy resolution of this conflict (the Oedipus complex) results in the ego internalizing the psychic control of the father, who represents societal norms (the superego), and a fully autonomous heterosexual adult. Failure to successfully master

delusion—are explained in terms of failures in achieving healthy conflict resolution. Once the patient understands the cause of his behavior as a failure to resolve the Oedipal conflict between himself and his father (whom he both fears and loves), he can subsequently learn to accept the father within himself, thereby becoming a free moral agent.[27]

Critical social theory resembles psychoanalysis in its appeal to a general theory of social evolution that shows how human society must proceed through stages of class domination and conflict before achieving resolution in a free democratic society. It explains regressions and fixations in terms of contradictions between conflicting cultural and systemic demands. Capitalism, for instance, is premised on cultural ideals celebrating freedom, equality, and happiness. However, the system of private property and wage labor is undemocratic, exploitative, unjust, and dehumanizing. The suppression of the ideal demands a substitute gratification, which is readily provided by ideologies touting consumer freedom and fulfillment.

In sum, psychoanalytic ideology critique seeks to restore the narrative integrity of divided and repressed selves by emancipating them from compulsions and delusions that have a systemic origin in class domination. Diagnosing these disturbances requires simultaneously understanding their deeper meanings and causally explaining their etiology—tasks that depend on general theories of social evolution, such as Marx's historical materialism (see chapter 11). Marx and Freud converge on the idea that false consciousness (or false self-understanding) prevents people from becoming autonomous masters of their own history (or autobiography). Both see false consciousness as a symptom of domination and repression. Although Freud speaks of the repression and sublimation (redirection) of libidinal yearnings and Marx speaks of the alienation of humanity from its natural desire for freedom and communal solidarity, both of them recognize that society (civilization)—and especially class

---

this conflict leads to oral regression (narcissism and homosexuality) or anal regression (retentive and expulsive behavior). Interestingly, Freud speculated that the original feeling of guilt that children experience in loving and hating their parents—a sense of guilt that paradoxically precedes the formation of a guilty moral conscience through the process of internalizing parental authority—could be explained only by postulating an archaic memory, hidden in the recesses of humanity's collective unconscious, of the betrayal and murder of a patriarch by his sons who were jealous of his exclusive possession of women within a "primal horde." The subsequent matriarchy and its celebration of incest and polymorphous sexuality, Freud reasoned, must have been overthrown, in turn, by the remorseful sons, who restored the primacy of patriarchal rule in a more egalitarian form. The compulsion to "repeat" this historical narrative, which has been suppressed from consciousness, explains why children traverse the stages of psychosexual development and submit themselves to the increasingly painful (Freud uses the term "sadomasochistic") denials of pleasure and love demanded by an overly aggressive superego. In Freud's late masterpiece *Civilization and Its Discontents* (1929) this hyperrepression of the libido—the principal drive underlying the constructive life instinct—permits a destructive death instinct to triumph in ever-greater explosions of hatred and aggression, a fact that Freud found to be amply confirmed by the rise of fascism.

27. Freud also noted that girls traverse a different dialectic with respect to their fathers, one revolving around penis envy (the Electra complex).

society, in which the laboring classes shoulder a greater share of the burden of alienated labor—is the primal source of repression. Unmasking false consciousness therefore involves laying bear the primal mechanism of repression, retracing the genealogy of domination as it operates in psychosexual conflict or in the history of economic class struggle. Lifting the veil of false consciousness awakens us to our own agency, free from the frozen routines of neurotic compulsion and commodity fetishism. But to lift the veil we need to see how the conflict-ridden dynamics of psychosexual development and social evolution can be resolved in a healthy and happy manner, thereby restoring both individual and community to a state of wholeness.[28]

A Critique of *Knowledge and Human Interests*

We might well question the soundness of psychoanalytical theory and practice, especially when extended to social science. And we might question the coherence of *KHI* as a defense of it.

To begin with the last question: *KHI* identifies three kinds of knowledge. As we have seen, the notion that different types of knowledge correspond to different methods of inquiry is a controversial one. Positivists sought to reduce all knowledge (even interpretation) to an empirical procedure based on observed correlations between behavior and belief. Although some philosophers (notably Davidson) still propose a similar kind of reduction, others (such as Gadamer) propose a reverse reduction, arguing that all knowledge is intrinsically interpretative.

Certainly, the fact that all knowledge whatsoever involves a moment of theoretical interpretation suggests that Habermas's neat distinction between explanatory and interpretative science requires qualification, as he himself later expressly conceded. Furthermore, his equation of science and technology—summed up in the reductive formula that instrumental action is governed by a "technical" interest—ignores the fact that technology is essentially developed or realized in the form of norm-, value-, and meaning-laden designs. Whereas science is exclusively defined in terms of a detached mode of observation and a reduction of experience to abstract mathematical relations, technology incorporates and elaborates this "primary instrumentalization" via a process of

---

28. Although Freud was critical of what he perceived to be the utopianism of Marx's communist ideal—arguing that aggression and domination were largely intractable features of human nature—he was nonetheless sympathetic to Marx's critique of capitalism as a system that imposed disproportionate instinctual renunciation on laboring classes. In *Eros and Civilization* (1955), Marcuse argued that eliminating the "surplus" repression demanded by capitalism's growth (the "performance principle") was feasible given the technological conquest of scarcity and would permit a nonregressive return to an aesthetically fulfilling form of polymorphous sexuality analogous to Marx's youthful characterization of communism as an emancipation of alienated senses.

adaptive design, or "secondary instrumentalization." As Bruno Latour notes, such designs embody norms and prescriptions, thereby fulfilling communicative functions as well (an automatic door closer embodies the command to "close the door" in its design, thereby unburdening us of the obligation to obey the command as a written directive). Following Jean Baudrillard, we might add that technology expresses meaning and symbolizes value (large American cars, e.g., express power and symbolize superior status). For this reason Andrew Feenberg concludes that it makes sense to talk about a "hermeneutics of technology" that discloses not only the purposes prescribed and meanings expressed but also the particular social and political interests (e.g., for hierarchical control or for democratic communication) that different technological designs serve.[29]

It is probably more accurate to say that during the late 1960s Habermas's understanding of technology vacillated between two approaches: an abstract, reductive approach and a more socially and politically sensitive approach. But working out the subtleties of his understanding of technology during this period would not advance our current study, for once he shifted from a cognitive to a communicative paradigm, his interest in technology and its ideological uses waned. (As we shall see in later chapters, this lack of interest signaled a lost opportunity to integrate a theory of technology into his account of democracy and modernization.) So rather than focusing on the question of whether there exists a fundamental methodological distinction between the different sciences and between science and technology let us instead ask a more basic one:[30] Does Habermas's own philosophical interpretation, as laid out in *KHI*, fit any one of these types? And if so, which one? A glance at Table 2, which divides different types of science and knowledge according to their respective methods, action frameworks, and guiding interests, shows that the question defies a simple answer. The problem is not that the method of critical reflection (psychoanalytic or ideology-critical) combines methods from both empirical

29. B. Latour, "Where Are the Missing Masses? The Sociology of a Few Mundane Artifacts," in *Shaping Technology/Building Society: Studies in Sociotechnical Change,* ed. W. Bijker and J. Law (Cambridge: MIT Press, 1992), 232; Feenberg, *Questioning Technology,* 84.

30. Hans-Georg Gadamer initially defended a strong distinction between natural science and social science, which presumed that the objects of natural science (unlike actions) exist independently of language. However, in the second edition of the English translation of *Truth and Method* (285), he argued that all facts and objects are theoretical constructs. As Linda Alcoff notes, knowledge is interpretive in that (1) facts are linguistic statements, (2) understanding is culturally conditioned, (3) inquiry is guided by authoritative texts, and (4) inquiry creatively applies general ideas to particular contexts. This has led Rorty and others to argue that there is no fundamental difference between natural and social/historical science. However, Habermas notes that social and historical sciences are *doubly* hermeneutical (we have observational access to things and events but not to actors' intentions) (*TCA 1* 109). See A. Giddens, *New Rules For Sociological Method* (London: Hutchinson, 1976); R. Rorty, "A Reply to Dreyfus and Taylor, *Review of Metaphysics* 34 (1980): 34–46; and L. Alcoff, *Real Knowing: New Versions of Coherence Theory* (Ithaca: Cornell University Press, 1996), 71–73.

Table 2
Taxonomy of knowledge

Knowledge	Science	Action	Method	Interest
Empirical-analytic	Natural and behavioral sciences (physics, biology, social statistics, experimental psychology, classical economics, etc.)	Instrumental plus Communicative (discourse/theoretical reflection)	Objectifying/noncircular Mathematical/deductive Experimental/observational/manipulative	Technical: oriented toward prediction and control
Historical-hermeneutic	Historical, cultural, and literary sciences (history, literature, cultural anthropology, sociology, clinical psychology, theology, ethical philosophy, etc.)	Communicative plus Discourse (theoretical and practical reflection)	Nonobjectifying (participatory)/circular-dialectical Part/whole circle (narrative interpretation) Ontological circle (subject/object)	Practical: oriented toward reaching mutual understanding with persons past and present; agreement with respect to shared norms and values for purposes of social cooperation; and self-understanding
Reflective (critical)	Social and self-evaluation (psychoanalysis and ideology critique)	Communicative (modified therapeutic dialogue between analyst/critical theorist and analysand/social agent)	Combination of objectifying and nonobjectifying methods enabling a deep interpretation of distortions caused by motives that have been suppressed by relations of power	Emancipatory: oriented toward the dissolution of unconscious compulsions
Reflective (theoretical)	Reconstructive philosophy	Communicative (theoretical and practical Socratic dialogue)	Reconstruction of universal presuppositions of communicative action	Theoretical

analytic and historical hermeneutic sciences: clinical observation/causal explanation and dialogical understanding. The problem is that the kind of reflection characteristic of *KHI* can be understood in three ways: as reflective (historical-hermeneutical) appropriation of tradition, as reflective (transcendental) philosophical analysis, and as reflective (therapeutic) emancipatory insight.

KHI presents itself as a critical interpretation of several philosophical traditions. To the extent that its criticism remains *internal* to these traditions, it can be understood as reappropriating them for purposes of practical guidance, broadly understood. In that sense it fits the description of a historical-hermeneutic science. However, five years after he wrote *KHI,* Habermas observed that its method was more reflective (critical) than interpretative, in that its aim was to dissolve a positivist ideology that suppresses its own genesis out of more reflective forms of philosophical thought in an effort to mask the human contribution to knowledge. Hence, like psychoanalysis (and Hegel's own *Phenomenology of Spirit*), *KHI* would appear to be a critical science aimed at dissolving false forms of self-objectification and self-alienation (PKHI 182).

Counting against this characterization is the fact that *KHI* does not mirror the dual interpretative/explanatory method deployed by critical science, and so Habermas eventually decided that *KHI* was mainly a pure form of transcendental philosophical reflection. Such a science aims at rationally reconstructing the necessary rule-governed competency that any person must master in order to speak and act in the world (see chapter 3). Of course, laying out the necessary conditions for and limits to knowledge and action does not directly serve any immediate practical interest (technical, moral, or emancipatory). Nevertheless, it does provide a philosophical grounding for those sciences that do. For instance, one cannot develop a conception of ideology or neurosis, conceived as systematically distorted speech and behavior, without a theory regarding the necessary conditions for and limits to ordinary speech and behavior (PKHI 182–85).

The conflation of two or three kinds of reflection—transcendental, critical, and hermeneutical—mirrors the conflation of knowledge and experience. Like Kant's *Critique of Pure Reason, KHI* equates knowledge with the constitution of objective experience (or experience that all normally functioning human beings have of their physical and social worlds), which it categorically divides into two domains that are correlated with instrumental and communicative types of action, respectively. Instrumental action constitutes a causally ordered world of things and events; communicative action constitutes an intrinsically meaningful, symbolically structured world of human agents, cultural artifacts, and meaningful interactions. These two domains of *categorical meaning* (objectivity) are unchanging and invariant throughout human history. But human knowledge is not. The way we interpret and describe our objective experience—the *theoretical meaning* that science (or reflective learning) superimposes on our categorically constituted experiences of nature and society—changes in a manner that appears to be progressive (PKHI 171–72).

How is this possible? According to Habermas (PKHI 180), scientific (theoretical) progress is possible precisely because having knowledge involves more than having objective experience. Empirical knowledge consists of facts, or states of affairs, that have been ascertained to be true after first having become problematic. States of affairs are not objects and events that we sensibly experience; they are the contents of propositions (or thoughts about objects and events). We ascertain their truth not by comparing them with objects—for thoughts and objects inhabit different logical and ontological spaces—but by justifying them. Contrary to Descartes, justifying the truth of a proposition involves more than feeling subjectively certain about it; it is not equivalent to having a personally indubitable experience or idea. For truth first becomes an issue for me only when my experience becomes uncertain, namely, when my experience is no longer deemed to be reliable by other persons with whom I interact. In other words, truth is a *claim* I make to other persons about my experience once it has become problematic and has been suitably translated into the linguistic form of a propositional state of affairs that can be justified by reasons. Like the raising of any claim, the raising of a truth claim implies an obligation or promise on the part of the speaker to convince others rationally. This activity of convincing others rationally—what Habermas calls *discourse*—is a kind of pure communicative action in which the normal assumptions and constraints of instrumental and communicative action are suspended and subjected to reflective questioning (PKHI 166–71).

I will have much more to say about discourse in subsequent chapters. It suffices to note that Habermas has detected an element of knowledge—discursive (or communicative) reason—that is common to all areas of science and knowledge (PKHI 172). Even natural science, whose experimental method is intimately linked to instrumental action at the level of object constitution, exemplifies this pure form of communicative action. Indeed, Habermas goes so far as to identify experimental action itself as a form of discourse to the extent that such "action" treats potentially problematic propositions as hypotheses that must be tested and justified collectively by a community of scientists who share a common theoretical paradigm (PKHI 169). Citing Thomas Kuhn (PKHI 159), he notes that experimentation involves more than simply "comparing" theory and raw sense experience (and deriving the former from the latter), since the experience that science deals with is already theoretically constituted. Over time, experimentation forces the discovery of anomalies that precipitate scientific revolutions in which the choice for selecting a new paradigmatic interpretation of reality is mainly decided in debates about prior theoretical commitments (PKHI 171–72).

In sum, Habermas's introduction of new conceptual distinctions into his theory of knowledge—between truth and objectivity, discourse and action, transcendental (theoretical) reflection and emancipatory (critical) reflection—helps eliminate certain confusions inherent in *KHI*. These distinctions do not undermine *KHI*'s principle thesis about the importance of transcendental cognitive interests in grounding distinct forms of knowledge constituting action. Still, it might be argued that the concept of a cognitive interest also rests on a confusion, inasmuch as it straddles the line separating natural and social evolution. Cognitive interests, Habermas says, "mediate the natural genesis of mankind with the logic of its cultural development." They "derive both from nature and from the break with nature" (KHI 196).

From one standpoint this seems correct. For instance, during the course of evolution, the natural human drive for self-preservation ceased to be merely biological. Interpreted through the cipher of religion and other cultural ideals, the struggle for bare survival evolved into a struggle for happiness. As the struggle for happiness met new resistance in the form of class domination, it evolved into a struggle for freedom. In short, the struggle to be free from toil was conjoined with the struggle to be free from domination. Thus, the causal mechanism of natural selection that drove human beings to evolve technically adaptable bodies also drove them to develop brains capable of instrumental and communicative reasoning. This new mechanism of reasoning impelled a different kind of social evolution premised on ideas of efficient production and order. Divisions of social labor and social hierarchy in turn called forth ideologies that justified the attendant inequalities. Despite the implicit desire for freedom from toil and domination underlying these ideologies, the struggle for happiness, even when it took the form of a political revolt against domination, still remained reactive, as if it were determined by the blind fate of natural causality. Hence Marx's ironic observation in The German Ideology that the historical struggle for freedom had yet to be made freely with conscious foresight.

Marx's remark about human history shows that, as a species, we have not entirely transcended the mechanism of natural selection, reaction, and blind adaptation, despite our evolved consciousness regarding our own freedom. It is thus understandable that philosophers have continued to view history as if we could know it from two points of view: as a natural process driven by the law-like causal determinations of selection and adaptation and as a cultural process freely and consciously determined by ideas of happiness and freedom. But this presents us with something of a contradiction. Of course, we can (and must) think of consciousness and freedom as having evolved along with the human brain, even as we think of their progressive development as a self-contained process of emancipatory reflection. But if Habermas is right about the opposed cognitive logics underlying natural science and emancipatory reflection, it is hard to see how we can do so consistently. In other words, we still seem to be stuck in the Kantian dualism between humans as material (biological) beings and humans as ideal (rational) beings.[31]

31. As Thomas McCarthy notes, Habermas's appeal to nature-in-itself (natura naturans) as a quasi-teleological ground of cultural evolution appears to be indefensible in light of the non-teleological conditions under which nature, understood as a domain of objects (natura naturata),

Our reference to the human species as a kind of supersubject touches on another difficulty. The epistemological point of view adopted by *KHI* still moves, in however attenuated a form, within the Cartesian problematic, in which a lone subject—in this case, the human species—is conceived of as trying to master nature, both its own and that of its surrounding environment, through transcendental acts of world constitution. The point of departure for transcendental philosophical reflection remains the subject: either the subject instrumentally engaged in fixing belief (Peirce) or the subject reflectively engaged in fixing its own identity (Dilthey). But in that case we have not avoided the very subject-centered approach that gives rise to the dialectic of enlightenment.

It would thus appear that the contradictions and tensions we encountered in Kant's subject-centered transcendental philosophy have not been entirely resolved in *KHI*. *KHI*'s account of the transcendental synthesis of natural experience as a product of embodied instrumental action, which it appropriates from Marx's theory of labor and Peirce's theory of knowledge, is more plausible than Kant's mentalist account. More plausible, too, is its account of the transcendental unity of apperception, that is, of the conscious identity and sense of self, which it attributes to embodied communicative action in the sense articulated by Hegel and Dilthey. Yet for all of its rejection of Kantian mentalism, the theory is still centered on the knowing subject. In the next chapter, we shall see how Habermas proposes to deal with this problem. Presently, it suffices to indicate how Habermas's continued reliance on a "philosophy of consciousness" led him to adopt questionable conceptions of ideological "false consciousness" and (psychoanalytic) ideology critique.

To begin with, it might be argued, as Popper did, that psychoanalysis and Marxist ideology critique are unscientific because their underlying theories about development are not susceptible to experimental falsification. Furthermore, the claim that reflection emancipates us from causal forces is questionable, even if reflection modifies our understanding of them (*OLSS* 102, 288–300).

While not disputing these points, Habermas emphatically denies their force. Neither Freud nor Marx believed that their theories could be confirmed or falsified by observation. Hence, Habermas concludes that only after those who use them successfully complete a process of reflection leading to enlightened practice might we infer their "truth" (*TP* 39). Reflection might then be said to dissolve if not the pathological causes of compulsive behavior then at least the illusion of natural fatefulness that attaches to the status quo (*TP* 31).[32]

---

appears to us. See T. McCarthy, *The Critical Theory of Jürgen Habermas* (Cambridge: MIT Press, 1978), 113–25.

32. Adolf Grünbaum notes (against Habermas) that Freud's own scientist understanding of therapy had the virtue of correctly recognizing that many psychopathologies are rooted in genetic disorders and not in repression. See A. Grünbaum, *The Philosophical Foundations of Psychoanalysis* (Berkeley: University of California Press, 1984), 7–43.

For his part, Gadamer raised practical questions about the capacity of persons to radically question their conventional understanding, and he doubted whether average persons would voluntarily submit to the wise authority of critical theorists in the same way that patients submit to the authority of their psychiatrists.[33] Indeed, the very presumption that critical theorists possess technical expertise in criticizing convention struck him as the height of undemocratic hubris. And yet, as Habermas noted, whole societies have succumbed to mass delusion (witness Nazi Germany), and so clinical diagnoses cannot be ruled out as inappropriate. At some point, our awareness that culture and information media are manipulated by the powers that be must surely entitle us to stand back and refuse to play the game of "conversationalist" with our cohorts, especially when the terms of conversation used by them carry so much questionable ideological baggage.

That, at least, was Habermas's opinion as of 1971, when he last debated Gadamer on this issue. Since then, Habermas's thinking about ideology and ideology critique has converged with Gadamer's (*TP* 25–40). By 1981, he no longer believed that ideology could be properly understood as *false consciousness*. *KHI* had evoked this notion in describing the illusory and distorted ideals of freedom, equality, and happiness postulated by defenders of capitalism. These ideologies could be criticized by appealing, as Marx and first-generation critical theorists had done, to a philosophy of history that asserted a different—and ostensibly truer—moral end point for humanity: a fully democratic society free from repression and capable of achieving reflective, transparent understanding of what a life of freedom and fulfillment would ideally require.

Habermas now agrees with Popper that such a philosophy of history is itself ideological in postulating humanity as a kind of supersubject (*TCA 2* 354). Post–subject-centered philosophy, he tells us, must be more modest in its pretensions. It can reconstruct necessary and universal structures of communicative action that do indeed contain normative ideals that loosely regulate our speech behavior. But these ideals are just that: *counterfactual* assumptions of a very abstract nature that do not embody any concrete notion of "the good life" capable of being practically realized. Habermas accordingly concludes that philosophers should resist the temptation to "enlighten" the rest of us about what "the good life" is. Assuming that the ideals of speech have any practical force at all, it is simply this: they compel us to decide for ourselves, in dialogue with our fellow human beings, of what this life consists.

33. See H.-G. Gadamer's "The Scope and Function of Hermeneutical Reflection," in *Philosophical Hermeneutics*, ed. D. Linge (Berkeley: University of California Press, 1976); J. Habermas, "The Hermeneutical Claim to Universality," in *Contemporary Hermeneutics: Hermeneutics as Method, Philosophy, and Critique*, ed. J. Bleicher (London: Routledge and Kegan Paul, 1980); and D. Ingram, "Jürgen Habermas and Hans-Georg Gadamer," in *The Blackwell Guide to Continental Philosophy*, ed. R. Solomon and D. Sherman (Oxford: Blackwell Publishers, 2003).

To be sure, this also assumes that everyday communication is a sufficiently reliable medium for achieving rational self-understanding. In Habermas's words, once "the form of understanding...becomes so transparent that the communicative practice of everyday life no longer affords any niches for the structural violence of ideologies" (*TCA 2* 354), something like democratic Gadamerian dialogue can come into its own as a method of critical enlightenment, even to the point of facilitating an *intercultural* global consensus on human rights (*DW* 17).

But is everyday communication as free from structural violence as Habermas thinks it is? By the early 1970s he had abandoned the idea that there could be purely transparent communication. Any modern, rational society, he noted, must institutionalize some form of welfare capitalism—with all the undemocratic economic constraints and administrative limits implied therein. To the extent that such societies manifest "structural violence," that is, "unconscionable social inequality, degrading discrimination, pauperization, and marginalization," they display all the symptoms of "systematically distorted communication...from misunderstanding and incomprehension, from insincerity and deception" (*DW* 15).[34]

Moreover, Habermas remarks, somewhat ironically, that the very process of modernization that makes it all but impossible to talk nonideologically about "the good life" in any philosophical or religious way finds a "functional equivalent for ideology formation." This functional equivalent is none other than the "impoverishment of culture" that prevents "holistic interpretations from coming into existence," which might enable average citizens to think critically about how all aspects of their lives—the legal, political, economic, cultural, social, and personal—are interconnected (*TCA 2* 355). As we shall see in chapter 10, such impoverishment occurs whenever economic activities and bureaucratic controls "colonize"—and thereby constrain and distort—domains of life, such as family, school, and the public sphere, properly integrated by communicative interaction. The symptoms that accompany this kind of colonization include a reactionary regression to premodern traditions, the most extreme example being intolerant religious and ideological fundamentalism and an uncritical fragmented (mass) consciousness that is easily manipulated by government leaders who cynically use single issues to divide the electorate in order to impose a particular dominant interest without any regard for a broader vision of the common good.

---

34. Habermas (*PSI* 131–70) defines systematically distorted communication (SDC) as pseudo communication masked by self-deception, as when family members unconsciously misidentify a strategic power conflict as an instance of equitable mutual understanding. Examples include preventing problems from being discussed (by ignoring or interrupting others, switching topics, etc.), altering the other's meaning, and contradicting oneself, either in word or in deed. Because socialization and language development are intertwined, SDC can cause personality disorders ranging from schizophrenic disassociation to neurotic compulsion.

If, on a personal level, we can still seek therapy or civil courts for working through our conflicts (*DW* 15), on a political—national or international—level we must resort to dialogue. Yet the terror unleashed by fundamentalist thinking of all kinds appears to impugn this remedy. Indeed, these conflicts appear to have polarized the world beyond any remedy short of war.[35] Habermas, of course, disagrees: the tragic existence of global inequalities and strategic power relations notwithstanding, dialogue remains our only hope. Concluding on a more balanced note, he reminds us:

> Communication is always ambiguous, suspect of latent violence. But when communication gets ontologized under this description, when "nothing but" violence is seen in it, one misses the essential point: that the critical power to put a stop to violence, without reproducing it in circles of new violence, can only dwell in the telos of mutual understanding and in our orientation toward this goal. (*DW* 18)

---

35. According to Habermas, the terrorism spawned by militant Islamic fundamentalism partly represents a reaction to the global imposition of a neoliberal economic and political understanding of progress, whose destructiveness remains unacknowledged behind the veneer of hypocritical declarations of moral principle—a clear case of systematically distorted communication.

3

The Linguistic Turn

In the 1960s Habermas wanted to show that psychoanalysis provided the best scientific method for understanding and explaining social action. Demonstrating this, he believed, would enable him to bridge the divide separating theory and practice, thereby defending critical theory against objections posed by positivists. By the mid-1970s, however, he came to believe that the direct connection between theory and practice he had defended in *KHI* was mistaken. As transcendental theory, *KHI* grounds but does not guide critical practice.

But Habermas also concluded that *KHI* was mistaken in another sense as well, namely in presuming that interest-guided action provided a sufficient transcendental grounding of knowledge. *KHI* had presumed that the experience constituted by interest-guided action was knowledge, when in fact knowledge consists of propositions whose truth is constituted (justified) outside of action, in argumentative dialogue. In order to capture the transcendental conditions underlying this discursive dimension of knowledge, which occurs entirely within the medium of language, we need to examine the transcendental conditions underlying linguistic meaning.

Taking up the "linguistic turn"—the expression used by philosophers to designate the twentieth-century turn away from psychological experience to language and logic as the proper place for investigating knowledge—Habermas set aside his earlier work on knowledge-constitutive interests and developed an entirely new philosophical approach, which he dubbed the *theory of communicative action* (TCA). However, by the late 1990s he felt compelled by difficulties implicit in his discourse theory to readdress the problem of knowledge from the standpoint of TCA.

TCA and the Dialectic of Enlightenment

According to Habermas, TCA has the unique virtue of avoiding the dialectic of enlightenment that had plagued earlier "philosophies of consciousness," among which he included *KHI*. By placing knowledge rather than social interaction at the center of philosophy, these "subject-centered" philosophies take as primary a question that is really secondary: How can a single subject acquire knowledge of objects and persons (minds) that lie outside the purview of her or his own mind?

This question, which has animated philosophy since Descartes, is based on a conceptual dualism between subject and object (mind and matter) that seems logically compelling from the standpoint of rigorous philosophical analysis. This kind of reasoning reflects the theoretical attitude of a detached observer. Hegel had already challenged this kind of abstract reasoning in his *Phenomenology of Spirit,* arguing that a coherent account of knowledge required a different, dialectical method of reasoning in which subject and object, theoretical understanding and practical life, could be shown to be part of a single, concrete totality. A century later Edmund Husserl renewed this critique of analytic reasoning by means of an entirely different method: experiential introspection. Husserl noted that the theoretical attitude of analytical reasoning artificially "freezes" and "objectifies" the world into static things possessing discrete properties and opposable *to* consciousness, thereby abstracting from our *lived experience* of the world as an already meaningful *phenomenon* of a temporally flowing and unified stream of consciousness.[1] But as Husserl's follower Martin Heidegger later observed in his masterpiece of existential phenomenology, *Being and Time* (1927), even the world as revealed to Husserlian phenomenological reflection evinces a level of detachment that is absent in one who is actively engaged with the world. Reflection and self-consciousness, he observed, only arise when our primary practical (existential) engagement with our environment gets disrupted—as when the head on the hammer I am hammering with suddenly breaks off. What was once a unified phenomena—consisting of an unreflective involvement (being-in-the-world) meaningfully foregrounded against an indefinite horizon (or background context) of aims, norms, and tacit understandings—now, on reflection, breaks apart into two separate phenomena: an isolated subject who stands passively gazing on an inert piece of dead matter, the resistant and opposing hammer object.[2]

Like Hegel, Husserl, and Heidegger before him, Habermas regards this subject-object relationship as an abstraction from the kind of holistic, pre-

1. E. Husserl, *Phenomenology and the Crisis of Philosophy: Philosophy as a Rigorous Science, and Philosophy and the Crisis of European Man,* trans. Q. Lauer (New York: Harper and Row, 1965).

2. M. Heidegger, *Being and Time,* trans. J. Macqaurrie and E. Robinson (New York: Harper and Row, 1962), 98–107.

reflective experience we have when engaged in our practical lifeworld. Yet, as he notes in *KHI*, the relationship itself is virtually inherent within any *reflective* process of *theoretical* knowing. Once knowing becomes a matter of stabilizing true *propositional* beliefs that attribute properties to things, the primary experience of things as tools, or extensions of action relative to a holistic background of practical understandings and know-hows, gets "covered up." Hence, instrumental action that does not originally involve a subject dominating an object becomes such as soon as it becomes part of a controlled experimental method aimed at testing propositionally formulated hypotheses by means of quantitatively calibrated measurements.

According to Habermas, allowing the subject-object relationship characteristic of analytic forms of instrumental action to dominate our understanding of what knowledge is, is both mistaken and dangerous to the extent that it excludes other, nonanalytical (dialectical or dialogical) forms of reason, action, and experience.[3] First, it misconceives the process of reflective learning as a process of *self-objectification*. This error occurs even when the philosophy in question masquerades as dialectical. Thus, for Hegel and Marx, the laboring subject is conceived as acquiring freedom from and dominion over nature by expressing her or his powers into a material substrate. Here the transcendental imposition of lawlike identity (objectivity) onto chaotic nature gets reflected back onto the subject, who now observes her or his powers in the form of an object.[4] Or, to take an example drawn for Kant's moral philosophy, the subject imposes a law of rational consistency on the subject's spontaneous desires, thereby exerting self-control over her or his now objectified inner nature.

Second, privileging the subject-object relationship misconceives the activity of reflective learning as the activity of a single, *supersubject* (the human species), whose purposive agency determines the otherwise unreflective activity of ordinary persons. According to this view, persons do not consciously direct evolutionary progress by combining their intelligence democratically; rather, progress is driven by the logic of ideas, technology, or class struggle.

As Michel Foucault noted in *The Order of Things*, this conception of a species that constitutes its own free agency through self-objectification is paradoxical.[5] Theoretically speaking, it is unclear how one and the same entity can be conceived simultaneously as an unconditioned, transcendental subject—the extramundane ground of the world—and an empirically determined object within the world. Practically speaking, the Promethean myth of humanity

---

3. The danger resides not in objectifying attitudes as such but in forgetting the more original care with which we disclose our world as meaningful and valuable. See A. Honneth, *Reification: A New Look at an Old Idea* (Oxford: Oxford University Press, 2008).

4. Marx remarks that "the great thing in Hegel's *Phenomenology*...is simply that Hegel grasps the self-development of man as...objectification." *Karl Marx: Selected Writings*, ed. L. Simon (Indianapolis: Hackett, 1994), 84.

5. M. Foucault, *The Origin of Things*, trans. A. Sheridan (New York: Random House, 1970).

perfecting and creating itself as an object of its own science would spell the very end of Man as a free and spontaneous subject. As Habermas notes (see chapter 5), our freedom makes sense only if it designates a spontaneous initiation of something new within parameters set by natural capacities that are not themselves freely created (and especially not by others).

Although Habermas in *KHI* might be accused of falling prey to the paradoxes of philosophy of consciousness as outlined here, his repeated references throughout his career to Hegel's early Jena lectures (1803–4) anticipate an alternative paradigm that avoids these paradoxes:[6] that of *communicative intersubjectivity*. Here Hegel identifies speech as the most original expression of consciousness. The social act of naming and classifying things makes possible the repeatable (remembered) conceptual identification of particulars prior to any split between subject and object; that is to say, the particular thing is already perceived as a general type of thing by the perceiver in accordance with conventional rules of classification. Laboring activity, he notes, likewise exhibits a primal unity of consciousness and nature. However, both speech and labor are aspects of consciousness that have been abstracted from a more basic experience, that of spirit, or social life. The fundamental structure of social life is *mutual recognition* involving two or more persons. Hegel cites the example of familial love to illustrate such a *nonobjectifying* relationship: "In love, each is like the other in the very same respect in which each is opposed to the other" (*TJ* 191). More inclusive forms of mutual recognition—individual rights at the level of civil society and laws at the level of the state—expand the scope of mutual recognition to include ever more universal relationships.[7] The immediate

6. In the philosophy of spirit (*Realphilosophie* I and II) Hegel talks about language as both medium of consciousness (representation and mastery of nature according to a system of names and concepts) and expression of a people's ethos. Language makes possible labor, the second formative medium, whose instruments reflect back to consciousness its own powers. Anticipating Marx's critique of alienated labor, Hegel here notes that modern industry "outwits" the "cunning" (tool-using) consciousness by reducing labor to mechanical routine. The intersubjective satisfaction of needs by labor results in a "struggle for recognition" (or dialectic of love and conflict) within a third formative medium: the family. Familial possession and economic exchange lead to the mutual recognition of property rights. However, class conflict undermines social recognition of needs, thereby calling forth government intervention—all of which anticipates Hegel's *Philosophy of Right* (1821). In an early essay, "Remarks on Hegel's Jena Philosophy of Mind," Habermas maintained that *only* in the Jena *Realphilosophie* did Hegel insist on distinguishing the dialectic of recognition that occurs within communicative interaction from the dialectic of self-objectification that occurs in labor. The *Realphilosophie* blurs these processes; imbued with meaning and purpose, nature confronts consciousness as both adversary (*Gegenspieler*) and object (*Gegenstand*). Habermas concludes that this reduction of action to an "absolute identity" led Hegel to assimilate both processes to a dialectic of self-objectification (*TP* 162–67). See G. W. F. Hegel, *System of Ethical Life and First Philosophy of Spirit*, trans. H. S. Harris and T. M. Knox (Albany: SUNY Press, 1979).

7. Habermas cites Honneth's interpretation of Hegel's Jena philosophy as articulating three struggles for recognition. At the level of the family, the struggle for recognition occurs against the backdrop of socialization, in which the child develops a sense of self (self-confidence) by entering into relations of loving concern with primary caregivers. The struggle for self-respect as an

upshot of this analysis is that knowledge and morality are themselves the product of socialization. A person becomes an independent and autonomous self with a distinct and stable identity only by reflecting on himself or herself *indirectly*, through the affirming eyes of another. It is this same nonobjectifying mode of reflection (from the second-person perspective of a fellow participant in shared communication) to which Habermas appeals in responding to Foucault's paradox of Man as a transcendental-empirical doubling:[8]

> The transcendental-empirical doubling of the relation to self is only unavoidable so long as there is no alternative to this observer perspective; only then does the subject have to view itself as the dominating counterpart to the world as a whole or as an entity within it....As soon as linguistically generated intersubjectivity gains primacy...this reflection undertaken from the perspective of the participant escapes the kind of objectification inevitable from the reflexively applied perspective of the observer. (*PDM* 297)

In sum, Habermas appears to dissolve the *conceptual* basis for the dialectic of enlightenment by showing that the subject-object relationship that it presupposes is derived from a more basic relationship of intersubjectivity wherein interlocutors affirm their mutual humanity. But this priority of moral reciprocity raises a new problem in that it seems to reduce subjectivity and objectivity to sociality. Having escaped from the private prison of consciousness (to which Cartesian mentalism had condemned us) into the public space of language, do we not find ourselves once again imprisoned in a closed system of self-referring meanings, cut off from other social domains and the single domain of an independent objective reality?

---

equal bearer of rights occurs at the level of state and society, as does the struggle for self-esteem in solidarity with other contributing members of society. These latter struggles are products of the modern break with feudal privilege. Robert Pippin argues that Honneth's (and by extension, Habermas's) interpretation of Hegel's dialectic of recognition wrongly tends to reduce Hegel's account of recognition to a social-psychological account of healthy and happy identity. He also takes issue with Habermas's tendency to treat recognition as a transcendental condition for consciousness. Finally, he rejects their view that Hegel's mature account of objective spirit, as contained in the *Phenomenology* and *Philosophy of Right*, has abandoned the earlier dialogical account of Spirit developed in 1803–4. Indeed, Pippin understands Hegel's mature view of recognition as establishing the necessary connection between *fully* free individual agency and mutual (dialogical) rational accountability of the sort that both Brandom and Habermas endorse. A. Honneth, *The Struggle for Recognition: The Moral Grammar of Social Conflicts* (Cambridge: MIT Press, 1996); and R. Pippin, *Hegel's Practical Philosophy: Rational Agency as Ethical Life* (Cambridge: Cambridge University Press, 2008), 184–86, 193n15, 207n30, 213–14, 255–58, 265n37, 276n3.

8. Foucault, however, argued that "techniques of self formation" do not proceed exclusively by means of self-objectification but incorporate practices that would have to be classified under the rubric of communicative action. For a detailed comparison of Habermas and Foucault, see D. Ingram, "Foucault and Habermas," in *The Cambridge Companion to Foucault*, 2nd ed., ed. G. Gutting (Cambridge: Cambridge University, 2005), 240–83.

In order to answer this question we need to first examine Habermas's theory of language. Once we have examined his version of the linguistic turn we will be better equipped to see how the primacy of intersubjectivity, which lies at its center, implies a transcending orientation toward a world of language-independent objects.

Situating Habermas's Philosophy of Language

Habermas sees his TCA as a progressive continuation of the linguistic turn in philosophy that has its roots in nineteenth-century German romanticism. Prior to this turn, philosophers dating back to Plato had generally regarded language as a mere instrument for signifying things and ideas that were presumed to be knowable apart from language. According to this view, natural languages played no role in shaping our ideas and experiences, which were thought to be universal and unchanging across time and place; at best, it imperfectly represented or expressed them. German Romantics—most notably Johann Gottfried von Herder (1744–1803) and Wilhelm von Humboldt (1767–1835)—reversed this priority by arguing that natural languages transcendentally constitute and express the discrete mental outlooks of whole nations, each of which understands the world after its own fashion.

Habermas names Humboldt as the grandfather of three great traditions of postmentalist philosophy that inform his own linguistic turn: *hermeneutics, formal semantics,* and *pragmatics.*[9] Each tradition in its own way articulates the three linguistic functions mentioned by Humboldt—expression, cognition, and communication. The hermeneutical tradition exemplified in the writings of Dilthey, Heidegger, and Gadamer emphasizes the *expressive* function of language. Language is here conceived as projecting an all-encompassing transcendental framework for interpreting reality. The formal semantic tradition exemplified in the analytic philosophy of Gottlob Frege, Bertrand Russell, and the early Wittgenstein emphasizes the cognitive or *representational* function of language. Language is here conceived as the totality of propositions whose atomic elements—names and predicates—derive their descriptive meaning from observable states of affairs. Finally, the pragmatic tradition exemplified in the writings of Karl Bühler, the late Wittgenstein, and J. L. Austin emphasizes the *communicative* function of language. Language is here conceived as the totality of speech acts by which speakers and listeners coordinate their actions by reaching a mutual understanding.

Each of these traditions overlap with the others, but none, in Habermas's opinion, has generated a truly synthetic approach that adequately accounts for

9. W. v. Humboldt, *On Language: The Diversity of Human Language-Structure and Its Influence on the Mental Development of Mankind* (Cambridge: Cambridge University, 1988).

all three linguistic functions. As I noted, Heideggerian hermeneutical philosophy dismisses the descriptive, propositional use of language as wholly derivative, abstract, and artificial in comparison to our always implicit expressive understanding of a practical lifeworld. Hence it reduces the cognitive function of language to the more original transcendental "disclosure" of a meaningful world (Being). This creative (poetic) act of world-making assimilates the experience of truth and objectivity to the self-contained linguistic expressions of a particular people or epoch. Even when this linguistic experience is not conceived as self-contained but as open to the linguistic experiences of other peoples—as it is in Gadamer's dialogical account of understanding—it still remains cordoned off from any language-independent experience that might arise from our practical dealings with resistant material objects. Hence, from the standpoint of hermeneutics, it is hard to understand how people can learn by modifying their descriptive language to better account for the practical resistance they encounter when working within the material world. How, for instance, could we say that the modern description of physical nature as law-governed matter-in-motion is a truer description than its premodern predecessors, which described the world as a realm of animistic personalities or divine ends striving for perfection?

Formal semantics succeeds much better in capturing the way in which language depends on correctly describing this world. However, it goes too far in the opposite direction. Rejecting the holistic idealism of hermeneutical philosophy, it reduces language to atomic elements that derive their meaning entirely from observed relations between objects. It thereby misses the important fact—well-documented by hermeneutics, pragmatics, and linguistic structuralism—that meaning is holistic. As Hegel already noted in his Jena lectures, *blue* is meaningful only in relation to the whole spectrum of color concepts.

Furthermore, it ignores or dismisses as meaningless nonrepresentational pragmatic uses of language. Pragmatics takes up this latter dimension. Wittgenstein in his later writings correctly noted that linguistic meaning must be understood in terms of spoken communication. Importantly, he also noted that such communication was intrinsically normative, or rule governed. However, by conceiving this dimension of language in terms of the model of discrete language games, he fell back into the same linguistic idealism that plagued hermeneutics. The norms governing meaning have no justification other than the mere fact that those who use them consent to them as a matter of socialization. This applies as well to the language games of science and mathematics. Hence, a purely hermeneutical (or contextual) pragmatic account of linguistic meaning succumbs to relativism as well as idealism since it recognizes no objective—that is, empirical and rational—basis for confirming or falsifying the truth of factual descriptions.

Habermas mentions a number of thinkers who have come close to transcending the limitations of these paradigms. As noted above, Gadamer extends the hermeneutical paradigm by recovering Humboldt's original insight that objectivity and truth ultimately depend on our anticipating an ideal expansion of our community of dialogue to encompass all of humanity. The influential philosopher of language Michael Dummett likewise extends the formal semantic paradigm to include dialogical consensus (acceptability) as a semantic truth condition. Finally, Habermas praises his close colleague and collaborator Karl-Otto Apel for having been the first to synthesize all three paradigms. As we shall now see, the distinctive feature of Habermas's approach, which it shares with Apel's, is the notion that linguistic meaning is always framed in terms of certain universal, transcendental-pragmatic presuppositions.

Transcendental Philosophy of Language as Rational Reconstruction

What precisely are these universal transcendental-pragmatic presuppositions and how do we discover them? To begin with *universal:* One can study the norms governing the languages and linguistic practices of particular groups, or one can study the norms governing any language and any linguistic practice whatsoever. Empirical linguistics and hermeneutics are of the former variety, Habermas and Apel's transcendental pragmatics are of the latter variety.

Now take *transcendental.* Kant introduced this term to designate innate forms of mental cognition that the mind imposes on sensory input in making experience of spatiotemporal objects possible. Following in the wake of the linguistic turn, we can talk about how particular natural languages, understood both as horizons of possible meaningfulness and as implicit backgrounds against which anything is foregrounded as an item of consciousness, combine with actions in making possible particular meaningful worlds. Habermas uses Husserl's notion of *lifeworld* to capture the way in which our implicit understanding of ourselves, our society, and our world hang together in a more or less coherent whole.[10] Although this dimension has been most stressed by hermeneutics, which seeks to interpret and make explicit this implicit understanding from the standpoint of a speaker of a particular natural language, Habermas observes that the lifeworld also consists of normative presuppositions and tacit understandings that *any* language user inhabiting *any* lifeworld would necessarily have to have at her disposal.

These reflections take us to an unmentioned concern of universal pragmatics: systemic structure. One can treat language as a system of rules governing the proper formation of meaningful sentences. This is the province of structural linguistics, whose most well-known exponents are Noam Chomsky and Ferdinand de Saussure. Chomsky is famous for arguing that children learn

---

10. See E. Husserl, *The Crisis of European Sciences and Transcendental Phenomenology,* trans. D. Carr (1936/1954; Evanston: Northwestern University Press, 1970).

to combine basic lexical elements such as noun, verb, adverbial, and adjectival phrases by means of an innate mental program (generative grammar); Saussure, by contrast, is most well known for showing how the meanings of terms such as *blue* acquire their meaning in relationship to terms that are similar and dissimilar to *blue*.[11]

In contradistinction to both of these varieties of structural linguistics is *pragmatics*, the last term used by Habermas to identify his philosophy of language. Pragmatics concerns not the formal structure of language as a virtual rule-governed system but its variable use (or actualization) in speech. What Habermas calls *universal pragmatics* (UP) can thus be understood as the science of just those universal rules that make possible actual spoken language. As such, it differs from both structural linguistics and, as we shall see, formal semantics, even while depending on them. Put simply, the ability to form grammatical sentences for purposes of stating facts does not guarantee the ability to use them in facilitating spoken interaction.

UP is the core of Habermas's entire philosophy—his theory of knowledge as well as his ethics. Without this philosophical foundation, his sociology of action, society, rationality, and modernity—the parts that make up the TCA—would be nothing. Given its centrality to his program, it is worthwhile asking what kind of science it is.

First, it is not formal logic, which analyses the meaning of concepts. Nor is it empirical science, which causally explains observed speech behavior. It is more like structural linguistics, in explaining the implicit know-how or competence that average persons must possess in order to generate grammatical sentences (or speech acts). This it does by showing how generative competencies can be reformulated as rules. It is also like hermeneutics in that the know-how in question relies on tacit understandings and normative expectations about speaking, acting, discussing, and knowing that seem unavoidable (necessary and universal) for us, insofar as we cannot imagine substituting for them any alternative set of norms that would not entail eliminating speaking, acting, discussing, and knowing as we currently conceive them (*OPC* 31–35).

According to Habermas, such reconstruction is transcendental in only the weakest of senses. Unlike Kant's transcendental philosophy, it does not purport to explicate necessary conditions for the possibility of consciousness or of experience as such (*OPC* 42). It does, however, purport to explicate some of the conditions necessary for the possibility of one kind of linguistic communication: *speech acts*, or uses of language intended to facilitate interaction (*OPC* 56–62). The specific conditions in question do not concern the successful formation of identifiable (meaningful) speech acts but pertain to the raising of claims and counterclaims that are necessary for the possibility of any communication between speakers who hold themselves rationally accountable to one

---

11. See N. Chomsky, *Aspects of a Theory of Syntax* (Cambridge: MIT Press, 1965).

another. Above all, UP selects just those contextually *unbounded* (universal) speech acts in which speakers claim to be expressing themselves *sincerely,* representing the world *truly,* and acting *appropriately* (OPC 51). What assumptions must they implicitly make about how to justify their implicit claims? What rules best explicate them?

Rational reconstruction takes for granted our certain knowledge that rational accountability (raising and defending claims) is key to understanding language use. More precisely, language use can be reconstructed rationally because the process of defending claims—convincing others that an assertion is true, a prescription is right, and an expression is sincere—is itself a rational process, distinct from rhetorically manipulating them into believing something. This we intuitively know to be certain. Reconstruction of this process is another matter, however, and requires the always fallible translation of intuitive understanding into propositions about rules. The only way we can test our translations is by questioning test subjects. We ask people to assess the rationality (or convincingness) of hypothetical examples of coordination and conflict resolution and extrapolate from their responses what appear to be the rules guiding their thinking. Given that rational reconstruction is tested against the responses of a broad range of test subjects spanning different cultures, its own conclusions are not impervious to potential falsification (OPC 28–35).

It might be objected that average persons' intuitions are unreliable and that the analogy between UP and the sort of structural (generative) linguistics defended by Chomsky is weak. Habermas responds to the first objection by noting that reconstructions differ from scientific explanations in one important sense: whereas scientific explanations contradict our common sense experience of the world and use theoretical "meta-languages" to radically redescribe phenomena expressed in everyday "object languages," rational explications merely clarify in propositional form—using the same vocabulary deployed by everyday speakers—their implicit know-how. As for the second objection, Habermas concedes that Chomsky's postulation of an exact correspondence between innate mental grammar (linguistic structure) and universal linguistic grammar does not obtain in the case of UP. The rules governing communicative competence that regulate the production of speech acts are not innate, even though they purport to be universal in a qualified sense. These rules are acquired through socialization into modern forms of life in which rational communication—making and accepting claims that are backed by reasons—has become the norm. Despite its historical contingency, this kind of communication, Habermas believes, can be shown to be superior to other forms of speech according to theories of cognitive and moral development. (See chapters 5 and 11.) So construed, all historical forms of language can be said to possess the same reason-based rules of communicative competence as their universal telos.[12]

___

12. The analogy between UP and generative grammar is stronger once we allow that Chomskian linguistic competence is also acquired in the course of learning psychomotor and perceptual

Universal Pragmatics and Formal Semantics

Now that we have a general idea about Habermas's philosophy of language, we can see clearly how the three varieties of the linguistic turn mentioned at the outset of our discussion all find their place in UP. Habermas himself illustrates this syncretic feature of his theory with reference to Karl Bühler's *organon* model of language.[13] According to Bühler, language simultaneously combines three functions: *expression, appeal,* and *representation.*

To begin with, speakers express themselves in language, exemplified by the use of exclamatory interjections such as Wow!, Ouch! and so on. This fact about language has led some philosophers, such as Husserl and H. P. Grice, to argue that linguistic meaning is essentially reducible to the subjective intentions of speakers.[14] In order to know fully what an utterance means, we need to know what the speaker intended to accomplish by uttering it.

Arguing against any intentionalist reduction of meaning is the fact that speakers represent, or convey information about, the world. However, by focusing exclusively on this representational function, formal semantics from Frege to Dummett neglects the way in which language is used to *do* things. As pragmatists have pointed out, speakers use language to engage their addressees in order to solicit their cooperation. The intentions they express are not merely subjective and self-referential but are aimed at soliciting responses from others. Meaningful speech thus involves such things as appealing, commanding, promising, and performing. Just as important, it involves, in Habermas's opinion, a process of simultaneously reaching both *mutual understanding* and *agreement* between speaker and hearer about these social acts.

Do expression, representation, and appeal exhaust the linguistic organon? Roman Jackobson, for one, has argued that language contains, in addition to the aspects of addresser (expression), addressee (appeal), and context (representation of world), three other elements that serve additional functions: code, contact, and message. Language is a code that can take many different forms (spoken, written, symbolic, etc.), including a *metalinguistic* form, by means of which speakers comment on their own speech (analytically, therapeutically, ironically, etc.). It is also a way of establishing initial social contact with others that is irreducible to engaging them socially. This *phatic* function is exemplified in the cries of infants and animals. Finally, language conveys its message aesthetically in a way that is exemplified by but not reducible to poetry. This *poetic* function is exercised in the simple choice of words we use to describe

---

skills instead of being a static program that preexists in the mind in some self-contained way (*OPC* 46).

13. K. Bühler, *Sprachtheorie: Der Darstellungsfunktion der Sprache* (Jena: Verlag von Gustav Fischer, 1934).

14. E. Husserl, *The Idea of Phenomenology* (The Hague: Martinus Nijhoff, 1973); H. P. Grice, "Utterer's Meaning and Intentions," *Philosophical Review,* 78 (1969): 147–77.

and designate things and therefore constitutes the core that produces the other functions.[15]

In some of his later writings Habermas acknowledges Jackobson's insights (*OPC* 389) regarding the ineluctable poetic features of everyday speech.[16] Nevertheless, he continues to emphasize the primacy of just those functions mentioned by Bühler, since it is precisely with respect to them that speakers raise universal claims that formally structure the kinds of spoken interaction that stand in need of rational justification. Hence, instead of characterizing UP as a theory of communicative competence (analogous to Chomsky's psycholinguistics) as he once did (*OPC* 47–50), he now describes it as formal pragmatics, in order to emphasize its connection to another normative theory of meaning constitution: formal semantics.

The principle attraction of formal semantics is its insistence that the meaning of sentences cannot be reduced to the private subjective intentions expressed by sentence users but refers necessarily (conceptually and logically) to a public domain of objects that is presumed to be truly represented. The verification theory of meaning exemplifies this approach: the meaning of a sentence is equivalent to the conditions under which it can be empirically verified as true. Given the problems with verificationism, Habermas prefers the formal-pragmatic and inferential-semantic reformulations developed by Dummett and Robert Brandom, respectively, which redefine sentential truth conditions in terms of how they are understood and justified by speakers. According to Dummett, I know the meaning of a sentence if and only if I can both establish its truth and infer the consequences that follow from my accepting it in the presence of others with whom I must reach mutual understanding (*TJ* 76, 126).

These positions largely avoid two fallacies of abstraction committed by formal semantics: the semanticist abstraction, or the assumption that linguistic meaning is to be analyzed primarily in terms of sentences that have been abstracted from the context in which they are spoken or asserted; and the objectivist abstraction, or the assumption that the cognitive (factual) meaning of an assertion can be analyzed in terms of directly observable truth conditions in abstraction from the truth conditions that speakers and hearers believe would have to obtain given their shared understanding of reality. They do not, however, overcome the cognitivist fallacy, or the assumption that linguistic meaning is exhausted by what gets factually asserted. (See appendix C for more on a comparison of Brandom's and Habermas's views.)

15. R. Jakobson, "Linguistics and Poetics," in *Style in Language*, ed. T. A. Sebeok (Cambridge: Harvard University Press, 1960); and R. Jakobson, *On Language* (Cambridge: Harvard University Press, 1990).

16. Habermas repeatedly underscores the metalinguistic, or self-referential, nature of ordinary language as well, chiefly with reference to argumentative discourse and its exemplary theoretical instances in philosophy, art, and literary criticism.

Formal Pragmatics and Speech Act Theory

Here Habermas turns to speech act theory. As I noted earlier, Wittgenstein in his later work had already argued that the meaning of spoken utterances was principally a function of use. J. L. Austin and John Searle developed this insight further, noting that the same proposition can be used to perform many different acts, such as promising, christening, commanding, requesting, warning, and the like that do not aim at describing so much as doing.

Habermas's main criticism of speech act theory is its initial tendency (pronounced in some of Austin's early formulations) to treat the interactive (or *illocutionary*) function of speaking as something separate from meaning. On Austin's early account, imperative speech acts such as "Sit down!" do not count as meaningful, even if they succeed in effecting the desired "uptake" in a hearer, because they do not assert a factual sentence. Conversely, constative speech acts such as "I know that it is raining outside" are meaningful only in virtue of their sentential (locutionary) content (It is raining outside), thereby leaving their illocutionary force inexplicable.

Following Austin's mature thinking, Habermas recommends that we make the following changes in the theory: First, the category of meaning must be extended to include illocutionary force, because performative verb phrases such as "I promise" are meaningful independently of what they say is to be performed. If the command Sit down! is taken up by the listener then that can only be explained by what she understands to be a meaningful connection between a command of this type, the authority of the speaker to issue it, and the appropriateness of the situation in which it is issued. Second, what an utterance means must take into account what is implicitly understood, as well as what is explicitly asserted. Sit down! does not expressly assert a factual sentence, but if the above analysis is correct, the listener will not take it up unless she implicitly assumes, along with the speaker, that certain facts obtain that make it appropriate to do so.[17]

The reference to background (implicit) meaning is crucial for understanding the next change Habermas proposes. Speech act theorists since Wittgenstein have been keenly aware of how important normative conventions are for

---

17. Habermas and Austin distinguish two different ways in which speech acts can be appropriate. First, they can be appropriate in the sense of being "in order," as when a judge appropriately concludes a sentencing hearing by addressing the defendant with the words, "I hereby sentence you to…" Asking whether a speech act is appropriate in this sense is a bit like asking whether it is true to (corresponds or fits with) the situation as it is defined by given institutional norms—a satisfaction of preparatory conditions that led Austin to misidentify appropriateness with truth. Second, however, speech acts can be right or appropriate in the sense of being justified relative to some implicit claim they raise. Austin remarks that advice given in appropriate circumstances can still be bad and a sentence handed down by a judge at the appropriate moment can still be unfair (*OPC* 74, 79, 101n86). See J. L. Austin, "Performative-Constative," in *Philosophy and Ordinary Language,* ed. C. E. Caton (Urbana: University of Illinois Press, 1963), 31.

explaining the success of speech acts. As Searle, notes, some "preparatory rules"—such as the prohibition against promising something that is done in the ordinary course of events—must already be in place before a promise can be made. Once a promise has been made, other normative conventions can be drawn on to guarantee its success (as when the law entitles a plaintiff to sue for breach of contract). Satisfying both of these institutionally bound, context-relative conventions suffices to guarantee the successful performance of a contractual promise.

But conventions like these cannot account for background conditions of acceptability associated with institutionally unbound universal illocutionary acts, such as asserting that something is true. Claiming to know something is an act that can occur in any context whatsoever. Indeed, we implicitly claim to know something whenever we speak or act. But the success of a knowledge claim does not depend on satisfying a convention: although institutional authority might suffice to guarantee the acceptance of a scientist's claim to know in the presence of lay persons, it would not do so in the company of her peers. In this latter instance, it is she alone who bears responsibility for securing acceptance of her claim by providing convincing reasons. Similar conditions of rational acceptability obtain whenever equals seek to coordinate their actions, thereby implicating a universal context-transcending basis for mutual criticism (*OPC* 82–85).

Using formal semantics as his model, Habermas proceeds to argue that expressive and normative speech acts also depend on the raising and redemption of universal claims to validity. Indeed, every speech act aimed at facilitating voluntary cooperation raises (implicitly or explicitly) three claims to validity with regard to the *truth* of the speaker's knowledge, the *normative rightness* of his action, and the *sincerity* of his intentions.[18] Although a speaker's behavior testifies to the sincerity of his utterance, it does not testify to its own rightness relative to accepted norms, and it does not testify to the rightness of these norms relative to more basic norms. In both of these instances the behavior in question must be justified by reasons.

To summarize: the standard form of a speech act consists of a mode of address *M* (illocutionary act) of the form "I hereby declare (promise, warn, request, etc.)," followed by a proposition *p*. Whereas the proposition and its corresponding claim to truth refer to something in the *objective* world, the illocutionary act and its claim to rightness refer to something in the *social* world. The claim to sincerity, of course, refers to the *subjective* world of the speaker's

18. In earlier formulations Habermas added a fourth validity claim regarding the meaningfulness of the utterance itself, which he now prefers to treat as a background, preparatory assumption. However, although there must be some background of shared understanding regarding the conventional meanings and uses of language in order for speech action to get off the ground, it is clear that Habermas's original intuition is correct, since we do challenge people to clarify what they mean.

intentions. Leaving aside the peculiar way in which Habermas now views the three validity claims as modifications of a propositional reference to three distinctive referential worlds, Habermas normally holds that only one of these three referential worlds and their corresponding validity claims are thematized at any given time, depending on whether the speech act in question is constative, regulative, or an avowal. However, regardless of its kind, every speech act ostensibly raises all three claims, if only implicitly. When implicitly asserted, these claims and their respective referential contexts are not clearly distinguished from one another, but they recede into the prethematic background of the lifeworld in which they form a holistic syndrome (see tables 3 and 4).

Discourse

Two further points round out Habermas's theory of meaning: his account of discourse and his distinction between types of actions and their corresponding speech acts. Let us begin with discourse. According to the model described above, a speech act is an offer to engage in social interaction. In making the offer the speaker takes on certain obligations to make good on the three claims to truth, sincerity, and rightness. The listener is free to say yes or no to the speaker's offer, depending on whether she entertains any doubts about the

Table 3
Components of speech acts

Illocutionary/ *performative force* *(act)* informs the listener that the speaker is willing to take on commitments and obligations to the listener in exchange for listener's willingness to accept speaker's speech act offer	*Locutionary/* *propositional* *content* refers to things and events in the objective world under a description of a state of affairs	*Perlocutionary effects* are intended by the speaker to move the listener apart from any claim that the speaker implicitly or explicitly makes	*Preparatory rules* presuppose comprehensibility of utterances and their acceptability vis-à-vis (a) institutional norms or (b) rationally justifiable universal validity claims
E.g., "I swear that…"	E.g., "John is evil."	E.g., frightening the listener into killing John	E.g., rules governing the formation of comprehensible utterances; rules governing the giving of sworn testimony in a courtroom; universal rules regarding the sincere and appropriate assertion of any knowledge claim whatsoever

Table 4
The formal pragmatic taxonomy of validity claims

Validity claim	Function of speech attached to	Mode of communication highlighted	Domain of reality (world or referential context)
Truth	Locutionary/ propositional (i.e., the represen- tation of facts)	Constative speech acts made from the standpoint of an objectifying attitude	The external world of objects and spatiotemporal entities
Rightness	Illocutionary/nor- mative (i.e., the establishment of legitimate interpersonal relationships)	Regulative speech acts made from the standpoint of an interactive/confor- mative attitude	The social world of shared and intersubjectively justifiable duties, rights, norms, values, interests, claims, and ethical understandings*
Sincerity	Disclosure of speaker's subjec- tive intentions, desires, feelings, etc.	Expressive speech acts made from the standpoint of an expressive attitude	The subjective world consisting of personal self- understandings, thoughts, inten- tions, feelings, and wants
Comprehensibility (later reassigned to the class of prepara- tory conditions)			Language

* The social world as it is here understood refers to the social world as it is expressly thematized in regulative speech acts. As such, it must be distinguished from the unthematized *lifeworld,* which designates a syndrome comprising personal self-understandings, competencies, and skills; societal norms and institutions underwriting solidaristic relationships; and cultural assumptions that enable a common understanding of a situation in all of its aspects (*PDM* 326). In designating personality, society, and culture as aspects of the lifeworld, Habermas intends to underscore the extent to which our conscious awareness of objective, social, and subjective worlds is foregrounded against a preconscious holistic background understanding, consisting of personality structures, cultural-knowledge schemes, and societal norms that are themselves sedimentations of previous "anonymous" accomplishments within the field of communicative action. Elsewhere, Habermas designates certain societal institutions, such as the family and the public sphere, as preeminently responsible for the lifeworld's symbolic reproduction of the meanings, purposes, and values that shape personal identity, cultural knowledge, and societal norm. In this context, what Habermas calls "the system" simply refers to that part of society that has managed to coordinate the actions of its members without mainly having to rely on communicative action or shared background understandings of the lifeworld.

claims made by the speaker. Suppose she says no and challenges one or more of these claims. The speaker may then terminate the exchange, continue it in a strategic mode (involving, for example, threats and deception), or "redeem" the disputed claim(s) by offering reasoned justification for them. Justification may occur as a simple extension of speech action, as when a speaker appeals to experience (for redeeming truth claims) or to accepted norms (for redeeming rightness claims). If this fails, both speaker and hearer can suspend their action and engage in a form of dialogue in which the experiential and normative warrant underlying a claim is itself questioned.

This special communication about communication is what Habermas calls *discourse*. Like communicative action, discourse is a rule-governed activity— one that demands the maximum inclusion, freedom, and equality of all partners. The reason why speakers must assume this particular model of justification (even if only tacitly) is partly a function of the kind of society they live in. In a modern society where individuals have lots of freedom to initiate action on their own, each competent agent is presumed to be rationally accountable for his or her actions. The presumption here is that persons cooperate with one another voluntarily on the basis of reasons that are at least acceptable to—if not strongly shared by—the parties involved. Strategic action and manipulation aimed at securing less than voluntary compliance certainly exists, but the default assumption in a modern, rational society cannot be constrained social action. Hence, the ideal of rational, unconstrained agreement seems normative for social interaction generally, and it is this assumption that underlies Habermas's conception of discourse.

I will have more to say about the formal structure of discourse in chapter 5, but here I want to stress the importance of this concept for the social theory held by Habermas. According to Habermas, one cannot understand the meaning of an utterance without in principle knowing the reasons for accepting it. This knowledge transpires in justificatory discourse in which certain ideal expectations—such as the inclusive, equal, and uninhibited representation of others' opinions—is presumed to hold sway. So construed, meaningfulness, rational accountability, and democratically structured practices of consensual discourse imply one another. That also explains why even "monological" forms of *epistemic* and *teleological* rationality, which are not directly rooted in communicative rationality, refer back to discursive rationality as their point of unity. Although I cope with reality on my own by reasoning consistently and calculatingly, underlying my reasoning are beliefs about what is true, good, and proper. Convincing myself of the truth of scientific propositions and the success of maxims of rational choice refers me back to processes of convincing others whose rationality is essentially discursive (*OPC* 309). Table 5 and the explanation that accompanies it clarify the distinctive roots of epistemic (formal logical), teleological (means-ends), and communicative (interactive) forms of rationality and how they are all mutually dependent on a fourth kind of discursive rationality.

Communicative and Strategic Speech Acts

Our analysis so far has hinged on the normative primacy of one kind of language use: the use of speech acts in communicative action. As we have just seen, language is also used "monologically" in *nonsocial* contexts. These uses,

Table 5
Types of rationality

Monological	Dialogical
1. *Epistemic* (a) logical (inferential) coherence obtaining between propositional beliefs (b) functional correspondence of propositional beliefs with reality (c) reflective achievement of conviction with respect to (a) and (b)	1. *Discursive* (reflection) (a) accountability: capacity to evaluate one's beliefs, goal evaluations, and moral judgments in light of reasons that can be accepted by others under conditions of unconstrained, inclusive, and egalitarian dialogue
2. *Teleological* (purposive) (a) ability to formulate clearly the ends of one's action and the means for achieving them (b) choice of efficient means for achieving ends (instrumental reason) (c) ranking and harmonization of ends so as to efficiently maximize their overall satisfaction (decision-theoretic reason) (d) use of reflection and epistemic rationality with regard to (a) and (b)	2. *Communicative* (a) ability to form comprehensible and acceptable speech acts for purposes of unconstrained interaction based on mutual understanding and/or agreement (b) ability to link (a) to the acceptance of validity claims (c) ability to justify these claims discursively if challenged by the listener to do so

Note: According to Habermas (*OPC* 309), epistemic, teleological, and communicative forms of rationality have different roots. Discursive rationality has no independent root but functions (reflectively) to integrate those forms that do. Whenever any foundational form of reasoning generates further questions that require deeper justification, the answers (justifications) it generates by reflecting on itself refer to other foundational forms of reasoning. Teleological reasoning about the instrumental choice of means rests on epistemic reasoning (inferences) about similarity, probability, causality, etc. In turn, communicative reasoning about appropriate speech acts—necessary for coordinating teleologically rational actions—rests on the discursive redemption of validity claims. Empirical knowledge and teleological action depend on discursive rationality in a less direct way than communicative interaction. Although self-reflection originates in the dialogical (discursive) encounter with other persons, it is subsequently internalized within the monological self-reflection of the lone knower or actor. In this sense, all of the above forms of rationality retain an indirect reference to discursive rationality. Habermas also discusses aesthetic and functional types of rationality, neither of which can be assimilated to the four kinds of rationality mentioned above.

Habermas claims, are parasitic on uses that occur *in* communicative action; their meaningfulness indirectly refers to a process of discursive rationality that principally derives from communicative rationality. Habermas makes a somewhat similar claim about literary and fictive uses of language as well.[19]

19. Some scholars have argued that literature can create a fictive world only by neutralizing the illocutionary force of communicative speech acts it "quotes" (Richard Ohmann). Conversely, others have argued that narratives (which can appear in communication) raise different illocutionary claims to tellability (Mary Pratt). Habermas accepts both views: although aesthetic claims to tellability and poetic (innovative) world disclosure are raised by the stories and metaphors that occur in everyday communicative action, they remain parasitic on illocutionary claims to truth, sincerity, and rightness; that is, their aesthetic functions are "tamed" and subordinated to communicative functions. This is especially the case in science, which also uses metaphorical images. Philosophy

Within social action we also detect speech acts that deviate from the model of communicative action. Do these speech acts invalidate Habermas's contention that the primary model for understanding meaning is communicative action? Habermas thinks not. However, if we understand communicative action to mean action in which "actors coordinate their plans of action with one another by means of processes of reaching understanding, that is, in such a way that they draw on the illocutionary binding and bounding powers of speech acts" (*OPC* 326), then we have to explain how speech acts that draw only partly on the illocutionary power of validity claims can still be meaningful.

Take the case of what Habermas calls *weak* communicative actions, in which persons coordinate their actions by reaching a *mutual understanding* (*Verständigung*) about their personal preferences, rather than by reaching *agreement* (*Einverständnis*) on shared values and norms. For example, simple commands ("Sit down!") and declarations of intent ("I intend to sit down") can succeed in coordinating action without depending on speaker and listener reaching agreement on the normative appropriateness of the action. As a listener, I know what these speech acts mean if I know what the speaker's reasons for uttering them are. I need not accept these reasons so long as I take the speaker seriously (sincerely) and accept his (true) understanding of the world (such as his assumption that there is a chair in the room).

Distinguishing mutual understanding and agreement seems correct. An atheist and a devout Catholic can agree that human cloning is wrong without understanding each other's conception of humanity. Conversely, persons can reach a mutual understanding about each other's different views without agreeing on their truth or rightness.[20]

Perlocutionary speech acts employed in strategic action offer a more serious challenge to the model of communicative action. For Habermas, all speech acts have what Austin called *perlocutionary effects,* or effects the speaker intends to have on the listener that could be achieved without recourse to language. Habermas insists that the perlocutionary effects of speech acts deployed in strategic action—no less than the perlocutionary effects of speech acts

---

and literary criticism, by contrast, use metaphor in order to accomplish the "paradoxical" task of translating, respectively, esoteric insights of science (specialized around truth claims) and of art (specialized around aesthetic claims) into the nonspecialized (and moral-ethical) vernacular of everyday life. Pure fiction, however, largely succeeds in suspending the illocutionary force of the speech acts it quotes (*OPC* 390–98).

20. According to Habermas, one must distinguish normative expectations accompanying the acceptance of *meaningful* utterances (illocutionary force in the broad sense) from normative expectations accompanying the acceptance of *morally binding* obligations (illocutionary force in the narrow sense). Even borderline cases involving *immoral* demands such as a bank robber's "Hands up!" accord with *norms* of correct speech *as a condition for their being successfully understood*. However, since the conditions of pragmatic (illocutionary) meaningfulness *ultimately* include the conditions for successful interaction as well (illocutionary broadly construed), Habermas says that the bank robber's demand remains *parasitic* on the structure of mutual moral obligation inherent in voluntary speech action (REPLY 239).

deployed in communicative action—depend on (but are not guaranteed by) the illocutionary force of validity claims.[21] They do so only insofar as strategic actors—who observe one another as obstacles or means to the pursuit of their private aims—rely on such claims to manipulate their interlocutor's behavior. In other words, a strategic speaker who "raises" claims to sincerity and truth does so not because she intends to justify them but only in order to get "the addressee to draw his conclusions from what the speaker indirectly gives him to understand" (OPC 332).

Some examples will suffice to clarify Habermas's point. The aim of an insult is not to coordinate action but to have an effect on the listener. Still, in order for such a *perlocution* to succeed, mutual understanding regarding two illocutionary claims made by the speaker, namely, about his sincerity and his factual assessment of the situation, needs to obtain. But this understanding is not directly advanced as a condition for the speech act, and the speaker assumes no obligation to rationally justify it. The same caveat applies to threats, in which the perlocutionary meaning of a deterrent effect overshadows the illocutionary meaning of an announcement. As before, the success of the effect depends on the speaker giving his listener to understand that he is sincere and has a true grasp of the situation, but without any commitment to reaching a rational agreement on these matters.

To conclude: the perlocutionary speech acts deployed in strategic action are meaningful despite their being "robbed of their illocutionary binding and bonding power." This fact does not invalidate the primacy of illocutionary speech acts deployed in communicative action as a necessary vehicle for perlocutionary meaning. To quote Habermas:

> [Strategic actors] feed parasitically on a common linguistic knowledge (that they have learned in contexts of communicative action). Because the presuppositions of communicative action are suspended, however, they now make use of this competence only indirectly to give each other to understand what they believe and want.... The truth values that guide each of them from the point of view of their respective personal preferences and goals are not transformed into truth *claims*, which have a built-in orientation toward intersubjective recognition, and which they therefore raise publicly, with a claim to discursive vindication. (OPC 332)

21. Habermas acknowledges that perlocutionary effects may function within communicative action to open up dialogue rather than to manipulate or deceive. Allen Wood's example of a teacher complimenting a student who is unconvinced of the merits of her own argument illustrates well the way in which an illocutionary act (complimenting) may be accompanied by perlocutionary effects designed to make the interlocutor more appreciative of her status as a rational participant in dialogue. Contrary to the suggestion by Habermas "that we conceive perlocutions as a special class of strategic actions...[in such a way that a] speaker can pursue perlocutionary aims only when he deceives his partner that he is acting strategically" (TCA 1 293–95), Wood notes that being openly announced may be a necessary condition for a perlocution's success.

Table 6 provides a complete taxonomy of the different varieties and subvarieties of communicative action (weak and strong, consensual and discursive) and strategic action (open and latent). Note that Habermas classifies ideological communication and understanding (systematically distorted communication) as a kind of strategic action in which speakers unconsciously deceive themselves and others in order to avoid rationally confronting one another with their own unhappiness and complicity in constrained and domineering relationships.

A Critique of Universal Pragmatics

I have barely given Habermas's theory of language the attention it deserves. Subtle differences between early and later formulations, as well as significant questions about the overall coherence of the theory, call for more a detailed account than I can provide here.[22] It suffices for our purposes that the overall trajectory of Habermas's theory as outlined here anticipates certain problems with respect to his theory of truth and knowledge.

As I remarked in chapter 2, Habermas was initially drawn to Gadamer's philosophical hermeneutics because it refuted positivism (objectivism) by linking the understanding of meaning to the assessment of validity (or truth), understood as intersubjective agreement. Gadamer assumes that understanding is only possible between speakers who already share a common tradition; however, he also shows that understanding is never complete or final. Because understanding always involves an element of interpretation, of openness and questioning, it is inherently dialogical. As such it opens up a critical space for evaluation; the resistance or otherness of the speaker or text forces the listener or reader to reflect on her own prejudices. In this sense, philosophical hermeneutics presupposes *two* grounds of agreement: the *factual* agreement that

22. Habermas's early universal pragmatics failed to make good his assertion that knowledge of what it means to justify a claim to rightness is just as fundamental to the meaning of a speech act as knowledge of what it means to justify a truth claim; it treated the claim to rightness as separate from the propositional content of a speech act and as referring solely to the speaker's own act rather than to a social norm requiring intersubjective justification. In *TCA 1* Habermas avoids this problem by attaching all three illocutionary claims to the propositional content of speech acts, so that a claim to rightness becomes a proposition about the social world and not merely about the speaker's relationship to her own speech act. But this later version of the theory seems to collide with a holdover from his earlier theory, namely, that all three validity claims are raised simultaneously in every speech act. But one can refer to only one type of "world"—and raise only one type of claim—at a time. Further difficulties surround Habermas's belief that truth claims and rightness claims are justified differently. Practical discourses involve giving factual as well as normative reasons, but whereas the conjunction of two separate true assertions is true, the conjunction of two separate right commands may not be right. In cases where both assertions and commands appear in the same argument, the logical connector "and" would appear to have entirely different meanings, thereby violating the context independence of literal meaning demanded by Habermas. J. Heath, "What Is a Validity Claim," *Philosophy and Social Criticism* 24/4: 23–41.

Table 6
Types of social action

Communicative Action (CA)		Strategic Action	
1. *Weak*: Oriented *minimally* toward mutual understanding (*Verständigung*) of speaker's *intentions* and toward mutual agreement (*Einverständnis*) on *only* claims to truth and sincerity. E.g., the utterance "I intend to leave you" succeeds when listener understands speaker's intention to leave based on a mutual acceptance of speaker's sincerity and factual understanding of the situation.		Oriented toward successful modification of the listener's behavior by means of threats, cajoling, and other rhetorical effects. It involves the use of perlocutions to bring about *indirect* mutual understanding (*Verständigung*) of intentions, whether sincere or not. E.g., "I have the desire and means to hurt you if you don't do as I say."	
2. *Strong*: Oriented *maximally* toward mutual understanding of speaker's knowledge of the facts of a situation as well as speaker's *convictions* about what is right in that situation and toward mutual agreement on *all* three claims to truth, sincerity, and normative rightness. E.g., the utterance "Under the circumstances, I should leave you (don't you agree?)" succeeds when listener understands speaker's intention to leave based on a mutual acceptance of speaker's sincerity, knowledge of the situation, and convictions about what is right.			
Consensual Action (weak or strong CA): understanding and agreement on validity claims are given	*Discourse (weak or strong CA):* understanding and agreement on validity claims *not given but generated by reasons*	*Open strategic action:* speaker makes clear his/her intention to modify listener's behavior through threats, etc.	*Latent strategic action:* speaker conceals his/her intention to modify listener's behavior
		Manipulation of the listener through deceit	*Systematically distorted communication* caused by mutual deception of self and other

must already be presumed uncritically in order for communication to begin and the *anticipated* agreement that results from critical dialogue.

The problem with philosophical hermeneutics, as Habermas understands it, is that it elevates the already accepted factual agreement to a position of unquestionable authority. It is unquestionable because it comprises nothing less than the entire holistic background of preunderstood meaning that, by its very nature, cannot be made an explicit object of consciousness *in its* entirety and all at once. Unlike particular repressed episodes that unconsciously compel the neurotic, the unconscious nature of traditional prejudice—which encompasses all of our linguistic habits in one interlocking, textlike totality and which forms the absolute horizon of all possible understanding—must remain unconscious. At least, this is how linguistic tradition is conceived by philosophical hermeneutics. To cite Habermas, "the pre-judgmental structure of understanding not only prohibits us from questioning that factually established consensus which underlies our misunderstanding and incomprehension, but makes such an undertaking appear senseless" (HCU 204). So, from the standpoint of philosophical hermeneutics, every critical dialogue between an interpreter and a text that generates a new understanding—and with it, a new agreement regarding the truth of any linguistic claim—still remains uncritically tied to a subconscious context of traditional meaning and its manner of understanding how the world truly is.

However, as Habermas observed in the *Logic of the Social Sciences* and in "The Hermeneutic Claim to Universality" (1970), everyday linguistic understanding contains a possibility for critical reflection that is more critical than the kind of tradition-bound, dialogical reflection envisaged by Gadamer's philosophical hermeneutics. Gadamer is right that one cannot leave language and adopt a totally detached, observational stance with respect to it without at the same time leaving the realm of meaningful experience. But Habermas notes that one need not imagine such a radical form of objective distancing in order to account for a more radical form of internal criticism. Quite simply, language users can talk about their language without ever leaving it or ceasing to participate in it. Such metalinguistic language can assume many ordinary forms—puns and ironic expression are among the most common examples. However, it can also take the form of theoretical reflection, as when linguists, grammarians, and lexicologists seek to formally "reconstruct" linguistic competence in terms of general rules of syntax and semantics that explain how language is applied.

> The system of natural language is not closed, but it allows the rules of application for any utterance to be determined ad hoc, commented on or changed...every natural language is its own metalanguage. This is the basis for that reflexivity which, in the face of the type rule, makes it possible for the semantic content of linguistic utterances to contain, in addition to their manifest message, an indirect message as to its application. (HCU 182–83)

Here Habermas anticipates the kind of context- (tradition-) transcending formal-universal analysis of meaning and validity he later developed in "What Is Universal Pragmatics?" The reflexive (or self-referential) use of natural language enables speakers to adopt a critical distance with respect to that same language. They can treat their language as an object of theoretical reconstruction and formal analysis without having to exit it as speakers and listeners, without, in other words, having to adopt the objectifying standpoint of a sociological observer.

We have traced the basic contours of Habermas's own theoretical reconstruction of language. According to his reconstruction, the meaning of institutionally unbounded speech acts can be explained as the outcome of applying (consciously or unconsciously) rules regarding the argumentative justification of universal validity claims. Taken together, these rules constitute an "ideal speech situation" in which it is assumed that those engaged in rational argument are free from prejudice and constraints of action, have equal chances to raise and contest claims, are moved solely by the force of the better argument, and include all who might contribute to the discussion. So construed, the already existing *factual* consensus that underlies the possibility of linguistic meaning consists of more than the particular prejudices of a given tradition; it also consists in the formal rule-applying competencies that are common to all languages, and these competencies essentially imply or anticipate a *counterfactual* consensus, understood as the outcome of an ideally rational form of communication. As Habermas put it in 1970, "a critically enlightened hermeneutics that differentiates between insight and delusion ... connects the process of understanding to the principle of rational speech, according to which truth would only be guaranteed by that kind of consensus which was achieved under the idealized conditions of unlimited communication free from domination and could be maintained over time" (HCU 206–7).

The formal pragmatic program that followed distinguished the formal conditions of ideally rational speech—productive of an ideal counterfactual consensus—from the always already "sustaining" factual consensus determined by particular tradition-bound contexts of meaning. As Cristina Lafont remarks, this duality between different levels of agreement—ideal and real—mirrors the duality of the speech act itself: for it is the illocutionary (or interactive) component of the speech act that harbors the universal formal structure of rational accountability and validity underlying all meaningful speech, while the locutionary, or referential, component remains bound to the unconscious holistic background context of parochial understandings, which represent nature and society according to tradition-bound categories and norms.[23]

The success of the formal-pragmatic program depends on two strong claims: first, that the relationship between meaning and validity can be understood

23. My reconstruction of Habermas's thought follows Cristina Lafont's in *The Linguistic Turn in Hermeneutic Philosophy*, trans. J. Medina (Cambridge: MIT Press, 1999), esp. chap. 2.

formally, that is, in terms of formal conditions of acceptability that can be established for types of speech acts whose basic illocutionary and locutionary sense can be given a literal meaning. Second, that the kinds of unbounded speech acts in which formal conditions are met are themselves universal, or primary, in comparison to which all other uses of speech are parochial, secondary, and parasitic. The first claim is necessary for resisting the contextualism (or holism) that plagues philosophical hermeneutics. As Dummett notes, "an acceptable theory of meaning must be at least molecular...(for) on a holistic view, it is impossible fully to understand any sentence without knowing the entire language."[24] In other words, according to linguistic holism, no sentence taken in isolation from the part-whole syndrome that defines textual meaning would be meaningful. Hence, no theoretical explanation of language in terms of rules—formulated as propositions—would be meaningful. Therefore, no ideal account of meaning and rational accountability would be meaningful either, and we would forever be condemned to live out our linguistic being in the dogmatism of unconscious prejudice. Resisting this catastrophic blow to critical theory, Habermas, like Dummett, insists that we must be able to distinguish, within any speech act, its absolute and unchanging *core* meaning—what can be literally and precisely formulated in the form of a single sentence, namely, a speaker's fully conscious, univocal intention or claim—and its contextually relative and shifting *unessential* meaning—what resists being expressed in a single proposition because of its essential connection to an indefinite, holistic background of unconscious meaning. That is, we must

> exclude those explicit speech actions in standard form that appear in contexts that produce shifts of meaning. This is the case when the pragmatic meaning of a context-dependent speech act diverges from the meaning of the sentences used in it....Searle's "principle of expressibility" takes this requirement into account: assuming that the speaker expresses his intentions precisely, explicitly, and literally, it is possible in principle for every speech act carried out or capable of being carried out to be specified unequivocally by a complex sentence. (OPC 61)

The second claim—about the universality and primacy of unbounded speech acts in everyday communication—is necessary for establishing the essentially normative and rational nature of speech. If strategic and poetic/literary uses of language were assumed to be primary (or no particular kind of use of language was assumed to be primary), Habermas could not establish that we are necessarily committed to being rationally accountable to others for our actions. Without this minimal concept of reciprocity, it would be difficult to refute

---

24. M. Dummett, "What Is a Theory of Meaning? (II)," in *Truth and Meaning: Essays in Semantics,* ed. G. Evans and J. McDowell (Oxford: Oxford University Press, 1999), 76–79.

moral and cognitive skepticism (or relativism), and without refuting skepticism the critical enterprise collapses.

Unfortunately, neither of the above claims seems warranted by Habermas's arguments. The first claim—regarding the possibility of restating the meaning of standard speech acts to truth, rightness, and sincerity *literally* in simple propositions, in isolation from their context of usage—presupposes (in the words of Lafont) a kind of "self-transparency" of meaning, or presumption that meaning can be reduced to pragmatic (or illocutionary) meaning. Thus we find Habermas saying:

> [In] the standard case of literal meaning, a speech act makes the intention of the speaker known; a hearer can infer from the semantic content of the utterance how the sentence uttered is being used, that is, what type of action is being performed with it. Speech acts interpret themselves, they have a self-referential structure. The illocutionary element establishes, as a kind of pragmatic commentary, the sense in which what is said is being used. Austin's insight that that one does something by saying something has a reverse side to it: by performing a speech act, one also says what one is doing. (*OPC* 217)

As Lafont rightly notes, this passage is either tautological or false. Clearly, we know that a speech act is employed as an assertion (that it announces its pragmatic meaning as an assertion) when we know what asserting is (or means), namely, when we know that a truth claim is being asserted. But we can know this without having the slightest idea about what is being said (as when we eavesdrop on an arcane lecture in astrophysics). Contrary to Habermas, the illocutionary act cannot determine the sense of what is said. That, Searle pointed out, is quite dependent on the holistic background (or context) of language, which enables us to "transcendentally" constitute our world as meaningful in a particular way.[25] The background cannot be formally explicated because (first) it consists of an indefinite number of holistically intertwined assumptions (i.e., assumptions that depend on other assumptions for their meaningfulness) *and* because (second) these assumptions refer to our knowledge of the world. By 1980 Habermas himself came to acknowledge the truth of these objections when he observed:

> The methodological limitation to the standard form goes too far in neutralizing context. The model of the speech act has to take into account not only such familiar elements as utterance, action situation, speaker, hearer and the yes/no position

25. "For a large class of sentences the speaker, as part of his linguistic competence, knows how to apply the literal meaning of a sentence only against a background of other assumptions....[T]his argument has the consequence that there is no sharp distinction between a speaker's linguistic competence and his knowledge of the world." J. Searle, *Expression and Meaning* (Cambridge: Cambridge University Press, 1979), 134.

he or she takes, but also the background of the lifeworld shared by speaker and hearer and thus the culturally transmitted, prereflexively given, intuitively available, background knowledge from which participants in communication draw their interpretations. (*CD* 271)

In this passage Habermas seems to have abandoned the peculiar link between meaning and validity he sought to defend against Gadamer. For Gadamer the link is provided by an authoritative tradition whose validity is taken for granted. Against this factual consensus Habermas opposes an ideal consensus established by speakers in rational discussion: it is we who determine the acceptability conditions of our utterances, not tradition. But now Habermas denies this. Hence, once the first claim (regarding the formal reconstruction of literally meant speech acts and their acceptability conditions) falls, so (it would seem) does the second claim (regarding the universal and foundational nature of communicative action). That follows from an indisputable fact: the illocutionary meaning of a speech act is partly determined by context, so that even the most formal and elementary description of what kind of act a speech act consists of is also unavoidably determined by a historically contingent context. Illocutionary, locutionary, and perlocutionary elements thus appear to be all but indistinguishable.[26] This explains why intentional and strategic uses of language are often literally indistinguishable from more robust speech acts oriented to the "unreserved" pursuit of a consensual coordination of action. In some contexts, for instance, insincerely praising a shy person's halting utterances about what ought to be done about the economy can be intended to manipulate them into cooperating in a sincere debate on the topic, so that the speech act of praising functions simultaneously as affirming a claim and as affecting a behavior.

By explicitly restoring the lifeworld (the always already taken-for-granted background of meaning) as necessary complement to the frontal, dialogical constitution of meaning, Habermas's later theory of communicative action returns us to the dialectic of factual versus ideal consensus implicit in Gadamer's philosophical hermeneutics. This seems eminently reasonable. The probability of speaker and listener coming to a mutual understanding of what they mean—and a mutual agreement on what is valid (rationally acceptable)—entirely on their own seems incredibly remote unless they already agree on a shared way of understanding that is largely beyond their control.[27] However, restoring the lifeworld to its rightful place has an obvious downside: it threatens to

---

26. Habermas himself recognizes instances, such as political rhetoric, in which these elements are indistinguishable (REPLY 254–59, 291n63).

27. Connected with this point is the emotional claim (or, as Jakobson puts it, the phatic function of engaging contact through gesture and speech) that even infants make on people. The ability to speak rationally—in the form of cognitive claims—is itself a sophisticated, reflective competence that builds on a primary emotional engagement (act of recognition) whereby each "interlocutor" empathetically identifies with (adopts the standpoint of) the other. For a sustained

reintroduce the very relativism and conservatism that pure formalism was supposed to circumvent. (In the venerable words of Wittgenstein, "If the true is what is grounded, then the ground is neither true nor false.")[28]

We thus find ourselves once again confronted with the Hegelian problem of a plurality of seemingly self-contained, linguistically constituted worlds. Or to restate the matter as a Kantian question: How can we have knowledge of an objective world if what we claim to be true is always justified in terms of our spatially and temporally limited frame of understanding?

The answer, as we shall see in the next chapter, hinges on the possibility that context-bound frames of meaning do not absolutely determine reference to the objective world. Against the "linguistic idealism" of philosophical hermeneutics Habermas must oppose epistemological realism, and against the consensus theory of truth that both he and Gadamer held he must oppose a nonepistemic (referential) conception of truth. In order to show that realism is viable from within the linguistic turn, he must show that conflicting ways of interpreting the world can at least agree on the particular objects to which they refer.

In sum: Habermas's critical theory must be pulled in two directions in order to be saved. On the one hand, it must weaken, if not entirely abandon, its claim to offer a universally valid formal reconstruction of meaning, validity, and reason (see chapter 5). It must, in other words, accept contextualism at this level of analysis. On the other hand, it must strengthen its commitment to realism so as to postulate the possibility of universal agreement about a common world of objects and a society of shared interests. Whether these directions are compatible with his Kantian grounding of morality and law in a formal (or procedural) account of autonomy remains to be seen.

---

argument against reducing communication to an understanding of cognitive claims, see Honneth, *Reification*, 50–51, 57–58.

28. L. Wittgenstein, *On Certainty*, sec. 205 (Oxford: Blackwell, 1969).

4

Knowledge and Truth Revisited

Habermas's philosophy of language raises questions about the extent to which our meaningful representations of the world can be shared across specific contexts of communication and the cultural lifeworlds that ground them. Whether these representations can be shared and communicated is obviously crucial to the possibility of knowledge. Habermas accepts the view, first advanced by Plato in his *Theaetetus,* that knowledge entails *rationally justified true belief.* According to this assumption, S knows p if and only if:

1. S believes that p
2. p is true
3. S is justified in believing that p

Statements 1. and 2. seem uncontroversial. Statement 3. has been challenged and defended, at least to Habermas's satisfaction.[1] But those who accept 2. and 3.

---

1. Habermas attaches two provisos to Plato's definition. First, the reasons in support of a belief must be logically connected to the experiences in which it was first acquired; second, some of these reasons will refer to causal explanations concerning the reliability of sensory organs in generating veridical perceptions. These provisos are motivated by paradoxes that were famously discussed by Edmund Gettier in 1963, when he pointed out that a person can satisfy all three of these conditions without being said to know that p. Gettier gives the following example: Smith has good reasons for believing that Jones will get the job he has applied for; Smith also has good reasons for believing that Jones has ten coins in his pocket. By the rule of transitivity of identity, Smith has good reasons to believe that the person who gets the job has ten coins in his pocket. By sheer luck Smith gets the job instead. As it happens, he also has ten coins in his pocket. Smith

still disagree on how to answer a fundamental question: What precisely do we mean by "true" and "justified"?

Take truth, the most elusive concept in the knowledge triad. Ancient philosophy conceived truth as a *one-place* relationship whereby the knower entered into a state of belief whose rational form was proportional to the rational form of the reality known. In Plato's philosophy, for instance, a belief counts as knowledge if it shares the same unchanging state of perfection as the ideal reality of logical and mathematical forms to which it aspires. The object justifies the knowledge status of the belief so that less rational forms of reality, such as changeable material things, correspond to states of belief, such as perception, that are subrational and inferior in knowledge status.

During the Middle Ages, philosophers known as *nominalists* rejected the underlying essentialism of this ontological paradigm of knowledge, which attributes intrinsic logical-conceptual form to a mind-independent reality. Their reduction of concepts (universals) to mental artifacts, however, rendered reality—in all of its contingent particularity—beyond the pale of rational (conceptual) knowledge. It was left to Descartes to resolve this crisis by turning a vice into a virtue, reversing the priority formerly assumed in the ontological paradigm. The subjective faculty of conceptual analysis (rational certainty)

---

cannot be said to know that the person who will get the job has ten coins in his pocket, despite the fact that his belief that this is so is both true and justified, because one of the premises on which it is based—that Jones will get the job—is false. Taking a different tack, Alvin Goldman has shown that S can be said to know that p without being able to justify p, so long as S can show a reliable causal link between p and its source (something that did not obtain between Smith's false belief that Jones would get the job and his true belief that whoever gets the job will have ten coins in his pocket). However, in a 1976 essay ("Discrimination and Perceptual Knowledge," *Journal of Philosophy* 73:771–91) Goldman gives an example that suggests that providing such a causal description might not suffice to replace or supplement justification. A passerby who accidentally identifies the only real barn in Barn Facade County (where, unbeknown to him, the other 999 barns are fake) can be said to know that he sees a barn even if his "good reason" for thinking so—that his perception and past experience are reliable sources of knowledge—appears to fail him in this instance. However, as Robert Brandom has persuasively argued (*Articulating Reasons* [Cambridge: Harvard University Press, 2000], chap. 3), this does not really refute the standard view of knowledge, since relative to the broader context of perception and experience (outside of Barn Facade County) his perception and experience have proven reliable, and this might well be a reason *we* can give for justifying to *ourselves* his correct identification as bona fide knowledge. It should be noted that Habermas (*TJ* 41) accepts Gettier's claim about the epistemic insufficiency of the three conditions but, like Brandom, he rejects Goldman's view that knowledge can dispense with justification. Following Lutz Wingert, Habermas argues that knower S must establish an "evident genealogy" between reliable learning experiences and his knowledge that p. Also, as Lafont observes (following Brandom's comments), "once it is recognized that the satisfaction of the justification condition should be endorsed by the assessor, one cannot get the Gettier problem off the ground. Gettier examples are grounded in situations where it is stipulated that we have a collateral commitment regarding the correct justification for the belief at issue (p) that is incompatible with the commitment of the speaker whose knowledge we have to assess." C. Lafont, "Is Objectivity Perspectival? Reflections on Brandom's and Habermas's Pragmatists Conceptions of Objectivity," in *Habermas and Pragmatism*, ed. M. Aboulafia et al. (New York: Routledge, 2002), 207n24.

now becomes the touchstone for defining what is objectively real. However, replacing the ontological paradigm of knowledge with a mentalist paradigm did not mean replacing the two-place relationship between subject and object that nominalists had introduced. The new mentalist paradigm therefore assumes that

1. we know our own mental states better than anything else;
2. knowing takes place essentially in the medium of representing objects;
3. the truth of judgments rests on evidence that vouches for their certainty (*OPC* 349).

Habermas contends that each of these assumptions rests on a myth. Assumption 1. rests on the myth of the *given,* which falsely presumes that our private mental experiences do not have to be formulated in some public language in order to be meaningful. Assumption 2. rests on the myth of *representation,* which falsely assumes that cognition involves forming clear images and representations of things rather than justifying beliefs. The idea that the correctness of mental images and representations can be determined by comparing their fitness to a mind-independent reality is incoherent, partly because we have no perceptual and theoretical access to reality that is not filtered by the mind or by language and partly because beliefs (propositions) are not anything like the material objects to which they refer. Finally, assumption 3. rests on the myth of *foundations,* which assumes that true beliefs must be justified by being derived from indubitable experiences rather than by being supported by fallible (revisable) reasons. This myth confuses truth with certainty, which, as Habermas notes, designates a subjective feeling we have about our experiences. Such experiences may be ranked along a continuum of reliability (as in the case of sensory perception), and anticipations of experience may be more or less predictable (certain). By contrast, truth obeys a binary logic whose ground transcends even our subjective certainty that a given experience is "objective," or shared by others. In sum, either a belief is true or it is false (so-called partial truths are really falsehoods); and the mere fact that all persons converge in their certainty about an apparently reliable experience—such as the appearance of the sun rising above a stationary earth—does not make it true. With few exceptions, questions of truth and knowledge only arise when appeal to direct observation proves problematic or inadequate, as in the case of negative, general, conditional, and counterfactual statements.

Of the three assumptions underlying the mentalist paradigm, it is the second that has troubled philosophers the most. By the 1930s, the difficulties associated with the mentalist model of truth as correspondence (implicit in the myth of knowledge as representation) led Alfred Tarski to propose a purely *semantic* conception of truth that preserved the realist presupposition implicit in the correspondence idea of truth without appealing to any ontological or mentalist connotations.[2] Tarski's insight can be clarified with reference to third-person statements about other persons' first-person statements, as when someone S says, "Everything that the witness W said yesterday is true." Here S simultaneously *asserts* the truth of W's statement as his own *first-person* statement and also *mentions* its truth in a *third-person* statement. Tarski exploits the dual perspective implicit in this kind of statement in developing his semantic theory of truth. According to Tarski's *Convention T,* a sentence X (e.g., "Snow is white") is true if and only if p (snow is white). Convention T translates the *vertical* correspondence between a sentence and the reality to which it refers into a *horizontal* correspondence between a factual proposition asserted in the first-person mode of objective reference (*p* as asserted by W in an object language) and the same proposition X mentioned by S in a metalanguage and quoted in the third-person (formal) mode. This relation of equivalence avoids the problematic correspondence between linguistic and nonlinguistic entities by framing the relationship as a purely semantic one, between object language and metalanguage.

Convention T proposes a *deflationary* account of truth that is philosophically satisfying. It enabled Tarski to define truth recursively, as the logical conjunction of all T-type schemes "obtained by replacing 'p' by a particular sentence and 'X' by a name of this sentence." However, as Habermas points out, it purchases its logical usefulness at the expense of any informative gain, for Convention T says nothing about what an average speaker means when he first asserts a proposition. In asserting a proposition, he no doubt also asserts its truth, but this assertion is meant as a claim directed toward others that cannot be logically analyzed in terms of an equivalence between propositions. In asking what this claim means we are not inquiring about the definition of truth or the method for discovering it; we are asking about the pragmatic conditions underlying our discursive justification of it (*OPC* 362).

The pragmatic connection between the concept of truth and the practice of argumentative justification leads Habermas to conceive knowledge as a *three-place* relationship. According to this model, claiming to know involves referring (1) a belief or proposition to (2) a mind-independent world of objects by means of (3) reasons that are convincing for a particular community. The tension between (2), which captures both our unavoidable practical belief in a common world of objects that is the same for everyone and our equally unavoidable theoretical belief that truth is an unconditional property of factual propositions that "cannot be lost," and (3), which captures our unavoidable belief in the fallibility and changeability of our always parochial knowledge, is never entirely resolved. Nonetheless, it reveals a dialectical complementarity: not only does the epistemic fallibility of a rational learning process only

2. A. Tarski, "The Semantic Concept of Truth and the Foundations of Semantics," in *Readings in Philosophical Analysis,* ed. H. Feigl and W. Sellars (New York: Appleton-Century-Crofts, 1949), 52–84.

appear meaningful in contrast to the transcendent reality it aims at progressively knowing, but the practical certainty of our beliefs as representations of that reality only appear as unconditionally true from within a process of reasoned conviction that has in fact refuted all available objections.

Thanks to this dialectic, skeptical doubts about the possibility of objective knowledge are incoherent. To doubt a belief is to raise a claim against it. But raising a claim implies a readiness to defend the claim with reasons that could in principle be convincingly accepted by everyone as true. So the skeptic cannot doubt the possibility of knowledge without implicitly claiming to know that there is no knowledge. As Habermas and others have pointed out, claiming this involves committing a "performative" (self-referential) contradiction (*OPC* 355–56).

Subject-Object Paradigms of Knowledge

Habermas differentiates his theory of knowledge from two theories that have hitherto dominated modern philosophy. Postulating the primacy of the subject-object relationship, these theories presume that knowledge represents or mirrors an objective reality.

The first theory, *naturalism,* explains knowledge from the side of the object. According to this theory, an independently existing nature causes us to have ideas of things. Knowledge is thus conceived as correspondence between idea and thing represented. The linguistic turn in philosophy retains this schema with slight modification. Knowledge is now conceived as correspondence between proposition and observed fact.

As we saw, verificationism holds that both the truth and the meaning of a proposition are defined in terms of empirically confirmed observations. Peirce's operationalism is naturalistic as well, insofar as it equates the meanings of propositions such as 'Diamonds are hard' with the observed effects of possible instrumental actions. Theories of meaning and knowledge developed by W. V. O. Quine and Donald Davidson in the late twentieth century also subscribe to naturalism. Both argue that understanding meaning can best be understood in terms of a process of radical translation. Crudely put, we match up the observed sounds and behaviors of others with our own speech behavior. Using a principle of charity, in which we assume that others are rational (consistent and prudential) and react to stimuli the same way we do, we construct a "passing manual" in which we translate the other's speech behavior into the first-person experience of our own meaningful behavior.[3]

---

3. Davidson introduces *triangulation* to explain how the interpreter herself *learns* language. Meaning arises when two organisms respond to the same stimulus the same way and observe this about each other: "The stimulus has an objective location in a common space; it's a matter of two private perspectives converging to mark a position in intersubjective space." But how do they

Davidson's approach explains meaning and knowledge in terms of observed causal (stimulus-response) relationships rather than in terms of normative expectations. This is its principal weakness; because it contradicts our lived experience that language as a rule-governed enterprise exists, it explains nothing. So there is nothing to recommend it other than theoretical simplicity (*TJ* 24). Yet it does confirm one of our practical intuitions, namely that our utterances and actions stand in some causal connection to an objective world.

The second theory, *transcendentalism,* has its roots in Kant's philosophy. Kant, you will recall, sought to explain how we can achieve knowledge of objects outside the mind once we concede that all knowledge is filtered through our own subjective experience. He explained the possibility of objective experience by reconceiving space, time, materiality, and causality as the mind's own modes of organizing its experience into a coherent consciousness of self. A residue of naturalism, however, still infected Kant's theory of knowledge, insofar as he held that the cause of sensory experience must lie outside the mind. His successors subsequently argued that such an "unknowable" cause was both incoherent and meaningless *and* that it contradicted Kant's own assertion that causation is a form of understanding imposed by the mind on its own experience.

Hegel, for instances, noted that natural sensations cannot even be indicated without using abstract indexical terms such as 'this,' 'that,' and 'now.' Hence there appears to be no meaningful language-independent reality to which we can compare our ideas and beliefs to see if they truly corresponded. In that case, true knowledge can only consist in the *coherence* of our first-order beliefs about reality and our second-order (reflective or philosophical) beliefs about those beliefs. The more coherent our first- and second-order beliefs are, the more coherent and objective is our knowledge of the world.

According to Habermas, Hegel's transcendental account of meaning and knowledge in terms of a self-contained circle of more- or less-coherent beliefs leads to skepticism of a new kind: contextualism. If we accept that natural languages purchase their coherence by being systematically closed and radically self-referential, then we cannot explain how one language can be translated into another. The incommensurability of natural languages would seem to imply cultural relativism: the way my language discloses the world is not

---

know they are responding to the *same* stimulus? Davidson responds to this Quinean problem of radical referential indeterminacy by noting that each can talk to the other about what stimulated them: "For people to know of each other that they are so related [to the same thing indicated by their common stimulus] requires that they be in communication. Each of the two has to speak to the other and be understood by the other." But, as Wittgenstein remarked, consistently holding a stimulus meaning identical across similar situations is a normative concept insofar as it implies correct identification. So Davidson's nonnormative derivation of meaning from solipsistic observation fails (*TJ* 116–20). See D. Davidson, "The Conditions of Thought," in *The Mind of Donald Davidson*, ed. J. Brandl and W. Gaombocz (Amsterdam: Rodopi, 1989), 198–99; and W. V. O. Quine, *Word and Object* (Cambridge: MIT Press, 1960).

reducible to the way your language discloses it. Furthermore, there is no way in the transcendental account to explain how knowledge and meaning arise from a learning process that is stimulated by resistances originating outside of language in our active engagement with (and sensory experience of) a natural environment. Thus, as Heidegger noted, we are "fated" by our language to understand the world a certain way and can only alter our understanding if an inexplicable change in meaningfulness somehow emerges from *within* the possibilities of our language.[4]

Internal Realism

Habermas situates his own theory of knowledge, which he calls *Kantian pragmatism* (or, following Putnam's usage, *internal realism*) between transcendentalism and naturalism. He accepts a weak transcendentalism to account for the fact that experience is filtered through language, but he counterbalances this with a weak naturalism, which presumes that language and action refer (and stand in a causal relation) to a language-independent reality.

The most salient aspect of this theory is its substitution of the model of active learning for the old model of representation. Pragmatically speaking, every action is an attempt at successful coping with others or the natural environment. Such action provokes learning by engaging either the normative resistance of others or the causal resistance of nature.

According to Habermas, it is the resistance of nature that bears on the dual function ("Janus-faced nature") of truth. To begin with, we hold our beliefs to be true so long as they continue to provide practical certainty in successfully predicting and controlling this resistance. Thus, he writes:

> Everyday routines rest on an unqualified trust in the knowledge of lay people as much as experts. We would step on no bridge, use no car, undergo no operation, not even eat an exquisitely prepared meal if we did not consider the knowledge used to be safeguarded, if we did not hold the assumption employed in the production and execution of our actions to be true. (*OPC* 364)

Yet, despite its relationship to successful instrumental action, true belief held in the mode of practical certainty is not equivalent to successful belief (where success is defined by community standards), as some pragmatists have

---

4. Habermas's rejection of coherence theories of knowledge presumes that such theories must be radically contextualist. However, his own view that knowledge claims anticipate universal agreement between knowers and their respective contextual frames of reference permits us to describe his theory as a variant of coherentism. Key to this understanding is the rejection of forms of contextualism that deny the possibility of cross-contextual understanding. See L. Alcoff, *Real Knowing: New Versions of the Coherence Theory* (Ithaca: Cornell University Press, 1996).

maintained.[5] Rather, truth as certainty refers our belief to another belief that Habermas regards as a transcendental condition for action: a belief in a world of objects that is the same for everyone. This belief, however, does not arise within action as such, but in the relationship between action and discourse.

Once a belief ceases to be successful it becomes a topic of discourse. Here its truth becomes a function of its justification. But justification, as we have seen, is relative to standards of reasoning that are inherently provincial with respect to the future. So the assumption of a common world of objects that is the same for everyone cannot be the correlate of a concept of truth understood in this cautionary way, as a property of an assertion that can at best be temporarily warranted by these standards.

Instead, the concept of a common world of objects that is the same for everyone is connected to the notion of truth in the form of a universal claim to validity:

> This mode of unconditionally holding-to-be-true is reflected on the discursive level in the connotations of truth claims that point beyond the given context of justification and require the supposition of ideal justificatory conditions—the resulting decentering of the justification community. (*OPC* 372)

When truth is conceived unconditionally as (in the words of Putnam) "a property of a statement that cannot be lost,"[6] we seem compelled (following Peirce) to redefine our notion of a warranted assertion in terms of standards of rational justification that a spatially and temporally unlimited community would agree to. It is this discursive ideal of truth that also warrants our belief in a common world of objects that is the same for everyone. However, this ideal warrants such a belief only when it is brought into relation with real discourse, and only when real discourse, in turn, is brought into relation with action:

> When, in the course of a process of argumentation, participants attain the conviction that, having taken on board all relevant information and having weighed up all the relevant reasons, they have exhausted the reservoir of potential possible objections to "p," then all motives for continuing argumentation have been, as it were, used up. At any rate there is no longer any rational motivation for retaining hypothetical attitude toward the truth claim raised for "p" but temporarily left

---

5. According to Habermas, Rorty forsakes "the pursuit of truth" in favor of pursuing "unforced agreement among larger and larger groups of interlocutors" (*TJ* 374). The result is contextual relativism. As Rorty puts it, "there is no way to get outside our beliefs and our language so as to find some test other than coherence." *Philosophy and the Mirror of Nature* (Princeton: Princeton University Press, 1979), 178 (*TJ* 357). According to Habermas, Rorty can't explain why we ought to expand our justificatory conversation unless we appeal to conceptions of learning that presuppose realist notions of truth.

6. H. Putnam, *Philosophical Papers*, vol. 3, *Realism and Reason* (New York: Cambridge University Press, 1983), 84–85.

open. From the perspective of actors who have temporarily adopted a reflexive attitude in order to restore a partially disturbed background understanding, the de-problematization of the disputed truth claim means that a license is issued for return to the attitude of actors who are involved in dealing with the world more naively. As soon as the differences in opinion are resolved between "us" and "others" with regard to what is the case, "our" world can merge once more with "the" world. (*OPC* 369)

By insisting that truth as a discursive ideal be brought into a relationship with truth in reference to a world of objects that is the same for everyone, Habermas emphatically takes leave of the Peircean *epistemic* conception of truth that he, Putnam, and Apel had all once accepted:[7]

No matter how the value of the epistemic conditions is enhanced through ideal-izations, either they satisfy the unconditional character of truth claims by means of requirements that cut off all connection to practices familiar to us, or else they retain the connection to practices familiar to us by paying the price that rational acceptability does not exclude the possibility of error even under these ideal con-ditions, that is, does not simulate a property "that cannot be lost." (*OPC* 366)

The epistemic conception of truth is paradoxical because no nonideal speech situation can guarantee the truth of a consensus, and yet any ideal speech situation that could do so would—by its very nature of guaranteeing a final consensus—contradict the nature of knowing as a never-ending learning pro-cess. Because the ideal speech situation implicit in discourse cannot be realized, it can at best serve as a critical *standard* for assessing the extent to which real discourses fail to satisfactorily approximate our rational expectations.

Reference and Meaning

Discourse can function as one half of a circular process of learning only if the new beliefs that it brings about refer to the same objects referred to by the older beliefs. But scientific revolutions—which involve replacing one definition of reality with another—appear to render such reference inexpli-cable. Subsequently, they appear to reinstantiate the problem of incommen-surable worldviews that plagues hermeneutics, which undermines our faith

---

7. Habermas credits Albrecht Wellmer and Cristina Lafont for disabusing him of the "con-ceptual connection between truth and rational assertibility" (*TJ* 37). An obvious reason to do so is that simple observation statements such as "This ball is red," which had formerly posed something of an anomaly within Habermas's consensus theory of truth because they either did not need justification or (as asserted facts) needed a justification that could only be provided by appeal to reliable experience (perception) (PKHI 170), now appear to be true simply by virtue of their sensible certainty.

in knowledge as a relationship of correspondence between our beliefs and a world of objects that is the same for everyone.[8] To counter this appearance, Habermas appeals to Putnam's theory of reference. Before examining this theory, however, it will be useful to discuss the problem of reference as it emerged in analytic philosophy of language.[9]

Propositions consist of two levels of meaning:[10] the thing that is talked about (what we refer to; e.g., the cat, that is designated or denoted by the term 'cat' in the sentence that expresses the proposition 'The cat is on the mat') and what is said about it (how the thing spoken about—the cat, say—is identified, described, and presented as being on the mat). Deictic propositional terms such as demonstrative pronouns ('this,' 'that,' etc.) and personal pronouns ('I,' 'you,' etc.) mainly refer. Expressions, such as verbal phrases containing general predicates ('walked home,' 'is green,' etc.), convey the sense of what is said. Other terms, such as proper names ('David Ingram,' 'Cicero,' etc.), names designating natural kinds ('water,' 'gold,' etc.), and definite descriptions ('the current president of the United States'), both refer and convey sense.

Without the distinction between reference and sense, learning about things, and changes in our understanding of what we perceive in our world, would be inexplicable. Gottlob Frege, who was one of the first philosophers to discuss this distinction, showed how the distinction enables us to appreciate the meaningfulness of identity statements, such as 'The morning star is the evening star' whose truth we ascertain, not by definition, but by learning.[11] Unlike noninformative (or tautologous) identity statements of the form 'a = a' (such as 'All bachelors are unmarried'), the above identity statement brings together two distinct senses with reference to one and the same thing. The names (or definite descriptions) 'the morning star' and 'the evening star' both refer to one and the same thing (the planet Venus) by identifying it under one of two specific senses, either as the morning star or as the evening star, neither of which definitely

8. The inability to explain cross-cultural learning also plagues Alasdair MacIntyre's view, which assumes that standards of rationality are inextricably enmeshed in thick languages-in-use that resist translation. As Davidson points out, this notion of linguistic incommensurability is incoherent, since knowledge of incommensurability presupposes having translated the incommmensurable into our language. Equally incoherent is MacIntyre's model of cross-cultural learning. In crossing over into an incommensurable worldview the interpreter experiences a split identity that also extends to her experience of the world. Against this relativism Habermas insists that "concepts such as truth, rationality, and justification play the *same* role in *every* language community"—even if they are applied and interpreted differently—so that learning across cultures is possible (*JA* 105). A. MacIntyre, *Whose Justice? Which Rationality?* (Notre Dame, IN: University of Notre Dame Press, 1988); and D. Davidson, "On the Very Idea of a Conceptual Scheme," in *Inquiries into Truth and Interpretation* (Oxford: Oxford University Press, 1985).

9. The following discussion tracks a line of argument developed in much greater detail by Cristina Lafont in *The Linguistic Turn in Hermeneutic Philosophy*, trans. J. Medina (Cambridge: MIT Press, 1999).

10. On a truth-functional semantic account, propositions are abstract objects expressed by sentences, which are concrete inscriptions. This distinction is important because we want to be able to say that different sentences ("It is raining" and "Es regnet") mean the same thing.

11. G. Frege, "On Sense and Nominatum," in *Readings in Philosophical Analysis*, 85–102.

exhausts its meaning. If referring to something meant to *definitely* identify it with some description (as, say, "such and such a thing"), then this would require knowing all of its necessary and sufficient conditions so that, in effect, nothing more could be said (or learned) about it.

Frege believed that identity statements such as the above are meaningful because they refer to something that really exists in the world, about which we can say something true or false. Other philosophers (notably Alexius Meinong) disagreed and argued that we could refer meaningfully to impossible entities as well, such as round squares (for which he postulated a nonexisting world). Bertrand Russell, by contrast, sought a middle path: like Meinong, he held that we could meaningfully speak about nonexisting things but that our doing so ultimately depends on referring to the one world of really existent things about which we can speak truly or falsely.

The problem with Russell's proposal is that it relies on a logical analysis that reduces names (for him, the ultimate referring expressions) to definite descriptions, which he then analyzes in terms of *general* sense-conveying propositions about what exists or does not exist.[12] In short, he proposes to do what Frege's analysis forbids: reducing reference to a general set of defining conditions.

Russell proposed precisely this reduction in order to avoid certain logical paradoxes. Consider one of Russell's famous examples: 'The present king of France is not bald.' According to its apparent grammatical form, this sentence appears to be a statement about a really existing thing. But it cannot be. If it were, then it would be both true and false: true because there is no bald king of France; false because asserting this presupposes that there is a present king of France about whom 'is (is not) bald' might refer. Russell therefore concluded that definite descriptions such as 'the present king of France' refer, not in virtue of the particular thing they denote (as the referential theory of meaning would suggest), but in virtue of their logical meaning. This logical meaning consists of a disguised set of general expressions:

1. There is some person who is the present king of France.
2. There is at most one person who is the present king of France (i.e., any persons X and Z who are the king of France are identical to each other).
3. Anyone who is the present king of France is not bald.

According to this logical reduction, 1. is false as an existential claim, and 2. and 3., which are not existential claims but claims about general classes of possibly existing persons who happen to fall under the description 'the present king of France,' are true.

The radical implications of Russell's theory of descriptions become apparent in light of his view that all proper names—the paradigmatic instances of referring expressions—could also be logically analyzed in terms of definite

12. B. Russell, "On Denoting," in *Readings in Philosophical Analysis*, 103–15.

descriptions that semantically contain only general expressions. According to this view, only indexical expressions such as 'this' and 'that' properly refer.

Despite their logical elegance, Russell's reductions appear counterintuitive. To begin with, his analysis is driven by examples that are abstracted from context and which are therefore misleading. When uttered during the reign of King Louis XIV, 'The present king of France is not bald' might very well have been true. We see that the capacity of this proposition to refer, and hence its capacity to be evaluated in terms of its truth or falsity, might simply be a function of *using it appropriately in the right context,* rather than a function of the complicated logical structure that Russell attributed to it. Accordingly, Peter Strawson argued that the Russellian view confuses pragmatic and semantic levels of meaning.[13] Indeed, taking Strawson's point further, others, such as Keith Donnellan, have noted that descriptions can even function like indexical expressions, which do not refer to (or mean) anything apart from their actual use within a particular context (as when a cocktail party guest, referring to "the woman over there drinking a martini," knows that it is immaterial whether she is in fact drinking a martini or a glass of water).[14]

Other critics of Russell, most notably Saul Kripke, have objected that names *rigidly designate* their referents independently of whatever descriptions cluster around them.[15] Names would rigidly designate their referents even if none of the descriptions that held true about said referents in *this* world held true about them in *other* "possible worlds." 'Richard Nixon' would rigidly designate Richard Nixon (that individual) even if Richard Nixon had been kidnapped at birth and raised in totally different circumstances.

Taken together, the above objections strongly suggest that at least one class of referring expressions—proper names—cannot be reduced to general expressions. Yet Habermas himself once thought they could:

> We denote objects by means of names or definite descriptions. To do this, we have to orient ourselves by characteristic features. That is why we can always replace a name with a definite description. (*PSI* 80)

However, after suggesting a purely semantic approach to the problem of reference, Habermas immediately follows with a passage that gestures toward Strawson's pragmatist view:

> If it is to function pragmatically, the definite description must contain an identifying description of the object. It generally depends on the context which feature is sufficiently characteristic for speakers and hearers to be able to pick out from

13. P. Strawson, "On Referring," *Mind* 59 (1950): 320–244.
14. See K. Donnellan, "Reference and Definite Descriptions," *Philosophical Review* 75:281–304
15. S. Kripke, "Naming and Necessity," in *Semantics of Natural Language,* ed. D. Davidson and G. Harman (Dordrecht, Netherlands: Reidel, 1972).

all the possible objects precisely that object which is being discussed. The less we can rely on contexts of pre-understanding, however, the more deictic expressions must bear the burden of denotation. (*PSI* 80)

Space limitations do not permit a thorough treatment of Habermas's contemporary views on meaning and reference. It suffices to note that it is now Putnam—not Russell or Strawson—whose theory of reference has captured his fancy. The key to this new approach resides in a view that might be described as intermediate with respect to the extremes mentioned above. On the one hand, in many situations context alone does not suffice in explaining how simple names and gestures pick out things without the help of descriptions. On the other hand, no description can be taken as definitely adequate in this regard either, since we can imagine anomalous cases in which the description fails to rigidly apply.

The point can best be illustrated if we shift our focus from names to common nouns. Common nouns within the realm of science shift meaning—but not reference—in the course of "progressive" changes from one scientific paradigm to another. This seems paradoxical. On the one hand, common nouns that refer to natural kinds, such as 'water,' 'gold,' 'tiger,' 'particle,' and the like, can be defined in terms of a finite set of properties. Triangles, for example, have their reference rigidly fixed by formal definitions that exhaustively stipulate their necessary and sufficient conditions. The same applies to the nonmathematical entities of physics (such as subatomic particles) when they are first introduced into scientific theories; their range of reference is also rigidly fixed by way of definition. On the other hand, if this were all that might be said about science—that it postulates its objects in the same way that mathematics does—we would be left with a difficult question: Why does science experimentally test its definitions against the resistance manifested by the properties of the entities it postulates instead of merely using these definitions to deduce said properties? And, if it should revise its definition of something in light of experimental results—thereby leading to a radical shift in the paradigmatic understanding of that phenomenon—why would we not say that we are talking about something entirely different? But if we are talking about something entirely different, in what respect is the new paradigmatic understanding a better understanding of the *same* thing?

Habermas solves this problem—which recalls the problem of relativism (incommensurability) affecting holistic versions of linguistic idealism—by turning to the theory of reference developed by Putnam (*TJ* 33–36). Putnam argues that scientists use theoretical expressions to designate theoretical entities in the same way that ordinary persons use *operational* "definitions" to designate natural kinds, such as 'water.' When we use an operational definition of the type 'Water is a clear, tasteless, odorless liquid that falls from the sky' we are not imposing a set of necessary conditions that must be met in order for something to be water. Even if water did not fall from the sky as rain, or, if under some other conceivable set of circumstances, it had a different taste and odor, it would still be water (recalling Kripke's point). Indeed, none of our lay stereotypes about natural kinds can be used to rule out abnormal occurrences in which a member designated as falling under a certain natural kind lacks a normal property: green lemons are still identified as lemons, and tame three-legged tigers are still identified as tigers. So our ordinary use of natural-kind terms to identify things is not *fixed* by any descriptive stereotypes or attributes.[16]

But then what does fix their role as designators, if not the attribution of a single defining set of ordinary properties? According to Putnam, it is the *scientific* essence of water (its chemical composition as H_2O) that remains rigidly fixed; in the case of the tiger, it is its genes. But if that is so, are we not saying that one attribute—the scientific one—exhausts the essence of each of these terms?

Yes and no. Yes, because a scientific definition—when first *introduced*— postulates a necessary set of conditions that the entire community accepts as normative.[17] Given the "division of linguistic labor" in our community, we turn to experts to definitely fix our designations (e.g., if I doubt whether my ring is really 24K gold, I go to a chemist). No, because within the context of scientific experimentation and debate, scientific definitions function more like lay operational definitions. As Putnam remarks, the scientific community that rejected Bohr's definition of a subatomic particle as having determinate position and momentum in light of tests confirming Heisenberg's indeterminacy principle did not reject the existence of subatomic particles but revised Bohr's understanding of them. If scientists had used Bohr's definition as stipulating an exhaustive set of necessary conditions, then they would not have been revising Bohr's description but discovering a totally new entity. In that case, we would not say that science corrected an error, and the notion of learning something new would not be associated with the notion of progress.[18]

If an aura of paradox still surrounds this process, it is because the metaphysical necessities that are formally introduced to rigidly designate water as H_2O are contingently discovered through experimentation. Although our initial and always provisional theoretical delimitation of reference conforms to the model of *conceptual realism* (whereby we assume that a theoretical description of an entity captures its defining property or essence), our subsequent testing and revision of theory in experimental and discursive practice conforms to the model of *nominalism* (whereby we assume that a theoretical description of an entity is but a reflection of our current convention).

16. H. Putnam, "Is Semantics Possible," in *Philosophical Papers* vol. 2, *Mind, Language, and Reality* (Cambridge: Cambridge University Press, 1975), 140–41.

17. H. Putnam, "The Meaning of Meaning," in *Mind, Language, and Reality,* 237–8.

18. H. Putnam, "Explanation and Reference," in *Mind, Language, and Reality,* 197; H. Putnam, *Representation and Reality* (Cambridge: MIT Press, 1988), 9–10.

Knowledge and Evolution

Now that we see how Habermas's theory of scientific reference can account for learning across conceptual paradigm shifts in science, all that remains to complete his pragmatist account of knowledge as something that is not driven solely by reason or ideas is a rearticulation of the relationship between natural and social evolution that had eluded him in *KHI*. Natural evolution, he argues, is analogous to learning. The natural selection of adaptive mutations responds to causal resistances within the natural environment but without the intervention of consciousness and its linguistic tools. Hence, we can understand *conscious* learning as in some sense *continuous* with more primitive stages of *preconscious* adaptation. At the same time, higher levels of learning that enable the linguistic (theoretical) articulation and argumentative testing of practical certainties break with this naturalism up to a point. Knowledge ceases to be a mere function of objective experience, or shared practical certainty, and becomes a function of rational truth. The failure of *KHI* to take into account this higher level of discursive knowledge also prevented it from explaining how knowledge-constitutive interests break with nature. Simply put, at the level of discursively achieved truth, causally conditioned natural evolution takes a backseat to rationally controlled social progress (*TJ* 27–28). At the same time, it must not be forgotten that reason (and language) depend, in turn, on naturally evolved sensory organs that refer us to a manifold of resistant forces—the ultimate "reality" against which we test our beliefs.

Moral Realism

Speaking of perceived "reality" as the ultimate criterion against which we test our beliefs raises an interesting question about the status of moral judgments. Although I will examine Habermas's views about morality in a later chapter, some indication of the status of moral judgments can be indicated here. Given the analogy between truth and moral rightness as universal validity claims, it might seem that Habermas must be committed to some version of moral realism. If what makes our propositions true (universally valid) is reference to a world that we have not mentally fabricated, then what makes our judgments true (universally valid) must likewise be the same thing: an "objective" moral universe, as it were. Accordingly, Lafont has argued that "the presupposition of the existence of a domain of generalizable interests is the condition of possibility for a meaningful discussion about the moral rightness of norms."[19]

19. C. Lafont, "Pluralism and Universalism in Discourse Ethics," in *A Matter of Discourse: Community and Communication in Contemporary Philosophies,* ed. A. Nascimento (London: Avebury, 1998), 68.

Putnam agrees,[20] and he has argued that moral discourse must make use of "thick" evaluative terms in testing the rightness of norms prohibiting such things as cruelty, which he believes denotes a descriptive property that can be perceived independently of any parochial cultural worldview.

Habermas finds these arguments in support of moral realism to be unconvincing, but not because he rejects what they assert. He concedes that moral discourse must make use of thick evaluative terms that have a descriptive sense, and he notes that prohibitions against cruelty, like prohibitions against other human rights violations, designate universal values that transcend social context.[21] The difference between Habermas and Putnam thus centers not on the existence of universal values but on their proper characterization. Putnam calls them perceptible "facts" and appeals to the social fact of their common acceptance in support of this characterization. Habermas, by contrast, resists this appeal to factual acceptance as sufficient justification. What justifies them, he avers, is the same thing that justifies mathematical propositions: their reference to a counterfactual (ideal) agreement (OPC 230–31). Furthermore, if this agreement imposes any constraint on our behavior, it is a constraint caused not by reference to objective reality, as in the case of truth, but by the projection of an ideally inclusive community of speakers—a community of which we ourselves are members.

According to Habermas, the projection of this community—analogous to Kant's moral Kingdom of Ends—underlies the very possibility of theoretical and practical discourse. To say that it constrains our behavior in the same way that a fact does overlooks a crucial difference: the moral community in question is defined solely by voluntary rational consent. It is I, who—in tandem with a humanity that must be made fully inclusive and the same for all—consent to my own constraint. This explains why Habermas thinks that normative rightness, unlike truth, is entirely epistemic—defined in its entirety by the concept of discursive agreement:

> [Moral beliefs] are implicitly corroborated...not by successfully manipulating otherwise independently occurring processes, but by consensually resolving conflicts of interaction....Corroboration does not occur in a practice that can be readily differentiated from discourse. Rather it takes place from the outset in the linguistic medium of communication—even though people first "feel" the consequences of moral injury....The resistance does not come from the objectively "given" that we cannot control, but from lack of a normative consensus with others....The resistance of "objective spirit" can be overcome by moral learning processes that lead the disputing parties to broaden their respective social worlds

20. H. Putnam, *The Collapse of the Fact/Value Dichotomy and Other Essays* (Cambridge: Harvard University Press, 2002), 127.

21. Habermas observes that social justice and social solidarity also designate universal values, in contrast to culturally relative values concerning child rearing (*TJ* 229).

and to *include* one another in a world they jointly construct in such a way that they can assess their conflicts in the light of shared standards of evaluation and resolve them consensually. (*TJ* 256)

As we shall see in the next chapter, the principle of universalizability that informs this community does indeed refer to generalizable interests. But this notion, Habermas insists, is not a fact but a moral desideratum. Unlike objects, interests do not inhabit any *natural* referential context; they are entirely products of social interpretation.[22] Generalizable interests are even more so, since their very existence depends on the willingness of moral agents to transform their initial interests in the course of critical discussion. Indeed, as we shall see, moral discourse requires that we at least try to do so in order to avoid imposing our will on others. It is just this mutual criticism and transformation of interests that emancipates us from pathological prejudices that have become second nature. Moral realism, with its appeal to society as second nature, would therefore seem to contradict the freedom of moral agents to refuse any constraint that they could not rationally impose on themselves (*TJ* 266–68).

Is Formal Pragmatism a Defensible Alternative to Realism and Contextualism?

In this chapter we have seen how Habermas constructs his mature theory of language and knowledge in order to avoid two extremes which, he believes, doom critical theory: contextualism and realism. Realism ostensibly denies our rational autonomy to interpret social and objective reality in accordance with our own rationally constituted interests. The object determines the subject (as in moral realism), or the subject corresponds to the object (as in metaphysical-epistemological realism), thereby rendering criticism of the object enigmatic. Contextualism, by contrast, allows that social and objective realities are not given independently of our sociolinguistic practices and interests. However, the holistic nature of belief commitments that are validated only with reference to one another and not in isolation gives rise to an invidious form of linguistic idealism that renders learning from nature and others enigmatic: what exists is what "our" descriptions meaningfully designate, and what our descriptions meaningful designate is a function of our web of belief commitments taken together. The image conveyed by holism privileges the *subject* in relation to the object, but only by enclosing the former within a closed system of self-referential meanings and denotations that remain incommensurable with respect to the meanings and denotations of other such systems. Furthermore,

---

22. However, given that Habermas's insistence that normative judgments about interests (which are distinct from personal needs) refer to a social world, it is hard to see why normative judgments could not be understood as factual assertions of a *nonnatural* sort.

since the theoretical holism of our beliefs mirrors the practical holism of our prereflective background understanding of the world, which essentially resists being made an object of rational reflection and critique, contextualism also threatens the autonomy of the knowing and acting self.

Formal pragmatism redeems our autonomy as rational agents by introducing a structural gap (or transcendental difference) between us and our factual "worlds." Although the idealizing assumptions of an objective world to which our assertions must refer arise from within our everyday lifeworld whenever we act, these assumptions also provoke a ceaseless discourse about the lifeworld, compelling us to critically reexamine our factual beliefs. Indeed, contrary to Habermas's fears, there is no reason why this "internal realist" presumption cannot be extended to our normative judgments as well. For the presumption that there objectively exist common interests that have yet to be discovered can be the only reason compelling us to criticize our current norms for failing to advance such interests.[23]

This concession to realism as a "regulative ideal" is precisely what enables us to "relativize" our own parochial assumptions about reality and expand our horizons to include perspectives other than our own. The use of referring expressions, names, indexicals, and deictic expressions (pronouns, demonstratives, etc.) that are not definitely fixed by any single inferential system permits communication to occur, even if that communication no longer necessarily involves the sharing of identical meaning.[24]

---

23. Habermas's objection to moral realism hinges on the Kantian notion that we can only be morally obligated by norms to which we all could freely consent. In this case, the only sign that we are mistaken in our moral judgments is the resistance of ostensibly reasonable others who disagree with us. Resistance then provides the cognitive motive to construct generalizable interests where none previously existed. In responding to Habermas's earlier criticism of her position, Lafont argues that this objection to moral realism suffers from two defects: (1) it confuses the *justification* of a norm with its *legitimacy,* or universal acceptance; and (2) it cannot explain that there are generalizable interests that all can agree on. With regard to (1), unless one builds infallibility and omniscience into the procedural ideals of discourse—which would render these ideals unfit for human beings—there is no reason why even universal acceptance by reasonable persons might not be mistaken regarding the validity (justice and rightness) of moral norms. Semantically speaking, it sounds just as strange to say that "cruelty is wrong" means "reasonable people agree that cruelty is wrong" as it does to say that "the belief that 'the earth is flat' is wrong" means "reasonable people agree that 'the earth is flat' is wrong." With regard to (2), moral autonomy consists in distinguishing which already existing interests are universal. This process may also involve reinterpreting (redescribing) interests, but we would not bother to do this unless we believed that people were already alike in their interests. C. Lafont, "Moral Objectivity and Reasonable Agreement: Can Reasonable Agreement Be Reconciled with Kantian Constructivism?" *Ratio Juris* 17/1 (2004): 27–51.

24. Habermas (*TJ* 145–47) here cites Brandom's discussion of *anaphora,* or the use of pronouns in referring to antecedent simple names (singular terms). Anaphoric uses of pronouns such as 'it,' 'he,' and 'that' (as distinct from nonrepeatable or merely reporting demonstrative uses such as 'this here') enable speakers to connect a secondary assertion about something to a more primary antecedent assertion about that same thing under a fuller denomination. So construed, anaphoras enable speakers to connect their assertions to other assertions (their own and others) about the same thing through *symmetrical* processes of substitution. Anaphoric commitments provide "spatiotemporal depth" to our chain of communication, ensuring that we can talk about

But this appeal to universal formal-pragmatic assumptions is quite limited, as we have seen. When it comes to determining precisely what is intended by a speech act, context and perspective (or speaker attitude) play a necessary role that cannot be formally bracketed. In the remaining chapters of this book we will see that Habermas continues to insist that a formal account of language, and therewith a formal account of discursive reasoning, is necessary for grounding moral and social critique. The question we must then ask is whether these assumptions suffice to ground critique in the way he thinks they do. If a formal-pragmatic account of *speech* does not suffice to explain meaning apart from substantive intuitions that are holistically intermeshed in our lifeworld, can a formal-pragmatic account of *reason* possibly explain moral right apart from substantive intuitions about the good? And if it cannot—if, in other words, all criticism is immanent to the very social existence it criticizes—do we critics not relinquish our critical autonomy?

---

the same thing despite our disagreement with respect to *asymmetrical* substitution commitments, or commitments "of breadth" regarding predicates (descriptions). Thanks to anaphoric commitments, two speakers who have different contextual perspectives on the world and different ontologies about what sorts of things are in the world (and how they are best predicated) can still talk about the same thing, as denoted by the pronoun to which they share an anaphoric commitment. What is of crucial importance is that, although the meaning of an anaphoric dependent is inherited from a previous link in the chain, there is no final or first link (such as a worldly object demonstrated by a 'this here now'). This is because even the meaning of the anaphoric initiator (a 'this' or a 'that') is determined by the entire anaphoric chain that it initiates. (Recall that according to the inferentialist account of coherence, meaning and reference are determined holistically, not foundationally.) The implications are quite startling: deixis (reference) presupposes anaphora. In the words of Brandom, "anaphora is more basic than deixis, for there can be languages that have anaphoric mechanisms but no deictic ones, while there cannot in principle be languages with deictic mechanisms but no anaphoric ones." *Making It Explicit: Reasoning, Representing, and Discursive Commitment* (Cambridge: Harvard University Press, 1998), 621. Again, to cite Brandom, "no semantically significant occurrence of a subsentential expression can be discerned unless it is governed by substitution inferences, which requires token recurrence: no (semantically significant) *occurrence* without (the possibility of) *recurrence*" (*Making it Explicit*, 465). See R. Loeffler, "Normative Phenomenalism: On Robert Brandom's Practised-Based Theory of Meaning," *European Journal of Philosophy* 13/1 (2005): 44; and J. Wanderer, *Robert Brandom* (Montreal and Kingston: McGill–Queens University Press, 2008), 136–45.

5

Discourse Ethics

Habermas's theories about linguistic meaning, action, and knowledge have as one of their aims the defense of a paradigm of moral reasoning, *discourse ethics* (DE), that has both *metaethical* and *normative* aspects. The metaethical aspect reconstructs what we intuitively mean when using moral expressions such as "ought" and "right." These expressions logically imply mutual respect between persons as free and equal agents. They also imply a standard of normative validity: only those moral norms are valid to which all persons could freely consent. The normative program tells us what we are obligated to do in order to reach agreement on valid moral norms. It does not prescribe any particular course of action, nor does it prescribe moral action as such (which under some circumstances may be too risky to reasonably demand of any agent). Rather, it shows that we cannot renounce our obligation to reach agreement on valid moral norms if we are to interact with others in a rationally accountable way. Furthermore, it shows that reaching moral agreement tacitly obligates us to enter into real discourse and, by implication, obligates us to conform our collective moral reasoning to the unavoidable presuppositions underlying discourse. Because these presuppositions demand that we treat all persons as free and equal agents, they already embody the moral point of view. Skepticism stands refuted: no rationally accountable person can deny her moral duty to others without tacitly contradicting herself. Ultimately, DE grounds critical social theory by providing an ideal standard of moral reasoning in comparison to which actual processes of moral reasoning can be judged to be more or less deficient.

Practical Reason: Delimiting the Domain of the Moral

Let us begin by looking at some technical distinctions Habermas draws between different types of practical claims, or uses of "ought." Sometimes we use the expression in a *pragmatic* sense, as when we say, "If you want to accomplish this end, you ought to employ these means." This minimal sense of practical reason is purely instrumental and in no way requires that I lead a good, fulfilling life. A more prudentially rational means for ensuring that my preferences are efficiently satisfied requires harmonizing them with the aim of achieving long-term success. But acting prudently does not yet require ordering my preferences around more enduring values associated with leading a good (as opposed to subjectively satisfying) life. Recommending that someone lead a good life correlates with an *ethical* usage of "ought." The goodness in question might be entirely personal, as when we say "You ought to be true to who you are." This ethical-existential usage concerns the choice of "authentic" values that define who I am: my core identity. If we think of values as consisting of higher-order preferences (preferences about preferences, or preferences about being the kind of person who has preferences of a certain sort), authentic values would be the highest-order preferences one can choose about one's life as a whole: such as living justly, behaving with integrity, acting with care and compassion for others, and so on. However, because such values refer to shared preferences (or as Habermas puts it, interpretations of preferences) that are esteemed by the community of which one is a member, they are not, strictly speaking, subjective preferences but objective standards. Both aesthetic judgments, such as "You (we) ought to prefer this experience/thing because it is objectively good, beautiful, tasteful, or desirable," and political judgments, such as "You (we) ought to prefer this policy because it advances our social and political values," imply shared standards. Having been socialized into us, these standards inform our identities, but not unconditionally. The identity a person "inherits" (as a Muslim Arab-American woman, say) can be modified by one's life choices (to be an agnostic feminist). Finally, we use "ought" in the specifically *moral* sense intended by Habermas (following Kant) as when we say, "Everybody ought to respect others' rights." This use of "ought" arises when discussing overarching (universal) norms of respect and justice that obtain even when all our other values conflict. Unlike ethical values, which can conflict with one another and be pursued in varying degrees by one person or community acting alone, moral norms form a coherent system of unconditional social expectations that regulate relationships between persons and groups (*IO* 55).

According to Habermas, each of these uses of "ought" (instrumental, prudential, existential-ethical, political-ethical, and moral) specifies a domain of practical discourse (rationality). In each domain, persons challenge and demand justification of others' decisions. In order to justify our prudential decisions, we undertake *pragmatic* discourses concerning effective strategies and techniques.

In order to justify existential or ethical-political decisions we undertake *ethical* discourses of a clinical-therapeutic nature concerning intrinsically fulfilling experiences and ways of life. In order to justify decisions regarding right (just) conduct toward others, we undertake *moral* discourses concerning universally acceptable norms.

In real life these levels of practical reasoning can scarcely be separated. Prudent actors will try to insure that the ends they pursue are the best ones given their self-conception. Authentic agents will try to insure that their self-conception sufficiently harmonizes with shared standards of value to insure the minimal recognition from others necessary to sustain a sense of self-esteem and self-identity. Political agents will try to insure that their conflicting standards of value can in some way be made to accommodate the universal interests of everyone. Finally, moral agents will have to consider how generally acceptable norms are to be applied and pragmatically implemented across a range of situations; how one describes (interprets) these situations will necessarily engage the value-laden standpoints from which we understand our world. Hence, debates about abortion, stem cell research (SCR), cloning, and preimplantation genetic diagnosis (PGD or PIGD) can be described equally well as debates about extending *universal* moral rights to the unborn, realizing a particular social good, or defending a universal ethical understanding of human nature.

The Priority of the Right over the Good

Although ethical conceptions of the good life are important in shaping the particular identities of individuals and groups, Habermas does not accord them priority over universal moral conceptions of justice. Indeed, he holds that moral principles constrain our ethical conceptions. In this respect, he sides with liberals in the so-called liberalism-communitarianism debate.[1]

Communitarians emphasize that our individual identities are shaped by our relations with other persons who care about us. Communities of concern are limited and bounded: they include those persons with whom we identify deeply. Members of our family, neighborhood, civic community, church, workplace, and nation constitute communities of concern in this sense; members of universal humanity, including strangers and outsiders, do not. Accordingly, communitarians hold that it is quite natural and morally acceptable to be partial in our dealings with others, depending on whether they are inside or outside our community (or communities) of concern. Helping distressed persons who

---

1. For a sampling of the rich literature on this topic, see S. Benhabib and F. Dallmayr, eds., *The Communicative Ethics Controversy* (Cambridge: MIT Press, 1990); and D. Rasmussen, ed., *Universalism vs. Communitarianism: Contemporary Debates in Ethics* (Cambridge: MIT Press, 1990).

are members of your own family (community) ahead of helping distressed outsiders is morally appropriate. Likewise, discriminating against outsiders—for example, by disallowing needy aliens to immigrate into your community—is not necessarily wrong if doing so is thought to be necessary for advancing the good of the community.

Liberals dispute the communitarian priority of the good over the right. Their argument hinges on the supreme importance of cooperation between communities. If communities are to cooperate with one another they must do so in accordance with universal moral norms that express the importance of tolerating and respecting persons as individual human beings, apart from their membership in any community. Habermas shares this sentiment. However, he agrees with communitarians on one crucial point: moral norms and rights must be justified discursively by a community of persons who care about one another's interests and cannot be justified by the isolated individual, reasoning alone. The communitarian linkage of justification and caring communication underscores the fact that one's own sense of self remains uncertain unless confirmed by others. Finally, given Habermas's belief that communicative action occurs within the context of a shared lifeworld, we should not be surprised to see him meet communitarians halfway in acknowledging the importance of particular values, traditions, and practices as concrete reference points for understanding and applying abstract moral norms.

Modernity and Moral Development

Before proceeding further it will be useful for us to situate Habermas's discourse ethics within the history of moral philosophy. Habermas presents his moral theory as one among many distinctly *modern* moral theories. He designates conduct as "moral" when individuals assume responsibility for freely harmonizing with their fellows, according to the dictates of their own conscience. This mode of conduct barely exists (if at all) in premodern societies, in which persons unquestionably accept their common status in life as dictated by religious authority. The emergence of modern freedom undermines such authority and generates conflicts that can only be resolved by individuals who relate to one another as equals. Although premodern ethicists were no strangers to conflict (witness Socrates), their solutions still revolved around theological-metaphysical conceptions of a good and just order that modern philosophers since Kant have impugned as rationally indefensible.

Like Kant before him, Habermas endeavors to justify morality on post-metaphysical grounds but without appealing to pure reason. One argument he presents explains how the normative core of morality—the so-called moral point of view, from which we regard others' interests on a par with our own (i.e., impartially)—can be adduced from the conditions of discourse and meaningful interaction. This argument, however, indirectly depends on two other interrelated ones, which appeal to sociology of modern society and developmental moral psychology.

As Habermas understands it, morality first arises within modern societies that have undergone a process of structural evolution impelled by what he, following Weber, calls *rationalization* (see chapters 10 and 11). Rationalization involves the gradual subordination of religious and metaphysical ways of understanding the world to a secular, scientific outlook. The disenchantment of nature as a domain of purposes and ends is coupled with the emergence of market and legal systems that center around contracts and private property. Accompanying this functional change in economy and law is a profound change in the way people understand themselves. People now understand themselves as *individuals* who must be rationally accountable to themselves and others. Fulfilling different roles in an increasingly complex society and judging their own highest religious and ethical convictions from the still higher tribune of moral conscience, persons develop conflicting interests and conflicting understandings about God and the good that God ordains for them. They eventually learn that ethical conflict can be avoided only if they pursue their conception of the good in a constrained way, by tolerating others and respecting their universal rights to worship and think as they please.

Besides holding that rights-based morality is a necessary precondition for modern society, Habermas argues that it represents a higher stage of development that enables us to solve conflicts more effectively. Here he draws from the developmental moral psychology pioneered by Jean Piaget and Lawrence Kohlberg (see appendix D). This psychology is premised on the idea that children proceed through an irreversible sequence of learning stages, with later stages incorporating and modifying elements of earlier ones.

Following Kohlberg's description, Stage 1, the earliest part of the *preconventional* stage of moral reasoning, only takes into account the consequences of actions in reasoning about how to seek pleasure and avoid pain. Stage 2, a higher level of preconventional morality, requires learning the rudiments of self-centered reciprocity, encapsulated in the maxim of "I'll scratch your back if you scratch mine." Social cooperation of this type, based solely on the momentary convenience of each party, is unreliable whenever one party decides that it is no longer in his interest to continue cooperating. *Conventional* moral reasoning solves this problem by taking into account the conventional expectations of others. Children at Stage 3 cooperate with their parents in order to make them happy; as adults, they learn to play the conventional roles demanded of them by society. Yet the highest level of conventional reasoning (Stage 4), demanding devotion to law and order, still shows no disposition toward questioning authority, as illustrated by the patriotic slogan, "my country, right or wrong."

Only at the *postconventional* level does the citizen question whether his nation's conventions are compatible with more general, abstract conceptions of right and wrong. These abstract conceptions already enter into the design of the nation's constitution. Such a constitution can be conceived in terms of a *social contract* in which persons distinguish between the equal rights and duties of general citizenship, on one side, and the different (unequal) rights and duties associated with the fulfillment of particular social roles on the other. According to this contractarian thinking (Stage 5), a person's basic right to life cannot be infringed by the majority. But society can still distribute burdens and benefits unequally according to the whims of the most powerful or the most numerous. Even when contractarianism endorses equal democratic rights and so permits the majority to pass laws maximizing overall welfare—the principle of *utilitarianism*—it still fails to respect the equal interests of all. Only at the *deontological* level of postconventional reasoning (Stage 6) do individuals interact in accordance with universal principles of justice that aim to advance the interests of all equally.

Modern morality is postconventional. The three main types of postconventional morality—social contractarian, utilitarian, and deontological—are therefore also postmetaphysical. That is, they provide purely rational procedures for ascertaining right and wrong that do not appeal to controversial metaphysical views about moral goodness and perfection. Unlike the four stages of preconventional and conventional moral development, which appear to follow an empirically confirmed progression, the ranking of postconventional stages of moral development continues to fire philosophical debate. Habermas accordingly provides philosophical arguments in support of deontological types of moral reasoning, and he advances his own discourse ethics as the best of this type, even entertaining (before eventually rejecting) the notion that it constituted a "Stage 7" on Kohlberg's scale (*CES* 89).

Kohlberg's and Piaget's developmental theories are controversial and difficult to confirm. Observing how children and adults reason when presented with moral dilemmas raises questions about cultural bias in the way these dilemmas are presented and formulated.[2] As Carol Gilligan has remarked, Kohlberg's

---

2. Habermas notes at least three main problems that plague Piagetian developmental theories (Kohlberg's especially). First, problems arise concerning the confirmation of these theories across cultures. Kohlberg asked persons to resolve hypothetical moral dilemmas, such as the Heinz dilemma, in which a poor man must choose whether or not to steal a drug that will save his wife's life. The responses were then scored on a scale from 1 to 6. But it is unclear whether these dilemmas can be extended to non-Western cultural contexts without altering their meaning. (Could the Heinz dilemma arise in a tribal setting in which goods, services, and the like are shared?) Also, cultures pursue developmental paths that are "more adaptive in a given environment and more culturally valued" than others. Piagetian theories propose a sequential developmental path in which more advanced stages dialectically incorporate earlier stages in a manner that is at once more differentiated and more integrated. In particular, Piaget held that stage 4's formal-logical operations (such as inferring that A is greater than C from the fact that A is greater than B and B is greater than C) are more advanced than stage 3's concrete operations (seeing that A is greater than C through direct visual comparison). Piaget also noted that the achievement of cognitive concepts (such as conservation) happens gradually, so that it might be applied to substance before weight and volume. However, the extent to which these concepts are grasped appears to be culturally determined. As Thomas McCarthy notes (*CD* 70–72), citing studies by Ashton (1975) and others regarding stage 3, "children from pottery-making families in Mexico perform better on conservation of substance than do

theory also appears to display a gender bias. According to Kohlberg's scheme, women generally scored lower than men in their responses, placing greater emphasis on interpreting contextual complexities and maintaining personal relationships than on resolving conflicts by appeal to general principles. Gilligan's hypothesis—that women are socialized into an ethic of care while men are socialized into an ethic of justice—suggests that deontological morality is neither as universal nor as straightforwardly superior as many think.[3]

As we shall see, Habermas formulates his discourse ethic to take into account the importance of both contextual application and care for one's interlocutors and their particular needs. That said, he gives compelling reasons why deontological moral theories should be preferred over utilitarian and social contractarian alternatives.

Modern morality obligates us to respect the inherent dignity of the individual. Utilitarianism regresses behind this standpoint by upholding the greatest happiness for the greatest number as the supreme standard for judging right and wrong. Although this standard might also justify respecting the rights of the individual—as it does in John Stuart Mill's *On Liberty* (1859)—its doing so is entirely accidental.

---

their peers from families that are not potters…nomadic, hunting populations…attain concepts of conservation of quantity, weight, and volume more rapidly…[and] among Australian Aborigines, performance on concrete, operational tasks is directly proportional to the extent of their contact with the dominant culture." Second, the theory has difficulty in explaining postadolescent "regression" among women and middle-aged persons. Studies by Gilligan and Murphy show selected women registering a preference for conventional solutions to moral dilemmas despite indications of their having reached a postconventional level of moral development. When presented with the Heinz dilemma, some of these women expressed regret that society could permit such a dilemma to arise in the first place; and some proposed different ways of staging Heinz's situation in which the prevalence of "conventional" norms of care would prevent the dilemma from arising at all. Likewise, many middle-aged test subjects preferred a relativistic or skeptical approach (scored as 4.5 on Kohlberg's scale) that acknowledged the limits of a rule-governed deontological ethic in dealing with the complexities and exceptions of real-life situations (a preference shown by many philosophically trained ethicists as well). Third, Kohlberg's theory has difficulty explaining the classical philosophical problem of cognitive weakness (cognitive insights failing to motivate action due to repression and the like). See P. T. Ashton, "Cross-Cultural Piagetian Research: An Experimental Perspective," *Harvard Educational Review* 45 (1975); P. R. Dasen, ed., *Piagetian Psychology: Cross-Cultural Contributions* (New York: Halsted, 1977); C. Gilligan, *In A Different Voice: Psychological Theory and Women's Development* (Cambridge: Harvard University Press, 1983); and C. Gilligan and J. M. Murphy, "The Philosopher and the Dilemma of the Fact," in *Intellectual Development beyond Childhood*, ed. D. Kuhn (San Francisco: Jossey-Bass, 1980). For an excellent discussion of Habermas and developmental psychology, see D. Owen, *Between Reason and History: Habermas and the Idea of Progress* (Albany: SUNY Press, 2002), esp. chap. 4.

3. For an early synthesis of Habermasian discourse ethics and an ethic of care, see S. Benhabib, "The Utopian Dimension in Communicative Ethics," in *Critical Theory: The Essential Readings*, ed. D. Ingram and J. Simon (New York: Paragon House, 1992), 388–99. Although he also incorporates care (solidarity) into justification, Habermas today sees the (universalizing) ethics of justice and the (concretizing) ethics of care as referring to justification and application, respectively. J. Habermas, "Justice and Solidarity: On the Discussion Concerning 'Stage 6'," *Philosophical Forum* 21/1–2 (1989–90): 32–52.

The main problem with social contract theory, by contrast, is its individual-ism. The classical variety associated with the thought of Thomas Hobbes and contemporary game theory, tries to derive a moral obligation to refrain from harming persons and their property by appealing to a minimal understanding of rationality, here restricted exclusively to instrumental and strategic reasoning. Hobbes assumes that persons are primarily interested in maximizing their own interests, and so he concludes that under conditions of scarcity they will fight with others in order to secure their well-being. Hobbes, however, argued in *Leviathan* (1651) that purely self-interested strategic calculators will limit their behavior on condition that all others do the same; in other words, they will enter into a social contract whose terms require respecting individuals' property rights.

Habermas has two problems with this theory. First, rational egoists would be hard-pressed to trust one another long enough to enter a social contract without a legal mechanism already in place that could compel compliance, and it would be strategically rational to break it if one calculated that the benefit from doing so outweighed the risks of being caught and punished. Second, Hobbes's concep-tion of the social contract runs contrary to our deepest understanding of what being morally obligated means. When we say that someone ought to obey the law—in the moral, as distinct from the prudential sense of "ought"—we mean that it ought to be done because it is right and just, not because failure to do so risks pain or punishment (*JA* 43). Moral duties extend to strangers, children, the disabled, and others with whom we do not or cannot enter into mutually ben-eficial cooperation (*IO* 15). Contracts made for reasons that all parties find pru-dentially compelling can still be unfair and, to that extent, coercive. For example, militant oil-consuming industries and militant environmentalists opposed to any form of profit-oriented market economy might eventually agree to a contract that struck a compromise between their extreme positions; but because it reflects only a strategic balance of power, it will be regarded by both parties as a neces-sary evil that can be dispensed with as soon as the balance of power shifts.[4]

Deontological Moral Theory and Universalizability: Kant and Rawls

Habermas advances his discourse ethics as the most adequate interpretation among a family of deontological theories that descend from Kant. The defining

---

4. Joseph Heath argues that Habermasian discourse ethics does not require *universalizability* since "there is a powerful incentive for agents to pursue moral argumentation until they reach some agreement—if need be through compromise or bargaining." *Communicative Action and Rational Choice* (Cambridge: MIT Press, 2001), 279–80. Heath's criticism misses its mark. DE offers no sociological explanation of why people engage in moral discourse but merely recon-structs the normative commitments assumed by persons who are already so engaged. C. Lafont, "Review Essay: Communicative Action and Rational Choice," *Philosophy and Social Criticism* 31/2 (2005): 253–63.

feature of Kant's moral philosophy is its insistence on the modern idea that moral subjects must view themselves principally as free, responsible agents who are *duty bound* to others and therefore rationally accountable to them. Our sense of moral self-respect is bound up with respecting others as ultimate ends, or autonomous agents, quite apart from their instrumental value to us (*JA* 44–45).

The emphasis on freedom and responsibility leads Kant to the radical conclusion that we can be duty bound to only those rules of conduct that we ourselves have legislated. Because I am responsible to others, these rules (maxims) must be capable of being willed by me as universal laws for humanity. The principle of *universalizability* (U)—Kant's categorical imperative—thus prescribes a procedure by which I can test my maxims, and in so doing become freer than if I were to act on them blindly, for only in this way can I take responsibility for (and take control over) my impulses. Because rational consistency—not making exceptions for myself and treating like cases alike—is the hallmark of morality, Kant concludes that what distinguishes a moral person is her possession of a good (or rational) will. Morality is about having virtuous *intentions,* not about producing good consequences (which, after all, can be the indirect side effect of selfishly motivated behavior).

Habermas accepts the basic idea behind Kant's moral philosophy—the connection between duty, moral responsibility, freedom, and universalizability—but rejects both the metaphysics behind it as well as the "monological" procedure Kant recommends for implementing it. Kant grounded his moral theory in a dualistic conception of the human person both as an embodied agent inhabiting earthly society, where persons' needs and desires clash, and as a disembodied member of an ideal Kingdom of Ends, where the rational will of each coexists in preestablished harmony with everyone else's. This conception is deeply problematic insofar as it opposes the causality of worldly inclination to the moral freedom of otherworldly reason. In particular, it overlooks the fact that socialization instills biological needs and desires with a rational form. Habermas accordingly concludes that the rational harmonization of wills is a never-ending learning process that must be accomplished in *this* world. Ultimately, it is questioning by others that enables us to become conscious of our interests so that we can responsibly change them in light of others' interests.

The relationship between autonomy and critical dialogue forces us to abandon Kant's procedure of moral universalizability in favor of one that is communitarian and democratic. Kant's method is *monological:* it requires that each person conduct a thought experiment within the privacy of her own mind in which she asks whether her maxim of action can be willed consistently as a universal law for humanity. This procedure—like the Golden Rule ("Do unto others as you would have them do unto you")—allows the moral agent to "project" her maxims of behavior onto humanity uncritically (*JA* 51). If I am a sadomasochist (I take pleasure in both treating others as slaves and in being treated as a slave in return), I will have little difficulty willing that all others behave sadomasochistically too.

Kant's procedure forbids assessing the consequences of actions for satisfying our preferences. Doing so, he believes, amounts to substituting a conditional imperative of the form 'If the consequences are good, then you may do X.' This rejection of utilitarianism appeals to our sense that it is wrong to harm others for the sake of bringing about an overall balance of good. Consequently, Kant makes our duty to others unconditional: morality demands that each and every person be treated the same way, consistently and without exception.

The price Kant pays for his inflexible rationalism is steep. Acting consistently regardless of consequences violates our intuition that it is sometimes OK to lie (make an exception to truth-telling) in order to avert great harm. It also violates our intuition that norms are intended to advance our common good. Hence, in *A Theory of Justice* (1971), John Rawls famously proposed to revise Kant's universalizability test. We are asked to imagine a hypothetical social contract (the original position) in which the parties concerned are asked to agree on norms for fairly distributing basic goods. Deliberating behind a "veil of ignorance" in which their own identity is concealed from them, contractors are forced to place themselves in the shoes of the worst off members of their society. They will therefore choose principles of justice prohibiting the violation of anyone's basic rights as well as any social inequality unless it can be made to work to the advantage of the least well off (e.g., through market incentives that encourage efficient productivity). By requiring that we consider the interests of each person, Rawls requires that we question norms—such as those prohibiting begging—that adversely impact the interests of the least well off.

A problem remains, however. By requiring me (as a hypothetical contractor) to abstract from all the particular interests that distinguish me from any other person, none of the real diversity that makes up the "social" in social contract remains. As with Kant's categorical imperative, the social contract of Rawls is a device by which each of us imagines herself to be a single, faceless rational chooser. Rawls assumes that any rational agent will reason the same way he does, that such a person will prefer his list of primary goods and his principles of justice. Even when these conclusions are supported by arguments, they are arguments whose strength has been tested against counterarguments that Rawls mentions and not against counterarguments that might be forthcoming from others within a fully inclusive dialogue.[5] But even if one used

---

5. Habermas argues that the strategy of justification employed by Rawls is incoherent: the original position is both an *ethical* (or merely prudential) model of value choice by a single "ideally rational" individual striving to "maximize" his share of primary goods and a *moral* model of intersubjective normative agreement. By reducing moral rights to the status of goods, Rawls cannot convincingly demonstrate the priority of the former as requirements for fair cooperation. Furthermore, by "imposing" impartiality through a veil of ignorance instead of by means of a discursive "enlargement of interpretative perspectives" (*IO* 57), Rawls renders his theory ahistorical and abstract. This "ideal" theory acquires "real" prescriptive value only when applied in constitutional, legislative, and judicial settings wherein the veil is progressively lifted. Concerned with showing that ideal theory can realistically secure a stable order, Rawls later argues in *Political*

a method that required empathetically adopting all conceivable standpoints (something like Adam Smith's "impartial spectator"), the problems associated with uncritically projecting one's own standpoint onto these other standpoints would still remain.[6]

Habermas argues that discourse ethics provides a better model of moral reasoning than Smithian, Kantian, and Rawlsian counterparts because only it overcomes structural "monologism," or moral self-centeredness. Instead of asking whether *I* can will *my* maxim to be a universal law for others without contradiction—the method proposed by Kant—discourse ethics asks whether *all* of those who are affected by the adoption of a proposed norm could agree to it in light of the likely consequences its general observance would have for the interests of each person affected by it (*JA* 32). Instead of asking what principles of justice a single ideal observer would choose, discourse ethics asks what principles of justice everyone would choose after having dialogically transformed their particular interests into generalizable interests.

Habermas therefore insists that the appropriate procedure for testing moral universalizability is *real*—not imaginary—discourse, in which even our shared interests can become topics of potentially transformative criticism. The intention here is not to debunk "advocacy discourses" and hypothetical thought experiments of the sort that are conducted inside the privacy of one's own mind, for such mental exercises are unavoidable—especially when deliberating about the interests of potential persons not yet born or about the interests of humanity as such.[7] Rather, the intention is to signal the rational necessity of

---

Liberalism (1993) that "reasonable" but otherwise conflicting ethical worldviews could endorse the theory's liberal democratic ideals for different reasons. Because this "overlapping consensus" is "observed" by each ethical community acting alone and not discursively reached by all of them acting together, its difference from prudential or strategic compromise remains in doubt. Indeed, Rawls at times comes very close to denying the existence of a universal morality that transcends parochial culture, so that his desire to achieve a politically neutral, "morally freestanding" consensus deprives that consensus of unconditionally binding force. Habermas concludes that, instead of trying to adduce substantively prescriptive principles of justice from monological procedures, Rawls should have merely reconstructed discursive procedures, leaving the construction of substantive principles to be discursively achieved by citizens (*IO* 72, 90). J. Rawls, *A Theory of Justice* (Cambridge: Harvard University Press, 1971); and Rawls, *Political Liberalism* (New York: Columbia University Press, 1993).

6. A. Sen, "Justice across Borders," in *Global Justice and Transnational Politics,* ed. P. De Greiff and C. Cronin (Cambridge: MIT Press, 2002), 37–51; and A. Smith, *An Inquiry into the Nature and Causes of the Wealth of Nations* (1790; repr., London: Home University, 1910), 159, 319.

7. Thomas Scanlon's contractarian principle, "An act is wrong if its performance under the circumstances would be disallowed by any system of rules for the general regulation of behavior which no one could reasonably reject as a basis for informed, uncoerced agreement" resembles Habermas's discourse theoretical formulation of the universalizability principle, despite the fact that it is presented mainly as a principle governing monological reasoning. T. Scanlon, "Contractualism and Utilitarianism," in *Utilitarianism and Beyond,* ed. A. Sen and B. Williams (Cambridge: Cambridge University Press, 1982), 110. See K. Baynes, *Kant, Rawls, and Habermas: The Normative Grounds of Social Criticism* (Albany: SUNY Press, 1992).

real dialogue and public accountability in a domain of reasoning that has too often been thought of as personal and private (*JA* 51).

As in social contract theory, discourse ethics asserts that valid (just) social norms must be freely consented to by all. Social norms are expected to either limit or shape the satisfaction of people's interests. An adequate interpretation of this feature thus requires taking into account the "consequences and side effects" of a norm, not only as these affect the interests of those directly involved, but of other persons as well. Consenting to an energy bill regulating our nation's consumption of fossil fuels endows this act with little moral legitimacy unless third parties in other countries also give their consent to it; for they will not consent to our consent if their interests are adversely affected by it. Finally, because norms impact our interests in ways that we are not aware of, we must examine their *unintended side effects* by questioning whether they produce interests that are desirable for everyone in the long run. For example, we must ask whether the norm permitting unrestrained freedom of contract produces a competitive market system whose incentives to produce and consume stimulate unsustainable (and undesirable) growth and global warming.

DE thus requires that universal consent to norms be fully informed and inclusive, but such consent can still be subrational. Suppose two persons who hold opposing views agree on a norm that advances both their interests—the model of an *overlapping consensus* defended by Rawls in his more recent work. An atheist and a theist could both consent to a rule separating church and state on the grounds that doing so either prevents or encourages the spread of religion among the general population, depending on one's point of view. We can also imagine agreement taking the form of a *compromise* based on a strategic balance of power, in which the interests of the most powerful party are unequally favored over the interests of the weaker (again, recall the example of the militant oil-consuming industrialist and the militant environmentalist mentioned earlier). Importantly, neither of these forms of agreement completely fulfills the expectation contained in a discourse theoretic account of rational consent—that the consequences and side effects of a norm must be agreeable to the interests and pursuits of all concerned—because there is no demand that those involved in the agreement actually inform themselves about others' needs and value pursuits and take a critical interest in them.[8]

Neither overlapping consensus nor compromise establishes a stable agreement based on moral trustworthiness; the former does not require that persons

8. Both Charles Larmore and Bruce Ackerman advocate models of moral discourse that favor principles of "conversational constraint" (Rawls's "method of avoidance"), according to which rational interlocutors set aside beliefs on which there is little chance of agreement in order to reach agreement on other, more pressing matters. This strategy is congruent with an overlapping consensus or compromise. See C. Larmore, *Patterns of Moral Complexity* (Cambridge: Cambridge University Press, 1987); B. Ackerman, "What Is Neutral about Neutrality," *Ethics* 93 (1983): 375; and Baynes, *Kant, Rawls, and Habermas*, 74–75, 115–18.

share or even understand the reasons why others happen to agree with them; the latter requires even less, since the sole concern of the parties is strategic: maximizing one's own self-interest as much as the current balance of power permits. In order for a stable social contract to emerge out of this temporary marriage of convenience (or modus vivendi), a party to the dispute would have to listen to others empathetically and adopt their perspective while at the same time expressing their own point of view in terms that these others in turn could empathetically understand and possibly accept. Contrary to the Cartesian model of reasoning, rational conviction can only be achieved collectively: my being rationally convinced that norm N is valid for us depends on my knowing that all of us have been rationally convinced of this fact.

Moral Cognitivism versus Moral Skepticism

But why should one adopt such a demanding understanding of (U)? In Habermas's opinion, neither Rawls nor defenders of ideal observer theory can tell us why. They have no response to the moral skeptic. Does discourse ethics?

Moral skepticism comes in two varieties: the strong view holds that there is no right or wrong answer to questions of the sort: 'Should P do X?' (or 'Is X right for P to do?'); even if there is a right or wrong answer to such questions, a weaker skepticism holds that there is no way for human beings to know (or rationally decide) what it is. As Habermas understands it, then, skepticism is fueled by two facts: the fact of unresolved moral disagreement and the fact that all attempts to conceive moral truth along the lines of factual truth (moral realism) have failed.

Let us begin with the latter problem. A classical argument against moral realism is that "ought" cannot be derived from "is." However, in his famous book, *Principia Ethica* (1903), G. E. Moore sought to defend a nonnatural variety of moral realism that did not involve defining moral expressions such as 'X is good' in terms of natural facts such as 'X is desirable (pleasurable, useful, etc.).' Because it makes sense to ask whether what is desired (pleasurable, useful, etc.) is good, Moore concluded that good is a simple property that cannot be defined. Nonetheless, Moore insisted that statements of the form 'X is good' are either true or false based on our intuition (or lack thereof) of X's goodness. Relying on the grammatical similarity between 'X is good' and other factual ascriptions, he maintained that moral judgments were *descriptions* that ascribed intuited *nonnatural* properties (good, right) to actions, persons, events, and things.

The problems with Moore's *intuitionism,* according to Habermas, are twofold: it conflates moral truth with factual truth, and it misconceives factual truth in terms of intuitive sense certainty (*MCCA* 53). Positivists were quick to point out both of these difficulties. How can we be so certain about the truth of our moral intuitions if others disagree with us? Does not such disagreement prove that moral judgments are *not* like factual assertions whose truth can be known with (sense) certainty?

Positivism's rejection of moral realism entails *moral subjectivism*. According to moral subjectivism, whenever I say 'X is good (right),' I am only expressing my positive attitude toward X. Now, moral subjectivism implies strong skepticism. One version of the strong view, known as *emotivism*, stems directly from the positivist claim that so-called moral statements are not meaningful factual assertions at all but expressions of personal taste that are accompanied by commands or emotional appeals designed to influence the attitudes and behaviors of others. For proponents of this theory, such as Charles Stevenson and A. J. Ayer,[9] a speaker might appeal to a factual reason to elicit a change in attitude in his interlocutor (e.g., if I convince my child that a stove his hot, I can get him to judge that touching it is not good).[10] However, agreement in factual belief does not necessarily guarantee agreement in moral judgment. Thus, for emotivists trenchant disagreements in moral judgment cannot be resolved rationally (*MCCA* 54).

Habermas here appeals to a powerful objection voiced by Peter Strawson.[11] When we say that something is right or good (or ought to be done) we are not merely expressing our subjective preferences. If that is all we meant by using these expressions, then we would not feel guilty about personal wrongdoing or feel resentful toward others who do wrong. When we demand accountability from wrongdoers we are not satisfied with just any factual reason they might give to excuse their behavior, and their personal desire to do what we believe to be wrong does not count as a relevant consideration on their behalf. Conversely, when we try to persuade others to accept our moral judgments we are not merely trying to move them emotionally for the mere sake of getting them to go along with us. Rather, when we make moral judgments we are implying that others ought to agree with us because we are right, in just the same way that we imply that others ought to agree with us when we assert that some fact is true. "Right" and "true" are claims to *intersubjective validity,* and that is why our efforts at convincing others to accept these claims appeal to reasons besides personal beliefs and desires.

Weak versions of skepticism can accept this *cognitive* interpretation of moral language and yet still deny the possibility of giving reasons in support of the most foundational moral principles. Take the *prescriptivism* associated with the moral philosophy of R. M. Hare.[12] Hare presumes that moral agents

9. A. J. Ayer, "On the Analysis of Moral Judgments," in *A Modern Introduction to Ethics: Readings from Classical and Contemporary Sources,* ed. M. K. Munitz (New York: Free Press, 1958), 537.

10. C. L. Stevenson, "The Nature of Ethical Disagreement," in *Readings in Philosophical Analysis,* ed. H. Feigl and W. Sellars (New York: Appleton-Century-Crofts, 1949), 587–93.

11. P. Strawson, *Freedom and Resentment* (London: Oxford University Press, 1963).

12. R. M. Hare, *Freedom and Reason* (Oxford: Clarendon, 1963).

can use reason in prescribing what ought to be done. The principle of rational consistency (universalizability) requires that like cases be treated alike, so that if norm N says that it is wrong to do X in situation P, then it also says that it is wrong to do X in situation Q to the extent that P and Q are sufficiently alike. Thus, if I can convince you that Q is sufficiently like P, I can also convince you that you should not do X in situation Q either, to the extent that you accept N.

According to Habermas, the problem with prescriptivism is that its conception of universalizability shows only how norms can be consistently applied, not how they can be rationally justified. Prescriptivism entails irrational choice (what Habermas calls *decisionism*) of the most basic norms. As Habermas sees it, the skepticism of this weak cognitive variety, no less than the strong skepticism of the emotivist variety, follows from a philosophical approach that abstracts from the first-person ("performative") standpoint of persons who resolve their moral disagreements through conversation. For example, prescriptivists pose the problem of moral argumentation as one of pure logic, namely, of deducing a particular judgment from a more general principle. The skeptical question thus arises: How can this basic principle itself be justified? At first blush, we seem to be confronted with the so-called Münchhausen trilemma in which justification leads to three possible dead ends: an infinite regress (the principle cannot be justified without appeal to another principle); a circle (the principal cannot be justified by anything other than itself); or an arbitrary suspension (the principle cannot be justified, period).

The above trilemma is based on a model of formal inference that cannot capture the logic of rational persuasion. Any conclusion (judgment) can be framed as a formal inference from premises, but any premise (a norm, say) must eventually be justified by reasons that are not already implied by it. It is this independent backing (informal inference) that our interlocutors expect when demanding convincing reasons in support of our normative premises. Habermas therefore prefers the model of substantive argument developed by Stephen Toulmin as more congenial to actual instances in which one person tries to persuade another.[13]

Moral Argumentation as Discourse

According to this model, a person justifies a conclusion C with reference to some reason, evidence, or datum D, both of which are inferentially connected by a general warrant W, supported by an evidential backing B. For example, I defend C ("You ought to give A $50 by the end of the week") by asserting D ("A loaned you $50 to be repaid by the end of the week"), which is inferentially

13. S. Toulmin, *The Uses of Argument* (Cambridge: Cambridge University Press, 1958).

(formally) connected to C by W ("Loans ought to be repaid within the specified period"). Notice that so far in our argumentation we have not deviated from the standard logical model of formal deductive inference. However, if my interlocutor demands a backing B for W, I must then assert reasons that are at best cogent or stand in some nondeductive relationship of support to W. This is because some of these reasons must appeal to certain factual and/or counterfactual assertions, whereas the moral judgment W they justify is normative, or nonfactual ("ought" does not follow from "is").

For example, I might justify W by asserting: "All affected persons would agree to W so long as the consequences and side effects of doing so (such as making flexible use of scarce resources) advances each and everyone's interests." If my interlocutor then challenges the validity of these interests, I can adduce the further premise: "These are interests that all persons would accept as their own after engaging in comprehensive discursive critique." Here the principle of universalizability (U) functions not as a premise but as a bridging principle in a way analogous to the principle of induction (I) in theoretical discourse. In both cases there is a gap between W (a general law or norm) and B (observed facts about the world and persons' interests) that is bridged by reference to an ideal, discursively achieved counterfactual consensus involving either an unlimited community of experimental investigators (theoretical discourse) or an unlimited community of moral agents (practical discourse), or both.[14]

Being counterfactual, neither (U) nor (I) can be conclusively realized in any temporally and spatially limited community, least of all one in which speech is constrained by domination and inequality. In an *ideal speech situation,* interlocutors would also be free to move back and forth between C, D, W, and B, as well as critically reflect on the appropriateness of the language they use to understand themselves and their world.[15] In addition to requiring sincere engagement with the other (a requirement common to all discourse), practical discourses also require authentic expression of one's needs and interests—a stipulation against self-delusion compelling each interlocutor to achieve transparent insight into his own inner nature (*TJ* 269).

Even with the aid of psychotherapy and ideology critique, no mortal can fully attain transparent self-understanding because reflection always relies on

14. The principles of induction and of universalizability, however, function at different levels. The former can be formulated in terms of rules of *logic* (such as John Stuart Mill's principles of elimination) that contingently require collective implementation by a community of scientists engaged in a collaborative process of inquiry in order to yield true conclusions (as Peirce argued). The latter, by contrast, refers to a norm of discourse as such. I thank Bill Rehg for this important insight.

15. In "Wahrheitstheorien," (1973) Habermas argued that just as practical discourse ultimately leads to theoretical discourse, so theoretical discourse ultimately leads to practical discourse (we must critically evaluate our scientific theories in light of their capacity to advance our rational interests). J. Habermas, "Wahrheitstheorien," in *Vorstudien und Ergänzungen zur Theorie des kommunikativen Handelns* (Frankfurt am Main: Suhrkamp, 1984), 175.

an unconscious background understanding, only some aspects of which can be consciously foregrounded at any given moment. That said, earlier in his career Habermas allowed for the possibility—since discarded as a misguided concretization of a transcendental idea—that the ideal speech situation might be realized as a "form of life." He later observed that the ideal might be approximated within institutions such as scientific academies, courts of law, and parliamentary bodies, operating as "an unavoidable supposition" of discourse—a transcendental condition that cannot itself be directly justified from within discourse. Defense of the principle is therefore indirect and circular. Any attempt to convince others of the illusory nature of the ideal is shown to be self-refuting—committing what Karl-Otto Apel (following Jaakko Hintikka) calls a "performative contradiction."[16] This defense is admittedly weak, since the ideal is not constitutive of the game of persuasion in the way that the checkmate rule is constitutive of chess (the game of discourse does not cease to exist when compliance with its rules is less than ideal). Yet we would not continue discussion if we thought that its conditions were seriously violated. So the ideal provides a standard for retrospectively evaluating the rationality of our conversations, even if it is silent on the circumstances in which conversation should be engaged (*MCCA* 92).

Having clarified the peculiar status of the ideal speech situation, Habermas continues with his refutation of skepticism by arguing the following points:

1. (U) follows "by material implication" from three premises referring (respectively) to (a) a principle of discourse (D) grounded in what it means to be rationally accountable; (b) a content premise (CP) that unpacks the meaning of moral disputes; and (c) a rational reconstruction of the normative content implicit in the rules of discourse (rule premise or RP).
2. Premise 1 can be justified by appeal to practical intuitions whose proper theoretical reconstruction can be tested in turn by questioning a broad range of persons.
3. One such test involves using counterexamples to show that no theory more accurately reconstructs these intuitions than (D), (CP), (RP), and, therewith, (DE).
4. Discourse is not a language game that persons engaged in communicative action can opt out of, unless they are willing to risk psychological suicide or schizophrenia.
5. Although the substantive interpretation, justification, and application of norms is relative to particular ethical (cultural) contexts of understanding, (U) represents an unsurpassable evolutionary advance in moral reasoning that transcends such contexts.

16. K.-O. Apel, "The Problem of Philosophical Foundational Grounding in Light of a Transcendental Pragmatics of Language," in *After Philosophy*, ed. K. Baynes, J. Bohman, and T. McCarthy (Cambridge: MIT Press, 1987), 250–90.

Premise 1 contains the most important subargument of Habermas's moral theory. Although he himself has not clarified the formal derivation of (U) from premises 1 a–c, others whom he cites (such as William Rehg) have, and so I will rely on their reconstruction. I begin with the principle of discourse (D), which specifies a condition of mutual rational accountability. Persons who are free to say yes or no to solicited offers to engage in acts of mutual cooperation must be willing and ready to propose terms of cooperation to which all can freely consent, the principle of discourse (D): "Only those norms can claim validity that could meet with the acceptance of all concerned in practical discourse" (*IO* 41).

Notice that (D) is a simple conditional that tells us only what is *not* valid—norms that have not been agreed on. (D) thus posits a necessary but not sufficient condition of normative validity. Also missing from (D) is an explanation of what norms are expected to do, namely, regulate (limit and shape) the harmonious satisfaction of people's needs (CP). For Habermas, (D) only "stipulates the basic idea of moral theory but [unlike (U)] *does not form part of a logic of argumentation*" (*MCCA* 93, emphasis mine). So (D) says nothing about what kind of norm can be generally accepted as valid (*MCCA* 66). Only when interpreted alongside (CP) does (D) require the discovery or creation of a norm that will maximize the harmonious satisfaction of everyone's interests. But now the question arises: What *rule of argumentation* should guide us in harmonizing interests? The answer is (U), which asserts: "A norm is valid when the foreseeable consequences and side effects of its general observance for the interests and value orientations of each individual could be jointly accepted by all concerned without coercion" (*IO* 42).[17]

Although the above formulation of (U) appears indistinguishable from (D)—both are formulated as simple conditionals—there is a big difference between them. First of all, as noted above, (U) is a rule of argumentation. It states that rational consensus is to be achieved by each and every person revising their needs and wants in light of the impact their satisfaction would have on the needs and wants of others (*MCCA* 67–68). It further states that this mutual revision of needs and wants is necessary for achieving a rational consensus on universalizable interests. Even when considered alongside (CP), (D) does not tell us whether—and if so how—a rational consensus on universalizable interests can be achieved. Without supplementation from (U), (D) cannot even provide us with any basis for distinguishing between a pseudo compromise, an overlapping consensus, an ideological consensus, and a truly rational consensus. Only a norm of argumentation such as (U) can regulate the process of

17. Habermas presents different formulations of (U) depending on context. Sometimes he adds that a valid norm must "be preferred to known alternative possibilities for regulation" (*JA* 32). This additional clause now seems redundant in light of his distinction between justification and application.

argumentation so as to guarantee that the common approval demanded by (D) be impartial with respect to *each* and *everyone's* rational interests and needs.

There is a second difference between (D) and (U). Although Habermas sometimes formulates (U) as if it were a simple conditional like (D), he elsewhere insists that it *defines* moral validity as such. In other words, unlike (D), (U) states conditions that are both necessary *and* sufficient for moral validity. So (U) tells us more than (D): it gives us a criterion for testing invalidity *and* validity.[18]

Now that we understand the distinction between (D) and (U) and the importance of (U) in explaining the possibility of (D) (which is foundational for discourse ethics), let us turn to Habermas's formal derivation of (U) from (CP), (D), and the rules of discourse (RP). Habermas (following Robert Alexy's interpretation of Aristotle's tripartite scheme) mentions three sorts of rules governing, respectively, the *logical product,* the *dialectical procedure,* and the *rhetorical process* of argumentation.[19] Rules of logic, which govern "the production of intrinsically cogent arguments," stipulate that no speaker may contradict himself, assign expressions meanings that are not shared by others,

18. Habermas is unclear as to whether (U) is a conditional or biconditional principle. In the essay presently under discussion it is formulated as a simple conditional, but in a later work, *The Inclusion of the Other,* the German expression that is translated as "when"—*nur genau dann*—actually suggests something stronger along the lines of a biconditional. I thank Bill Rehg for this clarification.

19. Alexy transposes Aristotle's distinction between *logic, dialectic,* and *rhetoric—perspectives* on assessing argumentative cogency—onto the distinction between *elements* of argumentation: *products* (arguments); *procedures* (decision rules governing discursive civility, division of labor separating authors from critics, etc.); and *processes* (rules of persuasion governing impartial discussion, possession of ethical competence and authority, and empathetic identification with opponent and audience).

Alexy's and Aristotle's distinctions are problematic. For example, the logical assessment of an informal argument (as product) requires dialectically assessing the presentation of competing arguments; this assessment, in turn, may require assessing the rhetorical competency of researchers' choice of standards for drawing statistical thresholds. The "rhetorical" rules governing the ideal speech situation can just as easily be located under the category of dialectic, since they organize a cooperative search for a decisive consensus. Distinctions also display contextual plasticity. In science, dialectical procedures can include "all the ways of critically testing and discussing hypotheses," including "laboratory procedures, meetings of a research team, referee procedures, conferences, published debates, and so on." W. Rehg, *Cogent Science in Context: The Science Wars, Argumentation Theory, and Habermas* (Cambridge: MIT Press, 2008), 26. Finally, we can distinguish higher (ideal) and lower (socially institutionalized) norms of logic, dialectic, and rhetoric. For instance, the consensus-orientation ideal can be institutionalized in different ways. The short-term needs of scientists who are concerned about achieving credit for their research may require them to maintain secrecy within research groups and compromise with their fellow team members, whereas the long-term needs of scientists to convince others outside of their group of the importance of their work will require them to openly collaborate with them on achieving durable consensus. This last consideration leads Rehg to propose a fourth perspective for evaluating arguments: the manner in which social institutions realize and sustain the ideals governing logical, dialectical, and rhetorical dimensions of argumentation. R. Alexy, "A Theory of Practical Discourse," in *The Communicative Ethics Controversy,* ed S. Benhabib and F. Dallmayr (Cambridge: MIT Press, 1990), 151–83.

or be inconsistent (by not applying the same predicate to actions, events, and objects that resemble one another in relevant respects). Hare's, Popper's, and Kant's consistency-testing interpretations of moral universalizability find their place among these rules, as do rules of informal logic and of induction. Rules of dialectical procedure, by contrast, regulate the dialogical "search for truth organized in the form of a competition." Such rules require that a speaker be sincere and accountable, challenging others' questionable statements and responding in kind to others' challenges. Finally, rules governing rhetorical process require that the sincere search for truth be rational, ruling out "all external or internal coercion other than the force of the better argument and thereby also neutralizing all motives other than that of the cooperative search for truth." Here Habermas cites the following process rules from Alexy's list:

1. Every subject with the competence to speak and act is allowed to take part in discourse.
2. (i) Everyone is allowed to question any assertion whatsoever; (ii) everyone is allowed to introduce any assertion whatever into the discourse; (iii) everyone is allowed to express his attitudes, desires, and needs.
3. No speaker may be prevented, by internal or external coercion, from exercising his rights as laid down in 1. and 2.

According to Habermas, the rules of logic "have no ethical content" and therefore cannot be used to infer (U). The rules of dialectical procedure do have ethical content—they guarantee mutual recognition between interlocutors—but they do not imply (U). That leaves us with the rules governing the rhetorical process. Rule 1 (the inclusion rule) states that "nobody who could make a relevant contribution [to the discussion] may be excluded" (OP 44). The requirement appears to be troubling because it leaves out young children and even adults who lack sufficient communicative competence. However, the requirement is less troubling when we understand that its aim is to guarantee that all arguments bearing on the validity of a norm are put on the table and that the validating agreement in question is universal in scope. Rule 2 (the symmetry rule) requires that "all participants are granted an equal opportunity to make contributions" (OP 44) so that each and every argument (or claim) will have a fair chance of being raised and rebutted. It also requires that "participants must mean what they say." Rule 3 states that each and every person will be able to exercise the "rights to universal access and equal participation" mentioned in rules 1 and 2 free from psychological or social constraints; interlocutors must be open-minded or "motivated solely by the force of the better reasons" (OP 44), and the terms of their discourse must not be ideologically distorted by covert relations of power. Taken together, rules 2 and 3 capture two moral ideas: justice and solidarity. *Justice* obtains by the fact that each person is guaranteed an equal right (freedom) to convince others and to be convinced by them in turn. *Solidarity* obtains by the fact that each person must empathetically identify with others' points of view while fashioning arguments whose value assumptions she knows can be shared by them as well. Moral norms, then, will secure both individual freedom (the right) as well as social recognition and solidarity (the common good), the one side complementing the other.[20]

Habermas claims that, when combined with the assumptions I have explicated under (D) and (CP), rules 1–3 (RP) provide all the ethical content that is needed in order to derive (U). (U) is not identical to these rules, since they apply to both theoretical and practical discourse. However, once one understands that everyone must discursively agree on a norm in order for it to be valid (D), where the norm in question aims at harmonizing interests (CP), in such a way that all arguments have been equally considered in view of a critical yet sympathetic (open-minded and self-reflective) examination of everyone's genuine needs (RP), it follows that (U). That is to say, a valid (unconditionally binding) norm must be based on rationally universalizable interests that have emerged out of an inclusive dialogue in which each and everyone's interests have been critically modified as far as possible to accommodate their equal harmonious satisfaction.

Habermas says that (U) *formally* follows from premises (D), (CP), and (RP) "by material implication" or *modus ponens:* If (D) and (CP) and (RP), then (U) (*MCCA* 97). But this seems odd, for Habermas's argument really amounts to showing that (U) is a necessary *pragmatic* condition for (D)—not conceptually entailed by (D)—*insofar as (D) could not validate norms that are specifically identified as moral norms without (U).* This is a transcendental argument (proving that X is a necessary condition for Y), but transcendental "arguments," Habermas insists, are *substantive* and not formal; in other words, they explicate, interpret, and reconstruct a *practical know-how* in the form of a *normative hypothesis.* In that case, Habermas is really arguing that (U) provides the best (and for the time being, only) hypothesis for explaining (D), whose other pragmatic presuppositions also include (CP) and (RP). Being a presupposition of argumentative justification, (U) cannot be argumentatively justified.

---

20. "From the perspective of communication theory, there emerges instead a close connection between concern for the welfare of one's fellow man and interest in the general welfare: the identity of the group is reproduced through intact relationships of mutual recognition. Thus the perspective complementing that of equal treatment of individuals is not benevolence but solidarity. This principle is rooted in the realization that each person must take responsibility for the other because as consociates all must have an interest in the integrity of their shared life context in the same way. Justice conceived deontologically requires solidarity as its reverse side.... Justice concerns the equal freedoms of unique and self-determining individuals, while solidarity concerns the welfare of consociates who are intimately linked in an intersubjectively shared form of life—and thus also to the maintenance of the integrity of this form of life itself. Moral norms cannot protect one without the other: they cannot protect equal rights and freedoms of the individual without protecting the welfare of one's fellow man and the community to which individuals belong." Habermas, "Justice and Solidarity," 47.

So Habermas appears to be mistaken in thinking that (U) can be *formally* derived from (D), (CP), and (RP).[21] But even if he were right about this, the skeptic might regard the rules that make up (RP) as mere conventions of philosophers living in modern Westernized societies, thereby still impugning the universal validity of (U). This takes us to points 2 and 3 of Habermas's five-step argument. Habermas argues that rules 1–3 explicate the practical understanding (know-how) that speakers implicitly bring to real discourse. To the extent that speakers make this supposition in order to engage in discourse at all, a skeptic who wishes to argue against (U) will be caught in a *performative contradiction*. Like Hintikka's example of a speaker who declares "I do not exist (here and now)" and in so doing contradicts a supposition of her performance, "I exist (here and now)," so the skeptic who argues against any of the three process-regulating rules mentioned above will have already presupposed them, thereby contradicting herself (*MCCA* 80). Assertions such as 'Using lies, I finally convinced H that p' or 'Having excluded persons A, B, C, from the discussion...we were able to convince ourselves that N was justified' indeed seem incoherent (*MCCA* 90–91).

At best, these examples show that the rules of discourse are "unavoidable"; they do not justify them (pace K.-O. Apel)[22] for the reason noted above:

21. Pace Habermas, the derivation of (U) appears to be circular insofar as (RP) already makes reference to (U) in its explicit language of universal "permissions" and "rights." In *The Inclusion of the Other* Habermas dismisses the circularity problem by claiming that rules of argumentation possess nonmoral normativity (*IO* 45); they regulate discourse not action. Unlike (U), they function only transcendentally; not derived from consent, their normative force is weak. But how can Habermas then claim to *derive* (U) by *material implication* from nonmoral normativity? Habermas argues that, although "(U) is indeed inspired by (D)...initially it is nothing more than a proposal arrived at abductively...from the implicit content of universal presuppositions of argumentation in conjunction with the conception of normative justification in general expressed in (D)" (*IO* 42–3). But an *abductive* justification, according to Peirce, involves a *nonformal discovery* of a hypothesis that makes sense of (hermeneutically synthesizes) a manifold of distinct phenomena. So (U) "follows" from (RP), (D), and (CP) as a hypothesis that explains how these premises hang together. (U) is therefore best interpreted as a transcendental explication (rational reconstruction) of these other conditions taken together. As such it is "justified" hermeneutically, in a circular manner. I thank Bill Rehg for this suggestion.

22. K.-O. Apel, "The A Priori of the Communication Community and the Foundations of Ethics," in *Towards a Transformation of Philosophy,* trans. G. Adey and D. Frisby (London: Routledge and Kegan Paul, 1980), 273. The debate between Habermas and Apel revolves around what postmetaphysical philosophy can accomplish. For Habermas, philosophy "has withdrawn into the system of the sciences" and must accordingly "renounce its privileged access to the truth" (*PT* 48). Thus, even if "fundamental notions of equal treatment, solidarity, and the general welfare" are "central to *all* moralities...(even in premodern societies)" and reside in the "universal and necessary pragmatic presuppositions of communicative action," such "normative obligations do not extend beyond the boundaries of a concrete lifeworld of family, tribe, city, or nation" unless, as in modern societies, these boundaries have been "broken through." Habermas, "Justice and Solidarity," 48–49.

Apel maintains that the above "strategy of avoiding a methodological distinction between philosophy and empirically testable reconstructive science [is] openly inconsistent," for only a transcendental philosophy can justify truly *necessary* and *universal* normative claims that transcend transcendental "arguments" are really hypothetical interpretations that presuppose (in circular manner) what it is they are explicating (*MCCA* 94). Furthermore, the very idea of an ultimate transcendental grounding implicitly appeals to concepts of subjective certainty. In practice, of course, speakers can be certain that these norms apply—that is what the hypothetical use of counterexamples and the corresponding discovery of a performative contradiction is supposed to show: there are no alternatives to these rules that captures what we mean by rational conviction. That said, the justification of a claim to truth or a claim to normative rightness appeals to notions of intersubjective validity that are incompatible with subjective feelings of certainty (recall chapters 2 and 3). Hence, the notion of a transcendental argument that aims at grounding presuppositions in indubitable experience is incoherent (*MCCA* 96). What is not incoherent, Habermas says, is the use of pragmatic (substantive) arguments that rely on cogent examples in justifying this or that *rational reconstruction* of an implicit "knowledge" (practical know-how) that we engage with necessity and accept with certainty (*MCCA* 97).

We now arrive at point 4 in Habermas's argument. The skeptic can still reject (U) by simply refusing to engage in discourse. Strictly speaking, there can be no moral obligation to behave rationally, and hence no moral obligation to adopt the moral point of view. However, since the discursive redemption of validity claims is an unavoidable possibility within everyday communicative action, refusal to enter discourse in any sustained manner cannot be practically maintained. A single-minded Hobbesian who only engaged others strategically would not be trusted for long. Of course, one could simply refuse to live in a society that demands rational accountability of its members. But the price for doing so—living without the recognition of others—would be psychological suicide. More important, because communicative action is the exclusive medium in which our own personal identities come into being and meaning

---

historically contingent lifeworlds. The debate between Apel and Habermas also extends to their understanding of the prescriptive content and motivational power of discourse ethics. Apel insists that the a priori principle of universalization (Part A of his DE) prescribes its own realization (Part B) through the establishment of legal, political, and social conditions that approximate an ideal communication community. Habermas denies this (see chapter 9 of this book), arguing that motivation for change must come from outside discourse: "Philosophy, even in its postmetaphysical form, will be able neither to replace nor to repress religion as long as religious language is the bearer of semantic content that is inspiring and even indispensable" (*PT* 51; *JA* 79). From Apel's perspective, Habermas's appeal to religion violates Kant's emphasis on rational moral autonomy; from Habermas's perspective, Apel's appeal to pure reason violates Hegel's estimate of ethical tradition in socialization (*MCCA* 207). K.-O. Apel, "Normatively Grounding Critical Theory through Recourse to the Lifeworld? A Transcendental-Pragmatic Attempt to Think with Habermas against Habermas," in *Philosophical Interventions in the Unfinished Project of the Enlightenment*, ed. A. Honneth, T. McCarthy, C. Offe, and A. Wellmer (Cambridge: MIT Press, 1992), 125–70, quote at 150; E. Mendieta, *The Adventures of Transcendental Philosophy: Karl-Otto Apel's Semiotics and Discourse Ethics* (Lanham, MD: Rowman and Littlefield, 2002), esp. chap. 4.

and value are created and transmitted, it is inseparable from a human mode of being (*MCCA* 100).

But the skeptic can concede all of this and still deny the universal (as opposed to ethnocentric) validity of (U). She can say that (U) reflects an unavoidable supposition of *modern* societies but not of premodern traditional ones. As is well known, Socrates' pioneering use of discourse ethics only recognized males of Greek origin as capable of meriting equal respect, and it is unclear how far he would have gone in questioning all traditional values.

Habermas's fifth point responds to this objection by invoking a theory of social evolution. Every society—tribal, traditional, or modern—is premised on some form of communicative action in which validity claims are raised, however much they may deploy dogmatic normative speech acts in everyday action and mythopoetic speech acts in religious rites and the like. Because validity claims to truth and rightness are already implicit in rudimentary form even in the earliest conceptions of validity—in distinctions between appearance and reality, sacred and profane—Habermas asserts that (U) (or unconstrained consensus) is the inherent *telos* of language as such. Furthermore, this assertion can be bolstered by showing that the kind of modern society in which (U) plays a predominant role constitutes the apex of social evolution. While practically possible, regression from this stage to premodern, postmodern, or antimodern stages is catastrophic (witness Nazi Germany). In the final analysis, modern societies are evolutionarily necessary for successfully solving certain problems of functional adaptation (see chapters 6, 10, and 11).[23]

Neo-Aristotelian Objections and the Abortion Controversy

DE presupposes that universal morality can be distinguished from culturally relative ethos. Neo-Aristotelians deny this. They argue that universal principles are too vacuous to guide action. So, whatever prescriptive meaning and force they have they acquire in being applied to particular situations. Application, however, qualifies and interprets norms in terms of the agent's understanding of these situations. And this understanding is informed by the agent's particular ethical and religious worldview.

---

23. The analogy between this (phylogenetic) theory and a Kohlbergian logic of moral and cognitive (ontogenetic) development is one that remains, by Habermas's own concession, quite imperfect. Primitive societies are not like infants in that they have already developed conventional moral aptitudes and fairly advanced capacities for cognitive abstraction and formal operation. For that reason the substantive argument in defense of a logic of social evolution is perhaps less cogent than Habermas would like it to be. That said, without such a logic it is inconceivable how a critical theorist could judge that liberal democracy, say, is more progressive than feudal aristocracy. For more on Habermas's theory of social evolution, see chapter 11 of this book and Owen, *Between Reason and History.*

The abortion controversy illustrates the way in which a universal norm, such as the proscription against murder, prescribes contradictory actions depending on who applies it. Suppose that a woman wants to abort an unwanted pregnancy and defends her decision on the grounds that the pregnancy was unintended (the result of rape or contraceptive failure, say) and limits her right to life. She might not recognize the embryo or fetus within her womb as a person, but even if she does, she could still hold that she has not taken responsibility for it and that its right to life conflicts with her own. I come along and object that this is murder—the deliberate killing of an innocent person. It does not matter whether my religion or my personal view about motherhood and family compels me to hold such a view. The important point is that I disagree with her about how to *describe* "abortion" (murder versus extraction of uterine tissues or some other supposedly defensible termination of life).

If we assume that our disagreement is a moral disagreement, we assume that it can be resolved according to the postulate that "every *sufficiently precise* question admits of just one valid answer," based on the assumption that rightness, like truth, does not admit of degrees (*JA* 59). However, when we try to resolve our disagreement we immediately realize that we mean different things by "person" and "right to life," so moral discourse between us is a nonstarter (*JA* 60).

Assuming that our disagreement is not merely verbal but reflects an ethical clash over how we understand unborn human life, our disagreement will not be resolved by adhering to moral principle (U). If we cannot extricate ourselves *completely* from the evaluative language that constitutes our identity, how can we reduce this embodied understanding to propositions that can be discursively criticized?

Habermas concedes that our capacity to transcend our ethos in cases like this is limited. Modern morality demands that we discursively bracket—and abstract from—our parochial evaluations. This ethical self-understanding involves a syndrome in which universal moral values and cognitive values are seamlessly interwoven with culturally relative ethical and aesthetic-expressive values. At the level of ethical practice, validity (*Gültigkeit*) collapses into the taken-for-granted social acceptability (*Geltung*) so essential to acting with certain conviction on the basis of an unswerving, forthright character. But rational accountability demands that we reflectively distance ourselves from our practice and in so doing make "razor sharp cuts between evaluative statements and strictly normative ones, between the good and the just" (*MCCA* 104). This cutting analysis involves abstracting lifeless propositions from our holistic value orientations. Once this happens, the intuitive moral-ethical understanding underlying our concrete practice loses its connection to the embodied habits and personal character traits that motivate action.

According to Habermas, when no agreement on the moral rightness or ethical goodness of an action (like abortion) is possible, we must turn to law in regulating our dispute. Law does not resolve trenchant ethical conflict. However, it can establish zones of tolerance based not on "moral solutions" but on "fair compromises" that have been democratically negotiated (*JA* 60).[24]

Justification and Application

Kant denies that the prohibition against lying admits any exception—even in applications where lying is necessary to avoid a worse harm. To make his prohibition less rigid and more acceptable, he could qualify it to allow for this exception: "Never lie except when doing so is necessary to avoid a worse harm!" But how could this qualification enter into the prohibition? The qualification accommodates another valid norm that conflicts with the prohibition in the application under consideration: "Avoid harming innocent people!"

The lesson of this example is simple: Pace Kant, the moral justification of a norm must factor in the precise situations in which it is valid. Those situations in which it is not valid—because it is overridden by another norm—must enter into its formulation as conditions, qualifications, or exceptions. Justification cannot be separated from application. But a new problem arises. We could not justify any norm without knowing beforehand all the justified norms that might conflict with it—including ones not yet discovered. Furthermore, we could not justify any norm without knowing whether any of these other norms would override it in some possible situation in which they both applied.

Given the impossibility of carrying out this strong conception of moral justification, Habermas prefers a weaker formulation that preserves Kant's distinction between *justification* and *application* without treating them as self-sufficient moments of moral reasoning. More precisely, Habermas presents them as two separate but complementary stages of moral reasoning. Each stage captures a different feature of moral impartiality: the satisfaction of generalizable interests and the integration of all perspectives on (descriptions of) a situation. In the first stage, we seek to determine whether we can *justify* the *prima facie rightness* (or universalizability) of a norm as it applies to typical broadly defined situations. Justification here operates with a time and knowledge index; that is, we consider only current knowledge about our needs and the impact the norm in question has had on them in the past—or will likely have on them in the readily foreseeable future (*JA* 39). In the second stage, we *apply* our system of norms to one particular situation in order to select the one prima facie norm that is most appropriate. We begin by taking into account all

---

24. Habermas criticizes Charles Taylor's attempt to resolve ethical disagreements nonprocedurally by appeal to a supreme, unifying good revealed in "epiphanic" aesthetic experience, partly because modern art can't perform this function and partly because aesthetic taste itself varies from ethos to ethos (*JA* 74–6). C. Taylor, *Sources of the Self: The Making of the Modern Identity* (Cambridge: Cambridge University Press, 1989). I discuss the relevance of aesthetic judgment to conceptions of political reasonableness and social welfare in chapter 11.

of the normatively relevant features of the situation from the standpoint of all affected parties; after we arrive at a single description of the situation that best incorporates all of these perspectives, we show why some of these features are especially weighty. This justifies choosing one among our prima facie norms as most appropriate for dealing with these features.

For example, suppose we have two prima facie valid norms: "Don't harm innocent persons!" and "Don't lie!" Both of these norms satisfy generalizable interests broadly understood. Now take this dilemma, familiar to bioethicists. If a doctor tells his easily discouraged patient who is fighting for his life the whole truth about his condition right now, he will likely worsen it. So he decides to lie (abiding by the "Do no harm" principle); the patient's best friend objects (abiding by the honesty principle). They then discuss the morally relevant aspects of the situation in order to determine whether and, if so, how they can reconcile their separate standpoints. Perhaps the doctor convinces the patient's friend that the patient will likely give up fighting and die if told the truth or the friend convinces the doctor that the patient would want to know the truth because he valued truth above life itself. Or perhaps they compromise their perspectives (they decide to wait and tell him the truth later, when doing so will not endanger his life). Combining their perspectives in qualifying the no-harm and honesty principles, they jointly arrive at a new norm: "Don't lie, except when it is necessary to avoid causing grave medical harm" or "Don't cause a person harm unless he would prefer that you do so rather than compromise his highest values!"

Two features of this case bear emphasis. First, a description of the morally relevant features of a situation that incorporates the perspective of involved persons is the outcome of real discussion. Discourses of application are essential in determining whether the situation being described is appropriately described as moral—capable of being described in terms of a single best set of relevant characteristics that all could agree on—or merely ethical.

Second, application discourses extend and feed back into justification discourses. Application discourses help specify norms and interests that, at the initial stage of justification, lack prescriptive content because they are too broadly formulated. However, once we have arrived at a more specified norm capable of being applied to a given situation, we must then reverse our tracks and ask whether it can be justified in more general terms. For example, we need to ask whether the norm: "Don't lie except when it is necessary to avoid causing the death of an innocent person" satisfies generalizable interests.

Only by repeating the cycle of justification—application—justification can we reach sufficient precision (qualification) in our moral norms to be able to say, conclusively, that they are right or wrong appropriate or inappropriate. The postulate that requires thinking that there is only one right answer to moral disputes depends on this hermeneutical circle.

This circle also enables Habermas to respond to Gilligan's concern that an ethic of justice cannot incorporate contextual caring for particular persons. In essence, Habermas regards justice and care as complementary aspects of any complete moral theory, not as distinct and opposed types of moral theory as Gilligan formulates it. As we have seen, DE already incorporates care in its rigorous requirement for empathetic role taking: it treats justice and solidarity as two sides of the same coin (*JA* 153–54). In addition to this dimension of care, DE also requires that we take into account how norms affect the concrete needs of specific persons in specific contexts of application. Care ethicists sometimes frame the caring relationship as a partial relationship that conflicts with moral impartiality. But this opposition is false. Gilligan herself acknowledges the complementarity of justice and care, and she stresses the importance of achieving a postconventional care ethic wherein, as Habermas puts it, one's scope of caring encompasses an impartial assessment of the impact that a decision (application) has on the concrete needs and perspectives of all persons involved.

Discourse Ethics Applied: Genetic Testing and the Future of Human Nature

Although DE is primarily introduced as a metaethical and normative theory, Habermas has occasionally applied the theory to particular moral problems. While acknowledging the limits of DE with respect to illuminating issues concerning animal rights and environmental ethics,[25] he notes that the theory sheds light on certain moral controversies.

Habermas's discussion of abortion is one of the areas in which he has talked about the application of DE. As noted, he insists that discourse ethics cannot in principle provide a single right answer in resolving this controversy. He maintains that any attempt to outlaw *all* abortions by extending a basic right to life to the fetus may conflict with the right to life of the mother as well as with her right to control her body. The legal and moral limits attached to this right, he believes, are proportional to the development of the fetus into a person who possesses the degree of sentience and consciousness requisite for us to imagine ourselves communicating with it (*FHN* 35). Before this developmental threshold is reached (a determination that is much disputed and beyond scientific demonstration), imposing a legal ban on abortion amounts to imposing a particular ethical-religious conception of personhood. Such an imposition, Habermas claims, would violate the moral principle of tolerance underlying liberal constitutions, which is itself an institutional embodiment of DE

---

25. According to Habermas, we acquire "quasi-moral duties" with respect to animals to the extent that we can enter into quasi-communicative relations with them. He adds that vegetarianism may prove to be morally correct (*JA* 105–11). Duties to the environment, he believes, reflect duties owed to others that ensure them "ecological" means to the enjoyment of basic rights (*BFN* 123) and a good life (*JA* 111).

(*FHN* 38). Any legitimate legal demarcation of personhood along a developmental continuum must therefore reflect a renegotiable political compromise.

Although Habermas denies that there are any *nonmetaphysical* grounds for holding that embryos possess personhood—a fact that also leads him to deny that they can be the subject of moral and legal rights—he asserts that they possess enough *ethical value* to warrant *some* legal protection. In what appears to be a striking departure from his earlier insistence that the domain of postmetaphysical, reason-based normativity is exhausted by the formal-procedural language of basic moral rights, he now ventures that the basis for this protection resides in a *species-specific ethical understanding of human nature* that is "the same everywhere" (*FHN* 39).

This expansion of the domain of ethical reasoning beyond what is merely relative to the personal (existential) and the sociocultural is guided by a peculiar philosophical intuition about the proper end and good of human life. For Habermas, human life possesses its own peculiar dignity, which is associated with values of freedom and individuality. We distinguish active subjects from manipulable objects. Indeed, Habermas accepts Hans Jonas's view that what distinguishes the self-emergent *grown life* that beckons our caring stewardship from the externally *made artifact* that a technician assembles from inert matter is a capacity for individuation and self-determination that exceeds the causal interventions emanating from the environment. Later, invoking Hannah Arendt's notion of *natality* as a defining feature of the human condition,[26] Habermas argues that freedom to initiate actions would be meaningless were it not for the contrasting experience of an utterly unplanned and contingent birth; in other words, it is only against the background of an impersonal natural existence that is beyond my control that I must assume responsibility for being the person I will become. Although we commonly believe that we are God's creatures and that our parents contributed to our growth, we distinguish these events of nurturing, which accord with a pregiven nature that must be respected, from the planned making of an object we control, dominate, and use according to our arbitrary whims (*FHN* 53–60).[27]

The upshot of this argument is this: while parental education of children into free, individual, and therefore "equal" moral agents accords with their pregiven nature, genetic engineering of children as designer objects does not (*FHN* 46–52). In Habermas's judgment, when human beings play God with

26. H. Arendt, *The Human Condition* (Chicago: University of Chicago Press, 1958).

27. This objection recalls the critique of reification developed by Lukács in *History and Class Consciousness* and later extended by Adorno and Horkheimer under the heading "dialectic of enlightenment." Like Lukács, Habermas is concerned with the "commodification" of human life that occurs when science engineers people for profit. However, the concept of reification he has in mind resonates more closely with the scientistic forgetfulness of values, emotions, and meanings that attach to beings in our caring relationships with them. T. W. Adorno, *Minima Moralia* (New York: Verso Books, 1984), Aphorism 79, 121; and A. Honneth, *Reification: A New Look at an Old Idea* (Oxford: Oxford University Press, 2008), 62–63.

their fellow human beings in this last way, they no longer relate to them as equals whose scope for autonomy is shaped only by nature, God, or some other common, equalizing fate (*FHN* 114–15). Those who know they are made by another will not only feel less free (because they will know that their agency has been constrained by the will of another and not simply by natural fate) but they will feel less equal (in comparison to their creator) and less individual (especially if cloned). The undermining of our ethical self-understanding will thus indirectly diminish a necessary precondition for participating in moral life.

Moral life, as we have seen, rests on social interventions that depend on the voluntary consent of all parties affected. So another problem with prenatal genetic engineering is that children will have their fates chosen for them without their consent. But this suggests that all forms of genetic intervention are morally wrong, even those we know are necessary for avoiding extreme suffering. Habermas gets around this problem by formulating a principle of *counterfactual consent*: "All genetic interventions, including prenatal ones, must remain dependent on a consent that is at least counterfactually attributed to those possibly affected by them" (*FHN* 91). Using this principle, it is reasonable to suppose that any person would have consented to undergoing prenatal genetic interventions in order to avoid great suffering. But in cases where eugenic technologies aim at *positively enhancing* genetic characteristics, such consent can hardly be assumed, since enhancements of this sort have unpredictable side affects that might not be in the long-term best interests of the person undergoing the intervention. We can imagine a case in which "the young person can call his designer, and demand justification for why, in deciding on this or that genetic inheritance, the designer failed to choose athletic ability or musical talent, which would have been vastly more useful for the career that she had actually chosen to pursue" (*FHN* 82–83). Habermas thus concludes that "we are not permitted to determine, according to our own ideas about other people's future lives, the range of opportunities these others will one day face in their attempt to give ethical shape to their own lives" (*FHN* 89–90).[28]

Problems and Paradoxes

The main thrust of DE is that we must enter into real discourses in order to determine whether a given norm is justified and applicable in a given situation. However, as the above example shows, the use of hypothetical or simulated dialogues in order to obtain counterfactual consent—even when they are not

28. Habermas argues that by using preimplantation genetic diagnosis and stem cell research we have already begun sliding down the slope that leads to positive eugenics, since these technologies do not permit their practitioners to clearly distinguish therapeutic intentions aimed at avoiding painful outcomes from instrumental intentions aimed at producing enhanced outcomes (*FHN* 97).

conceived as monologues—might be unavoidable when dealing with a host of norms that affect the lives of future generations and other indefinite populations. Like monologues, simulated dialogues (advocacy discourses conducted in the privacy of one's mind) lack the critical check that can only come from the resistance of real persons. They invite the person conducting this kind of thought experiment to project her own ideas about what future others would or would not consent to.

For this reason, it is far from certain that the principle of counterfactual consent invoked by Habermas to capture this thought experiment must yield the results he thinks it does.[29] Habermas argues that when we are uncertain whether consent or dissent would be counterfactually given, we must withhold intervention altogether.[30] But, as he later concedes, once we lose the innocence that comes with ignorance of genetic science, *withholding intervention* also produces uncertain consequences that might provoke future recrimination—in strict violation of the principle of counterfactual consent (*FHN* 82). So unless we banned genetic science—and we are too far along to do that—we risk violating the principle no matter what we do.

This is exactly parallel to cases involving socialization, where enhancing capabilities, shaping identities, and mitigating handicaps therapeutically blend together in one uncertain project. Habermas's argument that socialization differs essentially from genetic engineering insofar as the socializing medium of communication can later enable children to reverse the effects of socialization is hardly convincing, as even he himself later conceded (*FHN* 84).[31] But surely we cannot deny parents the right to make these necessary choices—despite the obvious asymmetry in power that it implies between them and their children. By parity of reasoning, it would seem that we cannot deny parents the right to shape their children's capabilities through genetic engineering, either.[32]

That this result appears so counterintuitive from the standpoint of DE reflects the paradoxical nature of the theory, which straddles ideal role taking and real dialogue. Ideally, DE demands that we take into account the interests

29. Contra Habermas, it is hardly obvious why genetically engineered persons would feel inferior, since entering into communicative action would require that others relate to them as autonomous equals (*FHN* 80, 124n54).

30. Lafont argues that Habermas endorses a "principle of abstinence under uncertainty" that conflicts with (rather than derives from) his principle of counterfactual consent. Persons normally consent to procedures whose happy consequences are probable, if uncertain. Precaution—not abstinence—should be the principle. C. Lafont, "Remarks on Habermas's *The Future of Human Nature*," *APA Newsletter on Philosophy and Medicine* 3/1 (2003): 157–60.

31. Habermas concedes that his argument against PGD seems weaker when it is used for sex selection, since what is at stake is personal identity, not capability. It makes little sense for someone to object to who they are. (Transgendered persons reproaching their parents for their gender-assigning decisions object to who they are, but only because they began as biologically *unintegrated* selves.) (*FHN* 88)

32. In which case the only way to avoid the slippery slope mentioned in note 28 is to disallow all forms of genetic research.

of future generations counterfactually, including their interest in whether they would prefer to exist under certain nonideal circumstances. But knowing who these future generations are is impossible to determine at the outset of our discourse because it depends on what reproductive policy we adopt at the conclusion. To try to avoid this paradox by restricting discourse to real dialogue among members of the present generation risks injustice. Our decision to allow eugenic policies that we think will be in the equal interest of future generations might in retrospect turn out to be misguided.

The tension between the ideal and the real reveals another paradox that looks ahead to Habermas's decision to move DE in the direction of law and politics. As our discussion of abortion shows, the range of social conflicts that can be resolved in moral argumentation might well be quite limited. If most conflicts center around faith-based ethical conceptions that are rationally incommensurable, then any possibility of social cooperation will depend on reaching political compromises. Postconventional morality would indeed secure our respect for the most basic human rights taken abstractly, but it would not resolve ethical disputes concerning their proper scope and concrete meaning. Absent some political and legal procedure for deciding on one authoritative interpretation, rights would remain abstract and without prescriptive force.

So, is discourse ethics irrelevant to solving problems of social cooperation in modern society? Habermas thinks not. Indeed he argues that it is central to our understanding of law and politics. But this raises a new problem. Law and politics are areas of life that appear to be ruled by brute power, in which real coercion trumps ideal freedom, hierarchy trumps equality, and special interests trump universal interests. What—if anything—is moral about this process?

Habermas's Ideal of Argumentation: A Final Assessment

We can pose this last question from the standpoint of Habermas's ideal of argumentation, since conformity to that ideal is what ostensibly makes our resolution of social conflict moral in the first place—a question of right rather than of might. But the question so posed could easily be reversed: What—if anything—is realistic about that ideal? Critical theorists emphasize the importance of grounding their ideals in the understanding of real social agents. But how accurately do these ideals track these understandings?

To answer this last question we must recall a point I made in the last chapter. Habermas's attempt to develop a general theory of meaning based on universal formal-pragmatic rules—of which the rules governing ideal argumentation are a subset—runs up against the inherent context-dependency of meaning. Taken in isolation from this context, speech acts do not tell us how they are to be understood. The same can be said of Habermas's theory of discourse.

Habermas partly concedes this point. The theory itself, he tells us, is largely meaningless until we have a better idea how it can be actually applied and institutionalized in specific contexts of science, law, politics, and so on. But expressing the problem this way is grossly misleading, because it presupposes an unequal division of labor between philosophers and sociologists. It presupposes that the job of sociologists in this collaboration is limited to showing how real processes of argumentation fall short of the ideal that philosophers have articulated. This way of proceeding contradicts the guiding insight of critical theory, which (to paraphrase Marx) is that the philosopher-educator must be educated by the social agents he or she is trying to enlighten. In other words, we must begin studying actual contexts of argumentation in order to determine whether it is even possible to arrive at a general normative theory of argumentation. If it is not possible—and our observation about the context-dependency of meaning suggests that it is not—then we must derive the norms of critical assessment from the local contexts to be assessed.

Habermas's general theory of argumentation is not without its virtues. To begin with, it goes a long way toward bridging an important gap between two seemingly incompatible approaches to argumentation, traditionally reflected in the opposition between logic and rhetoric. Logic is concerned with *normative* questions concerning right reasoning; rhetoric is concerned with *factual* questions concerning psychologically persuasive reasoning. In the area of formal (or deductive) logic the opposition between these terms is relatively weak because a valid deductive argument by definition proves that a conclusion necessarily follows from given premises. Rational insight—or normatively conforming one's psychology to the logical law of noncontradiction—suffices to guarantee the rhetorical persuasiveness of the argument.

But deductive arguments—which aim at preserving the truth of premises—are useless in discovering the truth. Discovering the truth requires the use of informal modes of argumentation—induction, analogy, narrative—that are aimed at establishing probable support for a hypothesis. Here the opposition between logic and rhetoric becomes significant. In science, assessing the strength or probable truth of a hypothesis based on experimentally observed results requires exercising *judgment* with regard to the reliability of instruments and research personnel; the interpretation, review, and presentation of results; and the critical reception of results by the wider scientific community and even the lay public. This extended process of argumentation—in which judgment plays such a crucial role—unavoidably touches on aspects of social psychology that cannot be reduced to logical insight. From a rhetorical perspective, these aspects touch on the role that power (broadly construed) plays in the pedagogical indoctrination of scientists and lay persons, the certification of expertise and authority, the system of rewards that motivate scientists to engage in costly and risky research, the maintenance and policing of long-term collaborative research, the institutionalization of critical review and oversight, and the formation of character. These factors—which from a logical perspective are external to the process of rational inference—nonetheless indirectly influence it, thereby undermining our faith in the logical cogency of argumentation.

Habermas's theory of argumentation has the distinctive virtue of showing that rhetorical processes positively contribute to—rather than detract from—the logical cogency of informal arguments. In this respect it establishes an *internal* link between logic and rhetoric (and also dialectic). For Habermas, the logical assessment of an informal argument cannot be undertaken in abstraction from a dialectical procedure aimed at achieving consensus (as Peirce taught). Even if we reject Peirce's epistemic (consensus) conception of truth (discussed in chapter 3), the link between justifying a hypothesis and seeking a broader (consensual) warrant for assessing the reliability of our justificatory procedure remains. Even geniuses who buck the established consensus eventually have to convince others that their revolutionary insights are relevant and potentially fruitful, and so must be confirmed as such by the community of scientists in order for them to count as science. Indeed, the ever-present gap between existing evidence and potential evidence based on improvements in experimental procedure, theoretical paradigm, and the like make such a collaborative dialogue on evidence-generating processes all the more imperative.[33]

Habermas's multidimensional (perspectival) theory also explains why a rational (valid) scientific consensus cannot be achieved in abstraction from rhetorical processes that guarantee that all relevant arguments and counterarguments have been freely and equally presented. Accusations of bias in science show that these rhetorical ideals are not without force in the real world.

Although Habermas's model of dialogue goes far toward bridging the logic-rhetoric gap, it does so, in part, by redefining the terrain of rhetoric. Since Aristotle, rhetoricians have focused mainly on the social psychological aspects of successful argumentation that touch on aspects of character, empathy, and emotion. Social scientists have supplemented this analysis with an examination of social institutions, focusing specifically on how they efficiently organize the collective pursuit of knowledge. Both of these dimensions are absent from Habermas's triadic model; yet without extending the model to incorporate them it cannot fully bridge the gap between logic and rhetoric.

Habermas's treatment of rhetoric focuses not on factual psychology but on norms that are intended to insure a maximum pooling of information and exchange of arguments. Insisting that all relevant arguments be given a free and equal hearing has more to do with dialectic than rhetoric, which is evidenced by the fact that his treatment of these issues is so narrowly focused on procedures (and ideal ones, at that). However, as Rehg notes,[34] it would not be difficult to extend Habermas's theory to include a social psychological dimension that is not only based in fact but capable of providing some normative guidance. Rehg has in mind what Aristotle called "proof from character."[35] In order to

33. Rehg, *Cogent Science in Context*, 148–51.
34. Ibid., 142–45.
35. *Aristotle's Rhetoric and Poetics*, trans. W. R. Roberts and I. Bywater (New York: Modern Library, 1954), book 1, chap. 2, p. 3 [1356a].

persuasively communicate one among several equally plausible arguments—
for example, resolving whether or not to pursue aggressive treatment involving
a terminally ill patient—it is not enough for a speaker to possess a reputation
as a reliable authority (a doctor, say) based on past history. One must also
be able to empathize with one's opponents and their counterarguments and
be able to adjust the emotional pitch of one's presentation in order to dispose
others to make responsible judgments about roughly plausible competing arguments. In the case under question, having worked with the patient intimately
over an extended period of time, a nurse might be thought to possess a privileged understanding of the patient's wishes and chances of improved quality
of life. This kind of knowledge—based as it is on face-to-face experience with
the patient—cannot be articulated literally (at least not all of it), and so its importance for enabling others to formulate a responsible judgment may require
presenting it with emotional emphasis.

The aforementioned rhetorical norms regarding the *ethos* and *pathos* of
argumentation are context-neutral and (unlike reputation) directly affect the
manner of argumentation. Less obviously intrinsic to the assessment of arguments are those factual and contextual constraints on dialectical procedures
(broadly construed to include rhetorical norms) that are imposed by social
institutions. Here we encounter the dialectic of logic and rhetoric in its sharp-
est form. On the one hand, the long-term argumentative pursuit of knowledge
(say) would be unimaginable apart from economic and government institutions that fund research, educational institutions that discipline research, institutional mechanisms that encourage research (by crediting researchers for
their discoveries), and personal interest. This suggests that such apparently
"argument-external" factors are more internally connected to the logical, dialectical, and rhetorical dimensions of argumentation than Habermas's ideal
model would suggest. On the other hand, if this is so, then the entire enterprise
of defending the rational cogency of argumentation is jeopardized by the inevitable influence that personal interest as well as social, economic, political, and
administrative power play in actual institutionalized arguments.

The dialectic between logic and rhetoric is now transposed into a higher
register—between the ideal and the real—that cannot be easily resolved. This
dialectic suggests two problems with Habermas's theory, once we take seriously the critical theoretical principle that the ideal must also be grounded in
the real rather than merely being imposed on it by the detached philosopher-
legislator.[36] First, it suggests that the theory is too optimistic in thinking that
ideals of argumentation can be conceptually integrated and coherently applied

---

36. That the ideal must be so grounded is reinforced by the fact that its meaning and force
is too abstract and indeterminate to stand alone, apart from observable contexts of institutional
concrete application; and so we have no real warrant that the ideal has been approximately satisfied other than by observing its application in real contexts of discourse (Rehg, *Cogent Science in
Context*, 156).

to all contexts of institutionalized research. Second (and related), it suggests that the theory is too optimistic in assuming that these ideals can (or even should be) institutionalized at all.

As for the first problem (concerning coherence), insisting on maximal inclusion of points of view can sometimes seriously jeopardize the attainment of institutionalized consensus. Science would be bogged down in endless strife if it deemed that the insights of creationists, say, were as relevant to questions about the origin of the universe as the insights of astronomers and astrophysicists. Yet who is to say what is relevant here? Has not the dominant majority within the scientific community simply imposed its own opinion on the minority without subjecting that opinion to full examination within a broader dialogue?

As for the second problem, given the fact that (1) different scientific subdisciplines often do not agree on methods, standards, and even what constitutes the pertinent objects of study; and (2) cross-disciplinary collaboration on scientific research is sometimes necessary, "strategic" compromise based on partial acceptance of findings and interpretations—rather than consensus (full agreement based on commonly accepted reasons)—may be unavoidable.[37] To take another example, the rhetorical ideal of a disinterested and open search for the truth—in which only the force of the better argument is allowed to enter—might be incompatible with the sustained (dialectical) organization of research, in which scientists' desire to achieve personal credit often leads them to conceal research from competing research teams.[38]

Habermas's theory of argumentation is too idealistic to provide a workable standard for assessing the rational cogency of scientific arguments. But can any general theory do so? I have suggested that general normative theories such as Habermas's founder on the shoals of reality: meanings must be contextualized

37. The evidence paper summarizing the results of the first run of collision detection experiments at Fermilab (CDF) designed to test the existence of a top quark shows that politically motivated compromises may be preferable to open admission of dissent. The CDF argument can be interpreted in three of four possible ways that can be ranked in descending order of Habermasian dialectical cogency: (1) full consensus on the existence of the top quark based on strict adherence to Habermasian norms (the evidence paper revealed no dissent); (2) absence of full consensus based on strict adherence to Habermasian norms (this possibility is ruled out by the evidence paper, which presented a solid consensus in favor of the existence of a top quark); (3) absence of full consensus based on Habermasian norms that is presented to the public as a full consensus; and (4) absence of a full consensus based on a violation of Habermasian norms that is presented to the public as a full consensus. Rehg points out that when indecision is potentially disastrous—as in the debate over the human contribution to global warming—masking over minor disagreement in a scientific report affirming human responsibility for global warming (parallel to option 3) might be justified. Even when the disagreement is caused by social pressures and biases that violate Habermasian principles (parallel to option 4), a false presentation of consensus might be justified if doing so is necessary for continuing fruitful collaboration. Balancing the advantages and disadvantages of different rhetorical strategies requires contextual judgment. Rehg, *Cogent Science in Context*, 184–93.

38. Ibid., 157–61, 180–93.

in any case,[39] and the contexts in which the meanings of discursive norms are institutionalized are inherently organized by top-down administrative bureaucracies in which power and strategic action unavoidably intervene. This double obstacle to a critical theory of argumentation might well resign one to postmodern skepticism.

Rehg, however, disagrees. Forsaking transcendent (external) criticism for immanent criticism, he notes that the very need to persuade others outside of one's immediate context of argumentation of the fruitfulness and relevance of one's research compels scientists to address an expanded audience that includes experts in other fields, and ultimately the public at large. The need to "transact" with others outside of one's narrow context means that the content of one's argument has to be made persuasive across a number of different venues.[40] The confrontation with different contexts of assessment provides a critical check on each microsocial context of argumentation.[41] Ultimately, the broader public must be included in the argument about the relevance and fruitfulness of lines of research. At this point in the argument, assessment shifts to the next level of analysis: the legal, political, economic, and social institutions that warrant confidence in the legitimacy of democratic deliberation.

39. As ethnomethodologists note, contextual indexicality is "irremediable, persisting despite our best efforts to translate indexical expressions into fully explicit, context-free 'objective' statements. Such explications always contain further ambiguities, and in some cases the explication actually loses the situated meaning of the original utterance by eliminating elisions that hearers depend on and expect as ordinary. For example, making a child's cry 'Mommy!' more explicit as 'My mommy!' changes its situated sense." Rehg, *Cogent Science in Context,* 219. Given the socially constructed nature of scientific meanings by individuals using ad hoc methods "here and now," contextual relativity must be qualified by admitting the widest range of perspectives possible. The new insights generated by the inclusion of women researchers in primatology and anthropology recommends this Habermasian norm (228).

40. Rehg endorses collaboration between sociologies of scientific knowledge (SSK) and Habermasian critical science studies (CSS) (Rehg, *Cogent Science in Context,* 200). A CSS practitioner enlightened by SSK asks whether a given consensus is based on relevant motives as these are normatively prescribed by the goals of particular institutions and modified by specific contexts (201). If relevant motives include advancing the good society (as Rehg thinks they must), CSS practitioners should make these topics of democratic deliberation. For example, in assessing arguments in behavioral biology, the CSS practitioner will make explicit the conservative policy implications of a "linear-hormonal" (LH) account of gender-associated behavioral patterns in comparison to those based on a "group selectionist" (GS) account that explains behavior in terms of experientially conditioned neural changes (204–7). H. Longino, *Science as Social Knowledge* (Princeton: Princeton University Press, 1990), 135, 165.

41. Rehg himself rejects the use of "idealizing reconstructions of tacit pragmatic presuppositions" in favor of "paying close attention to the actual case and the normative concerns of those involved" (Rehg, *Cogent Science in Context,* 266). The three-dimensional theory of argumentative cogency he proposes asks that the social critic focus not only on the logical merits of the texts produced but also on the dialogical merits of interdisciplinary transactions and their reception by the broader public. This last consideration marks the intersection of science and ethics (the good life). For example, we need to ask whether—among equally substantiated research hypotheses—certain lines of research will better promote our vision of society. Rehg, *Cogent Science in Context,* 284–95.

6

Law and Democracy
Part I: The Foundational Rights

Habermas's interest in law and politics is the single constant thread running throughout his career and predates his interest in knowledge and morality. His first book, *The Structural Transformation of the Public Sphere* (1962), examined the emergence of an independent political space for critical public opinion formation during the eighteenth century and its subsequent decline with the rise of mass media and propaganda in the nineteenth and twentieth centuries. Although the basic contours of his later discourse theoretic understanding of the public sphere are already present in that work, they lack a rigorous and systematic formulation. His second major book in this genre, *Legitimation Crisis* (1973), by contrast, reflected most of the theoretical innovations he would develop in his TCA and DE, albeit in highly schematic form. The central thesis of this book, which I discuss in chapter 10, is that the modern welfare state sits astride a contradiction between two of its presuppositions, a capitalist economic system that generates inequality and privilege and a democratic political system that aspires toward equality and inclusion. The government's management of capitalism's crisis of overproduction shifts the crisis onto itself: it must simultaneously assume the costs of economic growth and the costs of compensating the victims of such growth without siphoning off too much public revenue and without publicizing how it redistributes it. But the social interventions of the welfare state simultaneously erode work incentives essential to capitalism as well as repoliticize the population, who demand ever greater accountability from their leaders.

An important element in the above argument is the contradiction between postconventional moral expectations regarding democratic accountability and administrative requirements regarding unilateral planning and decision making. However, it was not until *Between Facts and Norms* (1992) that Habermas systematically defended a conceptual connection between postconventional morality and law as such, thereby showing how the very legal system that makes modern economies and governments possible also imposes internal limits on them.

Modern Law and Morality: A Paradoxical Wedding of Facts and Norms

At the conclusion of chapter 5 I noted that most value conflicts in modern society take the form of ethical disagreements that cannot find moral resolution. At best, people with irreconcilable ethical worldviews can learn to tolerate one another and live together in a legal regime that guarantees their freedom of conscience and fairly compromises their differences. This is paradoxical for several reasons.

First, the capacity of postconventional morality to resolve conflict at the level of everyday communicative interaction—the sphere in which it originates—is so limited that whatever impact it has on social integration largely depends on the extent to which it informs another domain of action, the legal system. Second, this system constitutes a domain of action that is thoroughly suffused with power politics, strategic action, and coercion—the very antithesis (so it seems) of action conducted in accordance with the moral point of view.

Finally, Habermas remarks that moral discourses are highly "improbable" in everyday life because the ideal expectations that they place on interlocutors are extremely demanding. No one checks to see whether participants in discourse have equal chances to speak freely; and no one checks to see how inclusive discourses are. Discourses come closest to being realized in academic, parliamentary, and judicial settings, in which participants are required to abide by formal rules of argumentation. Rules governing the election and representation of legislators and parliamentary rules governing debate are often designed to ensure that all major groups in society are given an equal opportunity to speak; rules governing courtroom procedure guaranteeing both sides a fair hearing before an impartial judge and jury are designed to bring out the truth and to represent all points of view. But this, too, is paradoxical. Because these institutions are assigned the task of making decisions, time constraints must be imposed on discourse. In legal and parliamentary settings, judges and legislators are not free to express their personal opinions as they wish (extremely partisan utterances violate the public trust we place in these officials). Indeed, in courts of law arguments are constrained both by legal precedent and by the adversarial structure of the legal contest, which forces opposing attorneys to behave strategically toward each other. In short, institutionalized discourses can be said to realize moral discourses only by compromising their implicit ideals. The question thus arises: How can one be morally obligated to respect institutions that deviate so much from the ideals that call forth that respect? Or, to reverse the question as I did in the conclusion of the last chapter: How can ideals that deviate so much from social reality merit our respect as realistic and workable?

Situating Habermas's Theory of Law and Democracy: Some Contemporary Debates

Before proceeding further it might be useful to stand back and ask what Habermas thinks he can add to contemporary discussions about law and democracy. Habermas is considered by many to be the founder of the *deliberative democracy* school that has emerged in the last twenty years. What chiefly distinguishes deliberative democracy is its emphasis on deliberation as a public process of justifying binding decisions through the giving of reasons.[1] Such democracy implies a civic duty to refrain from imposing coercive laws on persons unless they, along with the rest of us, have been publicly persuaded that doing so is in everyone's rational interest. The concerted search for common interests that have withstood the test of reasoned debate has the further implication that the interests and preferences that citizens initially take for granted as being in their mutual interests are liable to be replaced or transformed in the course of critical discussion. This contrasts with the dominant economic model of democracy as a power-backed form of bargaining, passive voting, and preference aggregation, in which citizens' unreflected interests and preferences are allowed free rein to influence the outcome. Yet aside from their common rejection of this model, advocates of deliberative democracy disagree about its justification, how substantively prescriptive it is, and how important consensus is as a goal.

Given these disagreements it might be useful to situate these differences in broader debates about democracy. Four debates seem especially pertinent in this regard. These concern: the justification of democracy, the relationship

---

1. Early defenses of the deliberative ideal are John Stuart Mill's *Considerations On Representative Government* (1861) and Dewey's. In *The Public and Its Problems* (1927), Dewey writes that "the means by which a majority comes to be a majority is the important thing: antecedent debates, the modifications of views to meet minorities.... The essential need, in other words, is the improvement of the methods and conditions of debate, discussion, and persuasion." J. Dewey, "The Public and Its Problems," in *The Later Works,* vol. 2 (Carbondale: University of Southern Illinois Press, 1993), 70–71. I here follow Amy Gutmann and Dennis Thompson in defining deliberative democracy as: "[1] a form of government in which free and equal citizens (and their representatives), justify decisions in a process in which they give one another reasons that are [2] mutually acceptable and generally accessible, with the aim of [3] reaching conclusions that are binding in the present on all citizens but [4] open to challenge in the future" (numbering mine). A. Gutmann and D. Thompson, *Why Deliberative Democracy?* (Princeton: Princeton University Press, 2004), 7.

between law and democracy, the meaning and importance of neutrality (impartiality) in governance, and the special recognition and protection of minorities. For now I shall focus on the first two debates and defer discussion of the other debates until chapter 8.

Justifications for democracy—by which I mean popular control over and/ or participation in collective deliberation and decision making[2]—fall into two broad categories: *instrumentalist* and *internalist*.[3] Instrumentalist justifications argue that democracy is preferable to other systems of governance because it is more likely to produce good outcomes or good effects on citizens. For example, some argue that democracy produces virtuous citizens who are civic-minded and care about the public welfare.[4] Popular will theorists see democracy as enabling the general will of the people to be exercised.[5] Others (notably utilitarians) believe that popular suffrage provides an optimal means for revealing the relative weights of people's wants so that government leaders can promote policies that maximize the public good.[6] Pragmatists also proclaim the epistemic value of democracy as a vehicle for social learning (i.e., for discovering social problems and resolving them).[7] Even those who find nothing good

2. Political theorists distinguish direct (participatory) from indirect (representative) democracy. In direct democracy the members themselves participate in matters of governance, broadly understood (deliberating and deciding on issues that affect them collectively). An example would be a town hall meeting in which every member of the community has an opportunity to debate and vote on the building of a library. In indirect democracy the members decide to delegate some functions of deliberation and decision making to some subset of the membership, whom they hold accountable by means of periodic elections. As a general rule, direct democracy seems best suited for smaller units in which all members possess roughly equal competence to decide, while indirect democracy is more efficient in larger, more complex units requiring expert leadership and governance. However, both types of democracy complement each other whenever citizens directly initiate and ratify popular referenda and influence *formal* legislative and executive bodies through *informal* channels of public opinion.

3. J. Arthur, ed., *Democracy: Theory and Practice* (Belmont, CA: Wadsworth, 1992), xi.

4. For a classical statement of this view, see J.-J. Rousseau, *On the Social Contract* (1762). For a more contemporary statement, see Carole Pateman's *Participation and Democratic Theory* (Cambridge: Cambridge University Press, 1970), 22–44.

5. See Rousseau's *On the Social Contract* (1762).

6. The classical statement of this view is James Mill's "Essay on Government" (1820), which argues that allowing the will of the majority to override the minority prevents tyranny and promotes the greater good for the greater number. Also see John Stuart Mill, *Considerations on Representative Government* (1861), which unlike the above (and in keeping with *On Liberty*), defends the view that majoritarian rule must be restrained by a healthy respect for minority interests. For a more contemporary utilitarian defense that recommends procedural safeguards guaranteeing the equal influence of citizens in influencing policy, see P. Singer, *Democracy and Disobedience* (New York: Oxford University Press, 1974).

7. This view, which was forcefully propounded by John Dewey in *Democracy and Education* (New York: MacMillan, 1916), has been defended more recently by Rorty and Putnam. Habermas's reservations about Deweyan democracy pertain to its limited application within a unitary ethical community that need only clarify, balance, and test its particular values experimentally in accordance with an unproblematic conception of the common good. In pluralist societies that lack such an orientation, a discursive notion of democracy emphasizing universal rights and

in democracy might prefer it over other systems for promoting social stability because it allows the masses to fight among themselves in the newspapers and ballot boxes rather than in the streets.

Most advocates of deliberative democracy appeal to instrumental reasons in justifying it. Although the chief aim of deliberative democracy is not the facilitation of strategic bargaining and preference aggregation, deliberative democrats (including Habermas) have suggested that deliberative democracy can help in these endeavors by encouraging bargainers to modify their preferences to the point where they are more rational and less antagonistic (see appendix E). Again, deliberative democrats (including Habermas) have pointed out that deliberative democracy encourages citizens to be less selfish and more civic-minded, or focused on the public good. In general, it would be difficult to justify deliberative democracy if it did not as a general rule yield outcomes that were on balance judged to be good. If it did not—and other types of collective decision making did (such as top-down decision making by less-partisan experts)—then there would be no compelling reason to prefer it. So most deliberative democrats (including Habermas) hold that deliberative democracy— because of its expansive pooling of information from the ground up and its subjection of that information to wide public and rational critique—is more likely to produce good results than other types of decision making.

Noticeably absent from the instrumentalist justification of democracy is any mention of its intrinsic value as an expression of and necessary condition for a fully human existence. For the instrumentalist, the act of deliberation has no value in itself. For the internalist it does. Aristotle, for instance, famously argued in his *Politics* that what distinguishes us as a species is our ability to use rational speech in persuading others to accept a course of action. For Hannah Arendt, deliberating and deciding in common arguably constitutes the very medium in which we express and give shape to our individuality, spontaneity, and equality. Habermas, too, endorses a similar kind of internalist argument; for, despite his recognition of the instrumental value of democracy for promoting virtue, knowledge, and the common good, he denies that these outcomes justify democracy. As he points out, the greater balance of good over bad produced by a perfectly benevolent and wise dictator would not compensate for the violation done to a citizen's moral dignity as a free and equal agent who is accountable to herself and to others for jointly conducting their otherwise separate lives.

Internalist justifications come in several varieties: *populist, proceduralist,* and *prescriptivist.* Populist forms (including some varieties of *civic republicanism*) see democracy as capturing the essential spontaneity of the human condition, the almost anarchic capacity of human beings to initiate new cooperative undertakings and reinvent who they are (their identities) through collective

---

cross-cultural moral perspective-taking of the sort highlighted by Dewey's colleague, G. H. Mead, is more applicable (*TJ* 232–35; *TT* 131–35).

deliberation and the clash of opinions. Informal, spontaneous demonstrations rather than organized institutions of decision making best exemplify what populists mean by democracy. By contrast, proceduralist justifications focus on the way in which democratic deliberation and decision making implicitly embody a fundamental moral value: justice. For a pure proceduralist, adherence to a just procedure suffices to justify the binding nature of a decision even to those who find it mistaken.

Procedures suffice to justify the binding nature of decisions only if they are recognized as just. But how does one recognize a procedure's justice, if not by the outcomes it produces? The fact that just procedures yield just outcomes cannot be the reason why these procedures are justified, for that would amount to justifying them instrumentally. Rather, these procedures are justified because they are just, evidence for which can be found in their tendency to produce just outcomes.

As I noted in chapter 3, it is possible to define procedural justice in ideal terms that would virtually guarantee the justice of a procedure's outcome. For example, we could define our democratic procedure to include—counterfactually—all logically possible points of view, advanced by persons who have undergone rigorous psychotherapy and training in logic, and the like. But no real procedure—just though it may be—could guarantee just outcomes all the time. This need not impugn the justice of a procedure, so long as the unjust outcomes it yielded were very few and of trifling import.

Unfortunately, the record shows that democratic procedures are very imperfect devices for achieving just results. To take an obvious example, the majority rule procedure based on a simple one-person, one-vote scheme comes as close as any procedure in encapsulating a fair collective-decision procedure since it recognizes the equal dignity of each citizen. Yet this procedure has repeatedly enabled the majority to tyrannize over the minority (even without violating its fundamental rights, which happens often enough).[8] In rare cases, it has enabled

8. Habermas (*BFN* 293) discusses cases in which the majority violates the rights of the minority. However, cases in which a minority group is repeatedly outvoted by a majority on a range of interest-related issues (in which compromise is ruled out) is not solved by granting the minority basic rights, or even (following Peter Singer) equally weighted votes, equal power to influence the outcome, or equal leverage in bargaining. Here, as Peter Jones argues, a principle of proportionality must be applied not only in determining fair political representation in legislative bodies but in resolving irreconcilable (noncompromising) issues, so that a well-identified minority that constitutes one-third of a voting population should be empowered to decide on one of three equally important issues that divide them from the majority. Supplementing the majority rule principle with this procedure would go farther in convincing a minority of the fairness in abiding by the majority's decision on the remaining two issues. However, from a Habermasian point of view, no compromise could provide a moral warrant for accepting this solution unless all parties to the conflict had first made a good-faith "deliberative" effort to criticize and transform their interests. P. Singer, *Democracy and Disobedience*, 30–36, 42, 64–65; P. Jones, "Political Equality and Majority Rule," in *The Nature of Political Theory*, ed. D. Miller and L. Siedentop (Oxford: Oxford University Press, 1983), 155–82.

the majority to abolish the procedure itself (as happened when German citizens voted to end Germany's short-lived democracy in 1934).

Prescriptivists seek to avoid these gravely unjust outcomes by prescribing (or proscribing) certain outcomes. Liberals, for instance, appeal to basic "inalienable" rights that outcomes must respect if they are not to be rejected as unjust (null and void). Some liberals (like Rawls) go further and supplement these rights with principles of distributive justice (the difference principle) that prescribe ideal principles for designing social institutions.

In order for these prescriptive principles to be effective, they must be entrenched in constitutional law (in the form of a bill of rights, say) and concretely defined in subsequent acts of legislation. To ensure that democratically elected lawmakers apply these principles correctly, without partisan bias, and otherwise heed them when engaged in normal statutory legislation, liberals entrust a supreme court—ideally composed of appointed judges who are tenured for life—to impartially interpret and apply them in reviewing and overturning, if need be, the decisions of legislators and executive officers. However, the rule of law, as it is here defined, poses a dilemma for the prescriptivist: What distinguishes this court from the wise and benevolent dictator mentioned earlier? Have we not substituted a nondemocratic decision procedure (judicial rule) for a democratic one?

Indeed, the above description of prescriptivism seems incompatible with an internalist defense of democracy. Democracy, the prescriptivist seems to be saying, cannot be intrinsically valuable given its threat to something that is: the basic rights of individuals. At most, democracy is instrumentally valuable in protecting those rights from tyrannical rulers. But its instrumental value in this regard needs to be balanced against its instrumental failure to protect against majoritarian tyranny. That is why judicial oversight of democracy proves to be more instrumentally valuable to the protection of rights than democracy itself.

Can we interpret prescriptivism in a way that can comport with the intrinsic value of democracy and thus support, rather than undermine, an internalist defense of democracy? Habermas thinks so. Although Habermas refers to his model of deliberative democracy as proceduralist, it is not *purely* so.[9] That is because he prescribes rights-based limits on majoritarian outcomes. However, because he thinks these limits are intrinsic to democracy—constitutive of democratic procedure in some extended sense of the term—he can argue that the prescribed outcome (respect for individual rights) is not really a limit on democracy but only a limit on imperfect majoritarian decisions.

---

9. In "Is Democracy Special?" in *Philosophy, Politics, and Society,* ed. P. Laslett (Oxford: Blackwell, 1955), 155–56. Brian Barry rejects "the notion that one should build into 'democracy' any constraints on the content of the outcomes produced, such as substantive equality, respect for human rights, concern for the general welfare, personal liberty, or the rule of law." Habermas, by contrast, holds that adherence to rational procedures justifies "the supposition that the democratic process as a whole facilitates rational outcomes" (*BFN* 285).

Stated differently, Habermas's proceduralist model rejects as undemocratic attempts to prescribe in advance any *concrete* interpretation of individual rights that goes beyond their abstract formulation. Prescribing abstract rights goes with prescribing democratic procedure; prescribing concrete rights, by contrast, limits democratic procedure (and usurps the people's right to define the scope of their own freedom). Habermas insists that nobody—not even the wise philosopher—has the authority to preempt the deliberation of citizens by telling them what substantively prescriptive rules they should or should not agree to adopt. At the same time, his fear of majoritarian tyranny leads him to adopt a *quasi*-prescriptive liberalism: majoritarian outcomes ought not to violate the basic rights of individuals—abstractly defined. The reason they ought not is *not* that individual rights possess an intrinsic value that outweighs the instrumental value of political rights ascribed to a democratically empowered citizenry. The reason they ought not is that violating the basic rights of individuals violates these political rights as well, thereby violating rights that are of equal intrinsic value.

To make a long story short, Habermas endeavors to show how (liberal) prescriptivism and proceduralism presuppose each other in such a way that "neither human rights nor popular sovereignty can claim primacy over its counterpart" (*MCCA* 261). Stated differently, no truly deliberative democratic procedure could conceivably exist if it did not have a basic respect for individual rights built into it. The fact that the majority rule procedure when taken alone can lead to the paradoxical violation of its own moral rationale merely shows that deliberative democracy entails a richer notion of procedure.[10]

Just as rights are built into deliberative procedure so, too, is deliberative procedure built into rights. Rights that are conceptually built into any deliberative procedure are too abstract when taken at this purely philosophical level of justification to provide much prescriptive guidance. Hence their prescription by the philosopher does not impose much of a constraint on citizens in choosing their actual institutional form. Because the fully prescriptive meaning, scope, and force of these rights is left to the citizens themselves to work out deliberatively, their binding quality (as moral claims and entitlements) remains conceptually dependent on deliberative consent.

---

10. Gutmann and Thompson argue that proceduralism needs substantive principles to exclude racial discrimination and other bad outcomes. Simone Chambers notes, however, that Habermas himself presumes that citizens deploy substantive arguments. She adds that some substantive reasons against racial discrimination—for example, that no morally relevant reason can be given for excluding any racial minority from participating in democratic legislation—depend on procedural norms requiring a full presentation of competing arguments. Also, equal individual rights are necessary conditions for the institutionalization of Habermasian procedures, thereby directly excluding racial discrimination. Still, Habermasian proceduralism cannot provide much support for social policies pertaining to questions that are less central to moral justice. Gutmann and Thompson, *Why Deliberative Democracy?*, chap. 3; S. Chambers, "Can Procedural Democracy Be Radical?" in *The Political*, ed. D. Ingram (Oxford: Blackwell, 2002), 168–88; and S. Chambers, *Reasonable Democracy: Jürgen Habermas and the Politics of Discourse* (Ithaca: Cornell University Press, 1996).

This general account of the relationship between rights and deliberative procedure touches on a much broader issue concerning the relationship between law and democracy. To begin with, not all human rights that make up the core of constitutional law can be conceptually deduced from the necessary conditions of democratic deliberation. If, by Habermas's own reckoning, they have a moral basis that lies outside democratic deliberation, then he needs to explain how they fail to violate the deliberative principle that all binding limits derive their rationales from the deliberative process itself. Another problem, to which I have alluded, concerns the legal institutionalization of deliberative democracy. Even if deliberative democracy could generate all constitutional limits on acceptable outcomes by simply looking to its own procedures, these procedures would have to be understood at a very high level of abstraction to capture the complexity of procedural moral requirements.[11] Any concrete "realization" of these "ideals" would perforce involve sullying them with constraints imposed by the very institutions in which they were embedded. Indeed, the biggest constraint would come from the administration of democratic institutions through mechanisms of coercive law. This returns us to the penultimate question: How can procedures of deliberation be linked to strategic uses of power without being compromised?

The Sociological Genesis of Modern Law

To answer this question we must first examine Habermas's sociology of law. Unlike *normative* philosophy of law, which understands law from the *inside*— from the standpoint of jurists and laypersons who are concerned about its moral authority to obligate individual actors to comply with its rules—sociology explains modern law from the *outside*—from the standpoint of social scientists who are interested in its historical emergence as a *factual* precondition for modern economic and administrative *systems* (see appendix F). Seen in this dual light, law facilitates both the normative integration of individual actors (social integration) as well as the functional coordination of systems (functional integration). On the one hand, it designates an organizational tool (strategic medium) largely deployed independently of moral concerns about justice, by which government bureaucrats exercise their *administrative power*

---

11. Habermas's proceduralism is similar in this regard to Charles Beitz's notion of "complex proceduralism," which goes beyond ensuring equal power to contesting parties and instead demands that "the terms of democratic participation are fair when they are reasonably acceptable from each citizen's point of view, or more precisely, when no citizen has good reason to refuse to accept them." C. Beitz, *Political Equality* (Princeton: Princeton University Press, 1989), 23. See. K. Baynes and R. v. Schomberg's introduction to the book edited by them, *Discourse and Democracy: Essays on Habermas's "Between Facts and Norms"* (Albany: SUNY, 2002), 6; and the essay by Baynes contained in the same book entitled, "Deliberative Democracy and the Limits of Liberalism," 15–30.

in coordinating the achievement of collective goals that are vital to maintaining economic efficiency and political order. On the other hand, it comprises *norms of justice* in accordance with which actors voluntarily coordinate their conflicting aims for the sake of social cooperation and solidarity.

Habermas is mainly interested in law as a normative institution. However, he directs much of his criticism against normative legal philosophies that are insensitive to the dual factual and normative aspects of law. On one extreme lies *legal positivism*, which proffers a functional or factual explanation for understanding why legal subjects obey the law. According to this view, persons feel obligated to obey the law not because it is morally just but simply because it *is* the law. They obey the law out of fear, or (adopting the viewpoint of a sociological observer) because they recognize that doing so contributes to an efficient and stable system. In Habermas's opinion, although this view may suffice to explain why some people feel obliged to obey the law—out of fear of the consequences for failing to do so—it cannot explain why most people do. Not only are the consequences of disobeying the law far from certain, but the long-term capacity of the law to command obedience depends on its being generally obeyed "out of respect for the law" as such.

Even when positivists like H. L. A. Hart concede the truth of this point, holding that most citizens in stable legal regimes obey the law because it is the "right thing to do," apart from its consequences, these positivists limit the normative, critical attitude that citizens can adopt with respect to the law. For positivists, if citizens recognize that they ought to obey the law because it is the right thing to do, it is because citizens recognize, in an *unquestioning* way, the "rightness" of the legal authority of the basic law, such as a constitution, from which all their nation's laws trace their rightful pedigree (what Hart calls a "rule of recognition"). Judges and jurists can criticize the wrongness of a piece of law making or a judicial decision for having deviated from the basic law, but they cannot criticize the rightness of basic law itself, inasmuch as this law defines what is legally right. They might, of course, criticize the basic law for nonlegal reasons, such as its ineffectiveness or moral unfairness. But there is something awkward about this, insofar as the basic law is supposed to provide *secondary rules,* or decision procedures, for resolving disagreements concerning our *primary* rules for acting, including moral rules.

For Habermas, the awkwardness of morally criticizing basic law can be removed only if standards of moral justice are both universal and necessary for understanding why citizens obey the law because it is the right thing to do. In other words, it is not enough for citizens to obey the law because it is the law (which they respect unquestioningly, as a matter of fact); they must also obey it because it is morally just and nonoppressive. Yet, despite its connection to justice, Habermas warns against viewing law as a simple instantiation of (or derivation from) morality—the view he associates with *natural law theory.* Unlike moral norms, which command specific actions as a matter of duty, legal rights command nothing. Instead, they *permit* a range of protected actions. These actions can be motivated by selfish interests and can even produce consequences that are widely regarded as immoral. The connection between law and morality is therefore at most indirect; in most cases it is not statutory law but the democratic procedure by which it is made that most directly refers to justice.

As I noted, the relationship between law and morality is complicated by law's factual connection to coercive administrative power, which threatens to undo law's legitimacy as a system of freely and universally accepted impartial norms. Despite the tension between legal power and legal justice, Habermas insists that these two elements are linked, functionally if not conceptually. To illustrate the historical contingency of this functional link, he observes that law and social power largely exist independently of each other in tribal societies. In these societies laws based on religion and custom suffice to coordinate the conflicting behavior of actors independently of the tribal leader's power to sanction deviant behavior with threats. The power associated with prestige also explains how tribal leaders can command the achievement of collective goals without recourse to sanctions or customary laws. This disconnect between law and power would be unthinkable in modern (complex and pluralistic) societies. In these societies custom-based law has been replaced by postconventional morality. But postconventional morality cannot motivate everyone to comply with codes of right behavior without the aid of coercive law. Modern morality has traded the sanction of divine retribution and the ritual observance of custom for the weak motivation of reasons. It has purchased its universal validity as a rational and abstract system of *knowledge* at the expense of its concrete motivational power to compel *action*. Hence, it needs to be supplemented by positive law, which, besides being a system of knowledge, is also a system of government-sanctioned action.

Habermas situates the preceding account of functional convergence within a lengthy discussion describing the two crises that mark the transition from premodern to modern society. In the first crisis religion-based morality loses its potency; in the second, power-backed law loses its legitimacy. The transition from premodern society to modern society in which these crises occur is explicable, in turn, as a response to economic and administrative crises endemic to premodern society.

Let me begin with the second point. Social scientists explain the evolution of economic and administrative systems as a response to problems of social conflict and economic survival. Simple tribal societies rely on customary habit and religious belief in securing social solidarity (*BFN* 139). Only when forced by social disintegration caused by population growth and survival threats stemming from such things as economic scarcity and foreign invasion do they develop a leadership class possessing centralized political power. The emergence of leadership roles eventually culminates in the splitting off of a specialized form of political power (tied to the prestige of a royal priestly lineage) that possesses authority to issue binding commands. Positive (noncustomary) law and political power thus emerge simultaneously. At a more advanced stage the simple command structure gives way to a complex state administration in which the process of command comes under regulation by standing legal procedures (*BFN* 142).

Because this new mechanism of social coordination constitutes the first form of class domination, with priests and military leaders living off the surplus generated by the labor of others, religion (divine law) is needed to legitimate it. This recourse proves inadequate with the advent of capitalism. First, capitalism emerges as a response to crises of underproduction, endemic to feudal and guild economies, that are partly caused by religious constraints on competition, usury, profiteering, and mobility. Second, once established, capitalism generates economic stratifications that, being independent of the older religion-based hierarchies, resist religious legitimation. Third, capitalism unleashes an economic egoism that operates independently of religious sanctions and altruism, thereby requiring a new system of law in order to be kept in check. Finally, this egoism has as its moral counterpart a personal ethic of conscience and responsibility (the Protestant work ethic) whose individualism explodes the unitary ethos of a single established religion.

According to Habermas, modern law and modern morality are "co-original" in that they both need one another in order to solve the new problems of social conflict posed by capitalism and modern pluralism (*BFN* 146). The capacity of morality to solve the problem of social conflict is limited by *cognitive, motivational,* and *organizational* factors. Modern morality designates a rational procedure for impartially resolving social conflicts. Individuals using this procedure shoulder the burden of adducing and ranking norms. The chances of their coming to agreement in this endeavor are rather remote. Agreeing on the most abstract rights is one thing, agreeing on their proper meaning and scope when applied to particular ethical disputes is quite another. The social pressure to resolve these disagreements requires institutionalizing a legal-decision procedure that will "unburden" persons of the need to endlessly deliberate on these matters without hope of closure.

Morality depends on the power of rational conviction to motivate normative compliance, but this power, as we have seen, is quite weak. Persons knowingly do wrong. Furthermore, capitalism opens up a domain of egoistic interaction in which nonmoral incentives prevail. Legal coercion is needed because morality alone cannot ensure that persons will honor their contracts and behave civilly.

Finally, morality lacks the organizational means necessary for its implementation. When it comes to my duty to forbear from harming others no problem need arise; it is I who am personally accountable for the harm I directly cause. Things get murkier when I consider my positive duty to aid my fellow citizens who are in distress—a duty that no society can deny, especially when my fellow citizens are the very ones who sacrifice their lives in defending me against external threats. Because morality requires that I use personal discretion in deciding the target and extent of my aid (based on my determination of what I can reasonably give or sacrifice), there is no guarantee that anyone will adequately fulfill their duty in this area (i.e., everyone will be tempted to "ride freely" in the expectation that someone else will take up the slack).

In the words of Hart, we need secondary rules (legal procedures) that precisely designate who is responsible for implementing our moral duties and in what manner.[12] As Habermas puts it, law defines a whole "system of accountabilities" (*BFN* 117). The legislative, judicial, and executive organs created by constitutional and statutory law ensure that shared moral duties to aid our fellow citizens are not only implemented but extended throughout civil society. In this way, areas of economic life, for instance, that are governed by relations of power and self-interest can become more just and stable, thanks to laws protecting collective bargaining, prohibiting discrimination, and providing for social welfare and income redistribution.

Our discussion so far has focused on a paradoxical fact—namely, morality needs law in order to be effectively realized: *legitimacy emerges out of legality*. This point is well established by Hart and other positivists: in modern complex societies primary rules governing conduct need to be ranked—and some of them need to be officially declared and enforced—by instituting secondary rules that establish legal procedures pertaining to legislation, adjudication, and enforcement. But the converse holds true as well: law needs to be intrinsically connected to primary rules of moral justice (rights and other principles of justice) in order for it to be effectively obeyed. Legality emerges out of legitimacy.

In order for law to guide our behavior effectively it must operate within the moral parameters set down by the rule of law. That it must be general in scope and consistent with other laws goes without saying. Beyond that it must be publicly and precisely formulated so that persons can know when they have overstepped it (*BFN* 143). In order for persons to assess its predictable effects law must be shielded from the arbitrary power of capricious lawmakers. Higher-order constitutional law accomplishes this self-limitation of legal power by imposing moral limits on the power of rulers to interfere with the basic rights of legal subjects.

Political philosophers typically explain the duty to protect a person's private autonomy (what Habermas calls subjective freedom) in one of two ways. First, following the *classical liberalism* famously articulated by John Locke (1632–1704) and other seventeenth-century natural law theorists, it might be thought that reason (acting as the voice of Nature or God) dictates a list of immutable rights. The problem with this approach is that it violates the principle of moral autonomy, which makes obligation contingent on free consent. Even if we think of reason as speaking on behalf of our higher (noumenal) selves (Kant's formulation) we are still stuck with the problem that the rights our

12. H. L. A. Hart, *The Concept of Law,* 2nd ed. (Oxford: Clarendon Press, 1991).

higher selves dictate to us (and to which we rationally consent) are unchanging. But rights are not unchanging; they evolve within a rational learning process in response to new social problems. Another difficulty with the classical liberal approach is its monologism. Habermas argues that he can feel confident that the rights he legislates to himself also obligate other persons only insofar as they are the product of a publicly demonstrable and *discursively* achieved *general* consensus.

The other popular way of adducing and justifying basic rights—the *civic-republican* approach most famously articulated by Jean-Jacques Rousseau (1712–78) in *On the Social Contract* (1762)—appeals to democratic consensus. This approach is also problematic. To begin with, it presumes that democratic consensus merely affirms what each individual has already decided in private. Consensus is then explained in terms of a convergence of private opinions that reflect a shared ethos. But modern pluralistic societies lack such an ethos. In any case, no particular ethos, or factual consensus by a limited group of persons, can establish the universality of basic human rights; indeed, given the fallibility of collective judgment, the rights they agree on might in fact unfairly discriminate against some persons in favor of others.

In sum, neither classical liberalism nor civic republicanism satisfactorily explains basic rights. As Habermas sees it, both explanations still bear the traces of a subject-centered philosophy of consciousness. That is, they view rights as the monological choice of a *unitary will*—either that of the private individual who appeals to her own rational intuitions or that of the public, regarded as a people who are already in agreement. By deriving basic rights exclusively from abstract moral reason or ethical life, they ignore an important fact: basic rights are legal rights and as such must be *discursively* defined in light of a particular polity's ethical self-understanding. Failure to appreciate this fact merely reinforces the impression that the freedom of the individual is essentially opposed to the democratic self-determination of the people.

The discourse theoretic strategy for explaining rights *does* appreciate this fact, and that is why it insists on regulating democratic discourse in accordance with the *unchosen* normative ideals of DE. DE cannot prevent democratic majorities from changing the law, which may not satisfy those who think that the scope and meaning of rights must be permanently fixed, but it can prevent these majorities from doing so in ways that violate the rights of individuals. Democracy constrained by principles of moral right thus provides some predictability in the law, just not the rigid predictability that liberal rationalism and civic republicanism once hoped to secure.

The System of Rights

We seem to have stumbled on a paradox: democracy cannot be a legitimate source of rights unless it in turn is limited by rights. In order to avoid the appearance of *bad circularity* (democracy limiting/legitimating itself) or *infinite regress* (democracy A being limited/legitimated by democracy B), Habermas proposes to trace the legitimacy of democratic decisions to two interpenetrating legitimating grounds: real (factual) democratic consent and norms of discourse that endow citizens with equal rights. Taken together these two legitimating grounds yield what Habermas calls the *principle of democracy* (PD). With respect to its ideal ground, (PD) specifies a *prepolitical* (necessary and unchosen) norm that limits democratic decision making from the outside. Habermas says that that each of us can ascertain the validity of this ideal on our own (viz., monologically). This can be done by deducing (PD) from the concept of *legal form* (LF) and the principle of discourse (D). In turn, (LF) and (D) can be derived from the conditions of modernity. (LF) is indispensable to the functioning of modern capitalist economies and administrative bureaucracies; (D), by contrast, is indispensable to the possibility of modern forms of discourse and communicative action.

Let us examine this argument more closely. (LF) states that the function of law is to permit legal subjects—a class left undefined—the right to pursue their ends in a legally limited manner, free from interference. In order for this function to be realized in a way that fulfills the minimal conditions for a rule of law, laws must be publicly promulgated, sufficiently defined so that legal subjects can predict their application, and applied to prospective conduct (thus ruling out retroactive laws). (D) states that "just those action norms are valid to which all possibly affected persons could agree as participants in rational discourse" (*BFN* 107). Taken together, (LF) and (D) imply (PD): "only those [freedom-granting] statutes may claim legitimacy that can meet with the assent of all citizens in a discourse process of legislation that in turn has been legally constituted" (*BFN* 110). While (LF) entails individual legal rights and (D) specifies their equal (universal and inclusive) application to all citizens, (PD) certifies their legitimacy: *everyone* affected by a statute that directly or indirectly bears on the scope of universally applicable rights must be capable of rationally accepting it as advancing the interests of each person *equally* or, when this cannot be done, as promoting the fairest compromise among competing interests. Legitimate statutes, in other words, cannot discriminate against the rights of any citizen and they must balance competing interests fairly.

Here we notice an important advance in Habermas's thinking. In earlier writings, he conceived of (D) and (DE) as ideas that could not be adequately understood apart from the moral principle of universalizability (U). Now, however, he conceives (D) as a more abstract norm that is neutral with respect to different types of discourse and bargaining. Most important, he regards (D) as informing both (U) and (PD).[13] Unlike (U), (PD) is not a rule of argumentation

---

13. Apel argues that Habermas's "branching architechtonics" creates problems for his defense of universal human rights. Because human rights are not directly derived from DE but from democratic law, their status is contingent on political power. K.-O. Apel, "Regarding the Relationship of

but a rule mandating that formal decision procedures for making and applying laws obey (discursive) norms of inclusive democratic deliberation. (PD) thus extends beyond moral discourses pertaining to universal rights and applies to the legal institutionalization of diverse kinds of discourses (moral, ethical, pragmatic, and judicial-applicative) and types of strategic bargaining that ought to inform decision procedures across a broad spectrum of political bodies: public spheres, legislatures, courts, and executive agencies. Unlike (U), (PD) does not explain the moral justice of norms that already have an intuitive (natural) force within everyday life. Rather, it explains the *legitimacy* of legal decisions that are expressly made for a variety of purposes, only some of which draw their content from natural morality. (PD) shows how communicative rationality is embodied in the laws that regulate parliamentary and judicial procedures, and it shows how law itself—or rather the rule of law—is conceptually constituted with reference to this same rationality. In this respect, (PD) is more *reflexive* than (U); whereas (U) constitutes a quasi-transcendental procedure that operates on an entirely different level than the substantive norms it tests, (PD) does not; that is, the rules it lays down for law making—such as rules for regulating political representation, electing candidates, regulating parliamentary debate, and so on—are themselves products of law making.

We here see how Habermas's trilevel discourse theoretic explanation of rights splits the difference between *liberal* and *civic-republican* explanations. The first level involves a philosophical deduction of basic categories of rights from the functional concept of modern law (LF) and the normative idea of rational justification (D), thus securing the minimal liberal requirement (the rule of law in which rights apply to everyone equally). The second level involves the political process of realizing (or interpreting) these abstract principles of right in terms of constitutional rights—the civic-republican founding where more robust liberal and political rights first make their appearance in accordance with a preliminary implementation of democracy (PD). The third level involves multiple processes of legislation, adjudication, and executive enforcement—the full implementation of (PD), in which liberal and political rights are statutorily defined by elected representatives (thereby enhancing the opportunity for their equal exercise through the provision of social rights) and further specified by judges and administrators.

Habermas begins by deducing three categories of basic rights that are essential to any modern legal code. The distinctive thing about this deduction is its procedural nature. Instead of appealing to substantive arguments about basic needs and capabilities that ought to be protected by right, Habermas appeals

---

Morality, Law and Democracy: On Habermas's *Philosophy of Law* (1992) from a Transcendental-Pragmatic Point of View," in *Habermas and Pragmatism*, ed. M. Aboulafia, M. Bookman, and C. Kemp (New York: Routledge, 2002), 17–30. Habermas concedes that he may have underestimated the extent to which human rights have a unique moral justification that transcends democracy (224).

only to the formal concept of modern law (LF) and the formal concept of discursive justification (D). Applied to legal rights, (D) functions as a premise from which the following rights categories can be derived (in descending order of necessity):

1. Subjective rights (permissions) to act freely, without constraint
2. Citizenship rights to political membership
3. Rights to have one's rights adjudicated according to due process
4. Political rights to participate in legislating rights
5. Social rights to the background conditions requisite for effectively exercising rights 1–4.

Categories 1–4 possess an unconditional conceptual necessity that Habermas characterizes as "equiprimordial." Applied to the modern concept of a legal right, (D) immediately yields the first and most basic category of *subjective* rights: equal (negative) rights to individual liberty, or noninterference in the pursuit of self-chosen ends. The second category of *citizenship* rights follows conceptually from the fact that liberty rights are claims recognized by a legal community. When combined with liberty rights, citizenship rights entail a human right to change one's citizenship status through emigration. The third category of *due process* rights follows conceptually from the fact that legal rights are claims that can be adjudicated and enforced through recognizable legal processes.

Taken together, rights to liberty, citizenship, and due process constitute what we mean by a valid *legal code*. Generated monologically (i.e., by conceptual analysis) the legal code comprises only a set of abstract principles or "unsaturated placeholders" for rights. In order to get a substantively prescriptive bill of rights, members of a constitutional convention need to apply this code to their own political deliberation. Here the principle of discourse (D) is applied a second time. Whereas it had been used to derive the bare category of an *equal* actionable legal right, it is now used to derive *legitimate* (binding) rights; namely, both the scope and binding force of rights must be conceived as being the outcome of democratic legislation. Although the categorical scheme of rights that limits democracy from the outside is deduced authoritatively from the bare concept of law and equal citizenship, its concrete interpretation and elaboration in the form of a system of prescriptive permissive rights must be adduced democratically. This entails a fourth category of political rights. Herein lies the basis for human rights to speak out, associate, and publish, all of which can be interpreted as negative rights, as well as positive rights to run for public office, elect leaders of one's choice, and vote in elections. Thus there exists, as Habermas puts it, an "internal relation between human rights and popular sovereignty" (*BFN* 123).

Finally, because rights 1–4 cannot be effectively and equally exercised by persons who suffer from extreme need or insecurity, Habermas adduces as a fifth category of rights—equal rights to the opportunities and resources necessary for exercising rights 1–4, including "basic rights to the provision of living conditions that are socially, technologically, and ecologically safeguarded" (*BFN* 123). Importantly, whereas Habermas insists that the first four categories of rights are "justified absolutely" in relation to the concept of modern law and as such must be entrenched in constitutional law, he observes that the last category of welfare rights—under which we might include subsistence—is justified only "relatively" and contingently. (As we shall see, this claim is problematic to the extent that Habermas regards *human rights* as extensions of *constitutional rights*.)

To return to the main strand of Habermas's argument, the lesson we learn from this derivation of rights disposes us to reject the simple views propounded by legal positivists and natural law theorists. The subjective right to do whatever one wants (*private autonomy*) does not require that one exercise one's political rights (*public autonomy*). One can simply relate to the law strategically as a coercive boundary condition that must be conformed to on pain of sanction—hence the apparent opposition between individual freedom and democracy. However, such a strategic attitude cannot be the *predominant* attitude that citizens have toward the law without risking considerable instability. It must always be possible for most citizens to relate to the legal system as a whole as morally just, even if we cannot relate this way to particular laws taken in isolation. For Habermas, this happens only to the extent that citizens see the law as the outcome of a democratic process in which they find their own will represented.

Negative and Positive Rights (Duties)

In deducing the system of *legal* rights, Habermas has shown that private and public autonomy are *co-original,* or conceptually linked. This implies that political rights are not conceptually secondary to rights guaranteeing individual freedoms. Still, as we have seen, the system of legal rights does imply a hierarchy, insofar as the fifth category of rights (to social welfare) is not as conceptually essential to the system as the other categories.

This hierarchy proves problematic when we later consider Habermas's theory of human rights, which he regards as a species of legal rights. As legal rights, human rights are essentially defined as permissions to act free from constraint. This formulation—in terms of a permissive notion of freedom—may not be very helpful in understanding our human right to participate politically (since it presumes an authority, higher than that of the people, who is permitting them to participate). The formulation may be even less helpful in trying to understand our human right to welfare; for example, how are we to understand that a child's right to education permits—rather compels—the child to be educated? In order to see why Habermas's assimilation of human rights to the category of legal rights is problematic for other reasons as well, we need to turn to Habermas's discussion of moral rights; for it may be that human rights are best understood as moral rights instead of as legal rights.

To begin with, in Habermas's account of legal rights, we note a symmetry between negative and positive rights that parallels a similar distinction in his account of moral rights. Corresponding to private moral autonomy is *negative freedom,* which is legally guaranteed by having the right to think, choose, and act free from interference; corresponding to public autonomy is *positive freedom,* which is legally guaranteed by the right to have the opportunities, capabilities, and resources that *enable* (or *empower*) thinking, choosing, and acting. For the sake of simplicity, let us call the two types of rights that correspond to negative and positive freedom negative and positive rights. Examples of negative rights include most civil rights (the right to freedom of conscience, the right to speak out, the right to move freely from place to place, the right to associate with whomever one wants) and some economic rights (the right to acquire and exchange property, the right to enter into contracts, etc.). By contrast, the political right to participate in democratic law making is a positive right, for law making involves protecting and defining the scope of one's freedom. So, too, are rights to education, health, welfare, and social security. Without these resources, the physical and mental capabilities that enable one to deliberate, to choose, and to act would be nonexistent.

Citing T. H. Marshall's famous essay "Citizenship and Social Class" (1950),[14] Habermas notes that negative economic rights were the first to be recognized, followed by civil rights, political rights, and welfare rights (*BFN* 503–4). From this genetic perspective, it might appear that economic rights (private autonomy) are more fundamental than civil and political rights (public autonomy), but Habermas denies this; from a conceptual perspective, political and civil rights are equally essential to realizing the concept of legal right. Nonetheless, he accepts Marshall's genetic subordination of social rights as conceptually correct. When we turn to his discussion of *moral* rights in *Justification and Application* (1991), a different picture emerges. In this work, he emphatically denies that there is any conceptual reason—at least from the standpoint of moral theory—for privileging one kind of right over the other. Indeed, his general view is that negative and positive rights are complementary and realize each other. Thus, economic rights cannot be *adequately guaranteed* apart from civil and political rights; and neither of these can be enjoyed by everyone equally unless everyone has equal rights to education, social security, and health care. Conversely, civil, political, and social rights are meaningless unless persons have property rights with respect to their own bodies and possessions (*BFN* 401–2).

Despite this complementarity, deontological *moral* theory since the time of Kant has traditionally privileged negative rights and duties over positive

14. T. H. Marshall, *Citizenship and Social Class, and Other Essays* (Cambridge: Cambridge University Press, 1950), 1–85.

rights and duties. In Habermas's opinion, this error follows from conceiving moral reasoning monologically. If, following Kant, we imagine that moral reasoning requires abstracting from contingent material interests (such as interests in health, education, and welfare) and identifying with a pure "rational will" that is given within each of us as a matter of preestablished harmony, then we must also imagine that the main rational interest each of us possesses in common with others is our interest in protecting our *negative freedom* against interference from others. By contrast, if we assume that moral reasoning reflects a higher (discursive) form of communicative reason in which the *integrity* of the individual is bound up with that of the society to which she belongs, then our rational interest will include preserving her political and social integrity as well, which will require protecting her *positive access to subsistence* (JA 64).

From this discourse theoretic perspective, the traditional reasons given for privileging negative over positive rights—that only the former are *unconditionally valid, determinate* in their prescriptive content, and *unambiguous* in their addressees—prove unconvincing. Traditionally, it has been supposed that our negative duty to refrain from harming or constraining others is unconditional in comparison to our positive duty to (say) provide needy persons with the material resources necessary for leading a minimally decent life. For Kant, the latter duties are "imperfect" in that individuals are permitted to exercise a wide degree of discretion as to when and to whom (and how much) they lend assistance, depending on their capacity to give aid. Furthermore, it has been argued that while negative duties are determinate in what they command and unambiguous with regard to whom they command—the command against killing other persons is unquestioningly addressed to each of us—positive duties are not. For example, if there is a positive duty to aid starving people, who among us is responsible for fulfilling it? And by what positive measures should it be fulfilled—famine relief, developmental assistance, elimination of incentives that produce corrupt regimes that rob from their own people, empowering more women in developing countries through education and better access to jobs, redistribution of social product, transformation of global capitalism, or some combination of the above?

Habermas argues that differences between negative and positive duties diminish once we realize that, from a discourse theoretic perspective, the most basic duty inscribed in the moral point of view is not the duty to leave others alone but the duty to *respect their integrity* as fellow participants in a communicative community structured in accordance with justice and solidarity. This duty entails not only a negative duty to refrain from harming and constraining others but a positive duty to treat others with equal respect. Even Kant's list of negative duties, such as the duty not to lie, retains a positive valence insofar as we are commanded to keep our promises and to tell the truth (JA 66–67).

Second, Habermas notes that the unconditional nature of negative duties is largely heuristic and not conceptual, since even norms that command negative duties at best possess prima facie (conditional) validity until they are applied to concrete circumstances. The command forbidding killing, for example, admits of exceptions in cases involving justified self-defense. Indeed, when the question of their positive enforcement arises, negative duties can be just as indeterminate in what they prescribe as positive duties. Persons not only have a right not to be interfered with, but they have this right as a claim against the rest of us, a claim we are obligated to positively guarantee. Questions about how to best guarantee this negative right raise pragmatic questions about who should be responsible for doing so and by what means. The need to safeguard populations from terrorist attacks shows that the law-enforcement measures and agencies best equipped for implementing security rights are costly and controversial to the point of being quite indeterminate (*JA* 64).

Indeed, all of these considerations simply reinforce a point made earlier. It matters not whether moral rights are conceived negatively or positively; all such rights are conditional, indeterminate, and ambiguous. For this very reason their capacity to effectively coordinate social life requires that they be supplemented by legal procedures that delegate governmental responsibility for defining and implementing them. As *legal* rights, they cease to be claims that are addressed only to other individuals and now become *institutional* claims addressed to society as a whole (*JA* 68). Once this transformation occurs, the distinction between negative and positive rights ceases to be hard and fast.

At best, we can say (following Habermas) that certain kinds of negative rights are generally more important than other negative rights and that certain kinds of positive rights are more basic than other positive rights. For instance, taking economic rights—or speaking in a more restricted manner, property rights understood as negative freedoms—the freedom to acquire resources necessary for one's subsistence is more basic to communicative interaction than the freedom to own productive assets and employ wage earners. Indeed, as I argue in chapter 9, the negative right to acquire and exchange "productive assets" is arguably less prior than a positive right of laborers (and of the broader community who also has a stake in the holding) to democratically order their productive assets and powers. In general, the most important rights revolve around securing just those conditions of individual agency that facilitate participation within a moral community structured by communicative reciprocity and solidarity. For this reason, the negative right to act without interference is not *morally prior*, even if it is more basic from the initial standpoint of what modern *legal form* requires (*JA* 66).

Constitutional Foundations

We will return to the preceding account of moral rights and their complementary relationship in discussing Habermas's theory of human rights. Before doing so, however, let us continue tracing the logical implications embedded in his system of legal rights. The system of legal rights provides the blueprint for a liberal democratic constitution. But this idea is paradoxical; if democracy bestows legitimacy on the law, then how can the law bestow legitimacy on *it*? Or, to reverse the question, how can democracy bestow legitimacy on its own constitutional foundation?[15] No doubt legitimate constitutional conventions are themselves small-scale exercises in democracy. But what could guarantee the legitimacy of this small-scale exercise in democracy—the popular constitution of a people's political will and identity—if not another constitution?

As we have seen, in order to avoid the infinite regress problem, Habermas argues that democratic constitution making is already legitimated *from the outside* by (D). He now argues that (D) informs the constitutional convention *from the inside*. Some constitutional rights—namely those that correspond to equal civil and political rights (equal freedom of speech and equal freedom to participate in political deliberation and decision) are *conceptually* (logically and necessarily) implied in the constitutive rules of democratic practice. Such rights do not regulate (limit or constrain) democracy after the fact—such as parliamentary rules governing the amount of time speakers can speak—but instead constitute it, or *enable* it to come into existence at the outset. They are present in some quasi-legal (or protolegal) capacity at the very moment of the constitution's democratic founding, thereby lending this founding the minimum degree of *procedural justice* necessary for establishing at least part of its legality and legitimacy (*TT* 118).

Procedural justice alone, however, cannot resolve all justice-related issues. Choices regarding political membership are only partly procedural. The all-white, male property-owning elites who drafted the U.S. Constitution may have violated a norm of inclusion when they excluded Native Americans and slaves from representation (the latter were only counted in determining the representation of Southern whites) and left the determination of who was permitted to vote for federal officials up to the individual states. But the dominant white population typically accepted the view—also shared by most Native Americans—that tribes were separate nations; and many whites (especially Southerners) were dubious about the full humanity of their slaves.

Procedural norms of inclusion cannot tell us whether or not the U.S. Constitution was legitimate at its founding. The fact that the constitution violated provisions for amendment laid down in the original Articles of Confederation, however, is the least of the many indictments against its legitimacy. In retrospect, the violent incorporation of Native American territories into the union and the Constitution's explicit reference to slavery and the slave trade count against its legitimacy. This follows once we assume, as Habermas does, that voluntary full inclusion is a necessary condition for legitimacy.

---

15. F. I. Michelman, "Constitutional Authorship," in *Constitutionalism: Philosophical Foundations,* ed. L. Alexander (Cambridge: Cambridge University Press, 1998), 91.

Habermas therefore maintains that, far from being procedurally legitimated once and for all at the moment of its founding, the U.S. Constitution—like any constitution that imperfectly embodies the discursive ideals implicit in democracy—acquired legitimacy in the course of future democratic emendations that made it more inclusive. The Philadelphia convention was but the first attempt at actualizing its normative ideals. Subsequent statutory legislation, adjudication, and higher law making (amendment) set in motion a never-ending cycle of (re)justification and (re)application in which basic rights were expanded and their beneficiaries made more inclusive (*TT* 122). This dynamic process—built into the very fabric of law as an expression of ideal principles—leads Habermas to conclude that a country's constitution, far from being a conservative deadweight on future generations' right to self-determination, is itself a *revolutionary project*. Future generations can feel bound by the original constitutional contract ratified by the Founders because they themselves are party to this contract as soon as they reinterpret its guiding principles in accordance with their contemporary understanding of their own political ethos and the deeper universal moral ideas that inform that ethos. In essence, future generations *retroactively* legitimate the constitution because they *progressively* constitute it. Instead of radically breaking with the constitution in a manner that would imply an interregnum in the rule of law—a state of legal anarchy that one normally associates with revolutionary foundings that often possess questionable legitimacy—"the continuation of the founding event," Habermas concludes, "can be understood in the long run as a self-correcting learning process."

Human Rights: Subsistence as a Test Case for a Juridical Conception of Rights

Let me now digress from Habermas's argument in *BFN* to conclude with a discussion that, while chiefly germane to international law and cosmopolitan governance (whose fuller examination falls under the purview of chapter 10), exemplifies the penultimate extension of Habermas's juridical conception of rights and, as such, represents a test case for determining the adequacy of that conception as a whole as it applies to the entire spectrum of legal rights. The discussion I have in mind—concerning the status of human rights in Habermas's philosophy—has already been touched on in my examination of his account of the differences between moral and legal rights. Habermas contends that modern human rights descend from the basic legal rights enshrined by the American and French constitutional foundations in the eighteenth century. The question before us is whether viewing human rights in this manner *exclusively* (as extensions of constitutional legal rights) does not bias them in favor of certain categories of human rights, thereby placing this view in opposition to Habermas's own understanding of *moral* rights, understood as *complementary and equiprimordial*.[16] The difficulty with this opposition is that the UN's Universal Declaration of Human Rights—which Habermas endorses—asserts that human rights are moral aspirations. Although this appears obvious in the case of some human rights mentioned by the UDHR (for example, human rights to recreation and leisure), other human rights—such as the right not to be enslaved, tortured, or imprisoned without trial—appear to be better understood as legal claims. Yet other rights—such as the right to education and the right to subsistence—are not easily translated into legal language of permissions that Habermas identifies with classical liberal and political rights.

In fact, there are several reasons why human rights should not be understood exclusively as legal claims. In addition to the above reason, certain kinds of human rights shortfalls stem from cultural factors that are often recalcitrant to legal remedies. Indeed, the impersonal and otherwise legal status of what I call structural injustices makes it impossible to assign legal responsibility to government officials for some human rights shortfalls. An examination of subsistence shortfalls in patriarchal sweatshop settings illustrates both of these limits. A moral concept of human rights, by contrast, conceives these shortfalls not as legal violations requiring intervention by policing agencies and court-supervised determination of personal culpability aimed at punishment, restitution, and compensation, but as shortfalls requiring potentially radical social reform.

Furthermore, as a related matter, the moral justification and meaning of human rights refers not only to harms that persons have endured at the hands of governments but also—and more fundamentally—to shortfalls in the secure enjoyment of basic goods that persons need in order to cultivate their basic humanity. The critical reflection (or deliberation) that progressively clarifies the meaning of basic human capabilities must unfold as the collective enterprise of humanity itself, as it stretches democratic impartiality beyond all spatial and temporal limits.

So construed, human rights designate goals or standards against which we judge *shortfalls in basic goods* that any fully civilized society ought to provide its citizens. This *exclusively moral* understanding of human rights thus designates an *aspiration,* as the preamble to the UDHR puts it, that is urged on all of us to realize at some unspecified time in the future, without regard to our citizenship or official status. In turn, the duties and responsibilities that flow from this aspiration emerge in the course of a global dialogue concerning our own human capabilities and society's failure to develop them equally and inclusively. In the words of Habermas, human rights "function...as sensors for exclusionary practices exercised in their name" (*PC* 120).

---

16. "Human Rights are juridical *by their very nature.* What lends them the appearance of moral rights is not their content, and most especially not their structure, but rather their mode of validation, which points beyond the legal order of nation states" (*IO* 190).

By contrast, when considered as a *decision procedure* for resolving current normative conflicts—and not as a process of enlightenment—Habermas's discourse theory inclines toward a different understanding of human rights. This is evident in Habermas's belief that human rights preeminently designate *legal claims*, reflected in his assertion that "liberal (in the narrower sense) basic rights make up the core of human rights declarations" and so "acquire the *additional* meaning of liberal *rights against the state* held by private legal subjects" (*BFN* 174). The fact that human rights are claims against juridical institutions is further underscored by Habermas when he asserts that "the discourse of human rights is also set up to provide *every* voice with a hearing," presumably in a court of law under the supervision of either a constitutional state or a constitutional international body (or both).

I argue that Habermas's failure to adequately clarify the moral status of human rights prevents him from appreciating the unconditional moral ground of subsistence rights in basic human needs and capabilities. In fact, his two-track model of democracy (as informal process of moral deliberation and as formal procedure for conclusively resolving disagreements) shows how political discourse as such—and not just the legal policies legitimated by such discourse—can remove ideological obstacles to the secure enjoyment of human rights. By focusing almost exclusively on the juridical notion of human rights as legal claims—and virtually ignoring the moral notion of human rights as aspirations—Habermas neglects what is perhaps most distinctive about a discourse theory of human rights, namely, the progressive genesis of human rights in a collective process of enlightenment.

Most philosophers have held that rights are claims of one kind or another. This preference is understandable given the gravity we customarily accord to rights as singling out our most important duties to act (or forbear from acting) in certain ways. Although there is much debate about whether all rights entail duties or whether rights are best understood as interests or aspirations, one thing is clear. An aspiration toward a good does not specify an agent responsible for bringing about that good. Thus, although many rights listed among the articles of the UDHR are best described as only aspirations, the rights that have been enforced through international peacekeeping intervention have been treated as legal claims that subjects have against governments and powerful leaders.

Habermas's deep appreciation for the necessity of a global human rights regime reflects this understanding as well. In the quotation cited earlier he designates "liberal rights"—or rights to freedom of movement, of property ownership, of speech and association, and the like—as the core human rights. These "negative rights"—or permissions to act without interference—are claims that are directed against governments. The most important institutions Habermas singles out in enforcing these rights—international courts of law (such as the International Criminal Court) and international peacekeeping bodies (the UN Security Council)—are instituted precisely to uphold these rights against severe and widespread "violations."

Here, then, is Habermas's main reason for holding that human rights are legal rights. The liberal rights that constitute the core of human rights as Habermas understands it are conceptually and functionally embedded in modern law, and their enforcement is so crucial to the very existence of society that it cannot remain contingent on the caprice of private "moral" conscience. As a related matter, human rights that are only moral rights suffer from the defects of a "state of nature": their precise meaning, individual application (adjudication), and coercive enforcement are uncertain and subject to the kinds of political opportunism that critics of human rights, such as Carl Schmitt, are quick to seize on. Without a legal decision procedure to resolve conflicting interpretations, judgments, and actions, the discourse of human rights quickly degenerates into an abyss of endless disputation.[17]

Finally, given the need to *legitimate* specific human rights interpretations, judgments, and enforcements, legal certainty is not enough. Discourse theory insists that these "decisions" find support in a universal consensus. Ideally, a global public sphere would persuade the leaders of nations and international law-enforcement bodies to interpret and implement human rights in accord with evolving public opinion.

We can argue the details of Habermas's vision, but probably most of us would agree that a global human rights regime that would interpret, apply, and enforce juridically conceived "liberal" human rights is highly desirable for the reasons he mentions. At the same time, it is important to note that, for Habermas, a juridical understanding of human rights is not freestanding of moral argumentation in the way that Rawls and some other prominent theorists have argued. Human rights, he notes, are *Janus-faced*: they are legal rights that are grounded not in the political values, ends, and policies of a particular people but in universal morality.

That said, it remains unclear whether, according to Habermas, human rights are moral rights that embody aspirations. Habermas's endorsement of Ronald Dworkin's understanding of law as "interpretation," which we will examine later, suggests an affirmative response to this query (*BFN* 197). According to Dworkin, the meaning of any concrete legal right (rule) is always circumscribed by a coherent body of abstract moral principles. Incorporating this interpretative account of law into his own discourse theory of law, Habermas underscores the "aspirational"—indeed "revolutionary"—nature of constitutional law as an indefinite project of dialogical reflection (*EFP* 45). Democratic public opinion "interprets" the moral content of its own legal presuppositions. This

17. A human rights regime must balance two conflicting demands for prescriptive specificity (fair-warning conditions implicit in the rule of law) *and* nonspecificity (flexible multicultural interpretation within local jurisdictions). Federal systems can reconcile these demands because national legislatures already specify the law in statutory legislation—legislation that Habermas finds wanting at the global level. For him, specifying human rights will fall to international courts that are representative of and sympathetic to a wide variety of global public opinion (see chapter 10).

content in turn circulates through parliamentary and judicial bodies, where further discussion sharpens its statutory meaning and force. The progressive inclusion and emancipation of legal subjects through the extension of rights increasingly expands and enriches the scope of democratic public opinion, thereby leading to a new cycle of moral enlightenment and political reform.

Habermas's understanding of human rights as "sensors" for exclusion, which I cited earlier, recalls this dialectic. Therefore, arguing on the basis of Habermas's discourse theoretical account of constitutional law (which he extends to cosmopolitan human rights law), it is not implausible to hold that human rights also designate moral aspirations. In any case, an understanding of human rights as aspirations does not obviously conflict with an understanding of human rights as claims.

The question now before us is whether a juridical understanding of human rights can adequately explain the importance of specifically second- and third-generation human rights that fall outside of the classical liberal model. Take the human right to subsistence. Assuming that such a human right exists and can be philosophically defended, it is far from obvious that its force and meaning can be explained juridically. As we shall see, this right is not as integral to modern law as liberal rights are. Nor can shortfalls in its secure enjoyment be as easily described as "violations" of laws (domestic or international) that have been perpetrated by governments.

The example of sweatshops illustrates how the right to subsistence can be diminished—without being violated—by impersonal economic and cultural structures for which no agent can be held responsible. In the case of sweatshops, we can distinguish between several layers of legal rights violations. First, there are violations of workers' *domestic* rights directly caused by employer disregard for national minimum wage, workplace safety, and collective bargaining laws. Second, there are violations of workers' *human* rights caused by government officials and their proxies in deliberately allowing—or in extreme cases, mandating—violations of international human rights conventions.

However, in addition to these legal violations we detect other causes contributing to a shortfall in sweatshop workers' secure enjoyment of subsistence. Some of these emanate from the *lawful*, normal operations of a market economy in which sweatshops are forced to operate on a precariously thin margin of profitability in order to meet the demands of multinational retailers and their affluent clients. The chain of sweatshop production often ends in a household where a family subcontractor (the family patriarch) is legally defined as self-employed—outside the framework of legal protections. Here the distinction between employer and employed is totally effaced; the patriarch functions as the boss who oversees his wife and children.[18] Working at the margin—or at

18. See Saba Gul Khattak's "Subcontracted Work and Gender Relations: The Case of Pakistan," in *The Hidden Assembly Line: Gender Dynamics of Subcontracted Work in a Global Economy,* ed. R. Balakrishnan (Bloomfield, CT: Kumarian Press, 2002), 35–62.

solvency, that is, minimum subsistence—the patriarch dominates and exploits his family, even as he is dominated and exploited by those who subcontract his "labor." In a context where collective bargaining does not apply, traditional gender roles function to maintain labor discipline. So here we encounter yet another institutional impediment to securing women's right to subsistence.

As a product of custom, the patriarchal family that anchors the domestic sweatshop is not exclusively a legal institution. This explains why the state encounters so much resistance when it intervenes in family life. As an institution that stands partly outside legal and economic systems, it conforms to a different logic: that of a more-or-less voluntary association based on mutual recognition, or what Habermas calls communicative reciprocity. Arguments in support of the family as an institution that properly belongs within the "private" sphere partly play on the social contractarian ideal of familial solidarity based on open and undistorted communication between constituent members. These arguments provide a prima facie warrant for subjecting any legal interference into the family to the highest scrutiny. However, the state's burden of proof in justifying its regulation of the family is often not hard to meet, for the traditional patriarchal family is anything but a consensual relationship based on open and undistorted communication.

Here we have what is perhaps the most direct application of discourse theory in the area of human rights enforcement. The most visible forms of familial domination are personal and interactional, often involving physical and psychological coercion. Less visible cultural structures that legitimate this interaction, however, are institutional, rooted in shared expectations about childbearing, child rearing, and the distribution of spousal roles. In cases where fulfilling these roles diminishes secure access to basic goods necessary for subsistence, we may speak of human rights abuse. Here the presumed claimant is seldom in a position to press her claim, and may not recognize it, due to her adaptive preference for maintaining the status quo. Even if she could, it would be unclear to whom she would press it. But an institutional account of human rights can remedy this problem: it is the religious or conventional institution in which these roles are imposed (through the sheer weight of traditional authority) that stands indicted.

A distinctly nonjuridical, pedagogical form of human rights discourse is required to remedy this shortfall. Women must come to see themselves and their relationship to their religion and community differently. Because the needs for community and religion (or an equivalent source for meaning, purpose, and identity) are basic needs as well as capabilities that can be more or less developed, simple emancipation from tradition is unrealistic. Instead, political pedagogy must be aimed at showing—in a manner that is respectful of women's cultural identities—that women can become economically self-reliant, or acquire roles that provide them with more secure access to subsistence and therewith provide them with greater equality within their inherited cultural identities. This is one measure that must be undertaken within the domestic sweatshop industry, where all too often traditional gender roles conspire to victimize women, who are under rule and thumb of their husbands (who, of course, are also victimized in turn by those who subcontract their labor).

The domestic sweatshop example perfectly illustrates two weaknesses of a juridical understanding of human rights: its tendency to emphasize what Thomas Pogge calls an "interactional" conception of human rights that cannot easily accommodate impersonal institutional impediments to the secure enjoyment of rights, and its corresponding embrace of a "liability" model of responsibility that focuses on punishment and compensation (distributive justice) rather than on political reform aimed at eliminating class and gender domination.

The interactional conception of human rights undoubtedly captures a significant class of human rights violations. The most visible human rights violations, involving genocide, ethnic cleansing, political repression of parties and collective bargaining agents, and so on, are perpetrated by governments and their unofficial proxies (such as civilian militias). These violations arise from person-to-person interactions that have been commanded (or permitted) from on high. The victims here have uncontestable claims against individual leaders whom they hold liable for depriving them of a basic liberty. So blatant and extreme is their suffering and servitude that we ourselves feel a deep solidarity with them. This "negative" solidarity, Habermas points out, is not similarly extended to the world's poor, for whom we feel a weaker "positive" solidarity (*DW* 79–80, 177–78, 139–42). For this reason, he endorses aggressive international "policing" intervention in grievous cases of violent repression but not in cases of poverty, whose remedies, he believes, fall within the province of a "global domestic policy" based on voluntary multilateral treaties.

Notice, too, that the interactional understanding of human rights assigns responsibility for human rights violations according to personal liability. This model defines harms as deviations from a *normal* background of conventionally sanctioned hazards that are causally traceable to the discrete actions of individual wrongdoers. The proper juridical reaction to holding someone personally liable for an overt crime is police intervention aimed at stopping the crime and apprehension, processing, and punishment of the perpetrator. Along with compensating the victim for her suffering, these remedies aim at restoring the status quo ante.

When we turn to the sweatshop example, we notice that the interactional/liability model only captures one aspect of a complex human rights shortfall. Following Henry Shue, let us provisionally describe a human right as a reasonable demand (claim or expectation) that others provide socially guaranteed protection against standard threats to a person's self-esteem as a human being.[19] In the patriarchal sweatshop, we see that government toleration of what

19. H. Shue, *Basic Rights: Subsistence, Affluence, and U.S. Foreign Policy*, 2nd ed. (Princeton: Princeton University Press, 1996). Shue criticizes Rawls's earlier neglect of a human right to subsistence (which Rawls later rectified in *The Law of Peoples*) by arguing that subsistence, security, and

at times amounts to forced confinement and labor (slavery) certainly fails to protect against a standard threat to a person's self-esteem as a human being. Here the interactional/liability model of human rights seems appropriate. It is not appropriate, however, when addressing the threats posed to the subsistence, freedom, and self-esteem of women workers caused by the structural workings of a capitalist economy whose law of competition forces a constant depression of wages to which only the most desperate submit. Add to this a patriarchal structure of domination that keeps women in slavelike servitude—partly with their own complicity—and we see that the standard threat to a person's self-esteem as a human being is also cultural and ideological.

The structural impediment to the reasonably secure enjoyment of a human right to subsistence implicates a complex web of global causes that are only partly explicable in terms of personal interaction and liability. True, one might hold liable the citizens who elect the leaders who appoint the bureaucrats who underwrite the multilateral treaties that maintain unjust trade, lending, and resource extraction agreements. But who does one hold responsible for capitalism and patriarchal culture?[20] These latter institutions arise from the

---

liberty rights complement one another (31). Although Shue maintains that political rights are al-most as basic as security and subsistence rights, he allows that it is theoretically conceivable that a benevolent dictator might guarantee the latter. Furthermore, Shue denies that cultural rights—the right to culture in general or the right to a particular culture—are as basic as rights to subsistence and security. However, in the second edition of *Basic Rights,* he concedes that access to educa-tion might be necessary for defending and securing basic rights. Following Habermas and Pogge (against Rawls) I would insist that liberal democratic rights are equally basic; following Kymlicka I would argue that cultural rights—and not just the right to education—are also basic, since an essential part of one's self-esteem, identity, and capacity for strong value judgment and choice (in the sense articulated by Charles Taylor and other communitarians) is freedom to practice the cultural folkways that one has inherited or chosen. For a defense of these claims, see D. Ingram, *Group Rights: Recognizing Equality and Difference* (Lawrence: University Press of Kansas, 2002), chap. 12; and D. Ingram, *Rights, Democracy, and Fulfillment in the Era of Identity Politics: Principled Compromises in a Compromised World* (Lanham, MD: Rowman and Littlefield, 2004), chaps. 6 and 7. See also Shue, *Basic Rights,* 74–75, 117–18, 163; and W. Kymlicka, *Liberalism, Community, and Culture* (Oxford: Oxford University Press, 1989).

20. Habermas (*IO* 122) opposes protectionism but endorses global regulation and redistribu-tion (see chapter 10). Thomas Pogge supports eliminating price subsidies and tariffs that enable de-veloped countries to protect their markets while dumping discounted commodities in poor coun-tries. T. Pogge, *World Poverty and Human Rights: Cosmopolitan Responsibilities and Reforms* (Cambridge: Polity Press, 2002), 18. He also supports an international ban on extending loans to, and purchasing natural resources from, undemocratic regimes (146). Finally, he and Charles Beitz have supported a tax on natural resources (what Pogge calls a global resources dividend), especially on resources whose consumption imposes environmental costs (196), the proceeds from which would be distributed to combat poverty. Alternative measures include reinstating import substitution models in place of export production (combined with protective tariffs) and replacing global capitalism with some form of global market socialism in which proceeds from tariffs would be returned to developing countries. D. Schweickart, "Global Poverty: Alternative Perspectives on What We Should Do—and Why," *Journal of Social Philosophy* 39/4 (2008): 471–91. Proceeding from discourse theoretic premises, Seyla Benhabib argues that theories (such as Beitz's and Pogge's) deploying Rawls's difference principle to justify elevating the world's worst off tend to misinter-pret the principle as a redistributive policy. Imposing such a policy on peoples, she insists, violates

unintended, aggregate effects of many actions extended over many centuries. Although their source is impersonal, their effect is not, for these structures create unequal opportunities for developing and exercising human capabilities between differently positioned groups of persons.[21]

I contend that the presence of unequal opportunities for developing and exercising human capabilities between differently positioned groups of persons can rise to the level of a severe human rights abuse. It suffices to note that what Iris Young calls the "social connectedness" of many differently positioned persons in contributing (however unwittingly) to the maintenance of, otherwise legal, human rights abusing economic and cultural structures calls for a nonjuridical response. To begin with, the abuse in question often does not rise to the level of a clear violation. Nevertheless, even when women are allowed a modicum of freedom and subsistence within the patriarchal sweatshop, so that there is no clear violation of their right to liberty and subsistence, we can hardly conclude that others have reasonably protected them against the standard likelihood that their liberty and subsistence will be threatened in the future. The degree of abuse is always relative, and protection against it never perfectly secured. Furthermore, the source of the abuse is not always susceptible to a legal remedy. It may be that massive legal reform is both necessary and sufficient to remedy the abusive injustices of a capitalist economy. However, it is unlikely that the same could be said of the abusive injustices of patriarchal culture. Changing culturally ingrained gender roles and misogynist ideologies in a way that might empower women to fight for improved working conditions has been at best only partly effected in places where it has been legally mandated. Change must also emerge from within a grassroots struggle over the meaning of culture itself, specifically regarding the basic capabilities whose equal development everyone is entitled to.

Is there a resource within Habermas's discourse theory that can justify a human right to subsistence as I have here presented it? Habermas himself recognizes that the right to subsistence is a human right, and there are important places where he develops what Pogge refers to as an "institutional" alternative to the interactional understanding of human rights that implicates the organization of society itself in abusing this right. Habermas specifically mentions legal institutions (specifically multilateral trade agreements and neoliberal economic agendas attached to lending requirements) in maintaining economic structures that contribute to poverty. For instance, despite his insistence that liberal rights

---

their right to democratic self-determination and neglects immigration as an alternative distributive mechanism (see chapter 8 of this book). Such applications of the difference principle ostensibly underestimate the diverse causes underlying poverty as well as the interpretative challenges in identifying the worst off. S. Benhabib, *The Rights of Others* (Cambridge: Cambridge University Press, 2003), chap. 3.

21. I. Young, "Responsibility, Social Connection, and Global Labor Justice," in *Global Challenges: War, Self-Determination, and Responsibility for Justice* (Cambridge: Polity, 2007), 159–86.

that protect negative liberty form the core of human rights, Habermas condemns neoliberal human rights regimes that restrict human rights to "negative liberties of citizens who acquire an 'immediate' status *vis-a-vis* the global economy" (*DW* 186). Combined with his scathing indictment of global poverty and inequality, this condemnation compels him to acknowledge a right to subsistence. Indeed, in addition to endorsing the UDHR,[22] he expressly mentions as basic "rights to the provision of living conditions that are socially, technologically, and ecologically safeguarded" (*BFN* 123).

But a problem now arises with regard to justifying this human right. Unlike Rawls, Habermas does not think that the mere presumption of an overlapping consensus among the world's peoples regarding a thin list of human rights suffices to secure them the proper respect they merit. A philosophical justification is necessary. Classical liberal and political rights, he believes, have such a justification without recurring to any grounds other than the a priori procedural categories specified by discourse theory. Social rights, by contrast, do not, and are at best contingent and derivative of classical liberal and political rights:

> From a normative standpoint, according "priority" to social and cultural basic rights does not make sense for the simple reason that such rights only serve to secure the "fair value" (Rawls) of liberal and political basic rights, i.e., the factual presuppositions for the equal opportunity to exercise individual rights.[23]

22. Article 25 lists a right to "a standard of living adequate for the health and well-being of [a person] and [his or her] family, including food, clothing, housing, medical care and necessary social services, and the right to security in the event of unemployment, sickness, disability, widowhood, old age or other lack of livelihood in circumstances beyond [one's] control."

23. *PC* 125. Habermas makes this assertion in response to a complaint made by the signatories to the 1993 Bangkok Declaration: Taiwan, China, Malaysia, and Singapore. This complaint questions the priority of rights over duties and, more important, the priority of civil and political rights over social and cultural rights. Reversing the Western privileging of classical, civil, and political human rights, the signatories to the declaration argued that postponing classical, civil, and political human rights for the sake of satisfying material needs is justifiable for two reasons: First, civil and political freedom is not as important to starving persons as subsistence, and therefore the former must be consequent on the latter. Second, civil and political freedom may obstruct economic progress by generating social conflict. Habermas does not deny that classical individual freedoms associated with modern capitalist conceptions of property and market exchange, as well as civil and political liberties, can cause the disintegration of traditional collectivist societies; nor does he deny that severely impoverished persons lack material resources and capabilities that enable them to enjoy classical, civil, and political rights. Rather than refute these objections to the Western conception and ranking of human rights, he notes that no country undergoing capitalist modernization can fail to institutionalize this legal conception of human rights. The unavoidable legal institutionalization of classical property rights and market freedoms that signatory nations to the Bangkok Declaration have already undertaken sets in motion an irrepressible demand for civil and political freedom. Free people demand not only efficient government but legitimate government. Furthermore, the prerequisites for democratic legitimation counterbalance the egoistic individualism unleashed by these rights; for they presuppose a high degree of solidarity among citizens who recognize themselves as masters of their own collective fate. It is this democratic equality that morally obligates citizens to guarantee everyone an equal right to subsistence in matters of education, health, security, and welfare.

Social and cultural rights, then, do not have the same status as liberal and political rights. At best, the right to demand protection against standard threats
to material well-being is a right that persons living within liberal and democratic orders can demand of their society to the extent that it is regarded as a
necessary condition for achieving civic equality. Another way of putting the
matter is to say that social and cultural rights are more conditional than civil
and political rights. Whereas the latter are necessary for possessing a minimal
degree of legal status, the former are not. Furthermore, given that Habermas
understands cosmopolitan human rights law in terms of an extension of constitutional law in which liberal and political rights are unconditional, we can
understand *these* rights as unconditional human rights. By contrast, the right
to subsistence as it is presented here is not justified intrinsically as an unconditional universal human right but instrumentally as a subsidiary right that
might be dispensed with without jeopardizing basic self-esteem.

Habermas's deduction of basic legal rights thus serves to reinforce the secondary status of subsistence rights once we take into account his further claim
that *human* rights are extensions of constitutional rights. Some constitutional
rights—namely those that correspond to equal civil and political rights (equal
freedom of speech and equal freedom to participate in political deliberation
and decision) are *conceptually* (logically and necessarily) implied in the constitutive rules of democratic practice, understood as a procedure of rational
discussion. Other constitutional rights—to private property, personal security,
freedom of movement, and indeed all the *classical* liberal rights that originally
occupied the attention of Locke and other liberal social contract theorists during the age of monarchy—are more directly related to the "grammar of the
legal code" (*PC* 117–18). These classical human rights, Habermas tells us, do
not "have [their] origins in morality, but rather bear the imprint of individual
liberties, hence of a specifically juridical concept" (*IO* 109). More precisely,
although such rights appear to be moral rights because of their universal validity, this is only apparently so. This is not to deny that classical human rights
are justified by moral arguments. But these arguments are unique in having an
institutional referent. Whereas moral arguments typically appeal to the respect
owed to persons in light of their humanity (i.e., their human capabilities and
needs), arguments in support of classical liberal rights arise in direct response
to violations of a juridical nature that emanate from the state (*BFN* 191).
Hence, unlike moral rights, which entail corresponding duties, liberal human
rights function as *permissions* (negative freedoms) to act without fear of government constraint. The positive freedoms (entitlements) that can be derived
from them take the form of citizenship and due process rights. Likewise, the
duty to secure these freedoms falls exclusively on governments (*BFN* 174).

Here we see how the procedural deduction of basic constitutional rights
(the paradigm instances of what will later be known as human rights) biases
Habermas's understanding of the human right to subsistence. The right to subsistence, if it exists at all, need not (and normally does not) find constitutional

support. What finds constitutional support is a liberal right (permission) to acquire and exchange property free from arbitrary governmental interference. Constitutionally speaking, the government has a duty to protect the political, civil, and property rights that make up the first principle of justice in the schemes of Rawls and Habermas. The priority accorded to liberty stands in marked contrast to the secondary status accorded to social welfare. The just distribution of material resources and opportunities requisite for the full and equal exercise of liberal rights is not constitutionally guaranteed, and its satisfaction cannot be permitted if it diminishes civil and political liberty overall (viz., while tradeoffs between liberties are permitted, tradeoffs between liberty and welfare are not). Only after the most extensive liberty compatible with equal rights for all has been legally guaranteed can government then begin to satisfy the "fair value" of civil and political liberty by adopting redistributive policies that improve the worse off. So satisfying the subsistence needs of citizens "fairly" is at best a duty that the government acquires contingently as a result of legislators and citizens voluntarily deciding to incorporate this right into statutory legislation.

What is disturbing here is not the fact that social rights, unlike civil and political rights, might not be legally guaranteed in a liberal democracy. My example of the sweatshop shows that some of the cultural factors influencing the secure enjoyment of subsistence probably cannot be legislated. Rather, what is disturbing is that the right to subsistence as it is here presented, within a juridical derivation of rights, cannot be treated as a basic (viz., unconditional) human right on par with other human rights to civil, political, and economic freedom. Poverty deaths caused by the *lawful* (constitutionally legitimate) workings of an unjust global economic order will not count as human rights violations but as regrettable (if avoidable) tragedies that can at best be reduced through acts of charitable assistance and developmental aid, which are by no means obligatory as a matter of human right. While utilitarians might have good reason to argue that our duties to assist others are as strong as our duties to not harm them (even requiring the self-imposition of burdens comparable to those who are the least well off), others, preferring a more libertarian approach, will demur, so that the radical political reform necessary for changing abusive structures will be replaced by superficial palliative efforts at voluntary redistribution.[24]

---

24. Human rights duties fall into three broad categories (in decreasing order of strength): duties to avoid harming a person in the enjoyment of a human right; duties to protect against other persons and institutions from harming a person in the enjoyment of a human right; and duties to aid a person who is deprived of the secure enjoyment of human rights, whether through human failure or through purely natural causes (Shue, *Basic Rights*, 165). As Pogge notes (*World Poverty and Human Rights*, 132), our primary duty to avoid harming strangers is at least as strong as our duty to avoid harming consociates. Likewise, the strength of our duties is conditioned by the resources, capabilities, and opportunities we have for realistically effecting relief. J. Waldron, *Liberal Rights: Collected Papers, 1981–1991* (Cambridge: Cambridge University Press, 1993), 25. For

To summarize: Habermas justifies the right to subsistence instrumentally. Its function is to provide opportunities for the equal exercise of constitutionally guaranteed civil, political, and economic liberties, not to secure protection of intrinsic goods. Second, the right to subsistence, as a statutory right, exists only as a legal right that is claimed against legal institutions. It is not a claim against oppressive economic structures or traditional systems of patriarchy and racial caste that have been imposed on the poor by the cumulative aggregation of unintended consequences extending backward in time over many generations. Not only may such structures and systems thrive within modern legal institutions, but efforts to legally reform them may be ineffectual. Third, the right to subsistence qua legal right is contingent. In an affluent society in which wealth is already evenly distributed, such a legal right would be unnecessary. Fourth and finally, the right to subsistence is understood as implying a positive governmental duty to redistribute opportunities and resources, contingent on citizens' sympathetic identification with their worse-off compatriots. As such, its enforcement cannot be subsumed under the central control of a global human rights agency, whose contributing members are not linked in democratic solidarity.[25]

Are there resources within Habermas's discourse theory of rights that justify a less conditional and fully human right to subsistence? There are if we factor in (a) his claim that a classical liberal right to property incorporates more inclusive, prelegal "rights to life and bodily integrity" (*PC* 125) that have "intrinsic value" apart from "their instrumental value for democratic will formation" and (b) his account of the complementarity of moral rights and duties, which would seem to imply that the right to subsistence is equiprimordial with other human rights. Unlike a classical right to property, which is clearly a legal construction, the right to life is essentially a moral idea. Its ground precedes the legal system and comprises nothing less than the most basic capabilities, needs, and interests that humans possess as a part of their universal nature. Invoking universal human nature as a set of universal needs, interests, and capabilities, however, immediately calls to mind the kind of moral realism (and moral intuitionism) that Habermas has labeled "metaphysical" (and prerational) and,

---

a further discussion of this complex issue as it bears on our duties with regard to effecting changes in sweatshops, see D. Ingram, "Of Sweatshops and Subsistence: Habermas on Human Rights," *Ethics and Global Politics* 2/3 (2009): 193–217.

25. Habermas's recommendation (*BNR* 333, 344) that a cosmopolitan human rights regime "achieve the goals of the UN Charter" and "overcome the differential in welfare within a highly stratified world society" through world domestic policy has been criticized by Lafont and others for being too decentralized and vulnerable to power politics. However, even if a global consensus were to emerge regarding the causes of and remedies for poverty *and* rich countries were willing to redistribute some of their income according to a workable plan, the structural injustices of global capitalism would need to be remedied. Because some of these injustices find cultural backing, ensuring subsistence requires going beyond Lafont's juridical recommendations. C. Lafont, "Alternative Visions of a New Global Order: What Should Cosmopolitans Hope For?" *Ethics and Global Politics*, 1/1–2 (2008): 41–60.

therefore, in opposition to the Kantian democratic procedural idea of self-determination (*TJ* 237–75).

Of course, there is no reason why we cannot think of human nature nonmetaphysically, as capabilities and functions that evolve contingently in response to our evolving self-understanding as a species. But there may be another reason why Habermas resists linking human rights discourse to the moral discourse of needs and capabilities. Viewing human rights in this manner also forces us to think of them in expressly nonjuridical terms. The fact that capabilities, interests, and needs imply indeterminate conditions for their actualization suggests that the concrete meaning of human rights is not exhausted by their *minimalist* claim structure.[26] Human rights qua moral rights remain essentially and interminably disputable—a project of discursive learning that is ill-equipped to function as a consensual decision procedure for resolving disputes generated by its own indeterminacy. Because the moral consensus that grounds human rights is ideal and counterfactual (forever deferred), such rights function as *utopian aspirations,* or evolving standards of civilization, progress, and critique, quite apart from (and even in tension with) their status as legal claims to a minimally decent threshold of treatment.[27]

As I have noted, Habermas himself regards the tension between morality and legality as productive; a bilevel model of democratic discourse in which the fruitful interplay between formal decision making (conflict resolution) and informal deliberation (learning) ostensibly explains how constitutional projects acquire greater legitimacy in the course of comprehensively realizing moral aspirations. However, in the absence of a global constitutional basis for cosmopolitan human rights law, it may be that acknowledging the moral rationale underlying human rights jeopardizes the legal consolidation of human rights under the auspices of the International Criminal Court and the UN (a consolidation Habermas strongly endorses). For, in that case, philosophical arguments—showing what human rights are about and explaining why they

26. Habermas, like Rawls, endorses a two-pronged minimalist approach to human rights. First, he views human rights as legal claims, or warrants for intervention. Avoiding intervention except for egregious rights violations requires trimming the list of human rights to those that are most essential to maintaining a free society. (Habermas accordingly mentions government-sponsored genocide, but not structurally induced starvation, as an actionable cause.) Second, Habermas complements *enforcement minimalism* with *justificatory minimalism,* or the exclusion of rights that cannot be justified in principle or by appeal to universal consensus. Legal grammar designates classical, civil, and political rights—but not subsistence rights—as human rights. A. Macleod, "Rawls's Narrow Doctrine of Human Rights," in *Rawls's Law of Peoples: A Realistic Utopia?,* ed. R. Martin and D. Reidy (Maldon, MA: Blackwell, 2006), 134–49; and J. Nickel, "Are Human Rights Mainly Implemented by Intervention?" in *Rawls's Law of Peoples,* 263–77.

27. Martha Nussbaum captures the distinction between rights as claims for minimally decent treatment and rights as aspirations in her distinction between *basic* capabilities, which are innate potentials, and *combined* capabilities, which are fully mature capabilities that possess additional environmental supports and "social bases" of an indeterminate and evolving nature. See M. Nussbaum, *Women and Human Development* (Cambridge: Cambridge University Press, 2000), 84–86.

are important—could no longer in principle justify the exclusion of a human right to subsistence from the pantheon of legally enforceable human rights.

But for proceduralists like Habermas and Rawls, any conception of human rights based on a comprehensive moral conception of basic human flourishing ostensibly violates the pluralistic tenets of political liberalism. In their opinion, such a teleological conception of human functioning would not be universally convincing to all human beings. Hence, appealing to this standard of human flourishing as a basis for legal action, critique, and reform would amount to imposing a particular nonshareable standard on the rest of the world.

I find this to be a strange argument from a philosopher who is convinced that cultures are conversationally open to one another, disposed to rational cooperation by the very telos of language itself, and therefore capable of converging toward—if not finally agreeing on—universal interests. As Martha Nussbaum notes in her critique of Habermas, if human rights can be justified apart from their instrumental value for subjective legal freedom and democratic autonomy, this is because they intuitively capture what we—in conversation with one another—have taken to be needs and capabilities that are so integral to our understanding of human flourishing that we insist on securing their protection and development through legal means. Put simply, Habermas has it exactly backward. There is no reason to expect that human beings would ever reach universal consensus on human rights unless we assumed, as a regulative idea, that they already shared general interests reflective of their human mode of existence; and there is no reason to expect that they would ever reach this consensus *impartially* unless the discursive procedure on which it was based was itself a rational reconstruction of *substantive intuitions* concerning essential human functioning.[28] In that case, the UN's increasing reliance on a revisable and cross-culturally negotiated list of capabilities in assessing progress in the achievement of human rights demonstrates a healthy respect for moral realism that first-generation critical theorists also shared, albeit not uncritically, and that Habermas would be good to acknowledge as well.

Final Thoughts on the Procedural Ideal of Deliberative Democracy

I began this chapter by noting that the procedural model of deliberative democracy defended by Habermas encounters a paradox. On the one hand, the

---

28. Nussbaum, *Women and Human Development*, 150n83. Nussbaum does not deny the value of a clarifying procedure—such as inclusive, fair, and uninhibited rational discourse—for adducing (basic) substantive rights and capabilities; she just thinks that the design of such a procedure must itself depend on a tacit appeal to our intuitive understanding of (basic) substantive rights and capabilities. The circular relationship between intuitive substantive "fixed judgments" and our qualifying procedures of rational deliberation is precisely what Rawls had in mind in introducing the notion of "reflective equilibrium."

model explains the legitimacy of democratic outcomes as an expression of their having been processed by fair procedures; consensus (or perhaps compromise, as we shall see) suffices to produce a binding decision so long as the process of deliberation leading up to it has been free, fair, inclusive, and respectful of others by not imposing any constraint on them to which they themselves could not have consented. On the other hand, no real-life deliberative process is perfect; even virtuous and well-intended citizens may reach decisions using approximately rational procedures that can be tyrannical. Because a judgment like this is always possible, we must look beyond procedural norms to explain it—hence the prescriptivist claim that procedural norms must themselves be limited by more substantive (i.e., concretely prescriptive) principles of justice that further define what can count as an acceptable outcome.

But then we are left with the "undemocratic" view that the limits on democracy must be imposed against the people's will, if necessary, by judges who have a better idea than actual deliberators about what these limits are. Habermas wants to avoid the taint of elitism by suggesting that what appear to be external limits on democracy—the inalienable rights of individuals that guarantee private autonomy—are really internal to democratic procedure itself, understood as an institutional expression of discursive norms that are already embedded in everyday communicative action. Therefore, if judges do overrule majoritarian outcomes, this need not be understood as an elitist, counterdemocratic act so long as the basis for their judgment is a conception of right that is constitutive of the democratic procedure itself. Judicial review, in other words, properly aims to protect democracy and nothing more.

I will have more to say about judicial review in the next chapter. For the time being I would like to focus on some difficulties that attend this solution. As I noted in the case of a right to subsistence, not all rights are conceptually constitutive of the democratic process. Some—like the right to subsistence—are only contingently so. Indeed, both the classical liberal rights to life and property, as well as the modern liberal rights to security, are at best indirectly "constitutive" of democracy. The former are conceptually linked to the legal form that modern rights must assume, as well as the concept of equality under the law, which Habermas claims is added by the discourse principle. However, these classical liberal rights can be more or less satisfied—if not fully realized as claims that demand corresponding social guarantees (which, of course, only democracy can provide)—outside of democracy. More tenuously linked to democracy are welfare and security rights (which fall under the fifth category in his system of rights), since these are entirely contingent. Habermas seems to suggest that a democratic society composed of rich people who provided their own material security in roughly equal measure would not cease to be any less democratic if it decided to dispense with these rights altogether.

This suggestion is problematic because there continues to be a debate, which I address in the next chapter, regarding how far liberal democracies need to go to protect these rights (if they should protect them at all). If Habermas wants to secure these rights more strongly, it is not enough for him to argue that they are contingently necessary for democracy. He must also argue that they have a deeper ground in the conditions requisite for a minimally decent life and, beyond that, a life that aspires to higher levels of flourishing. He might, for instance, appeal to more robust conceptions of human self-realization of the sort that have been worked out by Martha Nussbaum, in her neo-Aristotelian/ neo-Marxist account of basic and complex capabilities. Or he might appeal to notions of human self-realization that directly appeal to the importance of dignified, socially recognized work and consumption, as Axel Honneth and Carol Gould have argued.[29]

Taking deliberative democracy in this direction, however, would be tantamount to conceding that it has to incorporate substantive principles of justice and more robust accounts of human nature and human flourishing than Habermas has hitherto been welling to concede. His reluctance to do so, of course, is entirely understandable. For by conceding this, the democratic theorist appears to be prescribing limits on acceptable outcomes that are not directly internal to democratic procedure and that therefore do not directly proceed from the consent of those who are affected by it.

But perhaps I am being hasty. For what redeems this apparently elitist, counterdemocratic procedure of political theorizing is the same method of wide reflective equilibrium recommended by Rawls and incorporated into Habermas's own Socratic method of rational reconstruction. We inevitably come back to the idea that these theoretical insights are themselves the products of democratic deliberation between theorist and lay persons, in which considered judgments and reflected intuitions—but not a priori revelations—play themselves out in a circle of argument and application wherein deliberative procedure and substantive belief modify each other.

---

29. See A. Honneth, *The Critique of Power: Reflective Stages in a Critical Social Theory*, trans. K. Baynes (Cambridge: MIT Press, 1991); and A. Honneth, *The Struggle for Recognition: The Moral Grammar of Social Conflicts* (Cambridge: MIT Press, 1996). In *Globalizing Democracy and Human Rights*, Gould, like Honneth, defends workplace democracy. However, unlike him, she argues that justice proceeds democracy. In her opinion, democracy is instrumental to the equal development of capabilities essential to free agency. C. Gould, *Globalizing Democracy and Human Rights* (Cambridge: Cambridge University Press, 2004), 35. Although Honneth and Gould present their proposals as criticisms of Habermas's proceduralism, the proposals appear to be philosophical refinements of it.

7

Law and Democracy
Part II: Power and the Clash of Paradigms

In the last chapter I examined Habermas's application of DE to law, with its distinctive linkage of legality and legitimacy. Here, institutionalized legal coercion is shown to depend on normatively regulated democratic consent and vice versa. Saying that the consent in question is normative means that it approximates deliberative ideals mandating free, equal, inclusive, and reciprocal participation. These ideals, in turn, are legally codified in the form of basic rights. In this respect, basic rights and democracy are complementary rather than opposed, so that neither constrains the other in a way that would violate citizens' autonomy.

Whether this argument is entirely successful is disputable, for we saw that some basic rights have an extrajuridical ground, or intrinsic value quite apart from their instrumentality toward achieving autonomy. In the present chapter, however, we will be concerned with a different problem concerning the modification of discursive ideals in real-life democracy. Although some of these modifications derive from constraints of time and space that are imposed by the need to come to a decision, others derive from the impact of power on legal and political institutions.

Democracy and the Powers of Government

Although we can conceive of a democratic association of citizens implementing basic rights on its own prior to the existence of any state, we cannot conceive of it doing so *effectively* apart from lawful government (*Rechtsstaat*) (*BFN* 132).

The question thus arises: Whence arises the government's moral right to act on behalf of the community's interests?

Early modern social contract theorists from Hobbes to Rousseau answered this question by appealing to a mythical state of nature: persons living outside an established legal framework ostensibly agreed with one another to transfer their "natural" right to protect their life, liberty, and property to persons with whom they entrusted executive, judicial, and legislative powers. Given the implausibility of such a fiction, thinkers like Locke argued that persons tacitly consented to the protective custody of the governments in which they were already born. Such consent was made conditional on government protection of basic rights, later extended to include the right to participate in legislation through elected representatives. Here the tension between facts and norms that resides within the concept of law, namely, between its coercive and consensual nature and between its private and public aspects, is now repeated at the level of the state, in the form of a tension between two aspects of political power: the *administrative power* of government and what Habermas, following Hannah Arendt, calls the *communicative power* of public opinion (*BFN* 136).

Against Max Weber, Arendt insisted that the instrumentally efficacious power/violence (*Gewalt*) of the state derives its force and legitimacy from a form of public support that obeys an entirely different rationale, that of collective empowerment (*Macht*) generated through the discursive formation of a common will.[1] Indeed, Arendt maintained that the legitimacy of American and French constitutional conventions derived exclusively from such spontaneous political acts of empowerment.[2] Nonetheless, communicative power only explains the emergence of political power within an ongoing process of political debate and *deliberation,* not its administrative exercise in the form of binding legal *decisions* (*BFN* 150).

According to Habermas, deliberation and decision, communicative power and administrative power, mediate one another in several ways. Voting on referenda and electing officers captures one way in which administrative power mediates communicative power. Laws governing representation, voting, and running for office influence the quality and quantity of political debate.[3] In turn,

1. H. Arendt, "On Violence" (1969), in *The Political,* ed. D. Ingram (Oxford: Blackwell, 2002), 76–86.
2. H. Arendt, *On Revolution* (New York: Viking Press, 1973). Arendt says that the principle of "open discussion" (268) regulating "argumentative demonstration and political persuasion" (192) comprises the very "grammar of political action" (173). Habermas earlier criticized Arendt's view that political action rests on an agonal exchange of "opinions that cannot be true or false in the strict sense." J. Habermas, "Hannah Arendt's Communicative Concept of Power," *Social Research* 44 (1977): 22.
3. Habermas focuses on informal and formal democratic processes. In D. Ingram, *Rights, Democracy, and Fulfillment in the Era of Identity Politics: Principled Compromises in a Compromised World* (Lanham, MD: Rowman and Littlefield, 2004) I address *midlevel (quasi-formal) processes* pertaining to representation, voting, electoral campaigning, and institutionalized political struggles that mediate formal debates conducted by officials and informal discussions conducted

communicative power mediates administrative power, since procedures for representation, voting, and running for office are illegitimate unless informed by fair and inclusive acts of deliberation.

This symbiosis between communicative and administrative power has both cognitive and practical aspects. *Cognitively speaking,* public discussion "filter[s] reasons and information, topics and contributions in such a way that the outcome of a discourse enjoys a presumption of rational acceptability... [sufficient to] ground the legitimacy of law" (BFN 151). Compensating for the unregulated nature of public opinion—which permits inclusive but not equal contributions—is its relative spontaneity and breadth. For this reason alone, Habermas believes that legislatures should set their agendas around the problems highlighted by public opinion if they are to remain democratically accountable to the people. *Practically speaking,* public discussion "establish[es] relations of mutual understanding that are 'violence free' in Arendt's sense" (*BFN* 151). Because politics addresses ethical questions concerning collective goods as well as pragmatic questions concerning the means for implementing them, it is essential that it be sufficiently open, fair, and inclusive to generate the requisite degree of social solidarity necessary for citizens to feel motivated in complying with controversial decisions.

The principle of democracy (PD) implements the principle of discourse (D) in different ways depending on the logic of the matter to be discussed. The *process model* favored by Habermas answers the question "What ought we to do?" by breaking down the logic of political deliberation into three types of discourse distinguished by subject matter: *pragmatic, ethical-clinical,* and *moral,* as well as a fourth category distinguished by its manner of procuring agreement: *negotiated compromise* (bargaining). In pragmatic discourses interlocutors deliberate on the most efficient means for implementing shared values. Here technical experts give arguments in support of competing policies. Agreement on policies presupposes prior agreement on a description of the problematic situation to be remedied (*BFN* 164). Such descriptions are colored by values and interests not shared by everyone. So before a suitable

---

by citizens in forming public opinion. My approach adds a quantitative dimension (concerning the strategic aggregation and distribution of powers and resources) to Habermas's qualitative assessment of dialogue. Both measures can be used to assess the equality, autonomy, reciprocity, and inclusiveness of deliberation along six dimensions (spread over three levels): (1) *aggregative equality* (equality in distributing and weighing votes, funding campaigns, controlling and accessing media, and in representing opinions); (2) *aggregative autonomy* (independence of the public sphere from government and economy, independence [separateness] of government powers/functions); (3) *aggregative reciprocity* (mutual checks and balances between governmental powers, between political parties, between interest groups); (4) *dialogical equality* (equality in distributing capacities and opportunities to speak and listen effectively); (5) *dialogical autonomy* (freedom of speech and openness to arguments); and (6) *dialogical reciprocity* (mutual orientation to agreement in the interest of all concerned). J. Knight and J. Johnson, "Aggregation and Deliberation: On the Possibility of Political Representation," *Political Theory* 22 (1994): 277–96; M. James, *Democracy and Plural Polity* (Lawrence: University Press of Kansas, 2004).

description can be formulated for pragmatic consideration, political debate must proceed to the next level. First, the public must determine whether issues of moral justice are at stake. Habermas mentions tax codes and educational and health-care policies as expressly addressing problems of justice (*BFN* 165). But perhaps the situation is better described in ethical terms, or in terms of public welfare. Immigration policies that equally satisfy a moral duty to provide asylum to persons fleeing political and economic oppression also impact the good of the nation. Hence the question: To what extent does admitting refugees—as opposed to remedying their oppression abroad or relocating them in other countries with which we have bilateral agreements—harmonize with "our" views on environmental integrity, law and order, and the delivery of basic medical, educational, and other social services?

Suppose we cannot agree on what is in the country's best interests. North American agribusiness and consumer groups have an interest in maintaining high levels of low-skilled, low-wage immigrant farm labor. This interest is compatible with morality insofar as higher levels of immigration may well promote the fullest enjoyment of subsistence and liberty rights. In addition, it might also provide a local benefit in the form of increased tax revenues and lower agricultural prices. Agricultural labor unions that blame saturated labor markets for declining wages and environmentalists who blame population density for hastening environmental degradation might contest the moral justice and public benefits flowing from this policy.

When no agreement on the morality or ethical benefit of a policy can be reached *but* there is agreement that some agreement is better than no agreement, we have recourse to *bargaining*. According to Habermas, bargaining aims at *compromises* in which conflicting interests are balanced. Unlike a rationally motivated agreement, which "rests on reasons that convince all the parties *in the same way*, a compromise can be accepted by the different parties each for its own *different* reasons" (*BFN* 166). For example, the opposing sides debating immigration policy might settle on a compromise that permits farmers to hire modest numbers of foreign workers as members of unions, thereby providing them with cheaper labor, while at the same time increasing the bargaining strength of unions in negotiating higher wages and benefits for its members. In this respect a fair compromise is like an overlapping consensus except that the reasons motivating it are strategic and are backed by power (threats and inducements).[4]

Although political bargaining appears to disqualify (PD) as an instantiation of (D), Habermas notes that (D) can enter into bargaining indirectly, through procedures that give all interested parties "an equal opportunity for pressure, that is, an equal opportunity to influence one another during the actual bargaining, so that all the affected interests can come into play and have equal

---

4. But see note 12 for an important qualification of this point.

chances of prevailing" (*BFN* 167).[5] There are two reasons why bargaining presupposes a prior application of (D). First, it cannot be known whether a political dispute essentially resists consensual resolution until moral discourse has been attempted. The skeptical presumption that competing interests cannot be discursively transformed into shared interests must be challenged, otherwise we run the danger of imposing a false and unjust (pseudo) compromise (*LC* 112). A second reason why bargaining presupposes (D) is that it cannot be known whether the *procedures* under which compromises are negotiated are themselves fair until *they* are tested in moral discourse.

The Separation of Powers

Constitutional government aims at preventing law from becoming a tool of arbitrary power, be it the *administrative power* of the state or the *social power* of wealthy and influential elites within civil society. Jurists have traditionally invoked the constitutional separation of powers as a way to limit only the former (administrative) power. However, the traditional way of interpreting this principle—in terms of a horizontal system of checks and balances between legislative, judicial, and executive powers—ignores what Habermas believes is most important, namely, a constitutional circulation of power that establishes a hierarchy of legitimating discourses that descend from public, legislative, judicial, and executive levels of democratic deliberation. In keeping with this emphasis on *communicative power* as the source of legitimate law, Habermas extends the separation of powers principle more broadly to include the limitation of social power. Accordingly, he lists four principles for separating government powers from one another *and* from both social power and the communicative power of the public sphere. These are: (1) the principle of *popular sovereignty,* (2) the principle of *comprehensive legal protection for individuals,* (3) the principle of the *legality of administration,* and (4) the principle of the *separation of state and society.*

Habermas's discussion of these principles is designed to show how the horizontal separation of government powers serves to guarantee the vertical

5. Robert Dahl and Charles Lindblom argued that plural interest-group bargaining counters majoritarian tyranny more efficiently than a Madisonian separation of powers and "factions." They later realized that group-based "polyarchy" was ineffectual in checking corporate and government power. Dahl's recommendation for workplace democracy and public access to government information as remedies, Habermas believes, overestimates the degree to which citizens can undertake technical decision making—hence his preference for Bernard Peters's two-track model of democracy (*BFN* 315–21). See Dahl's *A Preface to Democratic Theory* (Chicago: University of Chicago Press, 1956); *Dilemmas of Pluralist Democracy: Autonomy versus Control* (New Haven: Yale University Press, 1982); and *A Preface to Economic Democracy* (Berkeley: University of California Press, 1985); as well as A. Downs, *An Economic Theory of Democracy* (New York: Harper and Row, 1957).

separation of administrative power from popular communicative power, thereby protecting the spontaneous creation of public opinion against state interference. At the same time—and somewhat counterintuitively—it also shows how the state must intervene in civil society to protect public opinion from the social power of economic elites. The entire argument is presented as if it were a deduction from the principle of discourse ethics and parallels (imperfectly) the deduction of the system of rights. The first principle articulates the concept of democratic legitimation (PD), or the conjunction of the principle of discourse and the principle of subjective rights. The second and third principles follow directly from the first principle by asserting the supremacy of the legislature over the judiciary, and the supremacy of both legislature and judiciary over the executive. The last principle asserts the autonomy of society from the state, which is necessary if influence is to be unidirectional from popular opinion to administration.

The *principle of popular sovereignty* affirms that "all political power derives from the communicative power of citizens" (*BFN* 170). The laws that government enforces must be seen as the outcome of unconstrained and inclusive discussion, both at the informal level of public debate and at the formal level of parliamentary deliberation. Habermas introduces five subsidiary principles that specify how this is to be done. The *parliamentary principle* requires that all interest groups be fairly represented. The *principle of majority rule* requires that all individual decisions (votes) be weighted equally and have equal impact.[6] The *principle of political pluralism* requires that "informal streams of communication emerging from the public spheres [be] open to all political parties, associations, and citizens." This principle, in turn, presupposes two additional principles requiring the *guaranteed autonomy of public spheres* and *competition between different political parties* (*BFN* 171).

The second major principle discussed by Habermas, the *principle of comprehensive legal protection for individuals*, follows directly from the first, insofar as "laws form the foundation for individual claims" and "from the actualization of these claims follows the guarantee of legal remedies" (*BFN* 172). Laws only function to protect persons equally if the claims that follow from them are adjudicated by an independent judiciary. Traditionally, the idea of an independent judiciary has been defended on the grounds of professionalism—in marked contrast to the example of ancient Athens, where average citizens performed both functions through forms of direct democracy. Rousseau later defended the independence of the judiciary by appeal to a basic distinction between legislation and adjudication. Legislators cannot mention particular

6. The principle of majority rule, when combined with the principle of equally weighted one person, one vote voting, seems to ensure equal respect among *individuals*. However, it can conflict with the parliamentary principle, which aims at ensuring the fair representation of *groups*. See my books *Rights, Democracy, and Fulfillment*, chap. 4; and *Group Rights: Reconciling Difference and Equality* (Lawrence: University Press of Kansas, 2000), chap. 9.

persons as addressees of the law without destroying the law's impartiality; judges, by contrast, can do so in their application of the law, since they have no role in making it and are otherwise free from normal political pressures.

Habermas appears to accept this view. What is essential to maintaining an independent judiciary is that it be removed from the overtly political process of legislation. Ideally, judges should be appointed (not elected) on the basis of their professional qualifications; and they should apply—not make—the law.[7] Obviously, this last requirement commits judges to a fairly narrow interpretation of the law, if not—as we shall see later—a mechanical application of it. Habermas thus accepts the traditional distinction between legislation and adjudication as a hedge against judicial usurpation of the people's democratic will as expressed through the legislative will of its representatives. Predictably, he reinterprets this distinction in terms of his own distinction between justification and application. For instance, he affirms the traditional view that laws by their very nature disallow exceptions, since they advance universal interests (*BFN* 154). It is application—of which adjudication is an instance—not justification (the universalizing function of legislation) that allows for exceptions in its consideration of the unique circumstances of a particular case or person. However, in a significant departure from the traditional model, he also notes that "private bills" applicable to individual legal persons (corporate or otherwise) are legitimate forms of statutory legislation (*BFN* 159). Indeed, he criticizes Rousseau (as well as Kant) for believing that the formal nature of a law (its commanding all persons without exception) guarantees its impartiality. What guarantees the law's legitimacy is its discursive justification, which is the proper function of legislation. But this function is not intrinsically opposed to the legislation of private bills that have exceptions built into them. As I noted in chapter 5, justification and application complement one another. No norm is valid without qualification, and that qualification is revealed only in its application. Judicial decisions already provide legislators with a history of legal applications that they can draw from in qualifying prospective laws. In this way exceptional circumstances can enter into their justification from the outset. The reasons that convince legislators to adopt a "private bill" still appeal to the general interests (or compromise between interests) the bill advances, even though the bill's scope is quite specific. Given the general rationale in support of a private bill, it always remains possible to regard the bill as a general precedent for decisions of a similar nature. Thus, the reasons that compel legislators to pass a private bill exempting an undocumented immigrant from deportation due to special circumstances also support a general amnesty policy for classes of immigrants who are deemed to be in similar circumstances.[8]

7. This principle would be qualified in Anglo-American private law, with its common law reliance on judge-made case law.

8. Thanks to Carl Schmitt's elevation of the state of exception in defending dictatorship—a principle that Georgio Agamben believes has been permanently instantiated in the modern security

But if justification and application essentially qualify each other, then there appears to be no compelling reason to vest these kinds of discourse in separate governmental powers. Indeed, Habermas himself endorses judicial review of statutory legislation both prior to and after ratification (*BFN* 173). If there remains a compelling reason in Habermas's mind for separating legislative and judicial powers it cannot be that each power only expresses itself in one kind of discourse. The compelling reason must be that judges should only apply the law; that is, they should draw their reasons—whether for purposes of justifying the general validity of a norm (as sometimes happens in judicial review) or for purposes of applying it to particular cases—from those that lawmakers have provided them (and which ultimately have their source in popular public opinion). This is the best way to prevent the judiciary from "programming itself": hence, the *principle of binding the judiciary to existing law*, which prohibits judges—who are often unelected officials—from making laws in the course of exercising interpretative license.

The *principle of the legality of administration* also "brings out the central meaning of the separation and balancing of powers" (*BFN* 173). As in the case of the previous principle, this principle requires that executive acts remain subordinate to the people's will, as expressed, first, by the legislature and, second, by the judiciary. Here again we find Habermas clarifying this concept by appeal to subordinate principles. The *principle of prohibiting arbitrariness in domestic affairs* (*BFN* 174) essentially prohibits the executive from intervening in domestic life without the express consent of the legislature. It upholds the rule of law (the *principle of the priority of law*)—as distinct from the rule of executive decision—and thereby protects against tyrannical forms of interference that render the predictable application of law null and void. It also requires that individual rights acquire a distinctive status. Whereas they initially appeared in the abstract conceptual form of permissions that the people give themselves, they now become claims against the institution of the state, as principally reflected in the executive acts of its leaders (*BFN* 174). The *principle of parliamentary oversight* gives the legislature the power to remove executive officers and suspend executive acts. (For Habermas, the power of the executive can only *enable*, not *restrict*, legislation.) This same condition applies to the executive's relationship to the judiciary, which retains a power of judicial review over executive acts. The *principle of judicial review* also enables citizens to sue the government in court for any harm its actions have inflicted on them.

---

state—no Kantian, except Habermas, has defended the legality of exceptions. (Kant even prohibits the right to pardon except when the executive is the aggrieved party.) I. Kant, *The Metaphysics of Morals*, in *Kant: Political Writings*, ed. H. Reiss (Cambridge: Cambridge University Press, 1970), 142, 160; C. Schmitt, *Political Theology: Four Chapters on the Concept of Sovereignty*, trans. G. Schwab (1922; Cambridge: MIT Press, 1985), esp. chaps. 1 and 2; G. Agamben, *State of Exception* (Chicago: University of Chicago, 2005); and D. Ingram, "Exceptional Justice? A Discourse Ethical Contribution to the Immigration Question," *Cultural Horizons* 10/1 (2009): 1–30.

Taken together, the above principles prohibit the collapsing of administrative and communicative types of power in ways that threaten the autonomy of public opinion formation, chiefly by means of government propaganda or by legal restrictions on freedom of speech and association. The protection of the public sphere against government encroachment (from above)—the aim of the *principle of separation of state and society*—finds parallel expression in the protection of the public sphere against social power (from below). Here Habermas is concerned about the social (or strategic) power that businesses, organizations, and pressure groups bring to bear in influencing both government and public opinion. Thwarting this danger may in fact require administrative interventions that guarantee "a civil society, that is, a network of voluntary associations and political culture that are sufficiently detached from class structures" (*BFN* 175). That the use of administrative power to offset social power might seem ironic is conceded by Habermas in his observation that what was often touted as a politically neutral state "was always ideological." For this reason he insists that civil society must retain a sufficient degree of autonomy from both state and economy to provide a medium in which undistorted communicative power can emerge (see table 7)(*BFN* 176).

The Transmission of Communicative Power: From Public Sphere to Government Administration

Persons assessing these dangers might doubt whether undistorted communicative power can ever emerge. They might also doubt whether such power, once emergent, can remain undistorted in its transmission from public sphere to legislature and from legislature to administration.[9] I will begin by addressing the first phase of this process. Habermas notes that (PD) institutionalizes "the public use of communicative freedom" differently than the way this is understood by two classical theories of democracy. According to the civic-republican (communitarian) theory descended from Rousseau, a general will or common good that exists prior to deliberation gets passively expressed in direct voting.

9. Jean-François Lyotard argues that an injustice (*différend*) haunts the transmission of communicative power from "people" to administrators insofar as the people's aims are unavoidably transformed into something different once they are inscribed in the discursive regimes of government officials. (Even the concept of a "people" is a constitutional fiction whose political right to exclude outsiders masquerades as a metaphysical human right.) Representatives transform "our" moral aspirations into compromises onto which administrators superimpose their own code of cost-benefit assessment. What begins as a discourse about injustice gets transformed into a discourse about balancing interests and then into a technoscientific discourse (about maximizing economic growth, legal order, etc.). What "communication" remains between technical decision making and public opinion is reduced to "data gathering." J.-F. Lyotard, *The Differend: Phrases in Dispute*, trans. G. Van Den Abbeele (Minneapolis: University of Minnesota Press, 1988), 157; "Memorandum on Legitimation," in Ingram, *The Political*; and Ingram, *Rights, Democracy, and Fulfillment*, 36–49.

Table 7

Levels of democracy: The flow of communicative, administrative, and social forms of power

Key:

- ● →= flow of administrative power from the administrative system to civil society and the economic system
- ◄ →= flow of social power from the economic system to civil society and government
- ■ →= flow of communicative power from civil society to government

Formal Democracy = (government)	Legislature ■ → ■ →	Judiciary ■ → ■ →	Executive
a. legally instituted discourses that provide procedural fairness b. assignment of discourses according to the separation of government powers c. decision as the aim of discourse	a. moral discourses that justify constitutional rights b. ethical discourses that justify general public policy ends aimed at advancing shared values and the common good c. bargaining that justifies fair compromises between equally compelling, conflicting value orientations and conceptions of the good d. pragmatic discourses that justify effective legal means for implementing (a–c)	a. discourses of application that apply laws (rights and policies) in adjudicating particular cases b. discourses of application that apply and interpret the constitution in reviewing (upholding or overturning) statutory legislation, lower court opinions, executive decrees, and prior constitutional rulings by the higher court	a. pragmatic discourses that aim at deciding instrumentally efficient means for implementing legislative and judicial decisions ■ → ■ → Administrative System Administrative Power ● → ● → ● → ● → ● → ●

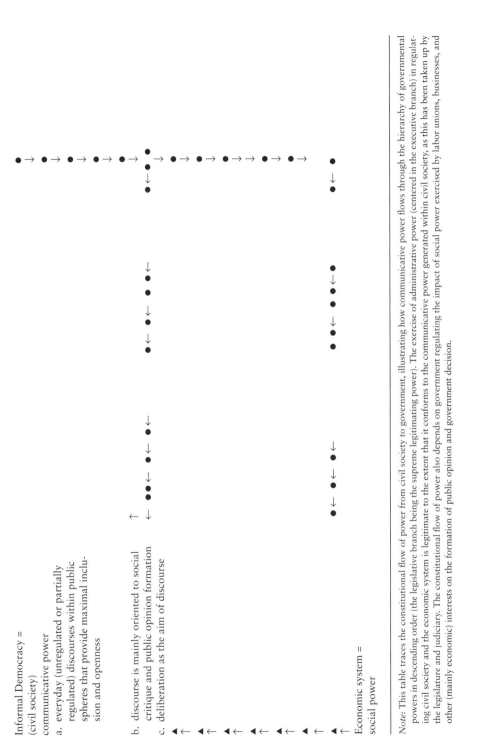

Note: This table traces the constitutional flow of power from civil society to government, illustrating how communicative power flows through the hierarchy of governmental powers in descending order (the legislative branch being the supreme legitimating power). The exercise of administrative power (centered in the executive branch) in regulating civil society and the economic system is legitimate to the extent that it conforms to the communicative power generated within civil society, as this has been taken up by the legislature and judiciary. The constitutional flow of power also depends on government regulating the impact of social power exercised by labor unions, businesses, and other (mainly economic) interests on the formation of public opinion and government decision.

This has the effect of rendering the election of parliamentary representatives obsolete: either they passively act on what the people have expressed or they do not, in which case they usurp the general will. According to the liberal theory descended from J. S. Mill,[10] there exists no common will among the public—just an anarchy of clashing interests—and so whatever common will gets enacted into law is entirely the product of agreements struck by wise legislators who have a wider vision of the public good than their constituents (*BFN* 182).

According to Habermas, both theories begin with a false view of public opinion and parliamentary deliberation. The liberal view is correct in discounting a preexisting consensus on all but the most basic constitutional principles. In a healthy democracy marked by a reasonable pluralism of beliefs and interests, the "people" do not speak in a single voice but in many voices that emerge spontaneously and anarchically. This apparent absence of a "sovereign subject"—the "people"—does indeed generate problems of rational collective choice that elected representatives must come to terms with. However, to the degree that everyday discourse critically filters the multitude of opinions that find expression, we cannot conclude that rational consensus, and therewith communicative power, are entirely absent from it.

In Habermas's judgment, the freedom and inclusiveness of informal public opinion formation—whose rational modus operandi is admittedly more critical (oriented toward the discovery of problems) and less constructive (oriented toward developing positive arguments in support of statutes)—finds its proper complement in the formal equality of parliamentary debates that are expressly oriented toward reaching decisions based on consensus. Parliamentary procedure accomplishes for political discourse what virtue accomplishes for moral discourse: the orientation toward an impartial consideration of interests.[11] It accomplishes this, however, by inhibiting a spontaneous and inclusive exchange of opinions. Habermas deploys Bernard Peter's notion of a *sluice* to capture this *two-track* model of democratic deliberation: the informal discourses circulating in the peripheral public sphere are rich in information but poorly organized and unfiltered; the formal discourses at the parliamentary center are rich in organized arguments but less expressive of a wide range of opinion.[12]

10. Although J. S. Mill supported extending the franchise to the working classes (albeit within a system granting property owners and holders of degrees additional votes while excluding the illiterate, the bankrupt, and the destitute), his low estimate of their capacity to deliberate rationally ("People will give...mean votes from the interests...of class") led him to entrust rational deliberation with bureaucrats. J. S. Mill, "Considerations on Representative Government," in John Stuart Mill, *Three Essays* (Oxford: Oxford University Press, 1975), 197, 311.

11. As Jon Elster notes, people must disguise their particular interests as general interests if they are to persuade others to accept them as their own. Virtue thus resides in the discursive procedures of bargaining (*BFN* 341). J. Elster, "Constitutional Bootstrapping in Philadelphia and Paris," *Cardozo Law Review* 14 (1993): 571.

12. B. Peters, *Die Integration moderner Gesellschaften* (Frankfurt: Suhrkamp, 1993), 340–52. Habermas first introduced the notion of a public sphere in *The Structural Transformation of the*

As Habermas notes, because representatives condense and prioritize the concerns of their own constituents, which they then selectively incorporate into policies that also embody the concerns of other constituents, they do not, strictly speaking, *represent* anything or anybody. For whether it be negotiating compromises, reaching understanding about the authentic good and identity of the nation, or achieving rational consensus on universal moral interests, parliamentary deliberation *transforms* the input it receives. In the discursive interchange between public sphere and parliament, interests are qualified and balanced, and horizons of understanding are expanded. Of course, the extent to which this happens varies depending on what is at stake. Representatives are less free to deviate from their constituents' interests when these are strictly local or particular. They will compromise these interests only for the sake of satisfying them as best they can. They are more free to deviate from them when representing the good of the nation; and they are most free to do so when representing the universal moral interests of humanity (*BFN* 178–83).

I want to now consider the transmission of communicative power from parliamentary statute to administrative decree. The "transmission belt" theory of communicative power states that executive officials cannot interpret or develop the law when enforcing it (*BFN* 189–90). This view is no doubt naive—every police officer, for instance, uses personal discretion in interpreting what the law requires of him or her in any given situation—but it seems especially naive when applied to welfare and regulatory law (what Habermas, following Weber, calls "material law"). Welfare and regulatory laws target specific persons and entities and do not apply to everyone in the same way. Not only does enforcement require discretion and judgment, but in the case of regulatory laws governing

---

Public Sphere; he meant a sphere—midway between (economic) civil society and state—in which critical opinion was formed. The public sphere depended on the communicative freedom of newspapers, writers, artists, intellectuals, and citizens in general. Thus it represented an institutional embodiment of "discourse." Habermas now defines the public sphere "as a network for communicating information and points of view (i.e., opinions expressing affirmative or negative attitudes)" wherein "the streams of communication are...filtered and synthesized in such a way that they coalesce into bundles of topically specified *public* opinions" (*BFN* 360). He has also refined the concept by accepting Nancy Fraser's distinction between "strong" and "weak" publics, which captures the difference between forms of deliberation that "encompass decision making" and forms that "consist exclusively in opinion formation." By "civil society" he now means—more closely in keeping with its original political use by Locke than with the one-sided economic interpretation developed by Hegel and Marx—"those more or less spontaneously emergent associations, organizations, and movements that, attuned to how societal problems resonate in private life spheres, distill and transmit such reactions in amplified form to the public spheres." So construed, civil society "no longer includes the economy as constituted by private law and steered through markets in labor, capital, and commodities" but rather comprises "those nongovernmental and noneconomic connections and voluntary associations that anchor the communication structures of the public sphere in the society component of the lifeworld" (*BFN* 366–67). See N. Fraser, "Rethinking the Public Sphere: A Contribution to the Critique of Actually Existing Democracy," in *Habermas and the Public Sphere*, ed. C. Calhoun (Cambridge: MIT Press, 1992), 134; and J. Cohen and A. Arato, *Civil Society and Political Theory* (Cambridge: MIT Press, 1992).

nuclear energy, environmental protection, genetic engineering, and national security, statutes are formulated so abstractly as to allow experts within the administration considerable leeway in interpreting them, thus lending the appearance that they—not legislators—are really making the laws (*BFN* 431–36).

Habermas submits that a discourse theoretic account of the separation of powers limits, without absolutely prohibiting, the administrative development of law. Strictly speaking, administrators should limit their development of the law to just those aspects that concern its pragmatic implementation; their "discourses" do not properly concern moral rights or ethical ends. Nonetheless, because pragmatic arguments invariably bring to bear value-laden descriptions of problematic situations, this statement must be qualified. An administrator, for instance, might be forced to choose between a statute that outlaws a source of water pollution and a statute that protects an endangered species that has become dependent on this very source for its survival, as in the case of manatees, which have adapted to the warm water generated by polluting power plants in Florida. Habermas notes that in cases like this, administrative agencies have no recourse but to reopen the question about what values are most appropriate for guiding their action. He adds, however, that their internal deliberation will not be legitimate unless it is submitted to public hearings that incorporate "quasi-judicial and parliamentary procedures, procedures for compromise formation, and so on" (*BFN* 193, 440).[13]

Discourse and Adjudication

As the preceding example shows, judicial review of executive actions is an essential part of constitutional law. Executive actions must remain within the law, and only judges have the competence to determine whether such actions do so. Indeed, binding the executive to the judiciary and the judiciary to the legislature as the principal organ of democratic legitimation directly follows from the discourse theory of law. But higher courts not only review executive acts and (conflicting) lower court decisions to determine whether they conform to law. They also exercise abstract judicial review of statutory law itself. Such review appears to reverse the ranking of powers (*BFN* 240). If, as Habermas himself concedes, the legislature can and should exercise its own constitutional review of pending legislation, then why endow the higher court with this seemingly antidemocratic power (*BFN* 242)? Can discourse theory justify giving higher courts the right to strike laws that the majority of lawmakers and citizens deem legitimate?

13. N. McAfee, "Three Models of Democratic Deliberation," *Journal of Speculative Philosophy* 18 (2004): 44–59; and D. Ingram, "Anti-Discrimination, Welfare, and Democracy: Toward a Discourse-Ethical Understanding of Disability Law," *Social Theory and Practice*, 32/2 (2006): 213–48.

Habermas answers this question affirmatively by noting that the supreme law of the land—the constitution—elaborates a system of rights whose ideal normative content is not entirely derived from the factual outcomes of democratic politics and therefore should not be left to the partial sympathies of elected politicians (*BFN* 242). This defense of judicial review, which amounts to acknowledging that the validating ground of basic rights is partially prepolitical, appears very close to that advanced by proponents of the classical liberal paradigm of law. However, Max Weber, Hans Kelsen, and other advocates of this paradigm were legal positivists.[14] They believed that basic rights could provide a neutral basis for coordinating action only if they were drained of any substantive moral content referring to controversial ideas of justice. This meant that basic rights had to be conceived in a narrow, formal way as negative rights. Such rights, they believed, could be derived from the *premoral* idea of legal form alone.

Habermas, as we have seen, denies that the concept of legal right follows from the concept of legal form taken in abstraction from the normative ideals implicit in discourse ethics. Not only is the legal code infused with normative content from the outset, the legitimation of rights implies positive political and social rights. So the meaning of law is not exhausted by written law as positivists maintain but also refers to a background of moral principles and legal paradigms. Hence, contrary to legal positivism, the reason why judicial review must be located in an independent higher court is not merely that judges possess a highly specialized technical knowledge of the constitution and its written history of statutory precedents that legislators and average persons simply lack (*BFN* 250).

Constitutional adjudication is not a mechanical exercise of technically subsuming a case under a rule that expressly contains it; if it were, then judges would have to invent new norms to apply to "hard" cases that are not so contained (*BFN* 261). Such invention would amount to judicial tyranny. Rather, judges must *interpret* the law they apply because the law implicitly refers beyond its express statutory meaning to moral concepts such as "equal treatment" and "freedom" that already reside in the abstract legal code informing the constitution (*BFN* 252).[15]

But such terms can be interpreted in two ways depending on how we construe them. If we think of them as instantiating *values* (goods), then constitutional interpretation would involve a forward-looking process of value maximization,

---

14. Weber realized that the binding character of law depended on its perceived normative legitimacy, by which he meant that "it is imposed by an authority which is held to be legitimate and therefore meets with compliance." G. Roth and C. Wittich, eds., *Economy and Society: An Outline of Interpretative Sociology* (Berkeley: University of California Press, 1978), 1:36. See also H. Kelsen, *Pure Theory of Law* (1934; repr., Gloucester, MA: Peter Smith, 1984).

15. Even a positivist such as H. L. A. Hart concedes this point. H. L. A. Hart, *The Concept of Law,* 2nd ed. (Oxford: Clarendon Press, 1991), 251. See also D. Ingram, *Law: Key Concepts in Philosophy* (London: Continuum Press, 2006), 42–47.

or value balancing.[16] Since the balancing and ranking of conflicting values is a political process, constitutional interpretation would again violate the discourse theoretical principle that limits the judiciary to applying—not making—law. This danger especially increases once we concede that basic rights include material rights to social welfare. Nothing in "value jurisprudence" inherently prevents judges from allowing, for instance, totalitarian public-safety policies advanced in the name of public welfare to trump individual rights to freedom of speech, freedom of association, and freedom of religion (*BFN* 259).

As I noted in chapter 5, Habermas emphatically criticizes the conflation of conditional values and unconditional norms and rights (*BFN* 255). Hence, he argues that constitutional interpretation possesses a different methodology from that of value maximizing and balancing. The proper methodology rather consists in applying universal norms and principles of right to particular cases. In this backward-looking jurisprudence, unconditional rights are presumed to preexist within the system of law, and the business of the judge is to find the single most appropriate assignment of a right given the most adequate description of the case being adjudicated, an assignment that (in the words of Ronald Dworkin) "trumps" any value-maximizing policy. Of course, this finding is also

16. Besides a value-balancing German jurisprudence, Habermas also has in mind the American school of "legal realism" (or legal pragmatism): "From the standpoint of Legal Realism... one can no longer clearly distinguish law from politics... because judges, like future-oriented politicians, make their decisions on the basis of value orientations they consider reasonable... [or] justified on utilitarian or welfare-economic grounds" (*BFN* 201). Deriving their inspiration from sources as diverse as John Dewey and Oliver Wendell Holmes, legal realists challenged the dominant school known as legal formalism, which held that judicial decision making could be modeled along the lines of a deductive science, in which particular cases could be unproblematically subsumed under legal precedents. (Formalism was enlisted by conservative judges to strike down income taxes and laws regulating work hours, wages, and working conditions on the grounds that these constituted illegal takings of "property.") By showing that general laws could be interpreted in multiple ways depending on the intentions, values, and interests of lawmakers, legal realists introduced a political dimension into the interpretation of law that encouraged judges to apply laws in accordance with models of economic efficiency (most were strong supporters of social legislation and the New Deal) and forward-looking democratic policies. Some, like Karl Llewellyn, saw law as a technical tool of efficient economic organization, but others (notably Dewey and his followers) thought it obeyed a "communicative" logic incorporating diverse perspectives on problematic cases. Habermas's discourse theory of law, however, assumes something that Dewey's does not, namely (as Klaus Günther puts it) that "all valid norms ultimately constitute an ideal coherent system which gives for each case exactly one right [i.e., appropriate] answer." Realists had a greater appreciation for the incoherence and patchwork nature of law, which they believed required judges to "balance" conflicting values and even principles. In note 7 I discussed how the principle of majority rule can conflict with the principle of parliamentary representation. Likewise, the cases that appeared before the U.S. Supreme Court during the 1990s concerning the constitutionality of racially designing electoral districts involved balancing the rights of individuals to have their votes counted equally against the rights of racial minorities to fair representation. See my essay, "The Sirens of Pragmatism versus the Priests of Proceduralism: Habermas and American Legal Realism," in *Habermas and Pragmatism,* ed. M. Aboulafia, M. Bookman, and C. Kemp. (New York: Routledge, 2002), 83–113; and K. Günther, "A Normative Theory of Coherence for a Discursive Theory of Legal Justification," *Ratio Juris* 2 (1989): 163.

partly reconstructive in the way that any act of interpretation is; for in hard cases, the norm and case mutually redefine each other (*BFN* 248, 259–260).

The interpretative nature of law thus places the question of judicial tyranny in a new light. If judging hard cases is not a mechanical application of technical expertise but is also partly an exercise in moral judgment, then it seems that the answer to the question, What gives judges the right to strike laws that we the people have made? can only be that they possess superior moral knowledge. This defense of judicial review, however, is clearly elitist and undemocratic, and it belies the actual lack of consensus that we often find among members of the highest court. Indeed, it is hard not to conclude that judges' opinions are as subjective and fallible as everyone else's.

Given these objections, Habermas argues that judicial review should be exercised sparingly, mainly in defense of just those democratic procedural norms that are essential for ensuring the legitimacy of the legal process as a whole. Courts should refrain from striking substantive statutes that have no bearing on the procedural fairness of the democratic process.[17] Nor must the legitimacy of the democratic process be judged in terms of excessively ideal standards of civic-republican virtue and discursive rationality that exclude reasonable forms of power-backed strategic compromise (*BFN* 278, 282). The high court's main concern should be to uphold basic rights by striking laws that unfairly discriminate against minorities and that prevent the fullest and most inclusive representation of voices. It should also safeguard the democratic process against the excessive intrusion of social power, for example, by striking campaign finance and lobbying laws that permit the wealthy and powerful to bribe or threaten government officials (*BFN* 264–66).

This response goes far in addressing the apparent contradiction between judicial review and democracy. However, it does not address skepticism about the moral authority of judges taken separately. Habermas responds to these

---

17. Habermas's position resembles John Hart Ely's. Ely understood "procedural values" broadly enough to include ideal principles embedded in any liberal democratic constitution. He argued that these values took precedence over substantive values, such as the protection of contractual freedom against public regulation, and gave legitimacy to nondiscrimination statutes. Frank Michelman, Cass Sunstein, and Bruce Ackerman support more aggressive judicial intervention on behalf of civil and political rights. Cass Sunstein's "reasonable analysis" requirement permits courts to overturn legislation whenever they deem democratic deliberation to be prejudiced. Less paternalistic is Bruce Ackerman's "dual democracy" approach, which permits strong judicial intervention during periods of "normal" democracy but only weak intervention (eventually ceding to nonintervention) during periods of "extraordinary" (or "revolutionary") democracy in which the people organize themselves under a mandate to advance the common good. In Habermas's opinion, these approaches underestimate the degree to which "virtue" is sedimented in the deliberative procedures governing fair bargaining; the court should therefore be "tutor to" but not "regent of" the public (*BFN* 279–80). J. H. Ely, *Democracy and Distrust: A Theory of Judicial Review* (Cambridge: Harvard University Press, 1980); B. Ackerman, *We the People,* vol. 1, *Foundations* (Cambridge: Harvard University Press, 1991); C. Sunstein, "Interest Groups in American Public Law," *Stanford Law Review* 38 (1985): 58; F. Michelman, "Law's Republic," *Yale Law Journal* 97 (1988): 1526–38; Ingram, *Law: Key Concepts,* 59–65.

objections by appealing to Klaus Günther's discourse theoretic model of adjudication, which describes judicial application as a dialogical enterprise.[18] Courtroom proceedings set in motion discourses of application in which counsel for the plaintiff (prosecution), counsel for the defendant (defense), jury, and judge search together for the most appropriate norm given the situation. However, unlike other discourses of application where everyone is an equal participant, judicial proceedings require that judges—and in the Anglo-American system jurors—occupy a privileged standpoint. It is they, not the contesting parties, who represent the impartial standpoint of the legal community as a whole and are responsible for synthesizing all relevant viewpoints in their interpretation of the case. Hence, the discourse conducted by the judge is not really between her and the litigating parties but between her and "a broad legal public sphere" (*BFN* 172).

Habermas's theory reminds us that judicial decisions are examples of small-scale democratic dialogue.[19] Judges—especially when serving jointly on appellate courts—communicate with one another in fashioning their opinions, and we must assume that they respond to one another's objections in reaching whatever consensus they can. Furthermore, they communicate with lawyers and other expert witnesses, and maintain a lively respect for public opinion.

That said, Habermas concedes that unconstrained consensual dialogue is only partly realized in courtroom proceedings.[20] Lawyers have limited time to plead their case; and when they do, they must appeal to existing law and relevant legal precedent, thereby forgoing any radical questioning of the law's justice. The adversarial nature of the proceedings so evident in Anglo-American courts—in which each side is obligated to try to win at all costs—injects strategic elements that further undercut the rationally disinterested search for justice.

Surprisingly, Habermas insists that these deviations from ideal discourse do not diminish the impartiality of court proceedings. Although contestants in legal debate are irrevocably partisan in defense of their positions, the rules of courtroom procedure guarantee all sides a fair hearing. More important, judges within an adversarial system are called on to participate as neutral intermediaries who represent the interests of the community.[21] Engaging in impartial and

---

18. K. Günther, *The Sense of Appropriateness: Application Discourses in Morality and Law* (Albany: SUNY Press, 1993); and Günther, "A Normative Conception for Coherence."

19. If the analogy with democracy seems a bit stretched, recall that in ancient Athens juries of up to five hundred formed the backbone of a vibrant participatory democracy.

20. O. Fiss, "Objectivity and Interpretation," *Stanford Law Review* 34 (1982): 744, 762.

21. This comports with Anglo-American procedure. Continental procedure permits judges wide latitude in questioning witnesses. The Nuremberg tribunal (1945–46), however, established a controversial precedent for combining both procedures, permitting defense attorneys to cross-examine experts testifying on behalf of the prosecution before a panel of judges who, in turn, cross-examined defendants and their attorneys. In the absence of a fact-finding jury, judges determined both the guilt of the defendants and their punishment.

open-ended dialogue among themselves, their proper aim is to "transform" or integrate the "perspectives" of the defendants and plaintiffs with those of the community at large (*BFN* 229).

In sum: judicial decision making testifies to the same tension between norms and facts observed elsewhere in law. As Habermas notes, judges must apply the law in accordance with the principle of legitimacy underlying the rule of law, which requires (in the words of Dworkin) that each person be treated with equal concern and equal respect (*BFN* 230).[22] They must also apply the law in a way that citizens can be certain of, consistent with past precedent. But precedents that lag behind evolving morality will eventually clash with and be overruled by principles. Moreover, changes in the law caused by discarding precedents will be as unpredictable as any dialogical outcome—hence the worry that a discourse theory of judgment sacrifices certainty on the alter of legitimacy. While not disputing this implication, Habermas offers the consoling thought that legal subjects can at least be certain of one thing: impartial courtroom procedure offers good prospects for reaching the right decision, so long as judges do their job well and existing law meets its implicit ideals of integrity and justice "halfway" (*BFN* 220, 232).

The Proceduralist Paradigm of Law and Democracy

Habermas notes that the outcomes of courtroom argument are less indeterminate (uncertain) than one might expect thanks to the judge's tacit reliance on commonly accepted *legal paradigms* that are less abstract and indeterminate in their application than principles. Such paradigms project "implicit images of society" that tend to uncritically freeze the meaning of rights—and therewith of equality and freedom—in a one-sided way. However, the growing complexity and diversity of modern society since the end of the nineteenth

---

22. In *Law's Empire*, Ronald Dworkin praises Habermas's "constructivist" approach to interpretation, which involves reconstructing the general procedures that make understanding and communication rational (i.e., fully coherent and "the best it can be"). Habermas returns the compliment by accepting the basic rudiments of Dworkin's theory of legal interpretation, including his important distinction between legal *principles*, which do *not* contain information specifying their application to cases, and legal *rules*, which do. This distinction enables Dworkin to argue, against positivists such as Hart (who view laws as explicitly formulated technical rules having no implicit reference to underlying moral principles) that "hard cases" (or cases resistant to subsumption under extant positive law) can be resolved by appeal to more abstract (moral) principles that underwrite the very idea of the rule of law (*BFN* 208). The choice of which principles (or paradigms) apply in interpreting a given hard case then falls on the judge. Whereas Dworkin imputes to the lone judge a Herculean task of selecting the most appropriate principle (or paradigm) based on an ideally comprehensive knowledge of all legal principles, laws, and precedents, Habermas imputes to the legal community (of which the judge occupies a privileged standpoint) a more fallible, dialogical interpretation of the case leading to a selection of the most appropriate principle (*BFN* 224). R. Dworkin, *Law's Empire* (Cambridge: Harvard University Press, 1986).

century—reflected in legal conflicts over the choice of these competing para-digms—have forced jurists to reflect on their limits and possibilities, and this reflection, in turn, has increasingly brought to light the conceptual link be-tween private and public autonomy, or the need to link the concrete mean-ing of subjective rights to an ongoing process of democratic interpretation. In Habermas's opinion, only a higher-order *proceduralist* paradigm embody-ing this discursive process accurately reflects a complex, fluid, and full-sided understanding of our "original idea of the self-constitution of a community of free and equal citizens" (*BFN* 393). Only this reflexive paradigm, he main-tains, can determine which concrete paradigm of rights is most appropriate for understanding certain types of situations or, if none is exclusively appropriate in dealing with a problematic case, how both of them might be applicable when simultaneously qualified vis-à-vis each other.

The two conflicting paradigms that Habermas asserts have shaped consti-tutional democracies over the last three hundred years emerged in response to the dominant forms of oppression of their day. The *liberal* paradigm emerged in the late seventeenth century in response to the problem of government tyr-anny, here identified with the expropriation and taxing of private property. The image of society it projects is an association of independent proprietors—farmers and small business owners—who contract with one another as free and equals under terms that are transparent and affect no one but themselves. This image defines legal situations in terms of individuals' negative freedom to pursue their good independent of government interference. It therefore has a strong purchase in, for instance, the common law of torts, which holds indi-viduals responsible for the reasonably foreseeable and avoidable harmful con-sequences of their actions.

The *welfare* paradigm that emerged toward the end of the nineteenth century responds to the problem of economic inequality, the very inequality that the liberal paradigm permits as natural and just. The image of society it projects—which corresponds to real changes in capitalism—is that of a complex system composed of organized corporate sectors, such as labor unions and sharehold-ing enterprises, that do not relate to one another transparently as free and equals and whose relationships impact the welfare of society as a whole in an indefinite number of ways. This image defines legal situations as opportunities for compensating individuals for the unavoidable side effects (such as unem-ployment and unequal bargaining power) intrinsic to a capitalist economy. It therefore holds a politically constructed economic system—not individuals—responsible for the determination of their economic fates; hence, it seeks to redistribute social liabilities and risks, assets, and securities equally.

Habermas's own understanding of the shift from liberal to welfare para-digms reveals several critical tensions. On the one hand, he insists that the liberal image of society—if it ever corresponded to reality—is now obso-lete in light of irreversible changes in capitalism. From this angle, the welfare paradigm does not "curtail" the negative freedom vouchsafed by the liberal paradigm so much as realize its equal and effective use for the first time. As he notes, "*no one* is free as long as the freedom of one persons must be purchased with another's oppression" (*BFN* 418). On the other hand, he observes that the implementation of welfare entitlements can be experienced as a paternalistic violation of an unsurpassed liberal understanding of private autonomy, not to mention a democratic understanding of public autonomy (*BFN* 404–9). Liberal and welfare paradigms of law can clash; and when either is applied in a dogmatic way to interpret all cases involving basic rights, some aspect of legal freedom or legal equality will be violated (*BFN* 410–14).[23]

To resolve these conflicts, Habermas introduces a higher-order proceduralist legal paradigm that does not define the content of rights so much as their reflective, democratic interpretation. More precisely, it requires that we—citizens

---

23. Here we have Habermas's response to both legal realists and critical legal studies (CLS). Whereas realist criticisms of formalism focus on the logical gap separating particular judgments and the general legal rules from which these judgments are "derived," CLS criticisms focus on the essential indeterminacy affecting all premises of legal reasoning, including the meaning and choice of general rules. Thus, whereas a realist would recommend turning to the concrete political intentions of legislators in determining whether a statute allowing capital punishment in cases involving the killing of witnesses applies to all murderers (since all victims of attempted homicide are potential witnesses), a CLS proponent would wonder whether defining "witness" broadly (to include all homicide victims) or narrowly (to include only those scheduled to testify in court) could be done in a way that was philosophically consistent. M. Kelman, *A Guide to Critical Legal Studies* (Cambridge: Harvard University Press, 1987), 11–13, 45–49. CLS scholars also deny that liberal and social welfare paradigms can be harmonized. Duncan Kennedy observes that "although there are no overall unifying principles of law which give a subject an internal necessity," there is a "deep level of order and structure to the oppositions between competing conceptions of doctrine and policy." D. Kennedy, "Form and Substance in Private Law Adjudication," in *Critical Legal Studies,* ed. A. Hutchinson (Totowa, NJ: Rowman and Littlefield, 1989), 16, 36–55. This structure—which roughly coincides with what Habermas calls the liberal paradigm—revolves around a dominant core, characterized by formalist types of reasoning that privilege individual responsibility and freedom, and a less dominant periphery—which resembles Habermas's description of the social welfare paradigm—characterized by substantive types of reasoning that privilege altruistic distributions of social burdens (risks) and benefits. Because each model of reasoning (or paradigm) is "potentially relevant to all the issues" (46) and neither can be harmonized with the other, no case can be decided in a rational, principled manner. As Allan Hutchinson remarks (in discussing torts), formalist types of reasoning will typically defer to rigid rules that fix responsibility individualistically, rules that hold individuals responsible for foreseeable harms they have caused, whether due to negligence or not (as in the case of strict liability). Substantive types of reasoning will defer to messier standards in assigning responsibility for harm (especially in cases involving incompatible uses of property rights) that involve the weighing of costs and benefits to society, the acceptance of complicated notions of multiple (alternative) causation, and the redistribution of liability among different parties. Habermas (citing Dworkin) rejects Hutchinson's analysis: the case itself dictates which paradigm of legal reasoning is most appropriate for interpreting it. Although concrete rules (statutes and cases) can clash, abstract principles cannot. On Habermas's model, a judge should instruct a jury hearing a tort case to weigh and reconcile formal issues of individual responsibility with substantive issues of social welfare. A. Hutchinson, "Of Kings and Dirty Rascals: The Struggle for Democracy," *Queens Law Journal* 9:273–92; Dworkin, *Law's Empire,* 444; A. Altman, *Critical Legal Studies: A Liberal Critique* (Princeton: Princeton University Press, 1990); Ingram, *Law: Key Concepts,* 194–205; and D. Ingram, "Dworkin, Habermas and the CLS Movement on Moral Criticism in Law," *Philosophy and Social Criticism* 16 (1990): 237–68.

as well as legal experts—collectively discuss on a case-by-case basis the extent to which a hard case (or problematic legal situation) can be defined in terms of either a liberal or welfare paradigm and in precisely what sense.

In order to explain the proceduralist paradigm of *law* we must recall what Habermas says about the proceduralist paradigm of *democracy*. Liberal and republican models of democracy presuppose a subject-centered conception of reason that postulates either isolated individuals or self-contained national communities as the proper subjects of rational self-determination and self-realization. The liberal model views citizens as private subjects who strategically pursue their interests in competition with others. They look to the state to protect their negative (subjective) freedom and to further their own interests. The political process is thus viewed as a market where vote tallies signal effective demand for governmental policies. According to this model, government is chiefly responsible for stabilizing conflict as well as for balancing and aggregating interests in an economically optimal way. Government's relation to civil society is therefore minimal: protecting economic freedom and ensuring economic prosperity. Its legitimacy thus hinges on enforcing constitutional rights that are presumed to have a neutral prepolitical basis in reason (*BFN* 269–74, 296).

The republican paradigm, by contrast, views citizens as political agents who identify with the state as a mechanism for promoting patriotic solidarity and the common good in accordance with a shared national identity. Here positive rights—especially the political right to vote and the social right to basic welfare—acquire preeminence over negative rights, since it is only through democracy that citizens define the proper limits of their own freedom. The political process accordingly serves to express and found an organic ethical unity in which mutual dependence is a condition for self-determination. Although the republican paradigm recognizes that national identity and solidarity are themselves partly constituted by communicative action, it gives special weight in this regard to ethical traditions and habits of a prepolitical nature. Hence, in contrast to the liberal model, state and public sphere (civil society) are here conceived as penetrating and constituting *all* aspects of society. The legitimacy of this "totalitarian" intervention rests entirely on its expressing the unified will of the people, which by definition cannot be bound by anything outside it (*BFN* 269–74, 296).

Habermas situates his proceduralist model of democracy between these liberal and republican extremes. Like the liberal model, the proceduralist model treats legal subjects as private persons who pursue their personal good within a relatively independent market economy. Like the republican model, it treats them as citizens who must be capable of jointly and publicly defining their collective identity. Unlike both models, the proceduralist model locates the source of legitimacy in discursive procedures rather than in transcendent reason or ethical virtue. Although it retains a liberal respect for individual rights and ethical pluralism—and so opposes the totalitarian tendencies of republican organicism—it endorses a republican critique of "possessive individualism" in its affirmation of public autonomy (*BFN* 297).

The conflict between liberal and republican models of democracy is partly mirrored within liberal democracy itself, in the form of a conflict between libertarians, who are hostile to any government save that of a "night watchman" state, and proponents of a welfare state, who argue that income redistribution and social regulation are necessary for including everyone equally under the same qualification of democratic citizenship. To a certain extent, this conflict—between liberal and welfare legal paradigms—tracks a distinction between negative and positive rights, neither of which can stand apart from the other. On the one hand, classical liberal rights to act without interference—and to speak freely and competently as a citizen in democratic debate—cannot possess equal value for all persons unless each person has equal access to the positive enabling conditions, capabilities, resources, and opportunities for exercising them. On the other hand, bureaucratically dispensing these entitlements involves classifying legal subjects as members of groups who, as individuals, have little control over the terms of their classification or its associated advantages and disadvantages. Accordingly, clients of a welfare state experience paternalistic government regulation as a personal violation of their negative right to be free from government interference (see chapter 10) (*BFN* 401–7).

In Habermas's opinion, the problem with liberal and welfare paradigms is conceptual: both share a "productivist image of a capitalist society" in which the question of rights is mainly focused on securing only the private autonomy of the lone subject. The liberal paradigm secures economic (market) efficiency by distributing equal negative freedoms—here conceived in accordance with the proprietary model of exclusive spheres of self-regarding wealth-maximizing behavior. The welfare paradigm secures the conditions of that freedom by distributing equal positive freedoms—here based on the client-provider model of average (normal) shares of benefits. Neglected by the liberal paradigm—and to a lesser extent, the welfare paradigm—is the co-originality of private and public autonomy: the necessity of democratically redefining the precise nature of freedoms and rights on a case-by-case basis so that negative and positive freedoms, liberty and welfare, can be harmonized with one another and with political self-determination (*BFN* 414–18).

A Concluding Assessment

The biggest challenge facing Habermas's discourse theory is reconciling the ideals of deliberative democracy with the realities of institutional democracy. In the remainder of this chapter I want to focus on three specific challenges. These revolve around Habermas's discussion of the circulation of power, the importance of strategic bargaining, and the justification of judicial review.

To begin with the democratic process: Habermas's description of this process in terms of discourse theoretical categories presumes that the public opinion generated within the public sphere has controlling influence over the problems that elected officials place on their agendas for deliberation and decision. Leaving aside Habermas's tendency to view public opinion formation as the work of a *weak* public, oriented solely to deliberation—as if elections and plebiscites, which certainly occur within civil society, were not oriented toward decision making—the presumption that public opinion functions as "input" for a government machine that processes policies as "output" is ambiguous. On the one hand, it suggests a kind of unidirectional flow of power, where the government remains dependent on the people for its agendas, arguments, and even policy options. On the other hand, it implies a cybernetic reprocessing of data according to programs and binary codes in which the basic input (content) is fundamentally altered and given a new form. Under this last description, it is far from clear what remains of the people's will after it has been aggregated and retranslated into policy legalese by technical elites. Seen from the standpoint of systems theory to which Habermas subscribes (see appendix F), the system is largely self-regulating (if not entirely self-enclosed) so that its selection of which input to process and by what code will be a top-down matter for elites within the system to decide. By the time the people's discontent is channeled through the sluices of the system and returns in the form of a technical statute that has more to do with maintaining the stability of the system, not much of the people's will remains. Does this sound like democracy?

In addition to Habermas's unfortunate use of metaphors drawn from systems theory to describe this process, which (doubly unfortunate) may have a ring of truth to it, there remains another problem that besets the circulation of power as Habermas understands it, namely, the distortions wrought on the circulation of power by social and administrative power. I will have more to say about this problem at the conclusion of chapter 9. It suffices for our purposes that Habermas's description of the circulation of power gives a certain—no doubt realistic—pride of place to strategic bargaining in which social power is most keenly felt. This should not surprise us. The broad areas of public policy on which there appear to be wide agreement concern constitutional basics, fundamental rights, and democratic procedures. Yet these provisions—formulated in general and abstract terms—must be applied and interpreted in light of concrete ethical values and interests, areas of public policy in which consensus is largely absent. So the most that can be expected in normal political deliberation is a mixture of discourse and strategic bargaining in which the effects of social power—inducements and threats—will distort the conversation.

Habermas's response to this reality takes three forms. First, he claims that all parties at the bargaining table ought to have roughly equal power in leveraging their claims (as required by discourse ethics). In some cases this principle can be legally institutionalized, as in the case of collective-bargaining law, which allows employees to engage in collective actions to offset the unequal financial power of their employer. However, in other cases the notion is unworkable. How, for instance, should government go about equalizing the disparity of bargaining power between animal-rights activists and the vast majority who are meat-eaters? How should it ensure that people are secure from losing their jobs when they deliberate on an environmental package that will impose higher taxes and regulations on the company that employs them? It is this unavoidable disparity in bargaining power (i.e., in having one's claims taken seriously by the majority) that justifies minorities' beliefs that they must resort to visible acts of civil disobedience in order to increase their leverage.[24]

Second, Habermas assumes that the need to clothe strategic self-interest in the civil language of public-minded deliberation will encourage people to discuss—and not just bargain. His hope is that by presenting public-interest rationales in support of their narrow self-interest citizens will be forced to empathize with their opponents to the point where they rethink, transform, and widen their interests to include those of their opponents. However, if Habermas is so confident in the "sedimented virtue" hidden in strategic bargaining to affect discursive deliberation, why does he then insist on the safety valve of judicial review for guaranteeing the right outcome?

This third response to the reality of democratic politics leads to final doubts about the compatibility of judicial review and deliberative democracy. Habermas's attempt to interpret adjudication in terms of a discourse of application is a way to accommodate the institutional realities of the legal system by showing how the privileged standpoint of an impartial judge and jury can offset the apparent counterdiscursive elements within the system, such as the strategic aims of contesting parties, the restrictions imposed on reasons (which must appeal to extant law or past precedents), and the tensions between competing legal paradigms, which prevent a mechanical resolution of hard cases. To a certain degree, these counterdiscursive elements can stimulate jurors and judges to engage in critical dialogue leading to deeper reflection on the meaning of law. However, they can also obstruct this endeavor: trial lawyers find that a winning strategy requires "gaming" the system as much as possible and manipulating judges and jurors by rhetorical appeals to their prejudices; available legal rationales may not conform to the highest standards of justice; and tensions within the law may contradict the presumption that a single right decision is in principle possible.

---

24. Habermas, like Rawls and Dworkin, defines civil disobedience as a form of public nonviolent lawbreaking in protest of what is perceived to be an unjust law. For them, civil disobedience is justified if and only if legal remedies have failed, typically due to violations of political and civil rights, but also whenever a groups feels that it has been made a "permanent" minority with respect to a wide range of issues in which compromise is unlikely. J. Rawls, "The Justification of Civil Disobedience," in *Collected Papers* (Cambridge: Harvard University Press, 1999), 176–89; R. Dworkin, "Civil Disobedience," in *Taking Rights Seriously* (Cambridge: Harvard University Press, 1977), 206–22; and J. Habermas, *Die Neue Unübersichtlichkeit* (Frankfurt: Suhrkamp, 1985), 79–99.

As Habermas notes, no amount of impartial dialogue within the courtroom (leaving aside external pressures emanating from the media) can overcome these obstacles unless constitutional, statutory, and judge-made law (legal precedent) already approximate rational legal integrity. For that to happen, society itself must possess economic, political, social, and cultural institutions that "meet" the legal system "halfway" (*BFN* 232). Beyond that, judges must play the taxing role of impartial spectator and conversational mediator with uncommon brilliance, especially at the highest echelons of judicial review, where tensions between legal paradigms demand new and creative resolutions.

It is one thing to exercise a mediating voice in the application of law, another to override the law. The former is necessary and unavoidable, and judges can do it more or less well. But the latter implies a great deal more than being an impartial spectator and mediator; it implies being a kind of legislative authority. Hence the question, Should the people entrust a privileged handful of people to override the people's judgment about what their rights should be? Does this not reflect—contrary to the underlying rationale for deliberative democracy—a combination of mistrust of one's fellow citizens (or skepticism of their capacity to deliberate rationally) and a confidence in the superior insight of elites? If we take Habermas's defense of judicial review seriously, should we not simply discard democratic procedure in favor of rule by the wise (as Plato recommended in *The Republic*)?

The force of this question stems from the fact that the people can be mistaken—that there can be a disjunction between what ought to be law as demanded by moral justice and what ought to be law as demanded by the principle of democracy.[25] But the question presumes, also, that there is an authority besides the people that is best suited to knowing what moral justice is. This presumption contradicts the spirit of deliberative democracy as Habermas himself understands it, which is that the philosopher (social theorist, or judge) does not occupy a higher ground on which to perceive what is true and right. If the elite decision procedure is at least as fallible as the democratic procedure—and Habermas's arguments show that we have every reason to believe that it is more fallible—then we have no good reason to disempower the people by invoking it.

Habermas tries to squeeze out of this dilemma by limiting the legitimate power of judicial review to laws that only directly impinge on democratic procedure, thereby leaving the people to legislate freely on matters of substantive justice. But this strategy fails on his account of the inherent "reflexivity" of democratic law making. Leaving aside the problem that some basic rights are not directly (or perhaps even indirectly) necessarily related to democratic

---

25. For classical discussions of this problem, see Richard Wollheim's *A Paradox in the Theory of Democracy,* in *Philosophy, Politics, and Society,* 2nd series, ed. P. Laslett and W. Runciman (Oxford: Basil Blackwell, 1969), 84; and J. Waldron, "A Right-Based Critique of Constitutional Rights," *Oxford Journal of Legal Studies,* 13/1 (1993): 18–51.

procedure, abstract principles of right—including participatory right—are without prescriptive force and content until their proper scope is defined by legislators in accordance with their substantive principles of justice. So we are back to where we started: if we have no good reason to disempower the people when it comes to matters of substantive justice then we have no good reason to disempower the people when it comes to matters of democratic procedural justice.

Habermas concedes this point when discussing Bruce Ackerman's distinction between normal and exceptional (or revolutionary) democracy.[26] As Ackerman points out, during those periods of revolutionary upheaval when the people are actively engaged in redefining their identity as a people—and redefining what it means to be free and equal—the courts should cede their authority. Not only must the people have a constitutional right to amend their constitution, but in times of crisis judges should allow a substantial majority with a mandate to reconstitute their constitution without obstruction. This revolutionary view toward law is mainly forward looking in that it constitutes a radical rethinking of—if not break from—the preceding constitutional paradigm. Yet Habermas's concession here is still too limited. For, according to him, it only applies to rare moments of truly deliberative, civic-minded politics when people are not self-consciously engaged in imposing their particular will on an opponent. Furthermore, it takes back what it concedes by conceiving revolutionary legal progress as a *continuous learning process* in which "on-going legislation carries on the system of rights by interpreting and adapting rights for current circumstances."[27] The gradual model of "revolutionary" politics invoked here is that of constitutional amendment and statutory refinement that still looks to the courts (who guard the past) for final authoritative approval, thereby depriving the present generation of its full democratic right to self-determination.[28] Only when Habermas redescribes this learning process as a "precautionary interruption of an otherwise self-referentially closed circle of legitimation" (*BFN* 318) does he intimate the kind of freedom from judicial review that revolutionary democracy with its forward-looking notion of democracy entails.

This last reference—to a learning process that no longer remains within the normal process of constitutional amendment and statutory change internal to a single legal paradigm but encompasses revolutionary leaps from one legal paradigm to another—raises new questions about the status of Habermas's

26. Ackerman's notion of dual democracy is developed within the context of his theory of constitutional revolution, which in turn owes much of its inspiration to Kuhn's distinction between normal and revolutionary science. See Ackerman, *We The People*, vol. 1.

27. J. Habermas, "Constitutional Democracy: A Paradoxical Union of Contradictory Principles," *Political Theory* 29/6 (December 2001): 774.

28. B. Honig, "Dead Rights, Live Futures: A Reply to Habermas's Constitutional Democracy," *Political Theory* 29/6 (December 2001): 792–805.

own proceduralist paradigm vis-à-vis its liberal and welfare predecessors. That these preceding paradigms have each undergone an internal crisis that cannot be resolved within them suggests that passage to a proceduralist paradigm is more revolutionary than Habermas suggests. Does a proceduralist paradigm fundamentally alter the way in which we understand our liberal rights and welfare entitlements, or does it merely provide a discursive procedure for applying them, more or less intact? Does it represent a more democratic understanding of judicial review which—if not overturning that office—requires that it be exercised less imperiously?[29] No answer to these questions will be forthcoming until we have a better idea how the proceduralist paradigm can be applied to specific areas of public policy, the topic of our next chapter.

29. Ackerman argues that it implies both: a radical rethinking of paradigms and a more democratic understanding of the process of constitutional amendment and change. Although he rejects the Hegelian idea that American society "is moving down some predetermined historical track," he nonetheless holds that "the court's use of the deep past is best understood dialectically...thesis, antithesis, and synthesis...each generation's dialogic activity providing in turn the new historical thesis for the next generation's ongoing confrontation with the constitutional future of America." See *We the People,* vol. 1, 304), and Ingram, *Law: Key Concepts,* 88–92; see also D. Ingram, *Reason, History, and Politics: The Communitarian Grounds of Legitimation in the Modern Age* (Albany: SUNY Press, 1995), 270–75ff.

8

Law and Democracy

Part III: Applying the Proceduralist Paradigm

We have examined the proceduralist paradigm in the abstract, but how might it be applied in the concrete? Habermas shows us how in a number of applications revolving around gender, multiculturalism, immigration, and separation of church and state. Our brief survey of these applications will provide critical insight into the capacity of the proceduralist paradigm to guide policymaking.

Separation of Church and State: The Public/Private Distinction

In his first major work, *The Structural Transformation of the Public Sphere* (1962), Habermas argued that the distinction between private and public life underpinning liberal society played a crucial role in maintaining the vitality of democracy. The middle-class family in the eighteenth century brought innovations in domestic architecture that created new spaces for reflection and conversation. The parlor and the private study emerged as perhaps the most important spaces for generating criticisms that reappeared in the political public sphere (*STPS* 43–56).

The development of private spaces went hand in hand with the personal cultivation of religious conscience, whose importance as an internal fortress capable of withstanding the assaults of government censorship was comparable to that of reason itself. This required, however, that religion, no less than reason, be extended beyond the private sphere to the public sphere, where it could become a powerful political force in its own right. Consequently, in England and

North America, private religious conscience became the focal point for framing political resistance against all forms of tyranny. This function, of course, depended on religion remaining separate from the state. Protestant denominations grew out of protest against a hegemonic church; their protest against tyrannical government, which first consisted of forbidden discussions held in private and later publicly delivered from the pulpit, continued the internal dialogue they had cultivated between their moral conscience and their God.

Having taken stock of religious conscience as a check on government tyranny, Habermas looks to democratic government as a check on *religious* tyranny. Belying what secularists (including Habermas) had once predicted, religion has neither withered away nor retreated into the private sphere but has once again become a major political force. Led by fundamentalists of all stripes, religions vie with one another as they seek to commandeer the state for their own purposes. Not surprisingly, Habermas condemns this desecularization of government, insisting that state and church remain separate if the former is to retain any "impartiality" with respect to competing confessions.

This view, of course, has been a mainstay of liberal political thought for almost three hundred years and has been given fresh impetus by Rawls's theory of political liberalism. Rawls insists that society can be understood as a mutually beneficial scheme of voluntary cooperation only if citizens believe that the public process of political deliberation is conducted in a manner that all can accept as legitimate or respectful of each and everyone's basic rights. This happens when discussion embodies "public reason." Public reason assumes a critical role whenever "constitutional essentials" concerning basic rights are at stake. Of course, not all of the reasons that legitimately circulate in what Rawls designates as the *background culture* (which is roughly synonymous with what Habermas designates as the informal, or *weak,* public sphere) can meet the minimum threshold of public reason as Rawls understands it. Most Christian fundamentalists probably agree that homosexual marriage should not be legal because it violates God's law, but this reason is simply not recognized as a reason by atheists who might otherwise be persuaded to ban gay marriage for secular reasons. Only if we were to suppose that these secular reasons were grounded in a neutral (or commonly accepted) authority, such as science or the Constitution, would they meet the threshold of public reason, even if the arguments in which they served as premises were not convincing to all persons.

According to Rawls, this threshold ought to be met when it comes to political discourse that occurs in the "public political forum," which consists of arguments delivered by judges, legislators, executive officers, and candidates who are running for office (the domain covered by Habermas's formal, or *strong,* public sphere). In these instances it is essential, Rawls believes, that the reasons given in support of policies publicly respect the divergent views of citizens by not appealing to reasons that cannot in principle be accepted by everyone. Such nonpublic reasons would, of course, include confessional beliefs of any kind, or any belief system that governs the lives of its adherents in some all-encompassing or comprehensive way. Given that the free exercise of reason inclines people to go their separate ways in choosing plans of life, "reasonable pluralism"—and with it, reasonable disagreement about the truth of any "comprehensive doctrine"—is unavoidable. So publicly acceptable reasons must only refer to beliefs that all can accept, such as those derived from science or from the very widely shared "free-standing" culture of political liberalism, which all *reasonable* citizens accept.[1] Thus, a believer who seeks to limit the right to abortion (and therewith the basic right of women to control their bodies) might appeal to the bad consequences that attend legalized abortion (such as a lowering of respect for life, say, or the psychological trauma women who have abortions undergo), but he could not appeal to the divine sanctity of life without imposing a "religious reason" on persons who are nonbelievers.[2]

Rawls later softened his view that political leaders, judges, and even ordinary citizens should refrain from appealing to comprehensive beliefs in defending policies that affect basic rights (at least within forums that could be described as public and nonsectarian). His "proviso" stipulates that they might appeal to such beliefs in good conscience so long as they eventually appealed (or intended to appeal) to public reason "in due course" of making their case to a broader public.[3] But this proviso would still be difficult to live under since some convictions (belief in an anthropomorphic God) are unsubstantiated by, or stand in tension with, science (e.g., the theory of evolution).

This is one of the reasons why Habermas resists requiring believers to justify their political beliefs in strictly secular terms (even if they do so "in due course"),[4] and it explains why he rejects the French republican principle of

1. Rawls appeals to the idea that reasonable confessions will overlap in justifying—from heterogeneous premises—the same universal values that make up a liberal-democratic political culture. Thus Habermas approvingly writes: "John Rawls chose the image of a module to describe this 'embedding' of the egalitarian universalism of the legal order in the ethos of the various religious worldviews: the module of secular justice should fit into each orthodox context of justification even though it was constructed with the help of reasons that are neutral toward different worldviews" (*BNR* 308). See J. Rawls, *Political Liberalism* (New York: Columbia University Press, 1993), 58–66.

2. Rawls observes that a comprehensive religious doctrine could reasonably affirm the "due respect for human life" only if it gave equal weight to two other competing values: the equal right of women to control their reproductive lives and the state's interest in the ordered reproduction of society over time. Doing so, he believes, would most certainly lead a reasonable person to conclude that a woman should have the right to terminate a pregnancy during the first trimester. Rawls, *Political Liberalism*, 243n32.

3. See J. Rawls, *The Law of Peoples; with The Idea of Public Reason Revisited* (Cambridge: Harvard University Press, 1999), 144.

4. Robert Audi, for instance, argues that "one has a prima facie obligation not to advocate or support any law or public policy . . . unless one has and is willing to offer, adequate secular reasons for this advocacy and support." Furthermore, Audi cautions that these secular motivations must guide one's voting behavior as well. See R. Audi and N. Wolterstorff, *Religion in the Public Sphere* (New York: Rowman and Littlefield, 1997), 25.

laïcité,[5] or why he rejects (alternatively) a weaker principle that permits religious reasons in all policy debates except those involving constitutional essentials.[6] Habermas also notes that the narrow secular requirement is impossible to fulfill. Ethically speaking, it forces believers who choose to participate in politics to behave dishonestly toward themselves and others by publicly disavowing their religiously motivated political commitments. Cognitively speaking, it requires them to separate their convictions from their very being—as if the religious convictions that energize the entirety of one's very existence were no different from cold scientific propositions. Even if believers could adhere to the ethical and cognitive demands of narrow secularism, doing so would be unfair, since it would require them—but not nonbelievers—to deny a substantial part of their identity as a precondition for active political citizenship.

Habermas therefore concludes that "we cannot derive from the secular character of the state a direct obligation for all citizens personally to supplement their public statements of religious convictions by equivalents in a generally accessible language" (*BNR* 129). However, this conclusion, he maintains, is consistent with the obligation imposed on *public officials* to *refrain* from asserting such convictions in *institutional* (parliamentary, judicial, or administrative) debates about public policies and laws.[7]

Leaving aside the severity of this latter form of self-censorship—Rawls's proviso permits officials to make officially recorded religious arguments in official settings so long as they later intend to supplement them with nonreligious arguments—one might here object that insisting on secular reasoning at the institutional level goes against the spirit of a proceduralist paradigm by privileging a liberal paradigm. This latter paradigm marks a hard distinction between an impartial domain of political values (public reason) and a sectarian domain of comprehensive creeds (private faith). By contrast, a proceduralist paradigm leaves the boundaries separating universal political values and particular social creeds fluid, assigning to a reasonable public sole responsibility for policing them according to its own democratic deliberation. From the standpoint of a proceduralist paradigm, the boundaries operating *even at the institutional level* are not hard and fast—determined by pure reason—but are publicly

5. The principle of *laïcité* provoked protests by Muslim women, who argued that banning head scarves and other religious symbols in schools and workplaces violated freedom of religious conscience. In 1989 the French supreme court (Conseil d'Etat) ruled that students could wear nonostentatious religious symbols that did not interfere with an orderly education. In 1994 the wearing of scarves was ruled to be in violation of the Bayrou guidelines interpreting this ruling. In the United States conflicts between disestablishment of religion and religious freedom favor the latter (see, e.g., the Religious Liberty Protection Act of 1998), although attempts to introduce prayers at school graduations have been repeatedly struck down by the Supreme Court as unconstitutional.

6. "I consider this reservation unrealistic in the case of modern legal systems in which basic rights directly affect concrete legislation and adjudication, so that virtually any controversial legal issue can be heightened into an issue of principle" (*BNR* 123n18).

7. "In parliament, for example, the rules of procedure must empower the house leader to strike religious positions or justifications from the official transcript" (*BNR* 131).

negotiable, so that, for instance, appeal to the dignity of the fetus as a human being might be thought (now or someday) to straddle the line separating moral reason and religious faith, and so could thereby acquire the status of an admissible institutional claim.

Admittedly, whether or not the public as it currently stands could accept Habermas's restriction on allowing religious reasons in parliamentary debates is a question that cannot be definitively answered. In some European polities the answer might be yes, but in a religious country like the United States the answer would likely be no. Habermas could still argue that Americans would consent to his stricture if they were fully informed and reasonable, but that response places a heavy burden on what is arguably a counterfactual thought experiment that remains foreign to the spirit of a proceduralist paradigm. However, in defense of his stricture, Habermas observes that no one—including believers—could ever be assured that public policies were neutral with respect to their faith unless institutional deliberation were radically secular (*BNR* 134).

But if believers' religious convictions cannot enter into institutional political debates, have we not then undercut their effective political representation at that level? Have we not continued to treat them unfairly? Habermas's response to this question is remarkably subtle, and trades on two somewhat conflicting responses. His earlier response asserted that believers can and must adopt an ironic stance toward their own faith commitments, splitting their identities into public and private aspects; his later response partially retracts this injunction, allowing that they can desist from doing so as long as others can *translate* their faith commitments into secular political reasons. As for the first response, Habermas insists that believers must learn from secular sources.

> Religious consciousness must, first, come to terms with the cognitive dissonance of encountering other denominations and religions. It must, second, adapt to the authority of the sciences which hold a societal monopoly of secular knowledge. It must last agree to the premises of the constitutional state grounded in profane morality. (*FHN* 104)

In a modern, secular society persons of faith must adopt a certain irony with respect to their beliefs; although they hold them to be true, they must acknowledge that others do not.[8] Whenever they engage these others in political debate,

---

8. Tolerance, Habermas, observes, only requires that believers refrain from imposing their way of life on others (*BNR* 308–9). As he puts it: "Every religion is originally a '*worldview*' or 'comprehensive doctrine' in the sense that it claims authority to structure a form of life *in its entirety*. A religion must relinquish this claim within a secularized society marked by a pluralism of worldviews" (*BNR* 307). More important, a religion must relinquish this claim with respect to its individual members, who retain basic rights that cannot be abrogated by their religious community: "When religious law supplements or even replaces civil law, especially within the sphere of the family, women and children in particular are exposed to repression by their own authorities" (*BNR* 297).

they must do so from *their* agnostic point of view; they must treat their own faith commitments as if they were not only potentially fallible but essentially nonshareable (*FHN* 105). Hence, "democratic common sense insists on reasons which are acceptable not just for members of *one* religious community" (*FHN* 108). Only under these secular conditions can the mutual toleration and respect demanded of us by modern morality be institutionally safeguarded. But in order for democracy to live up to these moral ideals, the believer must shift her reasoning to the only ground recognized by the agnostic: science. So construed, believers unavoidably carry a special burden that nonbelievers do not, "for only citizens committed to religious beliefs are required to split up their identities into...public and private elements" (*FHN* 109).

Contradicting this view, Habermas now says that religious citizens need not "split up their identity into a public and private part the moment they enter into public discourses" so long as their religious convictions can be translated into neutral arguments at the institutional level (what he calls the "institutional translation proviso") (*BNR* 130). In an additional effort to equalize the burden between believers and nonbelievers, Habermas mentions that *non*believers should shoulder equal responsibility for undertaking this "cooperative" translation (*BNR* 131).

This proceduralist response explicitly rejects the liberal distinction between reason and religion.

> But only if the secular side, too, remains sensitive to the force of articulation inherent in religious languages will the search for reasons that aim at universal acceptability not lead to an unfair exclusion of religions from the public sphere, nor sever secular society from important resources of meaning. *In any event, the boundaries between secular and religious reasons are fluid. Determining these disputed boundaries should therefore be seen as a cooperative task.* (FHN 109, italics mine)

A proceduralist paradigm requires that believers and nonbelievers adopt one another's perspective in an effort to learn from one another. This is a demanding if not impossible task. For not only must believers accept the political supremacy of the secular at the institutional level, nonbelievers must recognize the element of religious transcendence implicit in their own nonnaturalistic (nonscientific) commitment to the morally just and ethically good life. Needless to say, in the aftermath of 9/11 this task imposes a supreme challenge, especially to Europeans, who must now learn to tolerate the growing presence of Islam in their midst even while pressing Muslims to articulate a supreme loyalty to liberal democratic principles from within their own faith. As Habermas pointedly remarks, "Muslim immigrants cannot be integrated into a Western society in defiance of their religion, but only together with it" (*EFP* 71).

I will have more to say about Habermas's hypothesis about the persistence of religion in the modern age—a hypothesis that contradicts his earlier prediction that religion would simply wither away in an enlightened world.[9] It suffices to note that there is an aspect of this "postsecular" thesis that does not easily harmonize with his optimism about the translatability of religious reasons into secular reasons. Habermas says that the ethical core that forms the indispensable background to our secular morality *cannot* be completely translated into secular language. This explains the liberal belief—which Habermas endorses in a qualified way[10]—that "it is unreasonable to demand that people publicly justify their private ethicoreligious beliefs to others" (*TJ* 227). By invoking a split between the "untranslatable" embodied (experiential) ethos of religious practice and the theoretically translatable moral core of religious doctrine, Habermas again seems to have underscored the inevitable "identity split" that believers must endure in a modern liberal polity.[11] In this respect he has not gone much beyond Rawls.[12] Indeed, he insists that the resistance of religion to reason is a

9. "I would also admit that [in *The Theory of Communicative Action* (1981)] I subsumed rather too hastily the development of religion in modernity with Max Weber under the 'privatization of the powers of faith' and suggested too quickly an affirmative answer to the question as to 'whether then from religious truths, after religious world views have collapsed, nothing more and nothing other than the secular principles of a universalist ethics of responsibility can be salvaged, and this means, can be accepted for good reasons, on the basis of insight'" (*RR* 79).

10. Elsewhere Habermas notes that "citizens must develop an epistemic attitude toward other religions and world views" by "relat[ing] their religious beliefs in a self-reflective manner to the claims of competing doctrines of salvation so that they do not jeopardize their own exclusive claim to truth" (*BNR* 137). Achieving *mutual understanding* rather than *agreeing* on truth claims—except when these refer to the consequences of holding a belief—is what is expected.

11. Habermas once thought that someday philosophy might "translate" the "indispensable potentials for meaning into the language of public, that is, presumptively generally convincing reasons"—something that "for the time being" philosophy had "not yet" accomplished (*PT* 51). Yet scarcely had he penned these thoughts when he changed his mind, writing: "Philosophy cannot appropriate what is talked about in religious discourse *as* religious experience. These experiences could only be added to the fund of philosophy's resources...if philosophy identifies these experiences using a description that is no longer borrowed from the language of a specific religious tradition, but from the universe of argumentative discourse that is uncoupled from the event of revelation. At those fracture points where a neutralizing translation of his type can no longer succeed, philosophical discourse must confess its failure. The metaphorical use of words such as 'redemption,' 'messianic light,' and 'restoration of nature,' etc., makes religious experience a mere citation. In these moments of its powerlessness argumentative speech passes over beyond religion and science into literature, into a mode of presentation that is no longer measured by truth claims" (*RR* 75). This sentiment is later reiterated in his assertion that the "opaque core of religious experience" remains "abysmally alien to discursive thought" (*BNR* 143), despite his insistence that religion's "claim to truth" be taken seriously by nonbelievers.

12. Habermas's institutional translation proviso fails just as badly as Rawls's proviso in fully integrating believers into political life, once it is conceded that core elements of religious belief and practice cannot be translated into secular public reason. Lafont, for instance, observes that Habermas's demand for translation amounts to postulating a prior overlapping consensus, or agreement on a secular set of reasons by "different epistemic means." C. Lafont, "Religion and the Public Sphere: Remarks on Habermas's Conception of Public Deliberation in Postsecular Societies," *Philosophy and Social Criticism* 35/1–2 (2009): 134. Disputing Habermas's bias in favor of secular reason, Lafont recommends that citizens be allowed to state any reason they sincerely believe in "provided that they are prepared to address any objections based on reasons generally acceptable to democratic citizens that other participants may advance against such policies" (132). Maeve

sign of its durability and bears witness to the pluralism of belief in any *post*secular society. At the same time, he accords reason a privileged role in testing its own limits: only public discourse—prior to institutional debate and independent of postmetaphysical philosophy—can "decide what part of the religious doctrines is rational and what part irrational" (*BNR* 143). In light of this priority, Habermas concedes that "even these two expectations" (that secularized citizens may neither fundamentally deny that religious worldviews may be true nor reject the right of devout fellow citizens to couch their contributions to public discussion in religious language) fail to "fully counterbalance the *non-neutrality* in the effects of the principle of tolerance" (*BNR* 310, emphasis mine). This "residual imbalance," he concludes, "does not place the justification of the principle [of toleration] itself in question." Yet one wonders, with Rawls, whether deeply religious people will be willing to risk their faith and integrity by playing a game of political dialogue that places their faith at such a disadvantage.

The nonneutrality of liberal toleration still requires believers entering political careers to bracket what might be the main reason underlying their support for a policy—that God commanded it—and accept the paradoxical position advocated by Plato in the *Euthyphro:* that God commanded it because it is reasonable. In submitting to the trial of discourse, believers also submit to the trial of temptation—tempting their faith against the possibility of enlightened transformation. But a knight of true faith (as Kierkegaard taught) would never sacrifice his passion on the altar of reason in the way that a nonbeliever might.

Perhaps it is mistaken to insist on reciprocal transformative discourse as a condition for entering democratic political life. We allow religions to demonstrate the *depth* of their conviction through acts of *witnessing* without demanding that they justify their faith.[13] This kind of political speech (weak communicative action oriented solely toward mutual understanding) also

---

Cooke echoes a similar complaint when she notes that the demand for translation presumes agreement in advance, thereby undermining the whole point of Habermasian discourse, which is "to reach agreement on the single right answer through transformation of perceptions, interpretations, and evaluations." M. Cooke, "A Secular State for a Post-Secular Society? Postmetaphysical Political Theory and the Place of Religion," *Constellations* 14/2 (2007): 228–29. To Lafont's and Cooke's criticisms I would add a general reservation regarding Habermas's rule governing the logic of discourse generally, which requires that different speakers mean exactly the same thing when they use the same expression (a rule that again presupposes a priori translation).

13. In addition to witnessing, Rawls mentions *declaration* and *conjecture* as other forms of legitimate political discourse that do not express a public form of reasoning (arguing from premises we "think others could accept to conclusions we think they could also reasonably accept"). One can declare one's comprehensive doctrine to reassure others who hold different comprehensive doctrines that it comports with a reasonable political conception; one can openly conjecture that others' comprehensive doctrines comport with a reasonable political conception (correcting their misapprehension that they do not); and one can witness on behalf of displaying moral resistance, based on one's comprehensive doctrines, to public policies that one otherwise regards as politically legitimate (as when abortion clinic protestors, inspired by a belief in the divine sanctity of the fetus, seek to demonstrate the depth of their conviction in hopes that less passionate pro-choice supporters will relent). In a fully just society, these would be the only forms of legitimate political

informs identity politics in which cultural groups seek only to demonstrate to outsiders the importance (to themselves) of their way of life.[14]

Gender Difference and the Law

The private/public distinction also figures in discussions concerning gender differences and the law. With good reason, feminists proclaim that the personal is the political. The patriarchal family has been the focal point of women's oppression. Domiciled into child rearing and housework, women have been economically exploited and politically marginalized—even as they have struggled to find employment and political recognition outside the home. Conversely, the public domain—including the state and its bureaucracies—has been shaped by patriarchal structures emanating from the private sphere. The "welfare" doled out to single parents (almost all of whom are women) comes attached with all sorts of stigmas, requirements, therapeutic oversights, and interventions that are absent in the "welfare" claimed by mainly male pensioners as a matter of right (*BFN* 422).[15]

Although respecting the private/public distinction prohibits unwarranted state intrusion into the home—adult women who voluntarily choose to live in patriarchal home environments structured along a traditional gendered division of labor should not be prevented from doing so—the home is not a legally unregulated zone. Because of its important role in determining the capabilities and opportunities of family members as well as their access to basic goods such as income and self-respect, Rawls rightly includes it as one of the institutions—alongside the economic system and the legal system—that properly falls within the purview of what he calls the basic structure, or that part of society that is properly governed by principles of social justice.

Habermas does too; and both he and Rawls insist that women's rights must be respected both inside and outside the home. However, unlike Rawls, Habermas does not see the issue of rights in terms of distributive justice—as goods or possessions. Rather, citing the work of Iris Marion Young and Martha Minow, he observes that "rights are relationships" or (in the words of Young)

---

discourse; but in an imperfectly just society (such as ours) acts of civil disobedience would also be legitimate. Rawls, *Law of Peoples*, 155–56.

14. One is reminded of the Cynics, a group of philosophers who lived in ancient Greece and Rome during the fourth century (BCE) who not only spoke the truth but manifested it in their scandalous behavior. Discussing this kind of "veridiction" (*parrhesia*) in his last course at the Collège de France (1984), Foucault explicitly contrasted this aesthetic embodiment of ethical virtue as lived exemplar to the earlier Socratic variant, which emphasized political dialogue and reasoned justification. T. Flynn, "Foucault as Parrhesiast: His Last Course at the College de France," in *The Final Foucault*, ed. J. Bernauer and D. Rasmussen (Cambridge: MIT Press, 1988), 102–18.

15. N. Fraser, "Women, Welfare, and the Politics of Need Interpretation," in *Unruly Practices: Power, Discourse, and Gender in Contemporary Social Theory* (Minneapolis: University of Minnesota Press, 1989), 144–60.

"institutionally defined rules specifying what people can *do* in relation to one another."[16] The inherently political nature of rights as regulating relationships explains why the scope and meaning of rights has shifted along with our understanding of ourselves and our relationships. This applies above all to our understanding of the relationship between our private autonomy and our public autonomy, or between the relationship between our private lives and our public lives. Thus, not so long ago abortion was considered only a matter of public hygiene and eugenic policy, and forced marital sex was treated strictly as a matter of private patriarchal discretion. Here again we see how the question of boundaries that cropped up in our discussion of religion and politics reappears in this context as well.

Which legal paradigm (if any) should guide us in defining women's rights? The abortion controversy highlights the right to privacy, or the right of women to plan their "private" reproductive lives free from undue government interference. Liberal theorists since John Stuart Mill have sought to defend such private "self-regarding" acts on the grounds that they do not affect other persons or society and do not violate an assignable duty. But this solution begs the question about what (if any) acts are strictly self-regarding (abortion, for example, clearly affects the fetus, regardless of whether it is considered a full-fledged moral or legal person, and it affects society's legitimate interest in regulating the health of its citizens).

When viewed from the standpoint of this latter governmental interest, abortion highlights the public's right to welfare. But the public's welfare can hardly be considered apart from the private welfare of its individual members. Women will certainly identify their welfare with a freedom to choose whether or not to have children. Accordingly, welfare liberals like Rawls adopt a nuanced view of abortion rights that requires balancing the goods (or values) of privacy, personal choice, and public welfare. But Habermas, as we have seen, rejects this distributional calculus of rights as a top-down "instrumentalization of politics oriented exclusively to results" (*BFN* 426). The attempt to define the scope and meaning of basic rights monologically—from the standpoint of theoretical value balancing—misses what is more fundamental, namely, that the meaning and scope of rights properly unfolds only in an ongoing process of interpreting relationships and roles—the "identity politics" of everyday public life that is preparatory to any judicial or legislative act.

> If one starts with an intersubjective concept of rights, the real source of error is easily identified: public discussion must first clarify the aspects under which differences between the experiences and living situations of (specific groups of) women and men become relevant for an equal opportunity to take advantage of individual liberties. (*BFN* 425)

16. *BFN* 419; I. M. Young, *Justice and the Politics of Difference* (Princeton: Princeton University Press, 1990), 25.

Before clarifying Habermas's point about the relevance of a proceduralist paradigm in clarifying relationships whose interpretation is preliminary to any understanding of rights, let us look at another approach to defining women's rights. That approach focuses on the distinction between difference-blind and difference-sensitive law.[17] Advocates of a liberal paradigm see sexist discrimination, or gender-sensitive treatment, as the locus of women's oppression. Accordingly, they insist that women should have exactly the same rights as men and should be treated exactly the same way. Although this paradigm focuses on the equal humanity of women as rights bearers, it fails to address differences and inequalities in their social position—specifically, with respect to childbearing and child rearing, home care, and economic/patriarchal dependence—that persist after formal legal equality has been achieved (*BFN* 421).[18] It is women, after all, who are most affected by abortion law. It is they who shoulder the entire burden of childbearing, who shoulder the greater burden of caring for family members, and who typically shoulder the burden of dependency that comes from not being gainfully employed outside the home (which in turn renders them vulnerable to spousal abuse). Even if women manage to escape these burdens and vulnerabilities by entering the workforce, they continue to be discriminated against in a variety of ways, from being sexually harassed at work to being unqualified for jobs for failing to meet workplace codes that match up better with male physiques and temperaments.

Advocates of the welfare paradigm thus argue that labor and family law must be made sensitive to biological differences just as social law is made sensitive to differences in income and ability. As Habermas notes:

> Good examples are found in the protective norms pertaining to pregnancy and maternity, or custody rights in divorce cases. Such norms cluster around the clear biological differences connected with reproduction. The same holds for special regulations in criminal law dealing with sex offenses. In these areas, the feminist

17. For a classical statement of the alternative paradigms at stake here—a difference-blind approach versus a difference-sensitive approach—see M. Minow, *Making All the Difference: Inclusion, Exclusion, and American Law* (Ithaca: Cornell University Press, 1990).

18. See Susan Moller Okin's *Justice, Gender, and the Family* (Cambridge: Harvard University Press, 1989). Although Okin presents her position as a more gender-sensitive extension of Rawls's liberal theory of justice, she insists, more emphatically than Rawls, that the basic structure of society (the subject matter of Rawls's theory of justice) include the family, rectifying gender imbalances in child rearing and dependency and eliminating gender roles. Rawls later agreed with Okin that the principles of justice apply to the family, while he denied that they do so directly. Parallel to universities, churches, and other private associations, the law must protect family members' basic rights without dictating the family's division of labor. That said, he agrees with Okin that "should there be a divorce, [a wife] should have an equal share in the increased value of the family's assets during that time." Nussbaum, however, criticizes Rawls's assimilation of the family to a private association, which renders women's and children's basic capabilities insecure. J. Rawls, *Justice as Fairness: A Restatement* (Cambridge: Harvard University Press, 2001), 167; M. Nussbaum, *Women and Human Development* (Cambridge: Cambridge University Press, 2000), 270–83.

legislation followed the social-welfare program of promoting equality in women's legal status via compensations for disadvantages, whether "natural" or "social." (*BFN* 422)

But here the problem of paternalism emerges with a vengeance.[19] Appealing to false stereotypes about what is best for them given their "biologically determined needs," welfare laws have been known to prohibit women from working in traditionally masculine occupations (such as in the military, an occupation, Habermas notes, that exemplifies what it means to be a citizen). Often they come with a catch-22:

> Legal provisions for pregnancy and maternity have only increased the risk of women losing their jobs; to the extent that protective labor laws have generally reinforced segregation in the labor market or the overrepresentation of women in lower wage brackets; to the extent that liberalized divorce law has confronted women with the burdening effects of divorce. (*BFN* 422)

Given the discriminatory effects of paternalism, not to mention the dehumanization (deprivation of freedom) that women experience as a result of having their lives "colonized" by a therapeutic-welfare bureaucracy,[20] many (but not all) feminists are understandably wary of appealing to "essentialist" definitions of women's different nature. These feminists prefer to mark the difference between men and women in terms of *social positioning*. Here, differential rights—to affirmative action "preferences," for instance—are supposed to counteract the sex discrimination built into a patriarchal occupational system. Although these differential rights do acknowledge the importance of relational positions, they often neglect an important implication, namely, that the meaning and scope of rights must be interpreted democratically. Who ought to be entitled to what under affirmative action is often determined by legislators and judges according to their own theoretical balancing of values and interests. Even radical feminists have not been immune to this kind of theoretical balancing. To take one famous case, Catharine MacKinnon and Andrea Dworkin succeeded in having an ordinance enacted in Indianapolis that would make the production and distribution of pornography illegal. Although the purpose of the ordinance was to protect the civil equality of women against misogynist depictions that incite men to rape and abuse them, the court ruled that it violated

19. See Eva Feder Kittay's *Love's Labor: Essays on Women, Equality, and Dependency* (New York: Routledge, 1999). Kittay argues that the liberal social contractarian approach, with its emphasis on securing individual autonomy, is insensitive to the primary facts of relational dependency. Hence she urges strengthening welfare supports for caretakers and their dependents in addition to policies that redistribute care-giving responsibilities and protect paid caregivers from exploitation.

20. *BFN* 120. Habermas's reference to "colonization" in conjunction with his discussion of women's "preferential treatment" under the welfare paradigm touches on a technical theory of social pathology that is discussed in chapter 10 of this book.

freedom of speech—including the freedom of women who enjoy looking at misogynist depictions of women for purely recreational reasons (*BFN* 423ff).[21]

In Habermas's opinion, liberal and welfare paradigms err in predefining the needs (identity) of women by using *overgeneralized classifications* and *stereotypes of gender identity* (*BFN* 422–23):

> What is meant to promote the equal status of women in general often benefits only one category of (already privileged) women at the cost of another category, because gender-specific inequalities are correlated in a complex and obscure manner with membership in other underprivileged groups (social class, age, ethnicity, sexual orientation, etc.). (*BFN* 423)

This complaint about defining women's needs and identities according to a single dominant norm—what Habermas, following Foucault, condemns as a coercive form of "normalization"—has been forcefully articulated by radical "third-wave" (multicultural) feminists, who question the definition of two variables whose interpretation is taken for granted by both liberals and welfarists: the identity and needs of women and the gendered needs that revolve around specific roles (*BFN* 424). Abstracting from women's reproductive lives and social positioning, the liberal paradigm presumes that women's needs are fixed by the same rational agency they share with men. It therefore reduces women's needs to the same need for freedom that men have, and it defines job- and role-qualifications—especially in areas involving leadership and physical risk—in terms of traits that are stereotypically ascribed to men. Embedding them in their reproductive lives, the welfare paradigm presumes that women's needs are fixed by their peculiar biology and/or social positioning. It therefore reduces women's needs to domestic needs or needs for special protections, and it defines the roles that gravitate around domestic life in terms of traits stereotypically ascribed to women. Both paradigms thus end up defining women's rights too narrowly. In Habermas's opinion, only the proceduralist paradigm views women's rights and needs as *undefined, fluid,* and *political*—emerging within the crucible of a "struggle for recognition" (as Axel Honneth puts it) in which feelings of insult and disrespect motivate a collective recognition (social understanding) of persons as bearers of particular group and personal identities:

21. C. MacKinnon, *Towards a Feminist Theory of the State* (Cambridge: Harvard University Press, 1989). MacKinnon and Andrea Dworkin drafted several antipornography ordinances for Minneapolis and Indianapolis (both of which were later invalidated on constitutional grounds) that made the production and distribution of pornography a civil offense. They argued that pornography—by which they meant not obscene or sexually arousing content but sexually violent imagery that objectifies and demeans women and children—contributes to the violation of women's rights and hence to the denial of their equal protection under the law. Most controversial was their characterization of pornography as *action* (akin to violent assault) rather than *speech*, which is protected under the First Amendment. Some feminists agreed with the courts that the Dworkin/MacKinnon ordinances were too sweeping in defining pornography and too paternalistic in prejudging what pleasures were to be tolerated. See D. Ingram, *Law: Key Concepts in Philosophy* (London: Continuum Press, 2006), chap. 5.

Gender identity and gender relations are social constructions that crystallize around biological differences yet vary historically. In women's struggle for equality, as well as in the transformation of the paradigmatic understanding of the corresponding legal programs, one can observe that rights meant to guarantee the autonomous pursuit of a personal life project for women cannot be adequately formulated at all unless the relevant aspects for defining equal and unequal treatment are convincingly articulated and justified beforehand. The classifications of gender roles and gender-related differences touches elementary layers of a society's cultural understanding.... Therefore competing views about the identity of the sexes and their relation to each other must be open to public discussion.... This contest over the interpretation of needs cannot be delegated to judges and officials, nor even to political legislators. (*BFN* 425–26)[22]

In sum, respecting the equal rights of women will require expanding their participation in the democratic political processes in which they, along with other groups within society, define their needs and identity. But what happens when this right conflicts with a right that, at first glance, seems just as basic: the right of a cultural group to protect and preserve itself against external threats to *its* way of life, *its* identity? The radical multicultural feminists to whom Habermas appeals in questioning liberal equality (abstract sameness) and welfare inequality (biological difference) complicate the question of needs and identity and so, quite properly, alert us to the advantages of a proceduralist paradigm. Yet, as we shall now see, their claim that illiberal and patriarchal cultures can legitimately inform the identity of women appears to conflict with the freedom, equality, and inclusive openness built into that paradigm.[23]

Multiculturalism

The dialectic between sameness and difference that manifests itself so clearly with regard to the question of women's rights emerges again when we consider

22. The fruits of women's participation in protective legislation targeting their freedom and welfare are now well documented, ranging from proportional schemes of gender representation in governing bodies to rape-shield laws, gender-sensitive workplace designs and safety regulations, and reproductive rights. Habermas (*BFN* 424) cites Deborah Rhodes's inventory of what needs to be done in this area: "The question should not simply be whether women are, or are not, 'like men' with respect to a given occupation. Of greater significance is whether that occupation can be redefined to accommodate biological differences and whether gender as a social construct can be redefined to make those differences less occupationally relevant." D. Rhodes, *Justice and Gender* (Cambridge: Harvard University, 1989), 97.

23. Liberal feminists, such as Okin, have criticized multicultural feminists for affirming cultural identities that are illiberal. Multicultural feminists, such as Nussbaum (in *Women and Human Development*), have argued that respect for women's rights can go hand in hand with respecting cultural identities that are illiberal within tolerable limits. See S. M. Okin, "'Mistresses of Their Own Destiny': Group Rights, Gender, and Realistic Rights to Exit," *Ethics* 112 (2002): 205–30.

the rights of cultural groups to be treated differently.[24] On the one hand, people expect to be treated the same way in virtue of their humanity. On the other hand, they expect to be treated differently in recognition of their particular cultural identity. In some cases, this expectation is accompanied by a demand for group rights. Protecting the cultural identity (welfare) of a particular group with special privileges, however, allegedly contradicts the liberal principle of equality.

Habermas denies that group rights necessarily contradict liberal equality. He insists that affirmative action policies, bilingual education programs, and laws that exempt members of pacifist religions from military service are properly understood as protections against forms of discrimination. These policies aim at ensuring the *equal inclusion* of persons who have different needs. Group rights thus function to protect individual rights. Indeed, for Habermas, cultural groups are not self-acting agents that claim rights over and above the rights of their individual members (*BNR* 302). Rather, they designate conditions of agency to which their individual members claim a legal right. This right, in turn, derives from an individually held right to be treated with respect (*BNR* 300).

However, because culture is necessary for constituting personal identity, it is not merely instrumental to the pursuit of personal preferences.[25] In Habermas's words:

> The concept of a person acting instrumentally who selects from fixed options according to culturally shaped preferences fails to clarify the intrinsic meaning of culture for an individual's way of life.... Against this background it makes sense to derive cultural rights directly from the principle of the inviolability of human

---

24. Habermas notes one important difference between multicultural struggles over identity and recognition and feminist struggles of the same kind: "From the point of view of members of the majority culture, the revised interpretation of the achievements and interests of others does not necessarily alter their own role in the same way that the reinterpretation of the relations between the sexes alters the role of men" (*IO* 211–12). He now questions this assumption. Multicultural struggles for recognition that take the form of an assimilation-resisting, *identity-preserving* politics invariably *transform* how minority and majority groups understand one another and themselves. Sometimes, however, Habermas condemns identity-preserving politics for supporting illegitimate guarantees against such transformation. Here he fails to distinguish between different types of identity struggles, such as those involving oppressed ethnic groups, on the one hand, and those involving groups seeking cultural or national self-determination, on the other. Antiracist struggles typically aim at integration, whereas multicultural struggles aim at preserving cultural difference. Yet both target domination and discrimination (lack of inclusion). By contrast, struggles for national-cultural recognition (as in the case of French-speaking Québécois) typically defend a right to self-determination. See D. Ingram, *Rights, Democracy, and Fulfillment in the Era of Identity Politics: Principled Compromises in a Compromised World* (Lanham, MD: Rowman and Littlefield, 2004), chap. 2.

25. See W. Kymlicka, *Multicultural Citizenship: A Liberal Theory of Minority Rights* (Oxford: Oxford University Press, 1995), 34–48. For a critique of Kymlicka's concept of a societal culture, see D. Ingram, *Group Rights: Reconciling Difference and Equality* (Lawrence: University Press of Kansas, 2000), 80–85.

dignity (Article I of the German Basic Law): the equal protection of the integrity of the person, to which all citizens have a claim, includes the guarantee of equal access to the patterns of communication, social relations, traditions, and relations of recognition that are required or desired for developing, reproducing, and renewing their personal identities. (*BNR* 295–96)

According to Habermas, the distinction between culture as an involuntary condition of agency and culture as an instrumental good, or resource, that can be voluntarily acquired marks out a distinctive niche for "identity politics" (or the "politics of recognition," as Charles Taylor famously dubbed it). Siding with Fraser in her debate with Honneth,[26] he clearly distinguishes struggles for social justice that revolve around social status and oppression—the unequal distribution of goods and resources that is of chief concern to the welfare paradigm—from struggles for recognition that revolve around domination and unequal inclusion.

The discussion of "multiculturalism" calls for a more careful differentiation within the concept of civic equality. Discrimination or disrespect, nonpresence in the public arenas of society, or a collective lack of self-respect point to an incomplete and unequal inclusion of citizens who are denied full status as members of the political community. The principle of equality is violated in the dimension of membership, not in the dimension of social justice. The degree of inclusion concerns the horizontal relations among members of the political community, whereas the scope of the system of statuses concerns the vertical relations among citizens of a stratified society. Social strata are conditioned by patterns of distribution of social wealth…whatever counts as economic exploitation and social underprivilege…and whatever counts as deprivation….The inequality lies in the dimension of distributive justice, not in the dimension of the inclusion of members. (*BNR* 294)

---

26. See N. Fraser and A. Honneth, *Redistribution or Recognition? A Political-Philosophical Exchange* (London: Verso, 2003). Honneth argues that the struggle for recognition provides a unitary normative framework capable of explaining the struggle for economic justice (redistribution). Fraser, by contrast, sees these struggles as analytically distinct but empirically intertwined. In her opinion, recognition involves positively affirming another person's distinctive identity, while redistribution aims at securing parity of resources or capabilities. Still others, such as Brian Barry, reduce struggles for recognition to struggles for redistribution (voluntary access to and choice for goods), so that the injustice committed against Sikhs when they are forced by mandatory motorcycle helmet laws to remove their turbans is simply a "restriction in their range of opportunities for choosing one or another religious committee." In Hegel, by contrast, the category of recognition (as developed in the master-slave dialectic of the *Phenomenology*) is linked to nondomination. Despite Habermas's earlier acceptance of Honneth's reduction of all political struggles to a struggle for recognition, his position is closer to Fraser's; rather than classify misrecognition (or lack of recognition) as a simple form of domination or economic oppression, he understands it as an exclusion from equal citizenship. See B. Barry, *Culture and Equality* (Cambridge: Harvard University Press, 2002), 36.

To situate this passage within Habermas's discussion of paradigms requires drawing an additional distinction within the category of equality. Social equality (the equal distribution of wealth) forms the guiding principle of the welfare paradigm. Nondiscrimination, by contrast, forms the guiding principle of the liberal paradigm—that is, we think it wrong to discriminate (treat individuals differently) in areas of economic, political, and social life on the basis of categories of race, ethnicity, religion, gender, and so on that are irrelevant to successful performance in these areas. But there is another meaning of "non-discrimination" or civil equality that Habermas is gesturing toward that takes us beyond the liberal paradigm to the proceduralist paradigm. This other sense of nondiscrimination concerns recognizing and respecting persons' group-affiliated identifications (identities), identifications that may lead them to resist integration and assimilation into civil society. The right to be different and to refuse integration that some indigenous people and members of traditional religious sects assert nonetheless implies a kind of civil inclusion, or accommodation. A group right to special exemptions and benefits not enjoyed by other members of society promotes inclusion by not only permitting a group to exist (in a formal sense) but also by enabling its flourishing. This right, however, cannot be derived directly from liberal human rights taken in the abstract; and it cannot be derived from abstract considerations of individual and community welfare, either. The question of who belongs to a group and what kinds of protections it merits are political questions, and like all political questions they must be answered from within democratic discussion involving all concerned, that is to say, from within a proceduralist paradigm.[27]

Habermas complicates his discussion of equality further by noting that questions of distributive justice and cultural recognition "are almost always empirically intertwined." Indeed, his own account of cultural rights tends to blur these two aspects of civic equality, as when he observes that "[collective rights] empower cultural groups to preserve and make available the resources on which their members draw in forming and stabilizing their personal identities" (*BNR* 297). As we shall see, Habermas's conflation of culture as instrumental resource and culture as condition of identity is not without significance. On the one hand, it reinforces his view that a proceduralist paradigm should retain primacy in determining how liberal and welfare rights are balanced and made complementary. Group rights must respect individual rights, even as they enable resources that advance the group's welfare, and this balance must be negotiated democratically. On the other hand, Habermas's emphasis on culture as

---

27. In the United States the use of racial categories in affirmative action and electoral redistricting redresses the liberal paradigm's incapacity to deal with cumulative institutionalized disadvantages and polarized racial voting within districts where minorities are numerically weak. Antidiscrimination policies and formal voting rights, however, can not be supplemented by policies that consider the welfare of minorities without begging questions regarding the identity and interests of the groups they aim to protect.

"involuntarily acquired" identity leads him to stress the preservative function of collective rights, and these rights can limit the rights of individuals to appropriate culture according to their personal preferences. These diametrically opposed interpretations of culture render Habermas's account of group rights incoherent and lead him to stress the latter interpretation over the former in ways that seem inhospitable to the aims of multicultural identity politics.

Let us examine more closely the weaker current in Habermas's thinking about group rights. If the language community into which we are originally socialized remains, for most of us, a permanent part of our identity, whether we will it so or not, then protecting and preserving that identity—extending it into the future—will obviously be very important to us. Rights that "grant the representatives of identity groups to organize and administer themselves" also enable them to "police" the identity of the group by limiting membership to those who accept that identity. The right to associate with like-minded persons permits members of a group to exclude outsiders who reject that identity. Indeed, dissenters are viewed no differently than outsiders.

The right of the group to preserve and protect its identity is acknowledged by Habermas when he asserts that a group can legitimately restrict the freedom of its own members if it permits them full freedom to *exit* the group. Citing William Galston,[28] he observes that "realistic" conditions for exit must include the following provisions: First, members must have the freedom to inform themselves of alternative lifestyles. Second, they must have the freedom to reflect on these lifestyles. Third, they must not be coerced in their thinking by group programming. And, finally, they must not be denied skills that enable them to live outside the group should they choose to do so (*BNR* 303).

As we shall see, Habermas uses these conditions to argue against "strong" forms of multicultural rights on the grounds that they "violate" the rights of individual members. However, it is important to note that in this context his insistence on exit conditions implicitly acknowledges the right of groups to protect and preserve their identity even when it is not liberal or democratic.[29]

Although Habermas does not discuss the deaf culture movement, its demand for protective group rights exemplifies the problem of exit noted above. The use of cochlear implants in deaf children threatens the survival of sign language around which deaf culture is based. The smaller this community becomes the less political clout it has to get the resources it needs for its members, many of whom cannot speak or understand oral language with facility. At the

28. W. Galston, "Two Concepts of Liberalism," *Ethics* 105 (1995): 533.

29. Like Rawls, Habermas holds that principles of justice apply only *indirectly* to private associations. Private associations, however, must respect the basic human and civil rights of their individual members. The Catholic Church is a hierarchical organization that excludes women from the priesthood as a part of its dogma; but women are not officially treated or recognized as inferiors. Hence, the Catholic Church merits a group right to be tax exempt—unlike Bob Jones University, which was threatened with losing its tax-exempt status because of its racist admissions policy (*BNR* 298).

same time, denying deaf children cochlear implants violates the capacity and fitness conditions for exit stipulated above, since acquisition of an oral language must occur at an early age if deaf children are to have a good chance of learning it.

The example of deaf culture also illustrates four conflicts between group rights and liberalism that Habermas expressly highlights. Three of these conflicts involve violations of equal protection. These violations occur "(a) when different identity groups dispute each other's rights and privileges, or (b) when, as is typically the case with multicultural claims, one group demands equal treatment with other groups, or (c) when, as in a complementary case, nonmembers see themselves as disadvantaged in relation to members of privileged groups (white people, for example, by quotas for nonwhites)" (*BNR* 297). Taking deaf culture as our example, we observe these conflicts reflected in decisions concerning (1) whether scarce resources should be diverted to signers and other resources for the deaf, (2) whether deaf culture—which arises from a disability—has a right to exist at all; or (3) whether affirmative action hiring quotas for deaf people discriminate against the hearing.[30]

However, it is a fourth conflict between individual and groups rights that most worries Habermas. This conflict arises whenever "elites use their expanded organizational rights and competencies to stabilize the collective identity of groups, even if it entails violating the individual rights of dissenting members of the group" (*BNR* 297). This last case, Habermas believes, is fundamentally different from cases in which claims advanced by different cultural groups conflict with one another. In these latter cases, protecting groups from *external* threats by other groups can be justified because respecting others in their individuality can scarcely be accomplished without also respecting their cultural identities. Habermas therefore concludes that group rights that *make available* particular cultural resources—such as providing bilingual education, easing burdens of religious practice, and so on—are thus wholly in keeping with liberal demands for equal inclusion and may even be necessary to combat the spread of a mass-consumer Americanized monoculture (*PC* 75).

It is this fourth case, then, involving a group's right to protect its identity against *internal* threats—specifically against individual nonconformists—that Habermas thinks is most problematic. In this connection, Habermas expressly takes issue with a number of landmark legal decisions, including (a) the U.S. Supreme Court's decision to allow Amish parents to remove their children from school after nine years of formal education,[31] (b) the Canadian

---

30. For more discussion of these issues as they pertain to deaf culture, see Ingram, *Group Rights,* chap. 3; and Ingram, *Rights, Democracy, and Fulfillment,* chap. 3.

31. Writing for the majority in *Wisconsin v. Yoder* (1972) Chief Justice Warren Burger upheld the right of the Amish to remove their children from public school after the eighth grade as necessary to protect their way of life from "worldly influences." Citing evidence that "Amish are quite effective and self-reliant citizens," Burger denied that the state had a sufficiently compelling interest

Supreme Court's decision to allow patriarchal tribal councils to function as the last court of appeal for processing women tribal members' legal suits against gender discrimination,[32] and (c) Quebec's language laws that require French-speaking parents and immigrants to send their children to French-speaking schools. According to Habermas, in these instances *preservation* of cultural identity was allowed to trump the rights of (a) children to an education that would have enabled them to competently function outside of Amish society, (b) women to nondiscriminatory treatment, and (c) parents to choose whether their children might go to non-Francophone schools (*BNR* 298–304).

With the sole exception of tribal rights, which Habermas treats as morally justifiable "reparations" for past violations of sovereignty,[33] none of these

---

in educating Amish children beyond the eighth grade (age fourteen) that would warrant impeding the Amish in teaching their children skills of farming and domestic labor essential to their way of life. Writing for the minority, Justice William Douglas argued that removing children from public school at this age would "forever (bar them) from entry into the new and amazing world of diversity," thereby stunting and deforming them. Although this dissent explicitly addresses the absence of conditions—specifically the absence of knowledge regarding alternative lifestyles and the absence of reflective capacities that would enable Amish children to exit their religious community (despite their option to take a one-year hiatus from the community on turning eighteen)—it does not address what, according to Nussbaum, is perhaps the most salient concern: the inequality in education received by Amish boys and girls. Whereas Amish boys learn skills, such as carpentry and farming, that are highly marketable in the outside world (thereby satisfying the fourth exit condition of "fitness"), Amish girls learn domestic skills that are much less so. Studies have also shown that the psychological pressures faced by Amish children—knowledge that they will be shunned and will lose their inheritance should they choose to leave the community—conspire with lack of knowledge about the outside world (they are denied access to televisions, radios, most telephones, and the Internet) and their unusual style of behavior and language to discourage children from exercising their exit option (studies show that 75% of Amish children and 95% of Hutterite children remain in their communities after adulthood). Given these facts, Habermas's assertion that the Supreme Court "accepts a violation of the civil rights of juveniles to basic education that would enable them to make their way in complex societies" (BNR 299) is plausible if somewhat hyperbolic. See Nussbaum, *Women and Human Development*, 232–34; and Ingram, *Rights, Democracy, and Fulfillment*, 193–94.

32. Habermas has in mind a number of cases cited by Kymlicka in *Multicultural Citizenship* (38–40) in which patriarchal tribal councils denied women (but not men) who married outside the tribe the right to have their children included as members of the community in full standing. Another case, not mentioned by Habermas, involves Evangelical Christians who were denied access to their tribal threshing implements for refusing to participate in tribal religious ceremonies. In *Santa Clara Pueblo v. Martinez* (1978) the United States Supreme Court ruled in favor of the patriarchal council's decisions regarding patrilineal descent on the grounds that doing so "conformed" to the tribe's tradition. In the latter case the Court ruled in favor of the Evangelicals. For further discussion of these and other cases involving Native American tribes, see Ingram, *Group Rights*, chap. 5.

33. According to Habermas, the United States, Canada, and Australia are "morally compelled"—out of "equal respect for all"—to "rectify the historical injustice to indigenous peoples who were integrated, forcibly subjugated, and subjected to centuries of discrimination" by conceding "broad autonomy to maintain or restore specific forms of traditional authority and collective property, even though in individual cases these conflict with the egalitarian principle and individualistic character of 'equal rights for all.'" The result is that "an 'illiberal' social group is allowed to operate a legal system of its own within the liberal state" which "leads to irresolvable

efforts to preserve a cultural group identity appears justified. More precisely, they all threaten the kinds of individual rights that discourse theory of law regards as most basic, namely, rights to free and open communication. Any law that grants a group the right to resist changes in its identity by shielding the culture and language of its individual members from "contamination" by other cultures and languages seems to constrain the very communication by which persons, from adolescence on, undertake to voluntarily shape their identities in relations of free and undistorted mutual understanding. Responding to Charles Taylor's defense of Quebec's language laws, Habermas writes:[34]

> The protection of forms of life and traditions in which identities are formed is supposed to foster the recognition of their members; it does not represent a kind of preservation of species by administrative means.... The constitutional state can make this hermeneutical achievement of the cultural reproduction of worlds possible, but it cannot guarantee it. For to guarantee survival would necessarily rob the members of the freedom to say yes or no, which nowadays is crucial if they are to remain able to appropriate and preserve their cultural heritage. When a culture has become reflexive, the only traditions and forms of life that can sustain themselves are those that bind their members, while at the same time allowing members to subject the traditions to critical examination and leaving later

contradictions" (*BNR* 304). In contrast to this interpretation—which holds that the conflict in question "is reflected in law but does not emerge from it" since, ostensibly the episodes of subjugation and integration "predate the legal system" (*BNR* 305)—one might argue that the conflict in question rather stems from the liberal legal system's "colonizing" the indigenous community from the very beginning. The history of incorporating tribal peoples into the dominant liberal legal system occurred over a period of one hundred and fifty years during which tribal peoples first "lost" their treaty status as full-fledged sovereign nations, then lost their distinctive cultural identity, including their communal ownership of tribal property (replaced by individually owned plots of land), and then lost their status as aboriginals, having gained the rights of citizenship. Although the process of forced assimilation did not result in dissolving all reservations—tribal governments were often created and maintained by the government in order to justify its control over the extraction of mineral wealth—it did result in the eventual subsumption of indigenous peoples' tribal rights under the basic rights guaranteed by the federal constitution (in the United States this happened in 1978, in Canada it happened in 1982). Tribal law, then, cannot contradict basic individual rights. Contrary to Habermas's interpretation (*BNR* 305), the relationship between the federal government and semisovereign tribal governments seems more analogous to the relationship between the federal government and other private associations (including the family). That is to say, liberal principles apply indirectly to these associations, which have a right to limited self-determination—and therewith the freedom to adopt illiberal forms of governance and collective property—so long as they do not violate basic rights and permit dissidents a right to exit. For more on this, see Ingram, *Group Rights,* chap. 5.

34. C. Taylor et al., *Multiculturalism: Examining the Politics of Recognition* (Princeton: Princeton University Press, 1994). According to Taylor, "one has to distinguish the fundamental liberties, those that should never be infringed and therefore ought to be unassailably entrenched, on one hand, from privileges and immunities [i.e., the right of francophone and immigrant Québécois to send their children to English-speaking schools] that are important, but that can be revoked or restricted for reasons of public policy—although one would need a strong reason to do this—on the other" (59).

generations the option of learning from other traditions or converting and setting for other shores. (*IO* 222)

Quebec's language laws, Habermas fears, are designed to guarantee the preservation of Québécois Francophone culture by denying parents the basic communicative freedom to say "no" to a particular kind of education (and therewith a particular kind of identity) for their children (*BNR* 300). If we assume that parents ought to have a right to determine what cultural identity their children will initially acquire, so long as doing so does not deprive their children of the knowledge, critical aptitude, and psychological capacity that might enable them to later exit that cultural identity, then Quebec's laws must be deemed illegitimate.

The idea that parents should not have this right against the community appears to rest on a deeply flawed analogy between cultural identity and species identity. It might be argued that cross-cultural "contamination"—either through cross-cultural marriage or cross-cultural exposure of some other kind—"dilutes" and thereby "weakens" the identity of a culture as much as cross-breeding "weakens" the genetic identity of a species. But any weakening of a form of life is bad for it and—given the value of diversity for the ecosystem as a whole—bad for all of us. So cultural preservation—like species preservation—constitutes an overriding value that permits the dominant majority in a cultural group to limit the extent to which the group's members communicate with other groups.

Leaving aside the "preservationists" questionable assumption that cross-fertilization "weakens" rather than "strengthens" life forms and that the good of cultural preservation entitles groups to preserve their identity by whatever means, the very idea that cultural identities are self-contained and static—cut off from communication with other cultural forms of life—is deeply mistaken. As Taylor himself points out, members of any cultural group need *recognition* not only from their fellow members but also from members of other cultural groups. They need to know that their particular cultural identity is respected, if not fully affirmed, by others. More pertinent to our present concerns, Habermas argues that "the guarantee of the internal latitude necessary to assimilate a tradition under conditions of dissent is decisive for the survival of cultural groups." To be precise, "a dogmatically protected culture will not be able to reproduce itself, especially not in a social environment replete with alternatives" (*BNR* 303). Thus it is only by being freely interpreted—in dialogue with other cultures—that a culture can be adapted to ever new and changing circumstances; and it is only through change in the face of new cultural challenges that a given culture's practitioners relate to their own culture (and their own identity) with a degree of certainty.

To conclude, Habermas's proceduralist understanding of group rights seems ambivalent. On the one hand, the right to association and the right to democratic self-determination certainly justifies the right of the majority within that group to "support the continued existence of the cultural background of the collectivity directly," and this need not always happen "above the heads of its members" in a way that "would promote internal repression" (*BNR* 301). Even if we agree with Habermas and Brian Barry that, ontologically speaking, "cultures are simply not the kind of entity to which rights can be properly be ascribed," we can scarcely deny that "communities defined by some shared cultural characteristics (for example, a language) may under certain circumstances have valid claims...that arise from the legitimate interests of the members of the group"[35] (*BNR* 301). Perhaps it was this—wholly legitimate—democratic decision by the people of Quebec—and not, as Habermas contends, the postulation of Québécois Francophone culture as an "intrinsic value" grounded in a "metaphysics of the good...independently of citizens...maintaining their personal identity" (*BNR* 301)—that led them to want to preserve equal access to their provincial Francophone culture against the hegemonic incursion of the national Anglophone culture. These interests would have included maintaining a common political language against the threat of fragmentation, as well as protecting monolingual French speakers from potential discrimination in the workplace and in accessing public accommodations. Furthermore, the four "exit" conditions mentioned by Habermas would have been available to French-speaking and immigrant parents who preferred to leave Quebec or to provide special tutoring so that their children would be assured of an Anglophone upbringing.

On the other hand, Habermas's concern to preserve the procedural openness of communication that is so essential to free and undistorted identity formation leads him in the direction of a very different kind of identity politics: not the identity politics that is oriented toward protecting access to cultural resources intrinsic to a group's already (largely involuntary) linguistic identity, but an identity politics of transformation and destabilization. As he puts it, "the aim of multiculturalism—the mutual recognition of all members as equals—calls for a transformation of interpersonal relations via communicative action and discourse that can ultimately be achieved only through debates over identity politics within the democratic arena" (*BNR* 293). This identity politics has little to do with protecting, for instance, the exclusive group entitlement enjoyed by Sikhs to be exempt from motorcycle helmet laws—a protective privilege designed to ensure equal religious freedom—but it has everything to do with changing the way Sikhs and non-Sikhs understand their own identities.

In the end, Habermas is concerned that a politics of ensuring "equal access to cultural resources for any citizen who needs them to develop and maintain her personal identity" has already logically committed itself to a "politics of survival" in which the state undertakes to "ensure [the availability of these resources] in the future" (*BNR* 300). However, the politics of cultural

---

35. Barry, *Culture and Equality,* 67.

transformation that he offers as an alternative comes too close to abandoning the multicultural politics of equal recognition and equal protection that he himself regards as indispensable for maintaining a vibrant pluralistic society. Indeed, his criterion for a group's legitimacy—namely, that it pass the critical threshold "of the autonomous endorsement of every single potential participant" (*BNR* 302)—seems to retract the very thing that legitimates group rights in the first place, that is, that the cultural resources that such rights are supposed to protect are not voluntarily acquired and redistributed at will by individual members seeking to satisfy their own preferences but are constitutive of identity, having been acquired involuntarily through socialization.

Finally, Habermas's distinction between legitimate "enabling rights" and illegitimate "protective rights" is impossible to maintain in practice. Habermas himself observes that "this distinction ceases to be useful when the same collective rights simultaneously serve both functions, as in the Amish case" (*BNR* 299). But the point is not that collective rights sometimes serve both functions. The point is that internal dissenters are invariably regarded as external threats to group identity. It would therefore appear that what is most problematic is not that groups try to preserve themselves by policing their internal identities democratically but that they do so in a manner that fails to adequately respect their members' basic right to exit.

The conditions for exercising this right robustly cannot always be met—as can be seen in the case of women who live in patriarchal religious communities and Evangelicals who live on tribal reservations. In some cases, exit strategies, even when formally available, may not be optimal for those who might take advantage of them. In these cases, democratic self-determination and individual freedom may both have to be compromised in order to reach an equitable resolution. Indeed, there remains one striking case in which the conditions for exit are always problematic. Persons who want to emigrate from their native community due to cultural persecution depend on the hospitality of communities who will grant them sanctuary, even if this means risking the cultural identity of their new host. How does the proceduralist paradigm illuminate and resolve this contradiction? More precisely, how does that paradigm resolve the contradiction between the collective right to democratic self-determination and the individual right to relocate in pursuit of freedom and happiness?

Immigration

Habermas's comments on immigration suggest that a proceduralist paradigm could endorse the protection of a linguistic culture (such as Quebec's) without excluding or diminishing multicultural diversity—and, most important, without restricting immigration as a cultural threat to national identity. Writing in the wake of revisions (1993) made in Germany's Basic Law concerning the right to asylum, Habermas was alarmed by the xenophobic reactions he saw among his compatriots and Europeans in general. Reserving some of his harshest criticism for Germany's "exceptional" immigration law, he underscored the injustice of a policy that granted ethnic Germans' (*Statusdeutschen*) a constitutional right to citizenship while denying this same right to Germany's unmarried male guest workers, who were recruited from southern and southeastern Europe to work as cheap labor from 1955 to 1973 and forced to wait fifteen years before applying for citizenship. He also argued against Germany's restrictive immigration policy, which (with the exception of ethnic Germans) virtually cut off immigration from all but the wealthiest and most highly skilled.[36]

At issue in Germany's immigration debate were two distinct visions of national identity: communitarian and cosmopolitan (corresponding, respectively, to welfare and liberal paradigms). As I noted earlier, the communitarian vision privileges a particular (ethical) conception of the good over universal moral rights. Communitarians such as Michael Walzer argue that honoring rights to assist desperate strangers by granting them asylum or refugee status within one's own country is qualified not only by available economic and legal capacities but by an ethical demand to maintain the cultural integrity of the nation.[37] The cosmopolitan vision defended most forcefully by Joseph Carens and other cosmopolitan Rawlsians reverses this priority.[38] They defend a prima

---

36. Germany's *jus sanguinis* law still grants a privileged right of return to ethnic Germans residing in eastern and central Europe. However, following the reform of Germany's *jus sanguinis* citizenship law in 1999, any child born in Germany can obtain citizenship if one of his natural parents has been a legal resident in Germany for eight years. Shortly thereafter, Germany's law of asylum, which at that time was the most liberal in all of Europe, was revised to limit the flow of asylum seekers—a move strenuously opposed by Habermas. In still another development, Germany, like other member states of the EU, has been forced to open its borders to immigrants from other EU member states. The German Constitutional Court had ruled that Schleswig-Holstein's provincial law granting citizens of Denmark, Ireland, the Netherlands, Norway, Sweden, and Switzerland the right to vote in municipal and district elections violated Germany's Basic Law, which identifies citizens (persons with voting rights) as Germans sharing a "political community of fate." The Maastricht treaty (1993) overruled this decision by granting citizens of EU member states the right to vote in municipal elections in any other EU member state in which they resided. S. Benhabib, *The Rights of Others* (Cambridge: Cambridge University Press, 2003), chap. 4.

37. M. Walzer, *Spheres of Justice: A Defense of Pluralism and Equality* (New York: Basic Books, 1983).

38. In *The Law of Peoples* Rawls abandons the individual-centered, liberal version of the social contractarian approach he used in *Political Liberalism* and instead defends eight principles of justice that all law-abiding, human-rights respecting decent "peoples" (or nations) would accept as regulating their mutual relations. He then argues—following Walzer's own communitarian reasoning—that peoples have a right to secure their borders in order to "take responsibility for their territory" (no matter how "arbitrary a society's boundaries may appear from a historical point of view") and for their population and environment (8). Rawls maintains that open borders would result in a "tragedy of the commons" in which uprooted and perfectly mobile inhabitants would have no incentive to take care of the land. In making this argument Rawls assumes that peoples are "self-contained," that is, that members enter at birth and exit at death. Distinguishing peoples from the states that govern them, he also assumes, citing J. S. Mill, that peoples are "united by...common sympathies" that are "the effect of race and descent...community of language,...and possession of national history." Rawls, *Law of Peoples*, 23n17. These strong assumptions about a

facie right to immigrate that must be accommodated by an *open* immigration policy unless a government can demonstrate that honoring such a right would result in undermining its liberal-democratic political culture.

Habermas's proceduralist approach incorporates both communitarian and cosmopolitan visions of national identity, though in a manner that privileges the latter. Conceding that nineteenth-century European nation building forged a sense of democratic solidarity out of quasi-racial conceptions of ethnic-national identity, he observes that ethnic nationalism as such contradicts the universal moral foundations of the constitutional state. Janus-faced, the modern nation-state must now come to terms with its liberal multicultural status as a nation of immigrants and insist on a "post-national" identity rooted in "constitutional patriotism."

For Habermas, insisting that political identity principally revolve around a loyalty to human rights means that "the ethical substance of a political integration that unites all the citizens of the nation must remain 'neutral' with respect to the differences between the ethical-cultural communities within the nation, each of which is integrated around its own conception of the good" (*IO* 227). Granting that the state must remain neutral with respect to the various subcultures that make up civil society, even he admits that the "uncoupling of these two levels of integration" runs up against a hard fact: political integration involves more than loyalty to abstract constitutional principles; it involves loyalty to a particular culture-bound interpretation of these principles.

Habermas claims (out of deference to the principle of multicultural recognition) that immigrants should not be expected to assimilate to "the way of life, the practices, and the customs of the local culture across their full range" if this means having to give up "the cultural form of life of their origins," unless that form of life is politically unreasonable (in Rawls's terms) or intolerant of other reasonable cultural forms of life (*IO* 229). At the same time, immigrants can be expected to "enter into the political culture of their new homeland," which "safeguards the society from the danger of segmentation" and from a "separatist disintegration into unrelated subcultures." From this vantage point, expecting immigrants and their children to learn the language and history of their new homeland (one of the purposes Quebec's laws were intended to fulfill)

---

people's unity of interests, moral solidarity, boundedness, as well as the empirical assumption that open borders inevitably lead to a tragedy of the commons, have all been subject to extensive criticism (see Benhabib, *Rights of Others,* chap. 3). Cosmopolitan Rawlsians like Carens and Pogge, by contrast, apply the social contractarian device of Rawls to cosmopolitan individuals (viewed in abstraction from their particular status as citizens of nations) and argue that the moral arbitrariness of borders, coupled with a basic *liberal* right to move freely in pursuit of one's well-being, endows individuals with a prima facie right to enter a country, qualified only by considerations of political and legal stability. Rawls rejects this cosmopolitan extension of social contract theory out of deference to nonliberal peoples, arguing that migration is mainly propelled by political oppression and economic desperation. J. Carens, "Aliens and Citizens," in *The Rights of Minority Cultures,* ed. W. Kymlicka (Oxford: Oxford University Press, 1995), 331–49.

straddles the line separating common political culture and particularistic sub-culture (*BFN* 513).

Allowing immigrants to retain the reasonable cultural identity of their native country is not without risks. As Habermas notes, immigration cannot but alter "the composition of the population in ethical-cultural respects as well." Immigration may be unproblematic for multicultural countries like the United States that have no religious identity, but it can pose severe challenges to more ambiguously liberal democracies like Israel, which wants to retain its dominant Jewish identity in the face of demands by exiled Palestinian refugees to return to the homeland from which many were forcefully evicted.[39]

That said, discourse ethics helps us to frame the question that communitarian and cosmopolitan approaches to immigration must address: Where does a *common* political culture end and a dominant societal culture that extends "across the full range of life activities" begin? The citizens of a nation who confront this question together must first determine who *they* are and who they want to become. From a communitarian perspective, democracies must be politically bounded if they are to be legally self-determining at all. Because they cannot allow everyone who is affected by a norm to have an equal influence in debating it, the claims of potential immigrants in discussing immigration policies must weigh less than the claims of current citizens. Yet discourse ethics requires that anyone who is potentially affected by a norm be included as an "equal" participant.[40]

Given their inherently open nature, liberal democracies must acknowledge a basic right to emigrate, but they must also acknowledge a basic right to move and associate freely across borders. Anyone can therefore claim a prima facie human right to become a member of the polity. True to this cosmopolitan perspective, Habermas asserts that an inclusive moral use of a proceduralist paradigm requires that the problem of immigration be assessed impartially, "not just from the one-sided perspective of an inhabitant of an affluent region but also from the perspective of immigrants who are seeking their well-being there; [viz.] a free and dignified existence and not just political asylum" (*BFN* 511).

The above requirement means different things depending on whether the immigrants in question are current residents or prospective residents. A proceduralist paradigm would seem to justify giving residents an equal right to participate

---

39. Unlike Germany, which softened its "law of return" by liberalizing its citizenship requirements for nonethnic Germans, Israel has persisted in denying Palestinians citizenship, even after they have married Israeli citizens, thereby violating international legal conventions regarding the reunification of families across borders. This case is discussed (and denounced) by Benhabib (*Rights of Others*, 138).

40. Benhabib (*Rights of Others*, 205) pointedly notes that the German Constitutional Court's ruling in the Schleswig-Holstein case (*Bundesverfassungsgericht* [Federal Constitutional Court], 83, 37, 11, Nr. 3, p. 51), which denies that "the decisions of state organs must be legitimized through those whose interests are affected in each case" and instead locates the legitimating basis in "the people as a group bound to each other as a unity," expressly violates DE.

in political life (including, perhaps, an equal right to vote in elections),[41] since no one should be subject to laws that they have not coauthored democratically (*BFN* 509). Whether this amounts to weakening or effacing the distinction between citizens and permanent residents is a question Habermas does not pursue. Less clear is what a proceduralist paradigm would require of citizens in their consideration of prospective residents. The quote cited above leaves little doubt that prospective residents should have their perspectives represented "virtually" in all policy debates affecting them. Political participation—centered in the global formation of public opinion—should not be restricted to bounded voting rights. But what would this requirement actually entail?

Given its liberal and egalitarian thrust, it seem obvious, as Seyla Benhabib has recently argued, that a proceduralist paradigm would prohibit anyone from being barred from entering a country or from becoming a citizen on the basis of race, gender, religion, ethnicity, language community, sexuality, or other "ascriptive properties." For any reasons that might be legitimately adduced for limiting immigration would have to be ones that both would-be immigrants and inhabitants of the polities they seek to enter would find "reciprocally acceptable."[42]

In contrast to criteria based on ascriptive properties, Benhabib insists that criteria that

> stipulate that you must show certain qualifications, skills, and resources to become a member are permissible because they do not deny your communication freedom. Length of stay, language competence, a certain proof of civic literacy, demonstration of material resources or marketable skills are all conditions which certainly can be abused in practice, but which, from the standpoint of normative theory, do not violate the self-understanding of liberal democracies as associations which respect the communicative freedom of human beings qua human beings.[43]

Benhabib's comments leave open the question whether these criteria would not, in fact, be abused.[44] Furthermore, as Habermas notes, past historical

---

41. Noncitizen immigrants from EU member states—but not other resident immigrants—have a right to vote in local elections in the EU member state in which they reside. The Netherlands even allows immigrants from countries outside the EU to vote in citywide elections after five years of residency. Other models of flexible citizenship that have gained popularity in Mexico, Columbia, the Dominican Republic, and El Salvador include dual citizenship, which allows nationals residing or holding citizenship abroad to vote and even run for office in their native countries.

42. Benhabib, *Rights of Others*, 138. Although Benhabib introduces her criteria as if they pertained only to citizenship and not entry (admission), her later claim that "once admission occurs, the path to citizenship ought not to be blocked" (141) suggests that she intends them to apply to admission.

43. Ibid., 139.

44. In the United States, the issuance of temporary H2-A visas to "guest workers" may be taken by some as imposing reasonable length-of-stay conditions, despite Benhabib's own deep reservations about guest worker programs that do not allow the possibility of permanent membership

injustices have played a significant role in distributing assets and talents among the different races and nationalities of the world. Therefore, it remains unclear whether the nonascriptive criteria for restricting immigration that Benhabib mentions would in fact survive the discourse ethical test that she proposes in all circumstances.

Determining what sorts of immigration criteria withstand a proceduralist test is relatively uncomplicated in comparison to determining immigration priorities. Whose voice should be heeded the most? Distinctions must be drawn within the class of "all those affected" if the inclusion principle is to be workable.[45] Indeed, immigration policies would appear to affect some persons' interests more deeply and directly than other persons' interests. A policy that spells the difference between life and death for some persons obviously affects their interests in a deep way, and that might explain why Habermas thinks that economic refugees— and not just political refugees and asylum seekers—should have a relatively unconditional legal right to temporary residence in a safe country.[46]

---

and eventual citizenship (*Rights of Others*, 212). As Walzer notes (*Spheres*, 41), the fact that desperate foreigners consent to do the undesirable tasks that citizens refuse to do because of their low pay does not make these contracts morally acceptable, for, even if they are not coercive, they are certainly exploitative; and because they require workers to relinquish the normal rights of citizenship (such as organizing unions for better work conditions) and remain at the mercy of employers, who are only too willing to cancel their contract at the slightest sign of protest, they are also unconscionable.

45. The question, Who has the right to decide? has no satisfactory answer. Carol Gould mentions two equally compelling responses. One might extend voting rights to those who are directly involved in a common activity, such as a business enterprise; or one might extend these rights to all who are affected by an activity, whether they actively participate in it or not. These criteria differ from more traditional criteria that emphasize sharing a common political identity or inhabiting a common bounded territory. The problems with implementing a "common activity" criterion are twofold: (1) following discourse ethics, those who are affected by an activity to which they do not actively contribute have a prima facie claim to participate in decisions regarding the activity in question; and (2) globalization has rendered us less active agents in global economic activities and more passive objects of economic and environmental effects. The problems with implementing the "all affected" criterion are also twofold: (1) we must distinguish between degrees of affect (or between intensities in affect, as David Held puts it); and (2) we must distinguish between morally relevant and morally irrelevant affects (e.g., just because a couple's decision to live together and raise a family affects other people's interests does not obviously mean that these others should have a right to participate in and determine the decision). Furthermore, the criterion of who is affected is impractical for permanent structures, since the community of those affected changes depending on what is at stake. She therefore suggests that people at a distance are to be regarded as affected by a decision if their human rights—including economic and social rights as well as civil and political rights—are affected. Gould acknowledges that this relatively broad understanding of the scope of democratic participation has a cosmopolitan dimension that requires democratizing decision making in global institutions, such as the UN, which is the chief guarantor of human rights. At the same time, she stresses that "intersociative democracy" will also involve transnational—in addition to international and global—forms of democracy that pertain to particular cross-border communities of common interest and affect. See C. Gould, *Globalizing Democracy and Human Rights* (Cambridge: Cambridge University Press, 2004), chap. 7.

46. Kant, who was the first to recognize a cosmopolitan right to "hospitality," in the Third Article of *Towards Perpetual Peace*, insisted that migrants could not be turned away if it meant their demise (*Untergang*).

For Habermas, the obligation to assist the economically destitute through aiding them abroad or allowing them to immigrate is a general moral obligation that follows from the "growing interdependencies of a global society that has become so enmeshed through the capitalist world market." In this global society each of us assumes along with everyone else an "overall political responsibility for safeguarding the planet." Beyond this, Habermas notes that there are special obligations of compensatory justice owed by members of affluent nations to peoples of the developing world based on a past history of colonization and "the uprooting of regional cultures by the incursion of capitalist modernization" (*IO* 231).[47] For this reason, it is wrong to establish immigration quotas that are below those that are reasonable given extant capacities, resources, and necessities. Most important, quotas must be established "in accordance with criteria that are acceptable from the perspective of all parties involved" (*IO* 232). In particular, Habermas expressly questions quotas that are based entirely on the host country's economic needs and not on the needs (for example) of immigrants to be reunified with their families.[48]

In sum, although Habermas might be understood as recommending a concrete prioritization of duties and rights based on an ideal type of the immigrant as a desperate refugee, the logic of discourse ethics really takes him in a different direction.[49] People migrate for many reasons; the human desire to improve one's life or the lives of one's family or simply to live life differently

47. Benhabib and Habermas here touch on a peculiarity that compels us to look beyond the discursive justification of immigration law to its discursive application. This peculiarity consists in the irregular status of immigration law as a system of exceptions. As U.S. law amply testifies, special terms, conditions, and quotas apply to refugees, asylum seekers, and normal immigrants depending on their nationality, special needs, and special circumstances. Private bills granting individuals exemptions and deferments based on special circumstances testify further to this "exceptional" status. In order to justify these exceptions one would have to recall the dialectic of justification and application discussed in chapter 5. According to DE, lawmakers and judges are morally if not legally bound to attend to the life narratives of each person who solicits an exemption from deportation. Although the judge's (legislator's) rationale for granting an exemption partly appeals to the peculiarities of a life lived in desperation, it subsumes these peculiarities under a general law, thereby subjecting them to the logic of a general norm of consistency. The result is that all cases that sufficiently resemble the exception should also come under appeal. In this way, a law staying the deportation of single person can be expanded to larger classes of persons to the point where the decisive circumstance in question is seen as justifying a general amnesty. See D. Ingram, "Exceptional Justice? A Discourse-Ethical Contribution to the Immigration Question," *Cultural Horizons* 10/1 (2009).

48. U.S. immigration policy since the reform act of 1965 is unique in reserving the greatest portion of visas for family unification, thereby acknowledging the justice of compensating those who have hitherto contributed to the domestic economy without the emotional support of family. However, the U.S. quota for Mexican nationals seeking work visas is generally conceded to be too low. Interestingly, neither Benhabib nor Habermas mentions the negative impact of immigration on supplier countries. These effects include the well-known phenomenon of "brain drain" as well as the breaking up families and the decimation of rural communities.

49. The willingness (and right) of skilled persons to migrate for the sake of pursuing opportunities abroad suggests another reason for grounding immigrant rights in a cosmopolitan legal order. M. Pensky, *The Ends of Solidarity* (Albany: SUNY Press, 2008).

can hardly be disparaged as unreasonable. The conclusion reached by Rawls and many others that a just global order will "eliminate" the need to migrate is therefore premature. That said, the liberal demand for open borders is hardly more sustainable than the communitarian/welfarist demand for closed borders. In contrast, the proceduralist paradigm views global interdependency as both a challenge and an opportunity: a challenge because the paradox of democracy—the question regarding who is entitled to decide—appears all the more intractable given the effects our decisions have on the human rights of distant others and so reminds us, once again, that no democratically solicited answer could ever avoid begging this question; an opportunity because we are morally compelled—by the very need to safeguard our planet and protect those truly "stateless" persons who are without adequate legal protection in their adopted home—to extend the boundaries of democracy globally.

9

Law and Democracy

Part IV: Social Complexity and a Critical Assessment

Our examination of the discourse theory of law and democracy has focused on its normative philosophical implications. Yet the theory already incorporates sociology from the inside in its consideration of facts about modern legal systems. The norms underwriting discourse ethics must be modified when applied to social problem solving; they must be linked to positive law and the efficient administration of justice in such a way that administrative power now becomes a factor that must be legitimated and constitutionally limited.

Administrative power is legitimated only when it is linked to communicative power. But how do we know that the actual functioning of democratic societies permits this linkage? Habermas mentions two sociological facts that, impinging on the democratic legitimation of law from the outside, prevent us from answering this question definitively (*BFN* 375). First, the *social resources* that underlie the constitution of communicative power—including competencies, motivations, and opportunities for speaking and listening, acculturation in liberal political culture, access to information and sources of meaning, and time and energy requisite for deliberation free from the demands of everyday life—are scarce, unequally distributed, and partly beyond the political control of citizens. Second, and of greater concern to Habermas, the inequality in resources mirrors an inequality in *social power*, where the most highly organized sectors of society—businesses, labor unions, and technocracies—increasingly monopolize government policymaking, thereby circumventing the constitutional circulation of communicative power (*BFN* 358).

Technocracies, for instance, arise in response to the growing *complexity* of modern societies. Some of this complexity is social in nature and concerns the pluralism of beliefs and the differentiation of tasks. Some of it is systemic, and concerns the functional separation of specialized self-regulating spheres of action whose parameters are manipulated by specialists who possess technical expertise. Economic and legal systems most closely approximate this model of a self-regulating action system because of their specialized codes (money and power), but other spheres of action also possess a similar independence, insofar as those who act within them interpret the world using a specialized technical language (hence we can speak of the political system, the educational system, and so on). In short, wherever average persons have been relieved of responsibility for problem solving in a particular area by transforming that area into a technical sphere of action, we can speak of independent systems whose actions constrain our everyday behavior from the outside (*BFN* 342–52).

The challenge this technical expertise poses to democracy is obvious. Given the chaos of opinions circulating in the public sphere, the administration increasingly turns to technical elites for guidance in problem solving. Considering the close connection between technical elites, government officials, and big business, one cannot but conclude that government has largely dissociated itself from average citizens and forsworn the legitimacy their communicative power bestows.

Habermas does not dispute this diagnosis, but he is careful not to exaggerate its gravity, since a complete fragmenting of society into technical problem-solving systems is incoherent. If technical subsystems were as self-contained in their processing of information as systems theorists maintain, the experts within any one system would not be able to communicate with experts in other systems or with the public. But of course they do—and indeed must—communicate with one another because the side effects and externalities of one system cause problems for other systems and so threaten the reproduction of the social system as a whole. For example, economic recessions affect political stability as well as the availability of health-care services and educational opportunities. Yet it is unclear whether a simple market-based solution to the problem (in the form, say, of a relaxed monetary policy that aims at stimulating growth) will adequately increase stability and promote the availability of health care and education. So economists must learn to understand economic problems through the medium of noneconomic languages that do not reduce everything to calculable costs and benefits but which take into account, for example, noncalculable psychological and environmental "costs" associated with experiences of inequality and degraded life. In short, functionaries within any specialized subsystem, and not just economists, must communicate with the public and not restrict their communication to technical intercorporate consultations; for it is the public who first experiences problems of systemic imbalance in the form of social conflicts and feelings of discontent. Such conflicts, which address ethical values and norms of justice, fall outside the narrow purview of technical expertise, even while implicitly influencing it (hence the remarkable dissension among experts who read the same technical expertise through the lens of opposing paradigms). Even if the administrative system is but one subsystem among others and not a centralized planning agency, it must still rely on democratic input from the public in order to signal the functionaries within the various subsystems that their domains of action are in a state of disequilibrium with one another and with society at large (*BFN* 350–52).[1]

We will have more to say about such systemic imbalances in the concluding chapters. Suffice it to say, a democratic public sphere, with its reliance on a nontechnical common vernacular, remains a necessary condition even for a systems theoretical notion of society. But here we encounter another problem. Perhaps the discourse model has misrepresented the nature of democratic input. Perhaps economics hits closer to the truth when it conceives of democracy as a strategic competition for power and aggregation of interests signaling "effective demand."[2]

Here again, the partial truth of the economic model belies social reality. Bargaining, no doubt, constitutes a significant—and at times dominant—aspect of politics. Yet we must not simply reduce political bargaining to the issuing of threats. We have seen that an important part of liberal democracy—the basic system of rights—cannot be understood as the outcome of mere power politics. The majority accedes to basic rights that protect minorities—and limit majority rule—not merely because it fears that it too might become a minority some day (*BFN* 292–95). Furthermore, the economic description belies the actual negotiations that occur in constitutional conventions and legislatures when basic rights or the public welfare are at stake. These negotiations invariably involve an exchange of arguments that are designed to persuade others on the basis of impartial reasons (*BFN* 340).

Nonetheless, in *normal* political life consensus-oriented dialogue *does* take a backseat to both strategic bargaining and to top-down administrative agenda setting. The discourse theory of democracy appears unrealistically utopian if we consider that (a) deliberative democracy mainly exists at the margins of the political system and only then as an exceptional response to rare crises; and (b) the discursive norms of equality, freedom, and universal inclusion that inform its procedures cannot be fully realized throughout the entire political system given the constraints of social complexity and of social power.

Notwithstanding these sobering considerations, things appear somewhat differently, Habermas ventures, if we take into account two facts. First, as we shall see in chapter 10, the modern welfare state is subject to a permanent state of systemic crisis that continually erupts into social conflicts that interrupt the normal routines of politics. Second, although deliberative democracy can

1. Habermas's criticism of a systems theoretical account of the circulation of power (here directed against Helmut Willke) repeats a general objection he has about systems theory in general and Niklas Luhmann's in particular. See appendix F for more detail.
2. This deflationary view of democracy was famously advanced by Joseph Schumpeter in his now classic *Capitalism, Socialism, and Democracy* (New York: Harper, 1942).

never become the only procedure for problem solving in a complex society—
and hence can never be realized as a model of society as such—its norms can
provide a method (or thought experiment) for critically testing how far democratic deliberation can be realized given the exigencies of social complexity.

Habermas invokes Peters's model of deliberative democracy to illuminate
these constraints. As I noted earlier, the model presupposes a two-track system of deliberative democracy. The informal track revolves around the *public
sphere*—by which Habermas no longer means the limited bourgeois public
sphere addressed in *The Structural Transformation of the Public Sphere* but
the network of communication flows that extend from face-to-face egalitarian discussions to impersonal messages disseminated by mass media. In a later
formulation (2008) Habermas reserves the term "public sphere" to refer exclusively to that "intermediate system of mass communications, situated between
the formally organized deliberations and negotiations at the centre, and the
arranged or informal conversations which take place in civil society at the periphery of the political system," that is responsible for "filtering," "steering,"
and "keeping alive" political communications that originate in civil society
(*EFP* 159). At first blush, this three-tier model of political communication appears to reflect rather badly on the public sphere and public opinion in general,
in that it portrays the public as if they were consumers passively responding
to the most frequent messages that have been asymmetrically selected by the
media in favor of certain dominant viewpoints. The "abstractness" of communication that has been removed from the critical check of face-to-face question
and answer and the "asymmetrical" selection of weighted viewpoints appears
to lose all of the epistemic virtues that experiments, involving fully informed
deliberation—from the collective-decision discussions of Michael Neblo to
the focus-group polling by James Fishkin—have repeatedly confirmed to be
characteristics of robust face-to-face discussion (*EFP* 149–52). Yet Habermas
insists that a properly instituted public sphere performs an indispensable legitimating function involving the "filtering" of reasonable concerns voiced
within civil society, their "condensation" in the form of refined positions and
arguments (what Habermas calls "reflected" or "considered" public opinions),
owing to their being taken up by media "elites"—journalists, reporters, intellectuals, and lobbyists—and their public dissemination (*EFP* 161–67). As
Habermas describes it, although the public sphere is indeed as unresolved in its
deliberations as systems theorists portray it, its communication exchanges are
not as anarchic as those that occur spontaneously in civil society. This weakness—its incapacity to act decisively and resist the distortions of organized
social power—is also its strength; for it is precisely its unbounded diversity
that enables it to expand beyond borders and provide a global sounding board
for an indefinite range of issues, both domestic and foreign. The formal track
complements these strengths and weaknesses with its own. Only the legislature
is capable of negotiating and concluding agreements according to institutional
procedures that guarantee equal opportunities to speak free from the effects

of social power; and only judges and administrators can decisively act on its recommendations. But the procedural orderliness of government discourse is achieved at a cost: the filtration of public opinion to fit government agendas and the regulation of debate in conformity with rules of discursive decorum and "public-minded" civility (*BFN* 354–62) reduce the quantity and quality of opinions that get heard.

The legitimacy of this process depends entirely on whether the constitutional circulation of power obtains. At the point where political communication should originate—at the periphery—civil society must be structured in such a way as to encourage active and equal participation in political life. However, as Habermas notes, there exists the ever-present disabling of citizens' interest in and capacity for political communication caused by a lack of access to cultural capital (mainly affecting less educated, lower socioeconomic groups), the decline of partisan political attachments, and the subsequent rise of a fragmented voting public drawn to single issues and "niche" sources of information (*EFP* 178). A politically apathetic and fragmented civil society is no match for government and big business in their struggle to wrest control over the mass media for their own propagandistic purposes. But without the critical input and feedback from a politically vibrant civil society, the public sphere and its public opinion cease to be truly public. Somehow, the power exerted by government and business elites to manipulate the public must be resisted by the people. Ironically, for Habermas, it is partly because of the administration's *own* "countersteering" efforts to constitutionally guarantee the autonomy of the public sphere against its *own* administrative steering that such resistance is possible (*BFN* 327).

The question then arises whether autonomously generated public opinion can be taken up by the administration without distortion. Habermas's answer is not entirely encouraging. Habermas invokes Peters's center/periphery (or "sluice") model of the political system to explain how communicative power is "filtered" by the legislature and administration. At the center lies the administration, which possesses the power to *act* on statutes or solve problems in a technically competent way. At the periphery lies civil society, which can only *discover* problems through an endless process of deliberation. In between the center and the periphery lies the public sphere, which filters and condenses the opinions emanating from the periphery, and the legislature, which aims at *justifying* general policy solutions to problems highlighted by public opinion (*BFN* 307).

Let us leave aside the political center's unavoidably selective interpretation of public opinion and return to our initial concern. The autonomy of a liberal and rational public sphere is crucial for legitimating deliberations and decisions made within the center, but the public sphere is the interface for all kinds of associations and organizations. Those that harmonize best with the autonomy of the public sphere are the nongovernmental and noneconomic associations—mainly public-interest groups and social movements—that spontaneously emerge in response to social problems. Typically, these voluntary associations aim to revitalize the public sphere in addition to pursuing their narrower aims (*BFN* 370). Opposed to these associations, which make up *civil society*, are the businesses, labor unions, organized political parties, and other clients of the state that use the public sphere to advance their own particular interests.

These highly organized and well-financed sectors—whose "emissaries" already have close "insider" ties to government—are better positioned than the organs of civil society to grab the government's attention. Members of the media, however, can equalize the balance of political influence through independent reporting. Journalists, reporters, and functionaries of the mass media in general have professional duties to ensure the widest and most balanced dissemination of opinion—a duty that the government, through its regulatory oversight of the media—is constitutionally obligated to uphold. Their concentration in private hands, by contrast, renders the media vulnerable to manipulation by social power (*BFN* 376–79). Such manipulation in turn obstructs the free functioning of the public as a sensor for social problems; for economic elites are as unlikely as government elites to highlight social problems such as the ones I have discussed. Although Habermas insists that the mass media have yet to become a passive tool of "the system," or a mere medium of propaganda and mindless entertainment as he and first-generation critical theorists once claimed (*STPS* 181–251), he notes that their own independence—already severely compromised by the pathological demands of the market for more "infotainment" and less news analysis (*EFP* 180)—crucially depends on *social movements* that actively seek and demand publicity: hence the democratic significance of protest movements and public acts of civil disobedience (*BFN* 381–84).

Questioning the Proceduralist Paradigm

Habermas's theory of law links individual freedom and democracy more closely than political theory has traditionally done. It therefore stands as a strong refutation of libertarian thinking, with its privileging of unregulated markets over democratic governments as the favored mechanism for ensuring freedom, equality, justice, and solidarity. It also links legitimacy to discourse more closely than political theory has traditionally done. Although political theory has long recognized the connection between democracy and legitimacy, it has done so in the narrowest of ways, conceiving voting (universal suffrage) as a protection against incompetent or tyrannical leaders or as an expression of needs the public wants government to satisfy the most. Habermas's theory, by contrast, links legitimacy to the discursive formation of a rational will. Deliberation, not decision, is its preferred method for legitimation. Confronting problems of collective choice head on, it explains how conflicting preferences can be transformed and harmonized into laws that all can freely accept.

Doubts, however, remain regarding the autonomy of the public sphere. Furthermore, the sluice model of democracy, with its distinction between center and periphery, realistically endows elites with great discretion in selecting, filtering, and interpreting public opinion—all of which potentially runs counter to the constitutional flow of power as Habermas conceives it.[3] Aside from these empirical challenges, there are four philosophical concerns that merit special attention. First, one might object that Habermas's proceduralist paradigm is paradoxical: either discursive procedures possess sufficient normative substance to constrain the outcome of democratic deliberation, in which case they violate the autonomy of deliberators by imposing a philosophically predetermined result; or they do not, in which case they permit them to make irrational and discriminatory decisions. A related concern is that procedures only provide a subset of conditions that are necessary for deliberation to be just and rational. Other conditions—above all, a more equitable distribution of economic and cultural assets—seem necessary as well. Connected to this second objection is a third concern about the theory's narrow focus on law and politics—to the exclusion of the workplace—as the focal point of democracy. Of related interest is the mundane struggle against technical elites and technological hierarchy in pursuit of more democratic technical organizations. Finally, the theory's presumption of democracy as an institutionalized revolution provokes the further objection that it cannot justify revolutionary actions that aim to overthrow the political forces that prevent democracy from being institutionalized in the first place.

The first concern addresses an inconsistency in Habermas's application of the proceduralist paradigm. Unlike liberal and welfare/republican paradigms that constrain deliberation from the outside by appeal to prepolitical rights or goods, the proceduralist paradigm leaves the determination of legitimate rights and goods up to the deliberators. However, by not constraining the outcome of deliberation, the proceduralist paradigm seems to be normatively empty. For example, when applied to religion in politics, the proceduralist paradigm both is and is not accommodating (to religion). Habermas's attempt to have it both ways—recommending unconstrained religious politics in the public sphere, "filtered" and constrained secular politics in government deliberation—reinforces the impression that proceduralism is not so much a paradigm as a resolute refusal to think within a paradigm. This explains why, contrary to Habermas's own claims, the proceduralist paradigm fails to mediate liberal and welfarist/communitarian paradigms in conflicts between church and state. If anything, it assigns each paradigm its own proper sphere: the liberal paradigm (qua moral principle of nonimposition) prevailing in government deliberation, the welfarist paradigm (qua ethical principle of value inculcation) prevailing in the public

---

3. See William E. Scheuerman, "Between Radicalism and Resignation: Democratic Theory in Habermas's *Between Facts and Norms*," in *Discourse and Democracy: Essays on Habermas's "Between Facts and Norms"*, ed. R. v. Schomberg and K. Baynes (Albany: SUNY, 2002), 61–85.

sphere. Moreover, he cannot claim that his proposed compromise is better than the extreme alternatives it is intended to replace *because* it alone follows from a proceduralist paradigm. Claiming this would violate the very spirit of that paradigm, which asserts that citizens deliberating together—and not philosophers theorizing in isolation—have authority to make this decision.

Similar results obtain when the proceduralist paradigm is applied to multiculturalism or immigration; in neither of these instances does the paradigm obviously favor the solutions that Habermas tries to draw from it. Group rights that are intended to provide equal protection for discrete classes of persons appear to constrain identities in ways that seemingly violate the inherent openness, fluidity, and hybrid nature of identities set in motion by discursive procedures. The paradigm provides no definitive guidance in specifying what constitutes a legitimate group that is worthy of equal protection. Yet Habermas's somewhat tortured effort at distinguishing between legitimate "enabling" rights and illegitimate "protective" rights—classifying this or that group as falling into either one of these categories—presumes that it does. The same applies to immigration. When it comes to deciding membership, the paradigm at once supports and undermines territorially bounded national self-determination, so that the answer to the question about what distinguishes ascriptive from nonascriptive qualifications for membership—and what decides the legitimacy of appealing only to the latter—depends on what perspective one adopts.[4]

Substantive Economic Justice and Workplace Democracy

The problem of perspective crops up in Habermas's response to the second concern as well. On the one hand, he acknowledges that proceduralism abstracts from *substantive* principles of economic and social justice that any democracy would have to satisfy in order to be fully rational and legitimate but accepts this as the necessary price that political theory oriented toward the rational reconstruction of universal norms must pay. Citizens, not political theorists, must decide which norms of economic justice are necessary for realizing democratic institutions in their society. Political theory can only assert the obvious: that all citizens must have equal access to the conditions, resources, and opportunities necessary for equally exercising rights.

On the other hand, when speaking as a *political scientist,* Habermas observes that economic and social stratification necessarily yields forms of domination that are incompatible with exercising equal rights. Domination by definition entails that some persons exercise power over others in ways that would not

4. For further discussion of the paradoxes of associational inclusion and exclusion, see D. Ingram, *Group Rights: Reconciling Difference and Equality* (Lawrence: University Press of Kansas, 2000); and D. Ingram, *Rights, Democracy, and Fulfillment in the Era of Identity Politics: Principled Compromises in a Compromised World* (Lanham, MD: Rowman and Littlefield, 2004).

satisfy the test of universal rational consensus. If one accepts that capitalism necessarily presupposes economic domination (where those who control the means
of production dictate conditions of employment, production, consumption, and
life to those who do not), then Habermas's insistence on "equal access" to political resources condemns this economic form—hence, Habermas's assertion
that the "relationship between capitalism and democracy is fraught with tension" (*BFN* 501) and that pluralistic democracy flourishes "only in an egalitarian public of citizens that has emerged from the confines of class and thrown off
the millennia-old shackles of social stratification and exploitation" (*BFN* 308).

Given the political injustice of capitalism, one wonders whether any modern
market-based economic system could be compatible with democracy. Many
Marxists believe that all market economies generate inequalities that produce
"social stratification and exploitation"—hence their support for democratic
models of economic planning. But Habermas disagrees, partly because the
Marxist alternative is unthinkable. If taken to its logical conclusion, this alternative entails replacing the functional division of labor definitive of any
modern society with a simpler organization in which all action is coordinated
by means of face-to-face communicative action (*BFN* 479).

In claiming this, Habermas comes very close to equating modern society
with capitalist society—something that he had earlier chided Weber for doing.
"Like the bureaucratic state," he asserts, "the capitalist economy too developed a systemic logic of its own," so that "the markets for goods, capital, and
labor obey their own logic" (*BFN* 500). This apparent equation of modernity
and capitalism may explain why Habermas pitches his recommendations for
democratic reform at such a modest level of intensity: "to impose social and
ecological limits on the economic system without impinging on its inner logic"
(*BFN* 505). The collapse of the Soviet Union in 1989–90, in large part due
to the failure of bureaucratic socialism, merely reinforced Habermas's opinion that because "it has become impossible to break out of the universe of
capitalism," the "only option is to civilize and tame the capitalist dynamics
from within"—an opinion that he continued to hold as late as the economic
crisis of 2008–09 (*EFP* 187).

Habermas's assumption about the "markets for goods, labor, and capital" obeying their own capitalist logic seems problematic in light of recent
research on market-based forms of socialism, which retain a market in goods
and services without retaining markets in investment and labor.[5] It is certainly
problematic in light of his critique of capitalism and its destructive growth
imperatives (see chapter 10). Elsewhere, however, Habermas conjectures that

---

5. In a 1984 interview, Habermas asserted: "I no longer believe that a differentiated economic system can be transformed from within in accordance with simple recipes of workers'
self-management." However, he added that the "capacities for self-organization ... developed
within autonomous public spheres" regarding quality of life decisions was unimaginable short of
"abolishing capitalist labour markets" (*HAS* 187).

market systems *can* be incorporated into nonexploitative socialist models. As he puts it, models of market socialism, which abolish private control of the means of production and encourage workplace democracy, "pick up the correct idea of retaining a market economy's effective steering effects and impulses without at the same time accepting the negative consequences of a systematically reproduced unequal distribution of 'bads' and 'goods'" (*BR* 141–42).

Habermas's veiled reference to workplace democracy indicates how he would respond to the third objection. In his opinion, the "fragmentation of consciousness" generated by a hierarchical division of labor, splitting intellectual labor (management) from physical labor, is not only characteristic of capitalist forms of domination. Nothing in socialism requires that productive units be democratically controlled by those who work in them, either. But if every hierarchical division of labor generates cynicism, indifference, and an atrophying of "the need for normatively secured communicative agreement" within businesses, it must also generate these pathologies within the broader political arena. Hence, in addition to making a case for market socialism one must make a case for workplace democracy (RC 281).

The Technological Dimension of Democracy

Worker-controlled businesses doubtless have many advantages, including those of efficiency.[6] However, what chiefly interests me is the importance of the workplace as a primary locus of democratic struggle in a dimension of life that Habermas has—at least since the late 1960s—all but ignored: technology. The reasons for this neglect are no doubt complicated. To begin with, Habermas sometimes interprets his distinction between media-steered (system-embedded) domains of instrumental/strategic action and consensual (lifeworld-embedded) domains of communicative action as a distinction between types of *organizations* (see chapter 10). According to this interpretation, business organizations would appear to be both externally *and* internally regulated by instrumental steering media, such as administrative power and monetary incentives. Furthermore, since (according to Habermas) instrumental action obeys a singular technological logic of abstraction and differentiation, it follows that their technically "efficient" management would require unidirectional top-down "control" and coordination.

6. See D. Schweickart, *After Capitalism* (Lanham, MD: Rowman and Littlefield, 2002). Schweickart incorporates workplace democracy and entrepreneurial initiative into his model of market socialism, noting that socialist markets are less prone to the kind of ecologically disastrous "hyper-growth" and cycles of "over-production" characteristic of capitalist markets. Nor do worker-controlled businesses have any incentive to grow larger, unless a much larger economy of scale would significantly increase their market share and, most important, the profit share of each individual employee.

But elsewhere Habermas rejects this interpretation of the distinction between system and lifeworld, correctly acknowledging that organizations exhibit both media-steered and consensual aspects, although in differing degrees. Workplaces may be more integrated by steering media than families, and the history of technical modernization—from craft production to industrial production and beyond—may well reveal a tendency for workplaces to become increasingly more technically mediated. But that does not imply that workplaces are essentially resistant to democratic organization. Andrew Feenberg, for instance, argues that technology, which he insists should be treated as a steering medium alongside money and legal power, does not display a single logic, as Habermas seems to suppose. The process of abstraction, differentiation, and top-down control that characterizes the initial scientific elaboration of technical principles leaves the question of technical design undetermined. Capitalism fetishizes this initial stage of "primary instrumentalization" by building abstraction into its own industrial designs. But as Marcuse argued, more democratic designs are certainly imaginable (the transformation of the computer from information processor to communication medium testifies to this possibility).

Technological progress may require reversing the abstraction and differentiation of capitalist technological design. Rational development of technology would then follow a different logic: instead of incorporating a single function into a device in accordance with the logic of hyperspecialization, it would integrate multiple functions in accordance with the logic of economical means. We see evidence of this new logic emerging today in the use of solar energy panels that enable the generation of energy in ways that are environment-and-ecology friendly as well as empowering. In contrast to utility-operated coal-burning power plants, which are specialized to fulfill only one general need—the production of energy—solar technologies respond to other needs that emerge more directly from our everyday lifeworld: the need to live in harmony with nature and to control our lives.[7] By condensing multiple uses—popular control, energy production, environmental protection—into the same device, solar technology also resolves conflicts between environmentalists, populists, and industrialists.

Indeed, many populist struggles against bureaucracy and what Foucault called "technologies of discipline" are democratic struggles over the quality of life. These struggles are usually local—pitting patients against health-care providers, students and teachers against education bureaucracies, workers against managers, consumers against producers, environmentalists against business CEOs—but they occasionally rise to the level of general political struggles. (Feenberg reminds us that the May 1968 revolt in France was substantially motivated by a reaction against bureaucracy.) The important point is that these

7. See A. Feenberg, *Questioning Technology* (New York: Routledge, 1999), 209–25.

struggles, which Habermas describes under the heading of "quality of life" movements (*TCA* 2 392), are not struggles initiated by *citizens* against the juridical power of a sovereign government. They are not typically struggles over legislation (unless it is regulatory law). Rather they are "tactical" struggles in which small groups of professional providers and their clients seek to "reappropriate" technologies more humanely. In Foucauldian terms, the target of their resistance is a power relationship embedded in a technical practice. What they bring to bear against this relationship is not so much a set of interests as an embodied self-understanding, or "counterknowledge," that has been marginalized and "subjugated" by the dominant "professional" discourse.[8]

The example of patients fighting for control over their rare illnesses reveals something else about these struggles:[9] the space for political action is neither strictly public nor even geographically based. Uniting persons who feel isolated in their communities, computer technology makes possible a "virtual" public sphere. This technical extension of democracy may or may not advance the critical quality of discourse. Yet regardless of what we may think about using computers to organize tactical struggles democratically, it is obvious that technologies, no less than laws, embody prescriptions, norms, and values. In the words of Feenberg, "world-defining" technical designs—such as the dominant design style oriented toward top-down control—"are the technical equivalent of major legislative acts" and, therefore, given their all-embracing effects on our lives, constitute an important arena of democratic struggle in their own right.[10]

Revolution and Democracy

The idea that genuine democracy requires radical social change—democratization that is as technologically deep as it is politically broad—leads directly to the final objection. It might be argued (following Apel) that moral agents have a political duty to bring about the political and legal conditions for realizing their own (moral) autonomy, even if this requires doing so by means of revolution. Recall Kant's famous injunction that "ought" implies "can." According to Kant, it is unreasonable to expect persons to perform their moral duty unless they are legally protected from those who would take advantage of their goodness.

Habermas agrees that "ought" implies "can" but disagrees that "can" implies "ought" (i.e., that knowing the conditions that enable moral duty implies

8. See Feenberg, *Questioning Technology*, 120. Feenberg mentions the struggle of AIDS activists for more "caring" forms of experimental protocols in the testing of medicine: "The use of placebos, the requirements that subjects have no prior history of experimental participation, and the limitation of participation to statistical minimums were some of the arrangements that were challenged" (141).

9. Feenberg (*Questioning Technology*, 192) cites the Prodigy Medical Support Bulletin Board discussion group whose members suffer from ALS (amyotrophic lateral sclerosis).

10. Feenberg, *Questioning Technology*, 141.

a moral duty to enable these conditions). The principle of "can implies ought" only applies when minimal legal and democratic procedures are already present. In the absence of these procedures, there is no way to legitimate revolutionary political actions (even ones that aim to bring these procedures into existence). Like any teleological (goal-oriented) action, revolutionary actions produce consequences that affect a wide range of people. A norm obliging revolutionary action would therefore have to be legitimated by the democratic consent of all in light of their collective assessment of the negative and positive impact these consequences would have for each of them. Obviously, this consent can only be given retroactively, after democracy has been instituted. However, absent such consent at the beginning—which is impossible to give—no revolutionary action can be undertaken whose moral acceptability is not in doubt. Any attempt to legitimate revolutionary action by recourse to some other reason, be it historical necessity (the recourse taken by Hegel and, to a lesser degree, Kant) or strategic necessity, cannot but fail insofar as it bypasses morality.[11]

This does not mean that revolutionary action is necessarily immoral since individuals can find compelling reasons to undertake such action on their own. It does mean, however, that revolutionary action is beyond moral duty. This fact, Habermas believes, looms ever larger in today's globalized world of "haves" and "have-nots." For, with the growing debasement of democracy throughout the world and the continual allure of nondemocratic solutions to global inequities, revolutions and violent human rights interventions of questionable legitimacy are fast replacing the lawful legitimacies of political life as we know it (*TJ* 48–49).

11. Apel's position, however, is that a moral obligation to institutionalize morality is already implicit in discourse.

10

Crisis and Pathology

The Future of Democracy in a Global Age

The preceding chapters have been devoted to examining the normative (philosophical) foundation of Habermas's theory of law and democracy. This foundation and the proceduralist paradigm of law that follows from it provide a critical perspective from which to evaluate a variety of public policy issues that directly bear on social justice (equal treatment). However, this normative program represents only one half of Habermas's critical social theory. The other half, which we shall now explore, addresses a much more difficult and complex issue: the tension between capitalism and democracy. The problems that revolve around this tension are at best only indirectly related to questions of social justice. Yet they are normative insofar as they specifically address the psychological health of society as reflected in the kinds of identity crisis that persons inhabiting capitalist democracies—and nations in thrall to the impact of globalization—are apt to experience.

Discussing these crisis phenomena will provide a retrospective clarification of the dual nature of law as normative institution (embedded in a lifeworld structured by communicative action) and as instrumental steering medium (embedded in an administrative system structured by coercive power). It will also provide a forward-looking anticipation of themes to be addressed in the last chapter concerning the relationship between capitalism, rationalization, and modernity. These forward- and backward-looking themes are more intimately connected than one might suppose. As we have seen, modern law displays a deep tension between its democratic moral core and its instrumental function. The paradox of a medium that simultaneously institutionalizes and limits power becomes even greater when we realize how vulnerable democracy is to the forces arrayed against it. Sandwiched between the social power of economic elites and the administrative power of government bureaucrats, democracy appears to be an unachievable ideal.

Can the threat to democracy posed by the economic-legal system be parried? Habermas's predecessors in the Frankfurt school had no illusions on this score. They believed that the destruction of liberal democracy was preordained by reason itself. Habermas denies this and argues instead that it is neither reason nor its institutionalization in modern society that is to blame but, rather, capitalism. Contrary to the Weberian analysis of rationalization that informed the thought of his predecessors, Habermas denies that the logic underlying rationalization unfolds a unidirectional course of modernization that inevitably and everywhere culminates in capitalism. And he insists that it is only this contingent product of European history—not rationalization as such—that accounts for the objectifying (reifying) dehumanization that critical theorists since Marx have diagnosed. Capitalism, he believes, causes us to treat ourselves and our fellow humans as objects to be exploited for profit and therapeutic engineering, and it does this precisely by systematically expanding instrumental, strategic, and functional forms of rationality at the expense of communicative and discursive forms. But if that is so, Habermas must explain how capitalism can be surpassed or contained without abandoning the functional rationality of a regulated market economy.[1]

Capitalism and the Crisis of Democracy

Habermas's full explanation of why functional rationality is an essential feature of any complex modern society—progressive, liberating, and nonpathological when considered apart from capitalism—will only become apparent once we examine his theory of modernity, the topic of chapter 11. Here I will focus on

---

1. Although Habermas subtitles *Lifeworld and System*, volume 2 of *Theory of Communicative Action*, "Critique of Functionalist Reason," he nowhere tells us what functionalist reason is. The closest he comes to providing a definition is when he discusses system rationality: "The concept of instrumental reason suggests that the rationality of knowing and acting subjects is systematically expanded into a purposive rationality of a higher order. Thus the rationality of self-regulating systems, whose imperatives override the consciousness of the members integrated into them, appears in the shape of a totalized purposive rationality. This confusion of system rationality and action rationality prevented Horkheimer and Adorno, as it did Weber before them, from adequately separating the rationalization of action orientations within the framework of a structurally differentiated lifeworld from the expansion of steering capacity of differentiated social systems (*TCA* 2 333)." The expression "functionalist rationality" (or "system rationality") captures the sense in which the mechanical adaptation of systems to their environments—by maintaining their boundaries and preferred states of equilibrium (goal states)—mirrors the rational instrumental pursuit of goals by individuals. Functional rationality is distinct from instrumental rationality insofar as it works through an unconscious feedback loop linking actions and their unintended effects. Rational actions can produce effects that are functionally "irrational"—destructive of the very system that reinforces them. Conversely, irrational behavior—for example, religious taboos against incest—can be functionally rational (see appendix F).

a narrower set of issues concerning the relationship between capitalism, democracy, and functional rationality. To address these issues properly we must leave normative philosophy and enter the terrain of social science, specifically that portion of it that concerns the historical genesis of European capitalism. Capitalism emerged as the solution to an economic crisis besetting Europe's feudal economy during the High Middle Ages. The gradual substitution of a market economy based on private property and "voluntary" wage labor for a controlled economy, in which land was held in common or in public trust and craft production and commercial competition were severely restricted, increased productivity and consumption exponentially. Taking advantage of the economic efficiency of markets, capitalism marked an advance in the instrumental rationality of Western society.

Along with this advance came advances in morality and law that better institutionalized communicative rationality as well. Private and public autonomy—individual rights and democracy—emerged as complementary institutions alongside a market economy. New hierarchies of wealth based on market fortune replaced older hierarchies based on birth. So long as these inequalities were the by-product of contractual exchanges that were viewed as natural and fair, capitalism's legitimacy remained unquestioned. This changed, however, once the state began to take over the job of regulating the economy. To ensure that the concentration of wealth at the top did not generate a surfeit of production relative to consumption, the welfare state that emerged in the wake of the Great Depression assumed the role of investor of last resort, redistributing public tax revenue to businesses and consumers alike in ways that proved to be controversial (*LC* 33–40).

In Habermas's opinion, the welfare state diffuses capitalism's chronic economic crises of overproduction only by displacing them onto itself and other sectors of society,[2] in the form of *rationality, legitimation,* and *motivation* crises:

---

2. Habermas rejects the law of value that underpins Marx's belief that capitalist economies suffer from crises that cannot be displaced onto other systems. The law states that the rate of profit is proportional to the exploitation of labor. For Marx, profit is the difference between the value produced by labor and the wages necessary for reproducing it. (The cost of constant capital, or overhead, is transferred to the cost of the product.) The exploitation of labor is limited by the length of the workday, the cost of replenishing the workforce, and so on. However, Marx notes that the introduction of a labor-saving device within an industry can increase profits by reducing the total cost per unit of production. (The cost of adding the device is more than offset by the savings gained by reducing the wage bill.) The advantage gained from underselling one's competitors, however, is lost once they, too, acquire the device. The constant introduction of new labor-saving devices also reduces the source of profit: labor. The growing mass of unemployed workers, coupled with a sharp reduction in wages, diminishes demand for commodities, leading to their devaluation. (Alternatively, the increased cost of reproducing a more technically skilled workforce coupled with increased living expectations cuts into profits.) Also, given the accelerated pace at which machinery is rendered obsolete and replaced, the rate of profit falls as the machinery replaced fails to recover its original cost by the time it is depreciated. Although the falling rate of profit can be offset by transferring assets abroad where labor costs are very low or by acquiring government subsidies,

Functional Rationality Crisis: The state is charged with insuring steady economic growth while maintaining reasonably full employment, balance of trade, and stable prices. It must sustain economic growth through subsidies, tax breaks, developmental assistance, and infrastructure investment, while at the same time compensating for the unintended consequences of unplanned development, which include uneven development, systemic poverty, crime, and environmental degradation (including global warming, a problem Habermas noted as early as 1973) (*LC* 42). The state faces two contradictory imperatives here. First, it must act in the general interest of the capitalist class; and yet individual capitalists, free to invest as they see fit, may not see their particular interests as consonant with this "general interest." Second, the public expenditures necessary to compensate for the negative consequences of capitalist growth may lead to budget deficits that generate inflation, stifle growth, and provoke capital flight. Yet if public expenditures and welfare entitlements are cut back, the government loses public support (*LC* 40–50).

Legitimation Crisis: Because the government must be free to manage its rationality crisis flexibly, without having to rely on the contradictory signals emanating from a divided citizenry, it must find a way to mask its systemic crisis as a technical problem of managing economic growth. No longer defined as a political matter involving the fair redistribution of public tax revenues to private concerns, the problem is now consigned to the arcane machinations of economic experts, who are free to ply their sophisticated theorems away from the critical gaze of the public.

Habermas remarks that, with its social guarantees and division between unionized and nonunionized segments of the workforce, the welfare state has mitigated the worst economic disparities that encourage the growth of "class consciousness," thereby parrying the demand for radical change in the name of social justice. However, this strategy cannot entirely defuse the risk of a legitimation crisis. In attempting to offset the uneven side effects of capitalist growth, the welfare state must intervene in the everyday "lifeworld" of citizens, which includes those institutions responsible for socialization, social integration, and the preservation of culture: the family, the educational system, and the public sphere of mass information media. Because the lifeworld is essentially structured by communicative rationality, the state cannot guarantee "equal opportunity" in this area without once again provoking questions about its fairness (*LC* 71–75).

---

tax breaks (depletion and depreciation allowances), and research funds, Habermas believes that intellectual labor (research) aimed at increasing labor productivity can increase profitability (*LC* 40–44). How this explanation goes beyond Marx's remains unclear. J. Sensat, *Habermas and Marxism: An Appraisal* (Beverly Hills, CA: Sage, 1979), 150–53, 217; and K. Marx, *Capital*, vol. 1 (Moscow: Progress Publishers, 1963), 365–72, 386; and *Capital*, vol. 3 (Moscow: Progress Publishers, 1971), 241–66, 891–907.

Motivation Crisis: Habermas speculates that a legitimation crisis could be indefinitely forestalled if citizens became too distracted by their daily economic lives to pay attention to politics. But here too we find that state intervention undermines any single-minded attachment to work and its monetary rewards. To begin with, private life (civil privatism) is not, as such, antithetical to critical engagement in public life. Moreover, the ideology that

> family and job should consume one's attention (familial and vocational privatism),
> acquiring wealth and power is all that matters (possessive individualism and upward mobility),
> working and obeying one's superiors is both intrinsically rewarding and obligatory (the Protestant work ethic), and that
> the system is intrinsically fair because everyone has an equal shot at success (equal-opportunity education)

is no longer as convincing as it once was. The rewards of gainful employment often pale in comparison to the medical and welfare benefits provided by the state; and the higher earning potentials promised by college degrees have become depreciated as the cost of higher education rises. Rising affluence raises expectations for self-realization and control over one's life, which in turn leads people to question a life devoted to toil and consumption under the watchful gaze of bosses and "big brothers" (*LC* 75–92). Just as important, the expansion of the educational system, improved formal schooling, more egalitarian forms of child rearing, and the loosening of sexual prohibitions point to increasing difficulty in fitting young people smoothly into their "proper" roles. Education has been decoupled from "occupational success," and the new jobs are too monotonous to generate an adequate occupational identity (*LC* 91).

Social Pathologies and the Colonization of the Lifeworld

The crises associated with late capitalism affect society and individual and threaten—both objectively and subjectively—the *identity* of society and individual. Objectively speaking, late capitalism manifests an identity crisis or inner contradiction between incompatible steering imperatives. The state is caught in the midst of a system crisis in which it vacillates between behaving like a socialist state and behaving like a liberal capitalist state. Like a socialist state it funnels public revenue into welfare projects and the economy (through tax breaks, economic stimulus, etc.). Like a liberal capitalist state, it reacts against its mounting debt by reversing course, in effect "downsizing" and privatizing public services while deregulating markets. Seen from another perspective, the state behaves dictatorially (bureaucratically) and democratically, paternalistically and in a laissez-faire manner. Shifting its contradictions from one subsystem to another, the schizoid state also engenders a subjectively felt identity crisis within its own citizens, who experience themselves as active and passive, independent and dependent.

In his book *Legitimation Crisis* (1973) Habermas says that the "system" onto which the contradictions of economy and state are pushed is "society." Society becomes *anomic*—persons lose respect for the law and lose respect for one another; they lose respect for government, which they see as incompetent, *unjust*, and *illegitimate*, and, lastly (and most important) society fails to instill the *proper motivation* in citizens to produce and succeed (*TCA 2* 143, 386). Motivation crises reflect the limits of bourgeois ideology in motivating single-minded devotion to work and consumption. Yet, in principle they can be forestalled to the extent that socialization is "uncoupled" from a culture that encourages critical inquiry, aesthetic illumination of new sensitivities (through postauratic modern art that abjures authoritative representations of timeless beauty for the sake of social commentary), and autonomy and equality (universal morality). Habermas mentions the science fiction dystopia of a society of automatons who have been "programmed" through behavior modification, genetic engineering, or psychotropic drugging (*TRS* 123). But he notes that even in this dystopia, those who controlled the programming would still be subject to public accountability—at least among themselves.

Written almost a decade after *Legitimation Crisis, The Theory of Communicative Action* expands further on the identity crises besetting late capitalism. Here, however, Habermas has in mind something besides social crises reflecting a loss of respect for law, government, and social values, namely, two tendencies that directly undermine the reproduction of *cultural meaning and identity*, on the one hand, and *personal psychological well-being and reflective agency*, on the other. These tendencies exploit these other resources (cultural patterns and personality structures) in the process of temporarily "resolving" crises of anomie, legitimation, and motivation (*TCA 2* 386). In their place, they leave *psychopathology, stunted education*, and *alienation* (on the side of disturbances affecting the personality structure) and *loss of meaning, identity, and traditional continuity* (on the side of disturbances affecting the transmission of cultural patterns) (*TCA 2* 143).

The first tendency, which Habermas dubs the *colonization of the lifeworld*, involves substituting strategic forms of economic and legal action mediated by money and power for communicative forms of action responsible for socialization, cultural transmission, and social integration. Also directly implicated in the colonization of the lifeworld is the second tendency, which Habermas characterizes as *cultural impoverishment* caused by the splitting off of elite subcultures. This second tendency involves truncating or suppressing critical discourses within everyday communication in a way that produces a "fragmented consciousness" incapable of integrating cognitive, normative, and aesthetic understandings of reality in a critical way. Both of the above tendencies reflect the imperatives of a capitalist path of modernization that requires restructuring everyday life in accordance with the technical design of a hierarchical division of labor—a "functionally rational" separation of competencies and capacities in which top-down management, under the directorship of technical experts, reduces the "subjects" whom they control to appendages of a mechanical process of production and consumption. As Habermas puts it:

> We today have a "fragmented consciousness" that blocks enlightenment by the mechanism of reification. It is only with this that the conditions for a *colonization of the lifeworld* are met. When stripped of their ideological veils, the imperatives of autonomous subsystems make their way into the lifeworld from the outside—like colonial masters coming into a tribal society—and force a process of assimilation upon it. (*TCA 2* 355)

The Colonization of the Lifeworld by the System

Habermas frames his discussion of the colonization of the lifeworld in terms of a *bilevel* model of modern society as both *system* and *lifeworld* (see appendix F). The system refers to that aspect of society that is principally responsible for the *material reproduction* of life. This function is fulfilled by an economic system grounded in a legal system. The economic system establishes exchange relationships mediated by *money*;[3] it enables strategic actors to compete for scarce resources under terms established by a price system (the law of supply and demand). The legal system establishes property and contractual relationships, on the one hand, and coercive mechanisms for maintaining order and bureaucratic efficiency, on the other, both of which are backed up by administrative *power*. Money and power replace communicative action and function to relieve persons of the need to coordinate their actions through risky and time-consuming processes of consensus-oriented negotiation. Unlike money-mediated market relations, however, legal relationships do not merely stand

---

3. Habermas turns to the later systems theory of Talcott Parsons in explaining how economic and administrative systems replace normatively regulated communicative action with strategic "steering media" as consensual mechanisms for coordinating actors' behavior (what Habermas refers to as *system integration*, as distinct from *social integration*). In the early 1960s Parsons argued that money and power could be understood as specialized forms of communication. Money is a kind of code for sending and receiving information that presupposes a common set of expectations (cost-effective maximization of utility) and a generalized value (standardized medium of purchasing power). The redemption of monetary claims is backed up by banks and private law. Finally, money makes possible the reduction of all services, transactions, and properties to commodities whose exchange values and allocations are determined by a self-regulating market system following the law of supply and demand. Power also involves influencing behavior on the basis of shared expectations (the optimization of efficient performance through the unilateral threat of sanction). However, because it is not quantifiable, exchangeable, capable of being hoarded and concentrated without loss of value or circulated beyond limited organizational settings, it lacks the extensive system-building character possessed by money-mediated markets (*TCA 2* 265–82). See D. Ingram, *Habermas and the Dialectic of Reason* (New Haven: Yale University Press, 1987), chap. 9; and T. Parsons, *Sociological Theory and Modern Society* (New York: Free Press, 1967), 264, 307, 318, 361.

in for communicative action; they do not, in other words, simply steer behavior through coercive media (threat of power-backed sanction). Rather, legal relations are also embedded in normative democratic institutions that secure the voluntary acceptance of legitimate rules governing social cooperation. The intimate connection between law as a normative institution and everyday communicative action is especially evident in constitutional law, which institutionalizes the rights and conditions underwriting freedom of speech, freedom of the press, and freedom of association. Yet despite their artificial legal status (as Habermas understands it), constitutional rights have a compelling justification that precedes their legal institutionalization; reflecting a universal moral consensus, they remain firmly anchored in the solidaristic moral relationships underwriting communicative action in the lifeworld (*TCA 1* 72, 341–42, 359–60; *TCA 2* 113–18).

Both economic and administrative subsystems, then, are mediated by law (directly in the case of the administrative system, indirectly in the case of the economy). Because legal media that transmit the effects of coercive power are themselves legitimated by normative legal institutions that remain anchored in the lifeworld, the "uncoupling" of system and lifeworld that is definitive of modernization (see below) is at best partial, with the lifeworld retaining practical primacy over the system. The practical primacy of the lifeworld over the system appears even more compelling when we recall that it is the lifeworld that is responsible for the *symbolic reproduction* of humanly meaningful and purposeful life. This *tripartite* function—which includes the generation and *transmission* of cultural meaning and knowledge; the *internalization* of social roles, norms, and values through socialization; and the voluntary *coordination* of behavior (social integration)—is made possible by communicative action and its peculiar tripartite claim structure referring to truth, sincerity, and rightness (*TCA 2* 142).

I mentioned that the uncoupling (or differentiation) of lifeworld and system defines the trajectory of modernization. This process is propelled by what Habermas calls the *rationalization of the lifeworld* (see chapter 11), in which discursive problem solving becomes increasingly specialized in scientific, legal, and artistic discourses. Rationalization in turn makes possible technical knowledge for solving problems of order and maintenance without which authoritative and universally acceptable solutions would not be reached.

The uncoupling of the legal system (state administration) from the lifeworld marks the birth of *civilization;* the uncoupling of the economic system from both lifeworld and state marks the birth of *modernity.* According to Habermas, this two-stage uncoupling of system from lifeworld remains at best partial. The lifeworld retains practical primacy over the system, since the legitimacy of the legal system depends on its being anchored in the lifeworld. Nonetheless, the uncoupling of a capitalist market economy marks the beginning of a process by which the primacy of the lifeworld over the system is weakened, if not reversed. The birth of capitalism inaugurates the destruction of traditional ways of life and ushers in a new culture of material consumption and commodity exchange. Although the subsequent rise of constitutional and democratic forms of governance reinforces the primacy of the lifeworld, the transition from classical liberal (laissez-faire) capitalism to advanced welfare capitalism in the nineteenth and twentieth centuries reverses this trend. Even more damaging than the original destruction of traditional lifeworld caused by capitalism is the damage caused by the administrative system as it seeks to counteract this destruction. Protecting the family through bureaucratic regulation merely exacerbates the "colonization" of the lifeworld by the system. Whereas the juridification that established capitalist property and exchange relations destroyed customary statuses and altered the structure of traditional family life, the juridification associated with the therapeutic administration of public welfare threatens to undermine the symbolic reproduction of life as such (*TCA 2* 356–73).

Habermas's critique of colonization updates Marx's earlier critique of *commodity fetishism* and *alienation*. Marx had argued that capitalism transforms active human producers into passive objects of a market system. As human relationships become assimilated to economic relationships between buyers and sellers, they end up obeying the logic of the marketplace—the laws of competition and of supply and demand—in which money and profit, consumption and production, assume the status of "fetishes" that dominate all aspects of their lives. Marx also observed that the intense division of labor central to a modern factory system oriented toward an efficient and ever-expanding production of cheap products alienates producers from their humanity by forcing them to do mindless mechanical work (*TCA 2* 332–56).

Habermas agrees with Marx that capitalism encourages the hyperextension of money-driven economic relations into areas of life that are essentially constituted by relations of communicative interaction. Culture and politics, for example, are sold as standardized mass commodities produced by an entertainment industry. Instead of critical enlightenment, they now serve up a formulaic concoction of mindless spectacle, deceptive cant, and subliminal manipulation. The reflective privacy of the home has been replaced by the noisy din of television; leisurely moments of familial communion have been swallowed up by the demands of work and consumption. Education, too, increasingly mirrors the demands of the marketplace: getting a marketable degree has all but occluded learning aimed at personal growth and critical reflection.

But now, with the advent of the welfare state, it is not just the economic system that has colonized the lifeworld. Whole areas of life have become "juridified," or subjected to legal regulation by a welfare state intent on compensating for the destabilizing effects of a dynamic capitalist system.[4] In some cases, legal

---

4. The expansion of modern legal institutions—what Habermas, following first-generation critical theorist Otto Kirchheimer, calls "juridification"—is highly ambivalent. Habermas detects four stages of juridification. The first phase corresponds to early capitalism, whose extensive markets would not have been possible without stable currencies and (private) civil law governing private property, contractual exchange, liability, and so on. These legal conventions, which involved the nonnormative use of law as a power-backed steering mechanism, "liberated" peasants

regulation is experienced as less alienating and even partly liberating; collective bargaining law, for instance, empowers workers by permitting them to pool together in order to collectively leverage their demands against "coercive" threats made by powerful employers (*TCA 2* 367). At the same time, however, it disempowers workers by subjecting them to coercive regulations concerning union membership and organization, on one side, and collective bargaining terms and tactics, on the other. In other cases, most notably in the area of family and social law, juridification is experienced less ambiguously as alienating.[5] Unemployment and family-support benefits, for example, are intended to provide persons with the social resources necessary for gaining control over their lives and becoming active citizens. However, the legal processing of entitlements defeats this purpose; persons are reduced to "cases," in some instances forced to meet punitive eligibility requirements, and are subjected to forms of therapeutic surveillance, discipline, and control that effectively render them wards of a paternalistic and patriarchal state (*TCA 2* 367–73).[6]

---

by literally evicting them from the common lands to which they had held traditional title and by subjecting all persons—artisans, freemen, and even nobles—to the laws of the market. This phase of juridification—which involved the subsumption of the lifeworld under a bureaucratically regulated mercantilist system—was as coercive and alienating as it was "liberating." The next two phases of juridification—involving the constitutional limitation of government power (the implementation of the rule of law) and the extension of democracy—reversed this process. Both of these phases subordinated the system to a communicative lifeworld and hence were regarded as less ambiguously liberating. The final phase of juridification—involving the creation of the welfare state—again subordinates the lifeworld to the system. Like the first stage of juridification, it is experienced as both liberating (enabling citizens to exercise their democratic citizenship rights as social equals) and alienating (subsuming citizens under bureaucratic regulation). Despite this criticism, Habermas today defends the welfare state against neoliberal policies aimed at economic deregulation and government "downsizing" and "privatizing."

5. Most affected by "colonization" is the family, which in modern societies has taken on the task of socialization. In his earlier work on the structural transformation of the public sphere Habermas had focused on the penetration of the culture industry and its mantra of mindless entertainment and consumption into a private sphere that once served as a refuge for reading and reflection. In *The Theory of Communicative Action,* however, he focuses on the state's "therapeutic" oversight of the child's welfare, which has become increasingly endangered, thanks to the increasing demands and corresponding psychological stresses imposed on parents in a competitive economy. As divorce rates skyrocket, courts specializing in family law look to social agencies in resolving custody battles. Not only do parents and children find that their voices are ignored in the technical negotiations between judges, lawyers, and psychologists, in the case of severe family dysfunction, children become wards of the state, where their psychological and physical dependency is pathologically reinforced and extended. Meanwhile, in matters of education, the state responds to economic and social pressures by intervening in the development and implementation of curriculum and in the testing of children. Vocational demands take precedence over moral development, so that children come to identify themselves as producers and consumers rather than as politically engaged citizens (*TCA 2* 369–73). Habermas also cites a study by Christopher Lasch showing that the prolonged dependency of young adults on their parents due to poor employment prospects can produce narcissism, whose symptoms can be channeled into protest or countercultural lifestyles.

6. Habermas's diagnosis of modern social pathology stresses the debilitating impact of the economic-administrative system on family and public sphere, but little attention is paid to the debilitating impact of familial patriarchy on the system. The failure to see how closely lifeworld

The Splitting Off of Elite Subcultures

As I noted at the conclusion of chapter 2, capitalism has found a substitute for ideology in alienating us from our critical aptitudes. In order to develop a critical understanding of self and society, one must be capable of synthesizing different aspects and levels of experience as well as developing skills of analysis and argumentation. Capitalism frustrates this understanding by forcing us to "compartmentalize" our lives between work and leisure. The "good" employee all too often leaves her ethics at home when advancing the good of the company (to say nothing of the CEO who uses stockholders, employees, and the public purse to profit at the expense of the company and everyone else). People let the experts do their thinking for them; they become "deskilled" (craftsmen—who threaten management's control over the workforce—are replaced by easily trained machine operatives); or if they retain their skills, they become one-sided—good at technical-scientific forms of cognition, bad at moral-evaluative forms of cognition; good at micromanaging consumption, bad at critically relating their consumption patterns to the demands of a complex system (*TCA 2* 396–403).

In sum, Habermas's account of social pathology stresses the damaging effects that a capitalist system and its administrative regulation have on the symbolic

and system are codeterminative creates a blind spot in Habermas's analysis with respect to male domination, which has been subjected to extensive critique by feminists. According to Fraser, Habermas's diagnosis labels pathological any attempt to structure the family as a strategic conflict rather than as a consensual relationship of caring and nurturance. Doing so, however, pathologizes women homemakers' contractual claims to an equal share of income, which would guarantee them the financial security that would enable them to function independently of domineering husbands. Fraser also notes that the roles of worker, consumer, client, and citizen that figure in Habermas's analysis of the mediation of lifeworld and system—a mediation he depicts in the form of an input-output flow between family and economy, on one side, and between public sphere and administration, on the other—are also gendered in ways that qualify his analysis of pathological dependency (*TCA 2* 319–23). Habermas observes that the client-provider relationship that obtains between welfare recipients and the state undermines the freedom and dignity of clients. However, it is men who experience this pathological dependency more acutely than women, despite the fact that most welfare recipients are women. This is because the role of worker as it has been institutionalized within a patriarchal system is primarily masculine. Men are raised to be independent, self-sufficient breadwinners; women, by contrast, are marginalized as homemakers, part-time workers, or full-time, low-paying servants in "helping" professions involving care for others. Furthermore, the welfare system treats men and women differently based on this role distinction. Unemployment insurance, disability compensation, and social security pensions are regarded as entitlements that workers (mainly male) claim as a matter of right (having themselves contributed taxes to these insurance schemes); by contrast, aid to nonworking parents (typically women) is viewed as "charity" that the state begrudgingly doles out for the sake of maintaining therapeutic vigilance over dysfunctional families. The paternalistic oversight and punitive sanctions accompanying such aid exacerbates the dependency that poor mothers already experience. Finally, while the role of consumer is still essentially feminine—with women being responsible for maintaining the household economy—the role of citizen is chiefly masculine (as evidenced by the lower numbers of women serving in the military). N. Fraser, "What's Critical about Critical Theory?" in *Critical Theory: The Essential Readings* (New York: Paragon House, 1991), 357–87.

reproduction of everyday life. Capitalism's growth imperative impels the commodification of goods and services as well as the manipulation of culture for purposes of advertising, while the welfare state's therapeutic imperative impels juridical interventions in family and school that reinforce dependency, alienation, narcissism, and conformism.

The accuracy and comprehensiveness of this diagnosis is doubtless open to debate. Yet Habermas's reference to what Niklas Luhmann calls the *technicization of the lifeworld* (*TCA* 2 245) points to an indisputable fact: life has become increasingly mediated by automated technical systems, from vending machines and automated doors to automated exchanges of goods and services involving monetary transactions and legal claims. Most noteworthy for their dehumanizing effects—but largely neglected by Habermas—are the kinds of disciplinary *technical designs,* characteristic of a capitalist system, that range from automation to commodification and mass consumption.[7] In designs such

7. Building on Marx's and Lukács's ideas, Paul Thompson defines commodification in terms of four conditions. "Commodification and Secondary Rationalization," in *Democratizing Technology: Andrew Feenberg's Critical Theory of Technology,* ed. T. Veak (Albany: SUNY Press, 2006), 112–35. The four conditions are *alienability* (the capability of separating one good from another good or from the person of a human being); *excludability* (the capability of monopolizing ownership of a good); *rivalry* (the capability of reducing the number of times a good can be used, the number of persons who can use it at the same time, the number of alternative goods that can be substituted for it, and/or the purposes to which the good can be put); and *standardization* (the capability of a sample being treated as equivalent to any other sample of the same good) (116). *Structural commodification* involves changing rules, customs, and moral codes in ways that facilitate and legitimate the realization of the four conditions; *technological commodification,* by contrast, realizes these conditions by effecting changes in the goods themselves. The following example illustrates these distinctions: Prior to the twentieth century, people turned to family, friends, and clergy to deal with depression. The communicative relationships constituting therapeutic intervention were not yet commodified. With the advent of psychotherapeutic "science," these relationships underwent structural commodification in the form of purchasable therapeutic sessions with technical experts. Although technical commodification entered into the form of therapeutic dialogue, with the therapist controlling and interpreting the transference relationship according to technical rules and theoretical formulas, the most extreme commodification of therapy came with the emergence of a private health insurance network and the use of psychotropic drug therapies (Prozac, etc.). These were easily and widely dispensed, excluded or made redundant alternative interventions, and were under monopoly control (thanks to patents, copyrights, and other structures). A secondary consequence of commodification is the *autonomization* of the commodity form. Commodification produces system-building side effects that escape the intentional control of agents (described by Marx as a "fetishism of commodities"). Feenberg's distinction between primary and secondary forms of technological instrumentalization provides a highly useful framework for understanding this autonomization. Primary instrumentalization involves the removal of technically disposable elements from their natural contexts (*decontextualization*) and their analytic *reduction* to quantifiable variables that can be controlled in a top-down manner by *autonomous subjects,* who are detached from and *positioned* in relations of domination to objects. Secondary instrumentalization reverses this processes of *rational differentiation* by *realizing* abstract functions in integrated systems (*systematization*), *mediating* these systems with value-pregnant contexts, reintegrating actor and technology in nonobjectifying social ensembles, and democratically reinforcing technically creative relationships (*vocation* and *initiative*). What distinguishes capitalist technological commodification from other forms of modern technological realization is its truncated, exclusive focus on only one dimension of secondary instrumentalization: systematization. In

as these, *abstract function* (such as conveying nutrients through bottled baby formula) has replaced *concrete craft* (breast-feeding) in a manner that could be described as alienating.

Despite Habermas's neglect of the technicization of production and consumption, he does mention, as noted in chapter 5, one example of functionalism gone amok: positive eugenics. Fueled by market forces that increasingly reward only those who possess exceptional skills and talents, designer eugenics dispenses with the contingent craft of embodied conception, and it does so, moreover, in a manner that threatens to radically efface the boundary separating the human and the nonhuman (or posthuman). Habermas's fear is that the biotechnological functionalism that compels us to maximize our chances of having "successful offspring" may well end up separating us from our own humanity via a slippery slope that passes from prenatal diagnostic testing and selective implantation of embryos to in vitro gestation, cloning, and—as we approach the threshold dividing humans from cyborgs—behavioral programming. Indeed, extreme biotechnicization of the lifeworld would so fundamentally alter our ontological self-understanding that we would likely lose both our lifeworld and our humanity.

The technicization of the lifeworld raises other questions about Habermas's colonization thesis. Even if we concede that a partial uncoupling of lifeworld and system—and with it, the partial subsumption of life under semiautomated systems—is a hallmark of modern "progress," we might question Habermas's account of the extent and manner in which this process becomes reifying and pathological. The very term "colonization" suggests that a clear divide exists between colonized and colonizer and that the direction of colonization is one-way. The separation of colonized from colonizer is implicit in Habermas's attempt to define the split between lifeworld and system in institutional terms, with family and public sphere falling within the colonized colony of the lifeworld, on one side, and business and state falling within the colonizer empire of the system, on the other. This way of putting the distinction commits the fallacy of misplaced concretization. Families, no less than businesses, are responsible for the material reproduction of society; businesses, no less than families, are responsible for its symbolic reproduction. Integration of actors within these institutions is therefore dual. Families are already inserted within technical systems and mediated networks. The nuclear family, with its male breadwinner and female caretaker, was technically constituted by labor laws during the second half of the nineteenth century (when female- and child-labor practices were curtailed) so as to stabilize an increasingly automated capitalist economy that demanded fewer but more educated workers. Conversely,

striving to maximize only exchange value, technological commodification suppresses other values and dimensions of secondary instrumentalization: vocation (reciprocal relationship to meaningful affirmative work and things) and initiative (creative and collective care for work and things). See A. Feenberg, *Questioning Technology* (London: Routledge, 1999), 205–7.

familial patriarchy (which Habermas observes has declined since the 1970s) shaped these very same laws.

The reciprocal colonization of lifeworld and system requires a more nuanced account of social pathology than Habermas provides. We can no longer conclude that protecting housewives by legally guaranteeing them a portion of their husband's income would be experienced by them as an alienating form of juridification in the manner suggested by Habermas's colonization thesis. The objectification of women as dependents—to the extent that it still exists— precedes welfare state paternalism and capitalist patriarchy and so must be partly explained in terms of a process of misrecognition whose origins can be traced back to the earliest relationship between parent and child.[8]

Habermas's account of colonization as technicization provides yet another way to qualify his thesis without abandoning it. Habermas is surely right to resist the antimodernist temptation to demonize technology. However, he is wrong to treat it as a largely value-neutral, norm-free tool of instrumental action. Indeed, if Feenberg is right, modern automated technology—no less than money and legal power—functions like a steering medium.[9] Technological sys-

---

8. Honneth argues that libidinal attachment between infants and their caretakers establishes affective forms of communication without which cognitive acts of mutual recognition and communicative action would be impossible. Because adopting the perspective of the other (mutual recognition) is also necessary for experiencing an objective world, pathologies characterized by lack of affective attachment (such as autism) also produce cognitive and communicative impairments. Pathological patterns of socialization (child abuse, etc.) that prevent children from forming affective attachments can later lead them to treat others as objects, thereby depriving themselves of perspectives that would otherwise enrich their awareness of the concrete meanings things have for persons besides themselves. In addition to reification of others and of nature, Honneth also discusses the dynamics of self-reification that occur whenever we treat our desires and personality traits as if they were fixed objects knowable by inner perception or mere creations of the will. Although Honneth links the strategic manipulation of one's inner self in job interviews and sales talks to occupational imperatives, he assiduously avoids reducing social pathologies to system/ lifeworld disturbances. (As he notes, even strategic actors whose actions are mediated by money and power still recognize one another as legal and moral subjects, and even detached observers of nature and society never forget their primary affective involvement with and recognition of their fellow inhabitants and their lifeworld.) A. Honneth, *Reification: A New Look at an Old Idea* (Oxford: Oxford University Press, 2008), 42–45, 50–51, 57, 59, 80. For criticisms of Honneth's conflation of normative and nonnormative forms of recognition and his underestimation of sociopathic forms of manipulation that build on attachments, see the concluding commentaries in Honneth's book by Judith Butler, Raymond Geuss, and Jonathan Lear.

9. Feenberg, *Questioning Technology,* 166–73. Feenberg argues that modern (semi-)automated technology is not merely a technical means deployed by media of money and power but constitutes a separate steering medium in its own right. Like other steering media mentioned by Habermas, technology has a "generalized instrumental value," namely, productivity, or "enhanced control" over resources and persons. Although this value appears indistinguishable from the value of effectiveness secured by legal power, it is distinguished by its "operational autonomy," or complete detachment from normative claims. Second, just as money and power advance a "nominal claim"—to exchange value and obedience, respectively—so technology advances a nominal claim to prescriptive compliance. Finally, the value and claim "redemption" structure of technology

tems embody materialized "norms" and "prescriptions" that guide our behavior nonconsensually, thereby exhibiting the same ambiguity that characterizes money and power. Technology, too, liberates us from the risks and burdens associated with having to negotiate our shared life discursively but only at the risk of subjecting us to new constraints. Yet, no matter how functionally autonomous technological systems become in relation to the lifeworld—large-scale systems such as electrical grids, for instance, generate a momentum of their own that is hard to resist and control—their concrete design and implementation necessarily reflects the dominant values and interests of society.[10] That is why political struggle over the values and interests that inform technological design must be regarded as designating one important—if indeed limited—possibility for criticizing technological reification. However, precisely because large-scale technological systems unfold a momentum and logic of their own that resists transformation by a democratic politics of design, a critique of technology must also be pursued along a different track, one that insists on retaining the modern separation—however relative and partial—of dominant lifeworld and a subordinate system.[11] So, although the technicization of the lifeworld is not intrinsi-

---

possesses a "reserve backing" in the form of consequences (negative or positive) that parallels the reserve backing behind money (gold or national wealth) and power (enforcement). Feenberg responds to the objection that technology is not an analytically distinguishable steering medium but only a technical means informing media by pointing out that the same could be said of money and power. In real life, all three media "serve as means for each other." Just as money and power are implemented by technology, so technology is implemented by money and power (with money as a means for obtaining power and vice versa). According to Feenberg, the closest analogue to technology is legal power, which straddles the lifeworld/system distinction in constituting itself as both a normative institution that facilitates social integration (analogous to the way in which automatic door openers facilitate social interaction by embodying norms of openness and easy access) and as a complex medium that facilitates system integration (analogous to the way in which automated assembly plants facilitate top-down control of workers) (172).

10. Following Feenberg's instrumentalization theory, primary instrumentalization designates that feature of modern technology that imbues it with the abstract functional rationality characteristics of a system medium. By contrast, secondary instrumentalization designates that feature of technology by which abstract functions are shaped into concrete value-laden designs. According to Feenberg, modern capitalism and bureaucratic socialism prefer technical designs that deviate as little as possible from the singular requirements of abstract functional efficiency, thereby preserving the autonomy and hierarchy implicit in primary instrumentalization. Because the lifeworld is a source of democratic values, the same technological functions can be interpreted differently (energy generation can lead to impersonal hegemonic electrical grids or personal and widely disseminated solar panels). See Feenberg, *Questioning Technology*, 201–25.

11. For a discussion of technological scale and momentum, see T. P. Hughes, *Networks of Power: Electrification in Western Society, 1880–1930* (Baltimore: Johns Hopkins University Press, 1983); and D. J. Stump, "Rethinking Modernity as the Construction of Technological Systems," in *Democratizing Technology*. Stump argues that Feenberg's instrumentalization theory concedes too much to Heideggerian essentialism in its definition of modern technology in terms of autonomous (abstract) functionalism—a feature that Stump believes can be captured empirically in terms of technological scale and momentum. Feenberg agrees ("Replies to Critics," in *Democratizing Technology*, 188) that the concept of technological momentum can reconcile modernity studies

cally reifying—some automated systems, such as computers, can even enhance communication itself—it can become so. Here we can retrieve the valid insight contained in Habermas's colonization thesis: as the case of biotechnology run amok attests, modern automated technologies, no less than exchange relations of money and power, *can* produce pathological effects when "overextended" beyond their proper boundaries into domains of everyday life.

In sum, Habermas's discussion of crisis tendencies and social pathologies besetting the modern welfare state all point to a tension (or even contradiction) between capitalism and democracy. However, it seems that Habermas's own dualism of system and lifeworld serves to diminish this tension. Although he reminds us that capitalism is only one path that modernization can take, he never explains what he means by this, other than noting that one alternative— bureaucratic socialism—represents an obviously failed and truncated form of a modern rational society.[12] Indeed, his criticism of Marx for failing to grasp the inherent rationality of an uncoupling of system and lifeworld seems to protect market economies and bureaucratic administrations from direct criticism. So long as they are sufficiently "tamed" and do not "colonize" the lifeworld, they seem perfectly rational and unproblematic. The price Habermas pays for this concession to systems theory is steep, however. Much of what first-generation and third-generation critical theorists criticize in alienated labor—the use of technologies that reinforce compartmentalized thought and feeling, the de-skilling of human beings and their reduction to cogs in machines, the desensitization and blunting of consciousness and experience—drops out of his analysis or appears only at the margins of his thinking. If functional efficiency requires this kind of technical organization, Habermas seems to think, then so be it. Only by reformulating the concept of functional efficiency in terms that take into account the meanings and values of the lifeworld (and specifically the values of hierarchy and profitability informing capitalist culture) can we

---

(which emphasize functional differentiation of system and lifeworld) and technology studies (which emphasize the contextual mediation of system and lifeworld). However, he doubts whether Stump's constructivist empiricism (shared by Latour, Bloor, and others) is capable of developing strong theoretical criteria for criticizing the nature and limits of technology as such. For example, in the case of reproductive biotechnology discussed earlier, Feenberg notes that a critic using Stump's model might criticize gender selection technology on the grounds that it endangers women's rights but not because its design reflects patriarchal values and undermines our own self-understanding as human beings (190–91).

12. Habermas regards the Soviet model of bureaucratic socialism as a variant of the modern principle of organization characterized by a rational differentiation of lifeworld and system. The difference between advanced capitalism and bureaucratic socialism is that, under socialism, the economy is controlled by the state rather than the other way around. This means that social crises and pathologies assume a different form. Lagging productivity and consumer shortages reflect inflexible management of the economy coupled with information overloads (regarding planning options) and deficits (regarding consumer needs). Meanwhile social pathologies result less from the incursion of state administration into family planning and education than in the state's pretending to replace the political public sphere (CD 283). See also A. Arato, "Critical Sociology and Authoritarian State Socialism" in CD, 196–218.

deploy Habermas's (now softened) distinction between system and lifeworld to criticize alienating media that overstep their bounds.

Globalization: The New Challenge

Rather than pursue some of the alternative reformulations of Habermas's bilevel theory of society that third-generation critical theorists have proposed,[13] let me now turn to another crisis that has occupied Habermas for the past decade. Since 1981, the year that saw the publication of *The Theory of Communicative Action* in which Habermas developed his critique of capitalism's pathological tendencies, momentous changes have occurred in the global economy that rendered that account and his earlier account of legitimation crises partially obsolete. To begin with, the opening up of global markets and global competition limited the steering capacity of the welfare state to regulate its domestic economy. In addition, the pressure to deregulate, to lower business taxes, and to limit government spending forced the welfare state (especially in the United States) to scale back its damage-control interventions in the lifeworld, with the result that federal spending in health, education, and welfare declined. Declining wages (in response to loss of manufacturing jobs overseas, weakened unions, outsourcing, and de-skilling), slower growth, and an exploding income

13. If first-generation critical theorists were wrong to demonize instrumental rationality rather than the specific functional rationality of capitalism, then second-generation critical theorists are wrong to see in communicative rationality an adequate procedure for criticizing ideological delusions and social pathologies. So-called third-generation critical theorists (Fraser, Honneth, Benhabib, Bohman, McCarthy, Kellner, Feenberg, et al.) respond to this lack of critical edge in Habermas's theory by questioning his "essentialist" (all-or-nothing) distinctions between lifeworld and system, strategic/instrumental action (reason) and communicative action (reason), technology and experiential environment; likewise they shift the focus of critical theory from abstract theorizing about "logical forms" to concrete historical struggles for recognition pertaining to class, gender, race, and multiculturalism. Among those third-generation critical theorists who most deeply challenge the Habermasian paradigm are Honneth and Feenberg. As we have seen, Feenberg welcomes Habermas's refusal to demonize instrumental and technological rationality but questions his endorsement of an abstract technological functionalism that prevents him from appreciating how different technological designs can facilitate or obstruct democratic communication, enhance or frustrate the development of capabilities central to an integral life. Honneth, too, criticizes the failure of Habermasian theory of colonization to take up Marx's theory of alienated labor. Emphasizing the expressive and communicative nature of work, he reinterprets this theory in light of Hegel's dialectic of recognition, whose dynamics extend back the prelinguistic roots of child-parent interaction. A. Honneth, *Critique of Power: Reflective Stages in a Critical Social Theory*, trans. K. Baynes (Cambridge: MIT Press, 1991); Honneth, *The Fragmented World of the Social: Essays in Social and Political Philosophy* (Albany: SUNY Press, 1995); Honneth, *The Struggle for Recognition: The Moral Grammar of Social Conflicts*, trans. J. Anderson (Cambridge: MIT Press, 1995); Honneth (with Hans Joas), *Social Action and Human Nature*, trans. R. Meyer (Cambridge: Cambridge University, 1988); J.-P. Deranty, "Repressed Materiality: Retrieving the Materialism in Axel Honneth's Theory of Recognition," *Critical Horizons* 7/1 (2006): 113–40; and J. Anderson, "The Third Generation of the Frankfurt School," *Intellectual History Newsletter* 22 (2000). http://artsci. wustl.edu/~anderson/criticaltheory/3rdGeneration.htm.

gap between rich and poor, coupled with decaying public infrastructure and diminished public services, formed the backdrop to the global economic crisis of 2008–09. Thanks to deregulation in financial and investment markets and the growing value of real estate, stocks, and other assets (much of it inflated by speculation), banks and other financial institutions enticed investors to take advantage of mortgage-backed securities. Meanwhile these same institutions—so desperate to dispose of their excess capital—lured heavily indebted consumers with shaky credit to take advantage of low-interest adjustable-rate loans in order to purchase homes or to refinance the ones they already owned (for purposes of consolidating their debt) by borrowing against the inflated equity in their homes. This marriage of convenience between cash-rich financiers and cash-poor consumers sustained the high levels of consumption necessary for meeting the demands of a growing capitalist economy, despite the fall in wages affecting consumers in the lower tier of the economy. When the bubble burst (beginning with the collapse of the U.S. housing market) and the value of the mortgage-backed securities and other highly complex derivatives became impossible to determine, commercial banks holding these toxic assets were unable to sell them, and so sources of investment and consumer credit dried up, thus triggering a major recession.

I recount these facts—so familiar to most of us by now—because Habermas believes that they reconfirm important parts of his earlier prediction of legitimation crises in late capitalism (*EFP* 187).[14] That prediction is based on the welfare state's inability to manage capitalism's chronic crisis of overproduction (itself a result of treating wages as a cost of production that must be suppressed) without pursuing contradictory strategies: regulation and deregulation of the economy and of society. Although Habermas asserts that regulation—or as he is fond of putting it, "taming" the capitalist base (*DW* 43; *EFP* 187)—is necessary if the welfare state is ever to become a viable vehicle for realizing the discourse ethical ideals implicit in liberal democracy, he observes that globalization has increasingly rendered that option untenable. So we are stuck with a permanent crisis for which there is no real alternative—short of deregulation, whose disastrous consequences are now quite evident. That said, globalization opens up new possibilities,[15] for global governance of a global economy and environment, that Habermas finds promising.[16]

14. See the November 6, 2008, interview in *Die Zeit* with Habermas and Thomas Assheuer on the global economic crisis of 2008 titled "Life after Bankruptcy," reprinted in *EFP* 184–97.

15. Habermas defines globalization as "the cumulative processes of a worldwide expansion of trade and production, commodity and financial markets, fashions, the media and computer programs, news, and communications networks, transportation systems and flows of migration, the risks generated by large-scale technology, environmental damage and epidemics, as well as organized crime and terrorism" that extend beyond the borders of any state and "enmesh nation-states in dependencies of an increasingly interconnected world" (*DW* 175).

16. The extent to which the current era marks a fundamental change in global capitalism and a shift in the balance of power from sovereign states to supranational social, political, and economic entities is hotly debated. For a sampling of the debates between skeptics who see no fundamental change in the global order since the late nineteenth century and globalists who do, see D. Held

To appreciate the promise of globalization we must first take stock of its impact—both negative and positive—on the nation-state. Since the late 1990s Habermas has argued that the state no longer has control over the external environment that dictates what goes on inside its borders. To begin with, the state is faced with environmental and security challenges that it is ill-equipped to deal with on its own. It has failed to stem the tide of immigrants and refugees streaming across its borders due to economic dislocations and civil strife in developing countries; and the price it must pay for accepting them is a certain degree of multicultural instability and loss of national identity. At the same time, a reverse process of cultural assimilation and homogenization—the Americanization of the globe—threatens to destroy or permanently alter local traditions. Finally, the state has lost control over its own domestic economy.

The neoliberal policies adopted during the 1980s and maintained through the first decade of the second millennium by global financial and trade organizations such as the International Monetary Fund (IMF), World Bank (WB), and World Trade Organization (WTO) require that states embark on a course of structural adjustment, downsizing, privatization, and deregulation in order to become "competitive." Tight-money policies, coupled with tightly balanced budgets, make for stable currency and low inflation, but at the cost of gutting social services. To create a good investment environment, states must lower taxes and reduce social services. This dismantling of the welfare state weakens democracy in two ways: not only are economic decisions placed in the hands of global economic elites but growing social inequality between "winners" and "losers" threatens to undermine domestic solidarity.

Cosmopolitan Democracy and Global Politics as a Response to Global Crisis

Despite his concerns about the negative effects of globalization, Habermas is by no means insensitive to its positive side. First, it provokes a constant crisis that repoliticizes people and thereby corrects against tendencies that otherwise favor an "unconstitutional" flow of power. Habermas observes that threats to the "grammar of the lifeworld" caused by global warming, human migration, destruction of environment and tradition, commodification of culture, and so on have galvanized the formation of new social movements that, unlike earlier civil rights and labor movements, seek to change or conserve ways of life rather than merely fight for distributive justice. Even the transformation of tradition has its upside. For instance, in some places where the global demand for labor has increased, women have joined the workforce and have acquired organizational skills that have enabled them to challenge patriarchal domination,

and A. McGrew, *The Global Transformation Reader,* 2nd ed. (Cambridge: Polity Press, 2003), especially the authors' introduction.

reduce overpopulation, improve local economies, and become active citizens struggling for social change.

Second, Habermas believes that the increased vulnerability of isolated nations to economic, ecological, and security risks acts as a positive incentive for them to relinquish their unlimited sovereignty. In short, they are compelled by the threat of losing needed foreign investment to forgo nationalistic "protectionist" policies aimed at resisting outside cultural, political, and economic pressures in exchange for joining together in *postnational* constellations of shared governance. In this way, globalization meets halfway the normative ideal of bringing about a *cosmopolitan* rule of law in which everyone's human rights can be secured, if need be, against actions committed by their own governments (*DW* 177).

This bold idea has provoked a great deal of misunderstanding and resistance on the part of those who fear the creation of a monolithic global state or who believe that even a weaker, global enforcement of "human rights" will inadvertently increase mistrust and hostility between nations, each of which thinks it alone has moral authority to create a "humanitarian" world according to its own particular ethos (and in pursuit of its own particular interests) (*DW* 188–93). These critics therefore prefer the older European system of *international law* that prevailed from the Peace of Westphalia (1648) until World War I. This system presumes that nations exist in an "amoral" state of nature in which each nation is recognized by the others as possessing absolute internal sovereignty within its own borders and as having a sovereign right to advance its "national interests" abroad in whatever manner it sees fit, including waging war (*DW* 118–23).

Against this "realist" position, Habermas turns to Kant's seminal ideal of a cosmopolitan rule of law that began to inform international law beginning with the League of Nations but which only became dominant in the 1990s with intensified UN efforts in preventing genocide and ethnic cleansing and sustained international prosecution of human rights violations. Unlike international law, which relies on a balance of power between states to maintain peace, cosmopolitan law aims at protecting the human rights of individuals qua "world citizens." This goal conflicts with a right to war, which by its very nature demands that individuals sacrifice their lives to the nation, and replaces justified defensive warfare with policing operations directed against crimes against humanity and other gross human rights violations. It also requires remedying the economic and environmental causes that lead to social strife in the first place (*DW* 123).

Politics and the Rule of Law in International Relations

Before proceeding further, it might be useful to situate Habermas's theory of international law with respect to some of the philosophical questions that have been raised about international law in general. To begin with, some philosophers have questioned whether international law properly fits the description of law at all (the problem of legal fit). A related but somewhat different question has been raised concerning whether international law meets (or could meet) the exacting demands imposed by the rule of law as a norm that effective legal systems must aspire to (the problem of the rule of law). Finally, philosophers have queried the legitimacy of international law as a neutral (or impartial) framework for adjudicating disputes between states (the problem of legitimacy). Habermas answers all of these questions affirmatively, but with some reservation. The reservation stems from the fact that legality, rule of law, and legitimacy are all concepts that originally refer to the domestic legal systems of states (what, following Roman usage, is customarily referred to as municipal law). So the question arises: How much of their original meaning do these concepts lose when extended to the global arena?

The Problem of Legal Fit

What we today call international law (a term coined by Jeremy Bentham in the nineteenth century)[17] grew out of customs, some of which had been in force since the time of ancient Rome and the Roman Law of Nations (*ius gentium*). This law had been influenced, first, by the natural law philosophy of Stoic philosophers such as Cicero and later by the same philosophy as expounded by Christian philosophers such as St. Thomas Aquinas. From the seventeenth century until the nineteenth century natural law jurists such as Hugo Grotius (1583–1645), Samuel Pufendorf (1632–94), and Emmerich de Vattel (1714–67) sought to justify and codify these customs, the most important of which from our perspective concerned the moral justification and moral conduct of war ("just war" doctrine). The main difficulty these natural law theorists confronted involved reconciling the variety of human-made customs with timeless moral principles whose principal application was the internal ordering of self-contained states vis-à-vis the common good of their citizens and not the external ordering of states vis-à-vis their conduct toward one another. Many of the customs of international conduct did not appear to be morally grounded at all, and natural morality itself—resting on contestable metaphysical notions of human nature—proved to be elusive and impractical, especially when applied to states, the rights and duties of which were not derivable from the rights and duties of moral subjects. By the nineteenth century the natural law approach had been replaced by a more liberal and positivistic approach. This approach—which owed more to Hobbes's vision of a social contract—treated states as inherently free and equal sovereign subjects that rightfully pursued

17. J. Bentham, *Principles of Morals and of Legislation* in *The Utilitarians* (New York: Doubleday, 1973), XVII.25, n.1.

their own interests unconstrained by notions of justice. In this context, international law governed such matters as diplomacy, recognition of statehood and territory, and neutrality during wartime. However, the demand to regulate the conduct of war and outlaw aggressive war entirely—the peace mandate that emerged at the conclusion of World War I—once again led jurists to push for a more normative understanding of international law. The fruit of this labor was the voluntary League of Nations, which brokered a number of treaties banning aggressive war and inhumane weaponry and limiting armaments. After World War II the demand for a more effective international peace-keeping body led to the founding of the United Nations, which unlike the League of Nations provides representation for all states. With the founding of this organization and the earlier, precedent-setting Nuremberg Military Tribunal that tried former Nazi leaders with war crimes and crimes against humanity, what is known as *international humanitarian law*—the essence of Habermas's cosmopolitan law—emerges into full view for the first time. This law not only provided for the unprecedented indictment of individuals by international courts—a process that was made permanent with the later establishment of the International Criminal Tribunal for the Former Yugoslavia (1994), the International Tribunal for Rwanda, and the International Criminal Court. It also led to the adoption of the Universal Declaration of Human Rights in 1948 and other conventions concerning human rights and security.

Although few would deny that these documents and conventions impose obligations on states (in their conduct toward other states) and individual leaders (in their conduct toward their own citizens), many would deny their legally binding status. For most of the UN's life, the resolutions passed by its representative General Assembly and its elite executive body, the Security Council, as well as the decisions handed down by international courts, have not been recognized as legally binding by all states. Even when they have been so recognized they have not been rigorously enforced. Yet, despite what Hobbesian philosophy of law might lead us to believe,[18] the problem of enforcement—and the somewhat related problem that laws normally apply within well-bounded territories over which sovereign governments exercise an absolute monopoly of violence—are not as serious a threat to the legal status of international law as the problem of recognition. As H. L. A. Hart pointed out many years ago in arguing against the Hobbesian command theory of law, many laws consist of procedures, not commands, and their binding nature cannot derive solely from threat of sanction but also requires recognition of legitimacy based on some authoritative pedigree. Again, the mere fact that such resolutions are weakly enforced (if at all) does not distinguish them from many municipal laws, such as antisodomy statutes, which may also be weakly (if ever) enforced. Hart also

18. As Hobbes famously put it: "Where there is no common power [i.e., enforcement of a command emanating from a sovereign head of state] there is no law, where no law, no injustice" (*Leviathan [Indianapolis: Hackett, 1994]*, XIII.13).

observed that the application of law within a bounded territory over which a single sovereign state exercises an exclusive and absolute monopoly of violence is itself exceptional rather than normal. The notion of absolute state sovereignty, or the notion that states are only bound by their own laws, is a fiction. States depend on the recognition of other states for whatever limited sovereignty they possess, both in dealing with other states and in dealing with their own citizens.[19] Furthermore, many states appear to be evolving toward a model of *divided territorial sovereignty* of the sort exemplified in the U.S. federal model, where neither the federal government nor its member states can claim absolute sovereignty over all matters within a given territory. This model, which has taken hold in the European Union (and which Habermas finds to be so congenial to his own proposal for reshaping international and cosmopolitan law), also appears to capture the kind of "sovereignty" toward which the United Nations and its offshoot, the International Criminal Court, might be headed, a sovereignty divided between a supranational human rights regime, on one side, and a transnational system of governance, on the other.

These responses do not, however, staunch all of the skeptic's concerns. As Hart notes, the problem of recognizing what treaties and customs count as international law remains. Unless there exists something like a constitution that, in a manner analogous to a domestic constitution, explicitly lays out criteria for testing the "legal" pedigree of an international custom or treaty—for example, by establishing a supreme international legislative body—we will not have a legal system for recognizing, changing, and applying international law but only a hodgepodge of "primary" rules whose legally binding nature will remain uncertain.

As we shall see, Habermas responds to Hart's challenge by proposing the international adoption of something like Hart's secondary "rule of recognition," which will enable a constitutionalization of international law without a global sovereign state. So, even though international law as it currently exists is not yet fully law-like, it could conceivably become so (and, Habermas would add, is in fact becoming so). But even if the nations of the world adopted a constitution for a federal system of world governance, there would still remain a question about whether the legal system could live up to the stringent normative ideals associated with the rule of law.

The Problem of the Rule of Law

As noted in chapter 6, the rule of law entails the insulation of law from arbitrary forms of political power. The operant word here is "arbitrary." Habermas rejects the classical liberal attempt to insulate law by grounding basic rights in nature, God, or reason. In his opinion, legal rights are essentially the product

19. H. L. A. Hart, *The Concept of Law*, 2nd ed. (Oxford: Clarendon Press, 1991), 212–21.

of democratic politics, so in that sense all law—including constitutional law and its schedule of basic rights—is political. That said, Habermas insists that democratic politics is structured by discursive procedures that are themselves grounded in rational norms of communicative action that are not political or voluntarily chosen. Hence, these provide some neutral framework that is impervious to the vicissitudes of power politics. Although we cannot predict with certainty the outcome of any act of legislation or act of adjudication, we can predict that whatever outcome is reached will conform to relatively unchanging procedures and rights. Given the added weight accorded to precedent, we can conclude that a constitutional democracy might aspire to the kind of predictability and stability essential to the rule of law; it might, in other words, respect the freedom of legal subjects to rationally plan their lives in the knowledge that the law will not be imposed on them in an unpredictable and arbitrary manner.[20]

How far can this domestic understanding of rule of law be extended to international law? To begin with, if we suppose (as Habermas does) that a constitutional organization of international law will respect the limited sovereignty of states on the understanding that each embodies a distinctive cultural understanding of what promotes the common good of its own subjects, then it would be wrong to impose on any single state a concrete conception of the good that it cannot accept. The liberal, social contractarian pragmatism that has guided thinking on international law since the late eighteenth century—which assumes that states are free and equal agents that are bound only by what they freely consent to—thus dictates that whatever international laws they agree to will be either *abstract* and *indeterminate* in force (so as to accommodate widely differing cultural interpretations) or *concrete* and *contextual* (so as to effectively advance very specific government policies). In the former case, which typifies humanitarian law, international law provides very little prescriptive guidance and so falls short of providing a stable and effective framework for cooperation. In the latter case, which typifies multilateral treaties aimed at advancing particular interests of state, legal codification is virtually redundant, since it is mutual interest alone that forges and maintains the treaty. To the extent that humanitarian law normatively distances itself from the actual practice of states—for example, by insisting, as the UDHR does, that all persons have a right to leisure—it appears ineffectual and utopian. Conversely, to the extent that international law concretely and contextually codifies existing interests and practices, it appears apologetic. Both tendencies thus run counter to the concept of legal regulation, which simultaneously requires both a critical distance from and a factual closeness to actual practice. Unable to realize both normative distance and effective closeness simultaneously, international law

20. J. Raz, "The Rule of Law and its Virtue," *The Authority of Law* (Oxford: Clarendon, 1979), 210–29.

opens itself up to the play of power politics. The vagueness of humanitarian law makes it easy for states to claim they are living up to its mandates no matter how they treat citizens (their own or others who happen to suffer the collateral damage of their military interventions). The concreteness of legal treaties governing trade, environmental regulation, and the like merely codifies the unequal bargaining power of the most powerful states (as reflected, for instance, in the hegemonic control that the United States exercises over global financial and trade organizations). However, even concrete customs and economic treaties allow for multiple and conflicting interpretations. Cases brought before international courts and other international tribunals are often not binding or come with soft sanctions; in any case, the resolution of cases is highly unpredictable because judges are invited to use their personal discretion in balancing conflicting values of equity, autonomy, continuity, and so on.

The above dilemma—which starkly opposes a liberal (formal rules) approach to a social welfare (policy) approach—merely replicates at the level of international law a tension we noted earlier with respect to the clash of paradigms affecting domestic law.[21] According to Roberto Unger and many other critical legal studies proponents,[22] this dilemma cannot be resolved at the domestic level—and the liberal rule of law cannot be realized—unless the source of value conflict (capitalism, say) is eliminated or radically transformed in such a way as to reduce conflict and promote a consensus on common interests and values. Habermas's response to the dilemma is more ambiguous, as we have seen, and involves a strategy of discursively mediating liberal and social welfare paradigms. But in the case of international law, he (like Rawls)[23] appears to adopt a different strategy: to preserve the rule of law at the level of humanitarian law and security law by sharply distinguishing it from the politicized conflict zone of global economic redistribution (broadly construed to include the redistribution of costs and benefits associated with environmental regulation).

---

21. The dilemma as I have presented it closely tracks the CLS-indebted analysis developed by Martti Koskenniemi in "The Politics of International Law," *European Journal of International Law* 1 (1990): 4–32.

22. R. M. Unger, *Knowledge and Politics* (New York: Free Press, 1975)

23. Extending his social contractarian approach to international law, Rawls argues that a "law of peoples" must restrict itself to general principles that all minimally decent peoples would accept. These eight principles include the duty of peoples to respect one another as free and equal, to uphold treaties, to refrain from intervening in the affairs of other peoples and in engaging in war (except in self-defense), to honor human rights, and to assist "burdened" peoples who lack the resources to develop minimally decent social and political institutions. Although Rawls allows that economic assistance to burdened peoples might require a global redistribution of wealth, he insists that such redistribution have a strict cutoff point and not be tailored toward the kinds of egalitarian aims he proposes for domestic liberal democracies. As Rawls sees it, economic distribution for purposes of bringing about greater global justice between peoples, for providing cosmopolitan citizens with equal resources and opportunities to develop their capabilities, is not an international duty and therefore remains contingent on whatever voluntary arrangements nations and regional governing bodies might happen to adopt given their political interests. J. Rawls, *The Law of Peoples* (Cambridge: Harvard University Press, 1999), 37, 80, 105–20.

The politicization of international law is worse than in domestic law because of the greater cultural diversity among states, the vagueness and generality of treaties and conventions (itself a reflection of cultural diversity), and the weakness of international tribunals, which lack a substantial body of binding precedents that contain concrete resolutions. Habermas himself takes note of this problem when commenting on that portion of international law that concerns what he (following C. F. von Weizsäcker) calls "global domestic policy":

> The largely institutionalized procedures of information exchange, consultation, control, and agreement are sufficient for handling "technical" issues in a broader sense (such as the standardization of measures, the regulation of telecommunications, disaster prevention, containing epidemics, or combating organized crime). Since the devil is in the details, these problems also call for a balancing of conflicting interests. However, they differ from genuinely "political" issues that impinge upon entrenched interests which are deeply rooted in structures of national societies, such as, for example, questions of global energy and of environmental, financial, and economic policy, all of which involve issues of equitable distribution. These problems of a future world domestic policy call for regulation and positive integration, for which at present both the institutional framework and actors are lacking. (*BNR* 324)

Even with the appropriate institutional framework populated by regional federations (like the EU), the United Nations, Habermas concedes, will be suited to generating only "normatively regulated consensus-formation" with regard to human rights, security, and other areas of common interest and will not be suited to adjudicating "political struggles over conflicts of interest" pertaining to global domestic politics. The United Nations and its limited human rights and security apparatus will still be the focus of power struggles, but given the reform of the Security Council and the consensus on global security and human rights (not to mention the ongoing multicultural dialogue on human rights in the global public sphere), Habermas is more confident, at least, that this area of international law can aspire to the rule-of-law ideal. Prior to 2008 he was, with few exceptions, dubious about the possibility of establishing a world parliament that might provide further statutory definition of human rights principles outside the framework of a world republic (*BNR* 323).[24] However, by 2008 he had come to embrace (or reembrace) the possibility of transforming

24. However, as early as 1996 Habermas entertained the possibility that the UN General Assembly could be made into a bicameral parliament whose lower house would consist of popularly elected representatives (ensuring representation of national minorities, women, migrants, and indigenous peoples). He also recommended that the Security Council be restructured as an executive power or higher legislative house composed of representatives of all states (eliminating the status of permanent membership and veto privileges for prominent members) detached from national interests and seating regional bodies such as the EU (*IO* 187). Habermas moved away from this strong, institutionally conceived, cosmopolitan conception of global democratic governance in

the UN General Assembly into a world parliament, albeit one whose legislative function would be confined to the "interpretation and elaboration of the [UN] Charter" (*EFP* 120). With this change Habermas's model of international governance moves closer to the domestic ideal of a rule of law, for he now allows that such a parliament might be empowered to veto the resolutions of a reformed Security Council and even permit countries subject to Security Council sanctions to appeal these acts before the International Criminal Court. But these limited steps in the direction of the rule of law are, he concedes, "*more juridical than political*" (*EFP* 124). In any case, because "[t]he General Assembly, as the legislator under international law, (already) observes the logic of an internal elaboration of the meaning of human rights" (*EFP* 124), there is no reason to think that it would replace the one international institution best equipped to technically define, in the absence of statutory legislation, the "internal elaboration of the meaning of human rights law": human rights courts. International courts can develop abstract principles of human rights in their own concrete applications, thereby building up a history of case law that can lend definite prescriptive force to what are otherwise general and open-ended principles.

The Problem of Legitimacy

According to Habermas, the legitimacy of municipal law depends on its having been processed according to democratic procedure. However, in the absence of an elected and truly representative democratic world parliament, what warrant can there be for affirming the legitimacy of international law? Habermas's faith that the UN General Assembly might become an elected (possibly bicameral) institution composed of representatives of nations as well as representatives of "cosmopolitan citizens" provides some optimism that international law might be democratically legitimated. Certainly, nothing in principle would prevent the General Assembly, reformed in this manner, from transforming itself into a constituent assembly for purposes of establishing itself as a permanent world parliament (*EFP* 120).

But this response only addresses the legitimation of one kind of international law. Habermas divides the question of legitimation between humanitarian law and security-related legislation, on one side, and economic and environmental policy, on the other. Humanitarian law and security-related legislation, he believes, can be legitimated by appeal to two or three considerations. First, the democratic structure of a truly representative, elected world parliament would provide a degree of legitimacy. However, as in the case of domestic law, democratic legislation must be "programmed" by the concerns of the public

favor of a multilayered conception that places greater stress on transnational negotiation, global public opinion, and human rights courts.

(communicative power). So, second, there must exist something like an informal "democratic" background consensus that can be made discursively evident in the opinions circulating within a global public sphere. This threefold consensus—on the political desirability of a "substantively expanded conception of security," the legal necessity of human rights, and the concomitant commitment to democratic procedures for problem solving (relying, for instance, on resolutions passed by the General Assembly and ratified by many states)— "would be sufficient to confer legitimacy on decisions taken by [the UN's] two central but nonmajoritarian institutions": the Security Council and the International Criminal Court (*BNR* 343). Third and finally, legitimacy is bestowed on humanitarian law by the "'credit' of legitimation that is 'extended' to the collective memory of humankind by the exemplary histories of proven democracies," that is, by a venerable respect for judicial procedures that have an ancient pedigree (*EFP* 125).

Although Habermas concedes that "cultural pluralism" could pose problems for the legitimation of human rights law, its major impact would be felt in legitimating global economic and environmental policies that affect security and human rights indirectly, for here we are talking about conflicting conceptions of the good, about which there is little consensus (*BNR* 326). Despite Habermas's belief that a world parliament might legislate highly abstract guidelines for a just-world domestic policy (*EFP* 124–26), international law here appears to be more openly political than juridical (*BNR* 343), with regional federations and alliances entering into bilateral and multilateral agreements with one another and with other international organizations whose governing bodies are hardly representative and democratic. As we shall see, Habermas believes that the prospects for legitimating this layer of international law are less promising but not hopeless.

The Constitutionalization of International Relations

Now that we understand how Habermas situates his own theory of cosmopolitan law with respect to contemporary debates about the legality and legitimacy of international law, we can immediately proceed to the most important element of that theory: the constitutionalization of the world order. The fundamental question addressed by this concept is this: Can a cosmopolitan rule of law be brought about without creating a monolithic global state whose distant and impersonal rule over the world's peoples would be experienced by them as a loss of their national identity and self-determination? Habermas answers this question by noting that a global rule of law, which he claims would amount to the "constitutionalization of international law," need not, and indeed cannot, be conceived in terms of constituting a state.

According to the *republican* contractarian tradition, constituting a state amounts to removing persons from a state of nature (or from a "lawless" state of subservience to an absolute ruler), where they possess no secure rights, to a legal condition, where they do. The solidaristic identity of a particular people, as well as their individual freedoms and powers, are created in one act, with the state acting as the legislative and executive agency of their general will. This Rousseauian model, which inspired the French Revolution, misled Kant into thinking that a cosmopolitan constitution would likewise take the form of a single world republic that would seek to artificially create and impose its monolithic general will on culturally diverse nations (*DW* 128).[25] By contrast, the *liberal* contractarian model that informed the American Revolution grew out of an older tradition of limiting and dividing governmental powers that already exist. It is not conascent with the creation of state powers but with the limitation of such powers by means of constraining principles, such as individual rights (*DW* 138).[26] Once the world is populated with democratic, rights-respecting states, however, there no longer remains any need to constitute a new democratic state at the global level. What is needed instead is the constitution of a global democratic decision-making procedure by which already well-established liberal democracies can regulate pressing human rights concerns in tandem with other groups or individuals representing cosmopolitan interests (*EFP* 122).

25. Kant in *Toward Perpetual Peace* (1795) proposed the idea of a voluntary confederation of nations as a second-best alternative to his preferred ideal of a worldwide constitutional republic, for two reasons: first, he doubted whether states would abdicate their sovereignty; and, second, he feared that even a constitutional republic would inevitably degenerate into a "universal monarchy" in which all powers would have to be centralized in order to maintain order over a vast expanse. Yet Habermas notes that Kant's proposed confederation lacks the very thing—a constitution—that might enable it to become "a permanent congress of states," distinct from those voluntary treaties that had failed to prevent war by means of a balance of power (*IO* 169). Kant's proposal presumed that (1) republics, unlike monarchies, were peaceful, and would evolve as a matter of self-interest; (2) commercial interests incline toward peaceful relations; and (3) world public opinion would sensitize people everywhere to violations of cosmopolitan rights. Habermas finds the first two reasons only partly convincing in light of countertendencies toward nationalism and imperialism, but finds the third a potent force for moral learning that renders Kant's own metaphysics of transcendental reason, coupled with his natural historical account of evolutionary progress, unnecessary (*IO* 171–79). As Habermas notes, the UN Charter seems to have inherited some of Kant's inconsistencies, upholding the sovereignty of states except when this poses a threat to international security, while at the same time effectively endorsing intervention in a state's domestic affairs when gross and massive violations of human rights are concerned (*IO* 182). Contemporary international conflicts and human rights violations reflect the fragmentation of the world's countries into North and South, developed and underdeveloped—problems whose economic and ecological causes far outstrip the limited capacities of Kant's federation and the UN (*IO* 185).

26. Habermas remarks that "classical international law is already a kind of constitution in that it creates a legal community among parties with formally equal rights" (*DW* 133). However, it is "proto-constitutional" because the renunciation of war remains voluntary. The voluntary renunciation of war did not become obligatory for all nations until the Kellogg-Briand Pact (1928), which formally outlawed war. But the full emergence of cosmopolitan constitutional law would have to await the ratification of the UN Charter, which explicitly—albeit inconsistently—links the outlawing of war to the implementation of human rights and authorizes the use of force (pending Security Council approval) in sanctioning it (*DW* 102, 162).

Construed in this liberal manner, a constitutionalization of international law would not require the creation of a universal state possessing full powers to regulate all the conditions relating to social conflict and unfulfilled human rights. Nor could it, since the civic solidarity necessary for taxing and redistributing income—aspects of Habermas's "global domestic policy" that are necessary for combating the global poverty and social inequality that produce social strife and potentially violate people's rights to subsistence—exists only at the national or regional supranational levels. Instead, a cosmopolitan constitution gradually unfolds a decentralized rule of law limiting and delegating preexisting national, regional, transnational, and supranational powers according to a principle of *subsidiarity* (*BNR* 316). This federalist principle assigns problem-solving tasks to local (lower) jurisdictions unless more global (higher) jurisdictions can deal with them better (*BNR* 333).

This has momentous implications for reconsidering the legitimation crisis affecting the welfare state. The legitimacy of the welfare state depends on its advancing the common good of its subjects along three dimensions: the maintenance of freedom and security, the provision of economic welfare and distributive justice, and the fostering of social solidarity. Increased security risks, economic instabilities, and migratory flows caused by globalization overburden the meager legal media (power) that the state can deploy in trying to "manage" these "overflows." Hence the state is presented with an unpleasant alternative: either the state must abandon what is increasingly becoming an empty constitutional facade of "a self-administering association of free and equal citizens" or "we must detach the fading idea of a democratic constitution from its roots in the nation-state and revive it in the postnational guise of a constitutionalized world society" (*BNR* 333). In opting for the latter, Habermas believes that the state can still perform its constitutional integration function more or less well if it limits its competence to tasks it can manage. Although states are best equipped to guarantee education for their citizens, they lack competence on their own to combat global warming and regulate global financial markets and human migrations. In the worst-case scenario they cannot be trusted to uphold the human rights of refugees and other "noncitizens." These latter concerns are therefore better addressed by supranational entities, such as the UN or EU, or transnational entities such as international banks and nongovernmental organizations (NGOs).

Habermas applies the notion of subsidiarity to generate a *trilevel* cosmopolitan order. Each level designates a specific set of problems and organizational agencies for dealing with them (*BNR* 322–26, 333–34). The *supranational* level consists of one world organization: the UN and its sixty subsidiary organizations and the International Criminal Court. These entities are responsible for maintaining global security and protecting human rights by means of policing functions that can be carried out by using the military capacities of member states. By contrast, regional systems of supranational governance—which Habermas now locates at the transnational level—not only regulate the security and human rights compliance of their member states but also their domestic welfare. This last power, which currently remains undeveloped in the EU, requires the constitution of full-blown legislative and executive powers (including the power to conduct foreign policy). Legitimating these powers in turn requires the political cultivation of civic solidarity based on a distinctive shared identity.

Transnational agencies that are "intermediate...between nation states and world organizations" (*DW* 178)—ranging from global economic multilaterals (GEMs), such as the WB, IMF, and WTO, to regional (continental) economic and political blocs, such as the EU—address two kinds of problems: *technical* coordination problems associated with a complex world society, such as containment of epidemics, standardization of measures, disaster prevention, and regulation of communication; and *political* problems concerning global energy, environmental, financial, and economic policies, "all of which involve issues of equitable distribution" (*BNR* 324). Although consultation and softer forms of voluntary compliance can effectively deal with the former set of problems, Habermas denies that there currently exists any agency (save perhaps the United States) that possesses the competency to deal with the latter set of problems (*BNR* 325). Nonetheless, he believes that a world comprising democratically constituted regional/continental blocs like the EU might be able to address these problems through *intergovernmental negotiations*. To the extent that such blocs can legislate policies of health, education, welfare, and economic redistribution in accordance with shared conceptions of justice and welfare, they already embark on a transnational domestic policy that transcends the capacity of GEMs, which generally tailor their agreements to the functional and technical logic of the market rather than to the justice concerns of global public opinion.

Finally, at the *national level,* semisovereign states assume responsibility for their own domestic problems in tandem with other nations, with whom they have bilateral and multilateral agreements. For Habermas, they remain the principal conduits by means of which supranational and transnational decision making is *indirectly* legitimated (*DW* 141). Thus, the legally binding agreements struck in the Council of Ministers by appointed bureaucrats representing EU member nations are legitimated by the simple fact that the government leaders who appointed them were themselves democratically elected. Yet, as the recent failure to ratify the draft constitution of the EU through popular referendum poignantly testifies, average Europeans do not recognize the legitimacy of controversial justice-related policies that are processed through *intergovernmental negotiations* between government bureaucrats. Hence, Habermas insists that such negotiations, which presume a neoliberal understanding of European society as a market whose parameters are to be managed by technical elites, must eventually be replaced by more democratic procedures of legislation that only a more representative European Parliament can undertake (*DW* 73, 75–82).

According to Habermas, the reasons that explain the centrality of nation-states for democratic legitimation—and by extension explain the possibility of supranational democratic polities such as the EU—also explain why global democracy in the fullest sense of the term is impossible.[27] On Habermas's reading, the modern European nation-state emerged in the early nineteenth century as the solution to a unique problem: the conjoining of democracy to constitutional law—a conjunction, it will be recalled, that is necessitated by the logic of legitimation. This conjunction could initially occur only on the basis of an overarching shared national identity (nationalism); for only on the basis of patriotic attachment to a particular common good and cultural-linguistic ethos—in some cases artificially manufactured by nationalist propaganda— were strangers who lived miles apart, professed different creeds, and otherwise inhabited different worlds willing to die for one another. The multicultural welfare state has changed the meaning but not the structure of this democratic presupposition of solidaristic trust and sense of kinship. Civic solidarity based on constitutional patriotism has replaced the older, thicker form of ethnic-national patriotism; individual citizens are no longer required to sacrifice their lives in war for the sake of advancing the interests of the nation, but they are required to "sacrifice" their wealth for the sake of ensuring the security, welfare, and health of worse-off fellow citizens. So construed, civic solidarity is not exhausted by adherence to abstract principles that transcend political borders; for such universal rational principles alone cannot explain the peculiar preference and trust we bestow on those whom we believe care about us simply because we share a common fate (PC 101).

Habermas argues that the "learning process" acquired through decades of religious and factional strife that enabled Europeans to shed their parochial identities in taking on more inclusive national identities can be extended—at least in principle—to the formation of an even more inclusive European identity (PC 103). However, he doubts whether such a substantive form of democratic solidarity can exist in any robust sense at the level of a world organization whose proximate identifying feature is legislating and enforcing abstract principles of moral right, followed by a more distant commitment to just

27. Habermas has in mind David Held's early proposal for a single world state possessing a global democratic legislature. Echoing Habermas's concerns, James Bohman notes that this attempt to extend the model of the democratic nation-state in the direction of a global democratic state suffers from incoherence. Unlike reflexive forms of democracy that exist at the level of the nation-state, a global democratic state would likely have its democratic procedures fixed by an international convention composed of legal scholars, and so would not be subject to subsequent democratic revision by the global legislature. Second, because its cosmopolitan laws would supersede in rank the laws of nations, they would have to possess a level of prescriptive statutory definition and force that would render them somewhat less susceptible to flexible appropriation and interpretation by national democracies. Held has since come to accept a more decentralized and multilayered conception of global democracy of the sort proposed by Bohman. D. Held, *Democracy and the Global Order* (Stanford: Stanford University Press, 1995), 145, 154, 234; D. Held and A. McGrew, *Globalization/Anti-Globalization* (Cambridge: Polity Press, 2002), 95; and J. Bohman, *Democracy across Borders: From Demos to Demoi* (Cambridge: MIT Press, 2007), chap. 1.

principles of global domestic policy. Put bluntly, collective self-determination is meaningless where nothing remains to distinguish "us" from "everyone else" (*PC* 107). As I noted in chapter 6, the "world society" of "world citizens" is mainly *negatively integrated*: a gross violation of just those *negative duties* associated with classical human rights angers us all, no matter where it occurs (*DW* 143). To the extent that citizens of democracies also view themselves as world citizens who have positive duties to rectify, for instance, global inequalities between rich and poor and global warming, their loyalties are inescapably divided. Recognizing this Gordian knot for what it is—and refusing to cut it by proposing the simple solution of a single world state—Habermas insists that any design for a world parliament allow room for a house composed of representatives of governments as well as a separate house composed of representatives of cosmopolitan citizens and the common global good (*EFP* 118–20).

Prospects for more direct forms of democratic legitimation increase when dealing with regional supranational bodies such as the EU. Although the fate of the EU has yet to be sealed[28]—the proposed draft constitution leaves its

---

28. As of 2007 Habermas continued to endorse a democratic (if indeed "graduated") integration of the EU that would enable the EU to function alongside the United States as a partner in a bipolar coalition for global justice and stability (*EFP* 100). This hope appears less audacious when considered in light of the incredible advances toward unity the EU has made since its inception. The beginnings of the EU can be traced back to the Treaty of Paris (1951), which established the European Coal and Steel Community. Further expansion and integration occurred six years later when the Treaty of Rome (1957) created the European Economic Community and the European Atomic Energy Community. Additional members were added to the community in 1973, 1986, and by the time the Treaty on European Union (also known as the Maastricht treaty) was concluded there were fifteen member states. (Expanding toward the east and south, by 2009 the number of member states stood at twenty-seven). Following the plan laid out in the Lisbon Strategy (2000), the EU adopted a single currency (2002), the euro, and opened up free markets in goods, services, investment capital, and labor across the union. Political integration, however, has not kept pace with economic integration. Citizens of member states are reluctant to transfer sovereignty to the bureaucrats in Brussels, as evidenced by the failure of French and Dutch voters to ratify the European Constitution in 2005. To be sure, the Lisbon treaty that entered into force as of December 1, 2009, provides more democratic accountability. The European Parliament of 750 nationally elected representatives (plus the president of the parliament), distributed to member states on the basis of a new scheme of proportional representation, now has some law-making power in virtually all areas of governance and has the same degree of law-making power as the Council (see below) in areas involving the budget, immigration, and criminal and penal policy, and its assent is required for all international treaties involving trade and agricultural policy. Beginning in 2014 a "double majority" of 55% of the member states representing 65% of the EU population will be implemented. Furthermore, a million citizens joining a Citizens' Initiative can petition the Commission (see below) to bring forward new policy proposals. The treaty also creates several new offices: a president of the Council (elected by representatives of member states to serve a two-and-a-half-year term) and a high representative for foreign and security matters who reports to both the Council and the Commission. Although the Parliament's double-majority voting structure captures Habermas's view that both states and citizens (who represent more cosmopolitan perspectives) should have a divided share in legitimation, he does not think that its conception of the president and the high representative for foreign and security matters goes far enough in specifying the ultimate aim of unification. In Habermas's opinion, that should be a unified federal government, headed by a popularly elected president with the power to conduct foreign policy (*EFP* 80–88,

ultimate boundaries and functions undetermined—Habermas believes that it can and should become more than a monetary-economic union that is "negatively" integrated by market mechanisms in accordance with neoliberal thinking. In making this claim, he notes that a common European history of religious, class, and imperial warfare and of rising and falling colonial empires has given rise to a distinctive postwar European identity that can constitute the basis for distinctly European civic solidarity. This identity, which revolves around secularization, the priority of the state over the market, the primacy of social solidarity over individual acquisitiveness and choice, skepticism concerning technology and undialectical notions of progress, commitment to peace, and repudiation of national self-assertion, provides the ethical basis for a *positive integration* based on securing the full range of welfare rights (*DW* 46–48). Only a truly democratic European Parliament with expanded competency to tax and redistribute income—not a Council of Ministers engaged in intergovernmental negotiations—can legitimate the redistributive policies that guarantee these rights (*DW* 73).

The foregoing discussion explains why the main challenge to legitimation must occur at the transnational level. When the problems in question concern only technical matters of coordination, a consensus on knowledge by experts suffices to meet this challenge. However, as our earlier discussion of technology showed, technical expertise is not as value neutral as Habermas sometimes suggests, and it cannot, in any case, legitimate political decisions that impact social justice and the structure of decision making. Neoliberal policies, which aim to transfer coordination and integration problems from democratic polities to impersonal market mechanisms regulated by GEMs (with guidance from experts) are thus viewed by Habermas as the single greatest threat to legitimation. The so-called Washington Consensus that supposedly legitimates this transfer not only undermines the social welfare safety nets so essential to democratic solidarity but sets in motion an irreversible process of removing core areas currently under democratic control (however minimal):

> The political goal of switching from political forms of regulation to market mechanisms tends to perpetuate such a politics, since a change in policy becomes more difficult to the extent that the scope for political intervention is curtailed. The deliberate political self-limitation of the room for political maneuver in favor of a systemic self-regulation would rob future generations of the very means they would require for a future course correction. Even if every nation "consciously

---

101–5). That said, the EU represents an experiment in dual sovereignty in at least several senses: not only do member states retain sovereign control over some internal matters (the Lisbon treaty strengthens the EU's commitment to the principle of subsidiarity), but the federal organization of the EU reflects a complicated power-sharing relationship between an elected European Parliament, a European Council of Ministers representing member states, a European Commission composed of twenty-five commissioners, and a system of courts (including a Constitutional Court and a European Court of Justice).

and democratically decides to be more of a 'competition state' than a 'welfare
state'," such a democratic decision would inevitably destroy its own foundations
if it led to a form of organization that made it impossible to overturn that very
decision by democratic means. (*BNR* 351)

Even in cases in which this transfer is warranted—as in regulating global financial markets—the corresponding regulatory agencies and banks have hitherto remained unaccountable to the people whose decisions they most affect.
In Habermas's opinion, nations and regional economic blocs such as the EU
can make global financial institutions more representative, transparent, and
accountable while allowing Greenpeace, Amnesty International, and other
NGOs operating in global civil society a greater role in lobbying governments and multinationals through their cultivation of "world public opinion"
(*BNR* 341–43).

In sum, Habermas's defense of a cosmopolitan regime sans a global democratic state hinges on two assumptions, one normative, the other functional.
Functionally speaking, he believes that, once they are sufficiently motivated by
global crises to evolve political competencies requisite for dealing with them,
regional/continental supranational polities can solve pressing problems concerning the inequitable distribution of wealth and resources within their own
borders as well as without. Solving problems of global poverty and global
warming will require intergovernmental negotiations between leaders of these
organizations as well as negotiations between them and representatives of transnational organizations, including NGOs. Normatively speaking, he thinks that
a world security and human rights regime can be legitimated prepolitically, by
direct appeal to universally acknowledged human rights principles, and politically, by indirect appeal to a "weak" global public opinion and the democratic
procedures governing a world parliament and its member states. By contrast,
he insists that a world domestic policy be legitimated democratically—directly
in the case of intraregional politics and indirectly in the case of interregional
negotiations involving transnational organizations.

The Limits of Democratization: A Critical Assessment

Now that we have a more detailed understanding of Habermas's theory of
international and cosmopolitan law, we can return to the three problems I
mentioned at the outset of my discussion concerning legality, the rule of law,
and legitimacy. As I noted, Habermas responds to Hart's concern about the
absence of a rule of recognition that might definitively establish whether a
given decision or resolution counts as a legally binding instance of international law by proposing that international law be grounded in a constitution
that would definitively set forth a separation of law-making competencies and
powers. Hart noted the absence of an international legislative body that might
establish the legal pedigree of international statutes. Prior to 2008 Habermas

himself harbored doubts about the feasibility of a world parliament and, instead, proposed that an international court be the definitive source for identifying, changing, and applying humanitarian law. However, in the absence of a world parliament and until the nations of the world agree on the constitution of an international criminal court (as of this writing, the United States has not ratified the convention creating the International Criminal Court) the legality of international humanitarian law must remain in doubt. Needless to say, this doubt applies a fortiori to other international customs and treaties.

Suppose that international law were constitutionalized in the manner suggested by Habermas. Could it ever aspire to establishing the rule of law? Habermas's understanding of the dual sovereignty underlying international human rights law leaves some doubt on this score. If we assume that a single international court is delegated sole responsibility for defining the precise number, scope, and meaning of basic human rights in such a manner that it can render judgments against states that fail to respect these limits in fashioning their own statues, then the answer is yes. (This presupposes that the Critical Legal Studies critique concerning the dialectic of formal rule and substantive end that applies to any legal system can be circumvented, a fact that, to my mind at least, has yet to be demonstrated.) If we assume that such a court is only delegated limited responsibility for carrying out this task—allowing nation-states considerable freedom to define and apply humanitarian law within very broad limits set by the international court—then the answer is no. Allowing states to define and apply abstract humanitarian law according to their own cultural standards (as Habermas sometimes suggests) would effectively weaken, if not undermine, the normative, regulative force of international humanitarian law. If we insist that all nations voluntarily accept the authority of an international human rights court, and if we take seriously the reasonableness of the cultural (often religion-based) differences between them, then it appears that we must settle for the kind of culturally "neutral" human rights law proposed by Rawls, which does not favor an overtly liberal or democratic interpretation, or at least not one that defines liberal and democratic rights beyond the most basic and universally accommodating meaning that might be ascribed to them. As for the international regulation of world domestic policy, Habermas seems to concede that this area of international law, comprising as it does transient compromises that range from de facto practices to vague and utopian platitudes, will likely remain highly political and therefore poorly regulated in the normative sense of the term for a very long time, until citizens have learned to harness their nation's interest to the interest of the planet.

The problem of democratic legitimation is connected to the rule of law in this sense: that without such legitimation the law cannot be freed from the destabilizing effects of arbitrary political domination. Habermas believes that the decisions rendered by appointed judges presiding over international human rights courts—decisions which, in the absence of statutory legislation emanating from a world parliament, effectively define the concrete meaning and prescriptive force of humanitarian law—can be democratically legitimated indirectly by appeal to a broad consensus within the global public sphere. So long as the multicultural dialogue on human rights converges on only the most basic and general human rights principles, the scope for legitimate decision making (and "law making") will be quite narrow, mandating intervention in only the most extreme and grievous violations. Agreements regarding world domestic policy will suffer from a greater legitimation gap, since the agreements reached will take the form of political compromises brokered by appointed technical elites who have only a very indirect accountability to their respective governments, not to mention their own citizens and the people of the world. Here again, oversight and involvement by NGOs and a global public is supposed to mitigate the effects of self-interested powers.

Let me now turn my attention to some criticisms that have been raised about the capacity of Habermas's multilevel theory of global-governance and international cosmopolitan law to regulate global capitalism. As might be expected, Habermas's model of a cosmopolitan order has been criticized for underestimating the radical differences separating national, regional, and supranational constitutional orders—differences that render suspect any talk of extending democracy beyond the nation-state. Or so it would seem, if what we have in mind is a concept of global or cosmopolitan democracy that is understood as a gradual expansion of a national constitutional order, embracing regional entities such as the EU and eventually global entities such as the UN.

Habermas may have underestimated the extent to which the new global economy breaks with the older form of welfare capitalism and its state-centered presuppositions. The idea that the legal paradigms informing the welfare state can be preserved and extended to form the constitutional and social democratic framework of supranational regional systems of governance seems less plausible when we examine the current trajectory taken by EU consolidation. It may be that what we have is less a tendency toward a united federal system than a set of overlapping systems based on voluntary memberships. In this order some countries opt out of certain agreements (on common currency, defense policy, etc.) while opting for others (on free flow of labor and capital). Instead of the weak neoliberal model of negative economic integration or the strong social democratic model of political integration, one finds a growing tendency toward neocorporativist problem solving in which experts and persons most affected by particular systems consult one another and negotiate agreements among themselves—supervised, perhaps, by a central governing committee, but outside the normal legislative process and, more important, outside the public eye. This *sectoral-state* model, then, offers an alternative description of supranational and transnational democracy that does not see a trend toward the kind of top-down notion of a quasi-solidaristic, quasi-sovereign postnational democracy sometimes endorsed by Habermas. What the sectoral state loses in unity and direct public accountability it gains in local autonomy: those who are most affected by an intrasectoral (or even intersectoral) decision have the most direct say in deliberating on it.[29]

Conversely, Habermas's vision of postnational democracy has been criticized for being insufficiently postnational in an entirely different sense, namely, in its reliance on national governments and GEMs controlled by national governments in dealing with problems pertaining to global domestic policy. Here, Habermas suggests that the deficit in global social solidarity actually requires circumventing a global democratic (political) solution to global problems in favor of bargaining between technical elites, who are at best only distantly accountable (if at all) to the people. According to this model, the power-brokered negotiations that prevail at the transnational level remain within the framework of traditional international law, which is to say that average citizens cannot initiate proposals, set agendas, or bring suit—only government-appointed representatives who represent extremely limited economic and political sectors.

This nondemocratic structure makes it unlikely that such negotiations will effectively deal with world poverty and global warming. In short, the immediate interests of "national citizens" and government leaders in the developed world incline them toward self-serving policies that perpetuate inequitable trade relations and economic practices, condemnation by human rights groups within the global public sphere notwithstanding. Assuming that national and regional democratic polities behave in a self-interested way, then only a more ambitious global democracy of the kind embodied in Habermas's proposal for a world parliament could move the world's peoples—rich and poor, powerful and weak—to generate the sort of positive global solidarity requisite for changing unjust policies (*EFP* 125–26).

Perhaps we need an intermediary vision of supranational democracy that encompasses both of these objections to Habermas's conception of global democracy, which as we have seen seems to pull us in opposite directions. Reiterating these objections, James Bohman has recently argued that a *transnational* conception of democracy must reject the strong cosmopolitan ideal of self-determination in favor of a weaker but more realistic principle of nondomination.[30] Instead of imagining how social solidarity—or a united legislative will—can be institutionalized at the global level in the form of a global legal community, we need to imagine globally institutionalizing the core ideal underlying democracy—justice, or equal respect for individuals and groups that possess distinct identities and wills, in the form of a nonhierarchical (*polyarchical*), multilayered polity of porous democratic groups, whose members would be empowered to question and revise political boundaries and democratic procedures as well as contest policies and initiate debates.[31]

29. J. McCormick, *Weber, Habermas, and Transformations of the European State: Constitutional, Social, and Supranational Democracy* (Cambridge: Cambridge University Press, 2007).

30. Bohman, *Democracy across Borders.*

31. In chapter 7 I noted Robert Dahl's skepticism regarding the capacity of polyarchy to survive the hegemonic power of big business and big government—hence his skepticism regarding

In sum, global democracy would mark a *transformation* and not merely a gradual expansion of the traditional, state-centered democratic concept. Unlike proposals for global democracy that emphasize the bottom-up role that global public spheres (dominated by NGOs) play in contesting global institutions,[32] Bohman's proposal would give transnational democracy institutional effectiveness; it would enable citizens to translate their deliberation and contestation into effective political power. Like the open method of coordination deployed in the EU, his and John McCormick's concept of transnational democracy would provide for supranational committees that facilitate communication between dispersed publics and institutions in which citizens would be more empowered to deliberate on and decide matters that affect them most directly and locally, while at the same time participating somewhat less directly (differently, but not with diminished capacity) in matters that affect them globally.

I have argued that Habermas's own trilevel model of multilayered global governance is moving in precisely this direction, even if some of his formulations seem to vacillate between a top-down cosmopolitan legal order and a bottom-up international order involving negotiations between technical elites representing governments, GEMs, and NGOs. But the question with which we began this chapter—Can democracy survive capitalism?—has not been answered. Indeed, for first-generation members of the Frankfurt school, the threat to democracy goes beyond capitalism and embraces reason itself. The dialectic of reason encompasses a process of secularization that undermines meaning and value, thereby paving the way for the emergence of a deracinated humanity—"mass man"—whose thought and action have been completely absorbed into an impersonal economic-legal system. It must therefore be shown that something akin to the value and meaning that religion once provided can survive in modernity. In short, the question now arises whether modern emancipation and enlightenment can become *post*secular in a way that permits and encourages holistic sources of meaning and value to persist while resisting the fragmenting and alienating tendencies of modern life.

---

global democracy. Small homogeneous populations can reach agreement or approximate convergence on their public good more easily than large heterogeneous populations. As social complexity grows, the competence and interest in discussing technical matters falls to government elites, with the masses taking even less interest in foreign policy concerns, unless these touch on vital public interests, such as war, immigration, or transborder (regional) monetary consolidation. This skeptical argument is partly shared by Bohman and McCormick. However, they counter Dahl's skepticism by observing that international democracy must assume a different guise than the domestic model presupposed by Dahl—one that reflects a more radically decentered form of polyarchy. R. Dahl, "Can International Organizations Be Democratic?: A Sceptic's View," in *Democracy's Edges*, ed. I. Shapiro and C. Hacker-Cordon (Cambridge: Cambridge University Press, 1999).

32. See J. Dryzek, *Deliberative Global Politics* (Cambridge: Polity Press, 2006), vii.

11

Postsecular Postscript
Modernity and Its Discontents

The last two chapters have uncovered a profound tension in Habermas's theory of democracy: the ideal principles of freedom, equality, solidarity, and inclusion underwriting democracy are effectively realized only in *modern* institutions that emerge in response to the growing complexity of society. "Modern" is the adjective sociologists apply to the ensemble of economic, legal, political, and sociocultural structures that designate the passing of so-called traditional societies, or societies whose members chiefly relate to one another through customs and other shared understandings. Although philosophers and sociologists disagree about the specific limits and possibilities of this process[1]—with some defending the Western (European-descended) path as the preeminent one—they generally agree on the following sequence of mutual interdependencies: modern economies are driven by markets; markets are constituted by stable laws governing property, contract, and liability; laws are legitimated through constitutional procedures for generating popular consent (more or less liberal, more or less democratic) which, in turn, presuppose the widespread diffusion of postconventional moral aptitudes. These aptitudes uphold the inherent dignity of the individual, understood as a responsible,

---

1. Habermas insists that modern market economies logically and functionally presuppose a rule of law based on liberal rights. Taylor and Rawls, by contrast, allow that nonliberal rights might also work and that human rights ought not to be conceived in liberal terms (although Taylor has recently moved closer to Habermas's view). C. Taylor, "Nationalism and Modernity," in *The Morality of Nationalism*, ed. R. McKim and J. McMahon (Oxford: Oxford University Press, 1997); and *Modern Social Imaginaries* (Durham: Duke University Press, 2004).

rational agent who cooperates with others on the basis of commonly shared, rationally justified beliefs.

It is the mutual interdependence of the two poles of the preceding sequence—market-driven economy and morality-driven culture—that creates the dialectical tension to which I allude. This tension, in turn, can be formulated in terms of two competing conceptions of rationality.[2] Following the formulation proposed by first-generation critical theorists, economic rationality is exclusively oriented toward calculating the most efficient means for achieving one's ends. Economically rational agents aim at satisfying (if not maximizing) their preferences by ordering them by rank into consistent sets. Confronting others as if they were like any other controllable impediment or resource, they then calculate the one strategy that has the greatest policy for success.

The objectifying attitude according to which "economic man" understands his world is characteristic of modern science and technology taken as a whole; indeed, it is the dominant attitude underlying *all* forms of instrumental and strategic rationality. It is also radically limited in what it enables us to understand, for the whole world of meaningful life and value recedes from the cold gaze of the positivist who posits as real only those abstract facts that are reducible to measurable quantities confirmed by value-free observation.

Opposed to this attitude, which seems to view the whole world as an object for total (and totalitarian) domination, stands the moral attitude. The kind of rationality appropriate to this attitude is not instrumental but moral-practical. Its modus operandi is not the top-down inferential chain (deduction or explanation) executed by a lone technical engineer but the bottom-up discursive consensus achieved by all of us as we engage one another as free and equals.

Can the two competing modes of modern reason be reconciled? First-generation critical theorists thought not. Modernity, they noted, irresistibly unfolds a dialectic of enlightenment in which the institutionalization of instrumental reason in science—spurred on by the technological logic of economic competition under capitalism—gradually undermines its own moral foundation. The withering away of practical reason, coupled with the totalitarian domination of instrumental reason, produces a mass society of alienated human beings whose only aim in life is to consume more things and whose daily existence is controlled by bosses, managers, media manipulators, social engineers, and political elites.

Habermas disputes this diagnosis. Having located practical reason in the more resistant medium of communicative action, he believes that the outcome of the dialectic of enlightenment is hardly certain. Nonetheless, as we have seen, his sociological analysis of the forces arrayed against genuine deliberative

2. For Habermas, the opposition is not merely between instrumental and communicative forms of rationality but rather between functional and communicative forms of rationality. As I observed in chapter 2, even communicative action deploys instrumental rationality. The problem of opposition emerges when instrumental action is embedded exclusively in overreaching systemic media.

democracy—from the functional rationality of complex market, economic, and technological systems to the cultural irrationality of prejudice and parochialism—are not encouraging. However much they might be opposed in today's global world, capitalist economy and welfare state combine at every level to constrain—distort if not undermine—the ideals of democracy mentioned at the outset of this chapter.

But there is something more troubling in Habermas's account of modernity than what this superficial dialectic reveals. Taking his cue from Kant, Habermas conceives of modernity as a process by which different types of reasoning become radically differentiated into distinct and even opposed logics and methods. In antithesis to the old metaphysical and religious worldviews, modern thinkers, Kant insisted, must renounce the search for holistic explanations and frames of understanding. But having radically distinguished scientific from moral forms of reasoning, Kant could not explain the unity of human experience as both embodied (determined by physical causes) and spiritual (spontaneous and free). Habermas attributes Kant's failure to resolve the "determinism/freedom" problem to his metaphysics.[3] Yet Habermas also sees the failure to connect our objective knowledge of ourselves as "natural beings" and our subjective experience of ourselves as free beings to a distinctly capitalist form of modern alienation. As I noted in chapter 10, capitalism encourages the fragmentation and hyperspecialization of thought and action into technoscientific and ethicomoral compartments that no longer interact. Yet the interaction of these distinct modes of cognition and understanding is necessary if we are to be able to criticize ideology and alienation.

The question then arises whether Habermas's Kantian account of the modern differentiation of reason permits him to formulate a countermovement toward a distinctly modern integration of reason. Habermas insists that all forms

---

3. Like Kant, Habermas appeals to first-person phenomenological experience of our own freedom in arguing against a reductive form of causal determinism. According to Habermas, we experience ourselves as free in those moments when we are conscious of the reasons conditioning our actions. Reasons are not causes; they do not inhabit a physical space, do not temporally precede the actions they justify, and are not sufficient on their own (without the enabling conditions of body and social environment and other factors) to effect movement in any way that can be predicted. Nonetheless, they are not merely epiphenomenal, or without explanatory value in accounting for action. The two perspectives from which we always experience ourselves—that of third-person observer, on the one hand, and that of first-person speaker and second-person respondent, on the other—reflect two types of language games (cognitive and social) that have emerged in the course of human evolution. Appealing to the same studies of developmental psychology by Tomasello that Honneth cites (see chapter 10, note 8), Habermas notes that the social capacity to take the perspective of the other (Mead) precedes and transcendentally makes possible the experience (and cognitive language) of an objective world. Restated naturalistically (in causal terms), the "objective mind" (or culture) acquired along with the social acquisition of language structures the brain's neuronal pathways. The "subjective mind" (or "I") is not made redundant by the parallel processing of the brain because it is not an isolated ego controlling the process from above but a social construct that fully exists only in responding to others. See J. Habermas, "Freedom and Determinism" (*BNR* 151–80) and his *laudatio* for Georg v. Wright (*LPS* 46–56).

of reason share a common discursive logic despite having distinctive roots (see chapter 3). But is this formal (or procedural) concept of reason capable of grounding a critique of alienation? Can postmetaphysical secular reason alone critically illuminate the extent to which we have overstepped the ethical limits imposed on us by our human nature? If not, must we go beyond secular reason—back to religion and metaphysics—to recoup a utopian experience of fulfillment that can? In short, is a postsecular society—and a postsecular critical theory—still compatible with the logic of rational differentiation implicit in the Kantian project of modernity?

Marx on the Evolution of Modern Society

We cannot answer these questions until we have first examined Habermas's own theory of modernity, which he advances as a reconstruction of Marx's theory of historical materialism.[4] According to Habermas, the signal contribution of Marx's theory is its account of social evolution as a separation (abstraction or uncoupling) of a self-regulating legal and economic system from a meaningful lifeworld. That said, Marx fails to understand exactly how the social evolutionary increase in system complexity (and the cumulative increase in scientific-technological rationality that he identified with the forces of production) is dialectically related to another—distinctly moral—process of rational learning (roughly equivalent to what Marx describes as the relations of production). Hence he regresses behind his theory by failing to show how the moral ideals of freedom, equality, and solidarity constitutive of the lifeworld must be accommodated to the constraints, hierarchies, and distinctions imposed by the system. In short, Habermas claims that his reconstruction of Marx's theory of social evolution offers a more "realistic" assessment of the limits and possibilities of modernity than the analysis proffered by Marx and first-generation critical theorists (TCA 2 332–73).

Marx famously proposed that problems of exploitation, commodification, and alienation would disappear once economic decisions were brought under the collective democratic control of producers. Social relations would then be rendered fully transparent. As products of free, rational agents, they would

---

4. For the most complete theoretical statement of Marx's theory of historical materialism, see *The German Ideology, Part I*, trans. L. D. Easton and K. H. Guddat, in *Writings of the Young Marx on Philosophy and Society*, ed. L. D. Easton and K. H. Guddat (Garden City, NY: Anchor Books/Doubleday, 1967), 403–473; for Marx's historical account of capitalism as an autonomous system of exchange opposed to traditional ways of understanding life, see *Capital*, vol. 1 (Moscow: Progressive Publishers, 1963); for Marx's account of communism as a radical form of participatory and representative workers' democracy unmediated by state and market economy, see *The Civil War in France*, part 3; and *Critique of the Gotha Programme*, both in *Karl Marx: Selected Writings*, ed. L. Simon (Indianapolis: Hackett, 1994), 301–14, 315–32.

become (to paraphrase Habermas) pure communicative relations, unmediated by money-driven markets and power-driven legal systems.

Habermas rejects this diagnosis for underappreciating the emancipatory gain produced by economic and legal systems. In his opinion, modern economic and legal systems not only facilitate social coordination but liberate actors from the burdens of having to negotiate all aspects of their lives communicatively (*TCA 2* 339). Of course, these systems constrain and mediate our interaction in ways that also threaten our freedom. But that just means that modern society harbors an unresolved dialectical tension that must be maintained in a state of felicitous balance.

This view of modern society would seem to follow from Marx's own dialectical understanding of social evolution. Marx argued that social evolution is a dialectical process insofar as evolutionary advances resolve "contradictions" only by generating new ones. These resolutions, in turn, are dialectical in a secondary sense: the gains in freedom and equality they bring about at one level yield losses in freedom and equality at another level. Finally, the dynamic propelling evolutionary change is dialectical, reflecting contradictions between legally structured economic forces and relations of production.

Habermas affirms this basic account of historical materialism subject to several important qualifications. First, he notes that social evolution proceeds along two tracks, corresponding to increases in cognitive rationality and moral rationality, respectively. These distinctive paths of learning roughly map onto Marx's distinction between advances in the "forces of production" (scientific-technological innovations in the division of labor, the invention of machinery, etc.) and advances in the "relations of production" (innovations in property relations and property rights).[5] Importantly, both Habermas and Marx hold that these separate processes of societal rationalization can and do conflict with each other. Neither, for example, believes that growth in system complexity (impelled by a technical division of labor and scientific specialization) necessarily issues in more advanced (freer and more egalitarian) relationships between people at the level of everyday life (*CES* 138–42). However, Habermas diverges from Marx's view that social evolutionary developments are irreversible and culminate in a final stage of contradiction-free resolution. For Habermas, the uncoupling of system and lifeworld generates a productive tension between these two aspects of society that cannot be eliminated and that, under certain

---

5. Strictly speaking, Habermas analyzes social evolutionary processes into *three* components (not two, as I have presented them here). These processes revolve around the progressive institutionalization of (1) cognitive learning and instrumental rationality (leading to the development of efficient forces of production), (2) practical learning and communicative rationality (leading to the development of just relations of production and their democratic legitimation), and (3) organizational forms (leading to the heightened steering capacity and functional adaptation of social systems). Progress in (1) and (3) depends on progress in (2); however, problems in (3), reflecting a contradiction between (1) and (2), can stimulate progress in (2), leading to progress in (1) (*LC* 11).

circumstances, can produce crises that lead to regression (such as fascism) (*LC* 13). Second, and related, this means that advances in the morality of social institutions come with a price. The greater freedom and equality that individuals enjoy in modern liberal societies is alloyed with a certain degree of alienation from society and cosmos (*LC* 24–30). To cite *The Communist Manifesto:* "All that is solid melts into air, all that is holy is profaned, and man is at last compelled to face with sober senses, his real conditions of life, and his relations with his kind."[6] Third, the problems within the base of a social system that lead it to evolve a new superstructure are not always economic in nature. The institutionalization of a new system presupposes, rather than brings about, an evolutionarily advanced stage of moral knowledge. This means that moral learning—or the creation of freer and more egalitarian social relations—is the pacesetter for technological and scientific learning that gets institutionalized in economic and administrative systems (*CES* 144).

Habermas rejects Marx's social evolutionary scheme of six major *modes of production* that determine property relations and distributions of wealth. Instead of the Marxist progression—primitive communism, ancient slavery, European feudalism, capitalism, socialism, and communism—he introduces a more abstract scheme that focuses on changes in normative understanding that underwrite the *transition from premodern to modern societies*. These changes, in turn, are explicated in terms of three *principles of organization,* which determine the institutional boundaries limiting technical-instrumental and moral-practical learning and therewith functional, social evolutionary adaptation (*CES* 150–54). Finally, principles of organization are sequentially arranged in accordance with a developmental logic that is analogous to the sequence traversed by children during the course of moral development. So construed, the three main principles of organization institutionalize preconventional, conventional, and postconventional ideas of morality within their respective legal institutions (see table 8).[7]

The *kinship principle of organization* characterizes tribal societies in which the division of labor is minimal and persons do the same things and have more or less the same ideas (in Durkheim's words, they remain "mechanically" bound together in religious solidarity, each one internally replicating

6. *Karl Marx: Selected Writings,* 161–62.
7. Habermas concedes that the pattern of individual development cannot exactly mirror that of social evolution, since even the most primitive societies have institutionalized (at the adult level) relatively advanced interactive competencies involving reciprocity and generalized expectations. Also the kinds of crises that confront the individual differ from those that confront the social system and so call for different developmental solutions. Nothing comparable to the contradiction between moral-practical and cognitive-instrumental types of rationalization explains moral-cognitive learning at the level of the child, in which development of these competencies is more harmonious. In any case, the failure of a society to evolve a higher principle of organization that might resolve its crisis cannot be explained by the simple failure of that society's inhabitants to engage in higher-level moral and cognitive reflection. See M. Schmid, "Habermas's Theory of Social Evolution" (*CD* 162–80).

Table 8
Social evolutionary stages and their corresponding principles of organization

	Archaic (tribal) society	State-ordered civilization	Modern society
Principle of organization	Kinship (family/society)	State/political	Divided state/economy
Relationship between system and lifeworld	Incomplete separation of system and lifeworld	Separation of state system from kinship system (lifeworld)	Separation of economic (market) system from both state system and lifeworld: money and power emerge as market- and legal-driven steering media, respectively
	a. egalitarian tribal: systemic mechanism of exchange links similar family segments		
	b. hierarchical tribal: systemic mechanism of power generating stratification		
Class structure	Undeveloped	Political-economic	Economic
Ideological formation	Undeveloped	Religious	Economic/scientific
Degree of rationalization	Sacred prevails over profane; natural religion (totemism) and magic inform everyday action	Separation of sacred and profane action contexts; birth of rationalized monotheistic religion	Profane prevails over sacred; dissolution of unitary religious worldview into distinct cultural spheres and societal complexes
Form of mutual understanding	a. sacred: mythopoetic	a. sacred: uncritical acceptance of dogma coupled with its discursive interpretation	a. profane: fully rational purposive action informed by science and technology; normatively unbound communicative action with institutionalized discourses
	b. profane: prerational purposive action; communicative action with a holistic orientation to validity	b. profane: specialized professional discourses; norm-guided communicative action involving a discursive redemption of truth claims	
Dominant worldview	Mythopoetic	Religious-metaphysical	Scientific
Stage of moral consciousness	Preconventional (revealed) law oriented to consequences; mixed preconventional and conventional morality	Conventional legal and moral norms informed by an ethical conception of the good	Postconventional (formal) law informed by ethics of personal conviction and responsibility
Chief problem to resolve	Demarcation of society from nature	Internal social order in response to class conflict	Conflict between system imperatives and democracy

the same identical "collective consciousness"). The complexity of such societies, if we can use that term, consists in a horizontal division of more or less equally situated production units (families)—a form of social differentiation that Durkheim characterizes as *segmental,* in distinction from the *functional* differentiation associated with societies in which people who perform different kinds of tasks depend on one another and relate to one another through complex relations of economic exchange and contract. Increased horizontal differentiation (e.g., through population growth and the absorption of one tribe into another), however, creates new coordination problems that may require organization. Organization, in turn, involves functionally differentiating leadership roles, a form of vertical stratification that typically centers around the emergence of "prestige groups," or lines of descent that provide the tribe with chiefs who possess the authority to issue commands (*TCA* 2 153–63).

Before proceeding further with our account of the kinship principle of organization we must first take note of a feature intrinsic to the emergence of social organization that will later be seen to be a very problematic characteristic underlying Habermas's account of social evolution: *differentiation.* Differentiation proceeds on two, mutually interrelated, levels: lifeworld and system. At the level of the lifeworld, differentiation takes the form of what Habermas calls the *rationalization of the lifeworld.* The rationalization of the lifeworld proceeds on two sublevels. On the *cultural* level, we observe a rational (or logical) differentiation of distinct cultural-value spheres. This process, which Habermas explains as a *linguistification of the sacred,* not only involves analytically distinguishing types of claims (e.g., in the above example of the tribal chief, distinguishing commands to act from expressions of fear and signals of impending trouble), but it also involves *abstracting formal structures from concrete symbols* (e.g., distinguishing a formal illocutionary claim structure and the accompanying system of relatively common and constant meanings from the speech patterns of a particular person and the specific context of her utterance). Formal abstraction also brings to the fore analytically distinct cultural norms and ideas that have a common and relatively enduring validity (*universality*) that can serve as foundational reasons for justifying actions (*discursive reflexivity*).

On the *social* level, we observe a parallel process of differentiation involving the institutionalization of achievements stemming from cultural rationalization in distinct social structures and institutions. The *structural differentiation* of the lifeworld is reflected in the separation of culture, society, and personality. As culture becomes more rationalized (abstract, universal, and reflective) it acquires the capacity to be detached from the society in which it originated and can be reflectively modified and critically appropriated by other societies. As personality becomes more rationalized it, too, acquires the capacity to reflectively emancipate itself from cultural traditions and conventional social roles. The roles it increasingly identifies with are more abstract and general than vocational roles (e.g., that of citizen or bearer of universal moral rights) and also more uniquely individual and reflectively (creatively) self-generated. The *institutional differentiation* of the lifeworld—the separating out of rationalization complexes of science, law, and art—reciprocally builds on these other aspects of cultural and social differentiation and, in turn, paves the way for the *functional differentiation* of the lifeworld—the separating out of socialization, increasingly specialized around family and school, from material reproduction, increasingly specialized around the occupational system. The culmination of functional differentiation of this sort, of course, is the differentiation of lifeworld and system and the internal differentiation of distinctive subsystems (state and economy, for instance).

Now that we better understand the dynamics of cultural, social, and functional differentiation that mark the logic of social evolution as Habermas understands it, let us return to the three-stage sequence of social evolution that I began to elaborate, beginning now with the transition from kinship society to early civilization. This time, however, I will introduce the scheme of moral evolution discussed earlier in showing how the rationalization of morality acts as a pacesetter for the rationalization of knowledge and the functional differentiation of system and lifeworld. The decentralized authority that chiefs hold within archaic (tribal) society is limited in dealing with social conflicts and permanent crises calling for more centralized and more powerful means. Its reliance on *preconventional* instrumental reciprocity (exchange of favors/disfavors) and fear of punishment, such as ostracism, ignores distinctions between civil and criminal offenses, intentions and consequences, and provides few resources for resolving feuds beyond negotiated settlements and ostracism of losing parties (*CES* 162).

The *state principle of organization* can be understood as an evolutionary solution to these problems. Emerging at the dawn of urbanization and civilization, this principle of organization depends on *conventional* legal norms rather than personal prestige in maintaining order. Such norms transcend personal familial authority and its dependence on simple threats in resolving disputes and enforcing compliance. These norms—which are posited independently of the moral customs circulating within the lifeworld in accordance with more general principles of justice—incorporate fine-grained distinctions between civil and criminal offenses, intentions and consequences, and so need to be administered by literate experts whose qualifications are determined by merit rather than by familial descent (*LC* 20).

Finally, when the state principle proves inadequate in resolving social conflicts and regulating production and distribution according to ethical convention, it yields to the *divided state-economy principle of organization* typical of modern society. Just as the state principle unburdens individuals of the need to negotiate risky behavior among themselves, so too does the divided state-economy principle. The uncoupling of a self-regulating market from the state enables people to coordinate their economic lives by means of standard monetary and price mechanisms without having to negotiate the exchange of commodities. As we have seen, the moral bedrock underlying this norm-free strategic pursuit of self-interest is a system of individual rights rooted in post-conventional morality (*LC* 19–23).

Habermas qualifies this account of the divided state-economy principle of organization in his discussion of the four waves of juridification, which he later introduced in *The Theory of Communicative Action* (1981). As we saw in chapter 10, the differentiation of state and economy in the West was a gradual process marked by countervailing tendencies. With the advent of the welfare state, economy and system are not as rigidly separated from each other as they were during the heyday of liberal (or laissez-faire) capitalism. (Habermas even talks about the "refeudalization of the state.") Furthermore, in this later work Habermas also introduces the idea of the colonization of the lifeworld by the system, which again marks a certain reversal of the process of rational differentiation. Nonetheless, the general logic of social evolution reinforces the differentiation of lifeworld from system and economy from state. Indeed, neoliberal policies have encouraged this separation during the current phase of economic globalization.

Weber on Modernization and the Problem of Meaning

Habermas's reconstruction of Marx's historical materialism arguably provides a more plausible typology of evolutionary stages that dispenses with romantic yearnings for unalienated, system-free democracy. The plausibility of an abstract typology, however, must be balanced against the loss of concrete normativity. (Here, unlike in Habermas's Marxist account of the transition from feudalism to liberal and late capitalism in *STPS* [1962], capitalism appears as a possible terminus for a fully developed modernity).[8] Furthermore, the theory does not address the problem of modern nihilism highlighted by Max Weber and first-generation critical theorists that we discussed in chapter 1. Weber saw modernization as a process of secularization in which the cosmos is "disenchanted" and drained of purpose, value, and meaning.[9] Concomitant with secularization is the *fragmentation of culture and reason* itself into conflicting spheres of value. Science comes into conflict with morality, and both, in turn, collide with desire for pleasure and beauty. From this conflict comes skepticism

8. Habermas's later Weberian preference for an abstract logic of social evolution (modernization) in lieu of his earlier Marxian diagnoses of the concrete contradictions of capitalism in its specific historical manifestations is the subject of a withering critique by John McCormick in his *Weber, Habermas, and Transformations of the European State: Constitutional, Social, and Supranational Democracy* (Cambridge: Cambridge University Press, 2007), ch. 2.
9. See *The Protestant Ethic and the Spirit of Capitalism* (1904) and "Religious Rejections of the World and Their Directions," (1915) in *From Max Weber*, ed. H. H. Gerth and C. W. Mills (Oxford: Oxford University Press, 1946), esp. 329, 339, 342, 357; also see "Science as Vocation" (1919), in *From Max Weber*, esp. 144–56.

about intrinsic values, meanings, and purposes. Although all three cultural spheres bear witness to this process of relativization and devaluation, it is the moral sphere that suffers the most.

Habermas finds Weber's account of "rationalization" compelling as a description of modern culture and society but questions the implications he draws from it. Like Kant, Weber defended logical distinctions between types of value as well as the forms of reasoning that properly correspond to them. Scientific (experimental) method and mathematical logic serve as paradigms for reasoning about truth. This kind of cognitive-instrumental rationality is fungible for economic and administrative planning. By contrast, Weber noted that methods of practical reasoning that figure in morality, ethics, and law are less formally rigorous and certain in their outcomes. Indeed, Weber was even inclined to dismiss Kant's method of moral universalization as insufficiently rational, arguing that Kant's appeal to logical consistency betrayed an unspoken reliance on nonmoral, cognitive-instrumental forms of rational choice based on a calculation of consequences. For this reason, he was deeply skeptical about the capacity of morality and ethics to survive within a modern rationalized society. Crushed between the irrational hedonism of self-centered consumers and the rational calculation of methodical producers, morality and ethics become anachronistic, and their purveyors increasingly don the appearance of old-fashioned religious fanatics. Not surprisingly, this demotion of morality and ethics led Weber to endorse a positivistic view of law conceived as a neutral tool of coordination detached from any notion of moral justice or ethical well-being.

Although Habermas rejects Weber's pessimistic diagnosis, he does accept his depiction of rationalization as a process of cultural and societal differentiation. This depiction, which reflects the Kantian distinction between theoretical, practical, and aesthetic deployments of reason that informs Habermas's own triad of validity claims, corresponds to the modern sociocultural spheres of science, law (morality), and art. Beginning with the nineteenth-century art movement known as impressionism, modern artists ceased to think that their proper task was to represent reality "truthfully"; the eighteenth-century notion that art should convey moral and ethical insights also struck them as bizarre. Their call to arms—summed up in the slogan "art for art's sake"—rather expressed their intention to generate new and jarring experiences (often of an erotic nature) that would impact the viewers' cognitive representations and practical insights indirectly. Likewise, modern scientists no longer believed that it was their job to provide practical wisdom or self-enlightenment; far from setting us free, their knowledge bound us to efficient routines that were as mindless as they were unpleasant. And moral philosophers cautioned against confusing unconditional duties with factual constraints and sensuous desires.

Corresponding to this differentiation of cultural value spheres, Habermas argues, is a differentiation of social *rationalization complexes* (*TCA 1* 237–42). A rationalization complex designates an aspect of cultural life that can be *institutionalized* as a *methodical* learning process. As such, it designates a formal-pragmatic relationship to one of three possible world frameworks (objective nature, society, subjective person) that can become a topic of rational discussion centered around a single (cognitive, practical, or expressive) validity claim. Take, for example, *knowledge claims* (to truth). These claims can be meaningfully raised in discussing cognitive problems that emerge in dealing with the *objective world* of natural events, thereby giving rise to the rationalization complex known as *natural science/technology*. They can also be raised in discussing problems that emerge in dealing with sociohistorical events and structures in *society*, thereby giving rise to the rationalization complex known as *social (behavioral) science/social engineering*. Next, take *normative claims* to rightness/justice. Such claims can be meaningfully raised in discussing the legal norms and principles of justice regulating *society*, thereby giving rise to the rationalization complex known as *law*. Normative claims can also be raised in discussing *personal* duties and rights, whose proper domain is the rationalization complex known as *moral philosophy*. Finally, take *expressive claims* to goodness and aesthetic worth. These can be meaningfully raised in discussing *personal* desires, thereby giving rise to the rationalization complex known as *ethical (erotic-hedonistic) philosophy*. They can also be raised in discussing *aesthetic objects* and *natural beauty*, thereby giving rise to the rationalization complex of *art,* art criticism, and *aesthetics*.

Conspicuously absent from these rationalization complexes are cognitive-scientific learning processes associated with subjective desires and feelings, normative learning processes associated with objective nature, and expressive learning processes associated with society. The first two absences are easily explicable; the third, less so. According to Habermas, although there have been many psychological theories that have been advanced as scientific—these range from Freudian psychology to hedonistic-utilitarian calculations—none is truly so. What we call experimental and behavioral psychology is really a branch of social science. Freudian psychology, by contrast, is classified by Habermas as a form of theory-guided reflection, whose narratively structured accounts of stage-by-stage psychosexual development are neither predictive nor observationally verifiable. Likewise, Habermas contends that no quantifying method for ranking desires is sustainable in light of problems concerning the reflexivity of desire (our desire to have desires different from those we have now). Finally, he observes that no normative learning is possible with respect to nature once nature ceases to be perceived as an expression of divinely ordained moral commands (as in teleological conceptions of natural law).

The absence of an expressive learning process associated with society is somewhat more problematic. Following Hegel, first-generation critical theorists (notably Benjamin, Adorno, and Marcuse) saw art as a medium for reflecting on the rational integrity (or disintegrity) of society as a whole. For them art embodied utopian experiences, or illuminations of life lived authentically, intensely, and in perfect harmony with spirit (reason) as with nature (feeling). Accordingly, they believed that art could serve as a touchstone for critically judging the extent of alienation and fragmentation in society—hence the importance (in Marcuse's thought especially) of the politicized countercultural movements of the 1960s, which demanded that society be transformed in accordance with a new ecological, economic, and technological aesthetic (or aesthetic reason).

Despite the obvious attraction of a social project aimed at sustainable ecology in harmony with nature and community, Habermas warns that the endeavor to remake society as a work of art is redolent of the worst forms of top-down social engineering. (One need only recall the dangerous attraction that Nietzsche's notion of the superior "overman"—the great transvaluer of values—had for the Nazis and Italian Fascists in their efforts at creating a new society, not to mention Josef Stalin's depiction of artists as "engineers of human souls.") Even the more progressive modern art movements that sought to defend the social and practical function of art, such as surrealism, failed to show, in Habermas's opinion, how the disparate aspects of life (society, nature, and person) could be reconciled without retreating into the dark abyss of the unconscious (MUP 350–52).[10] Yet, despite his skepticism toward avant-garde art movements and heroic attempts at refashioning society as a work of art, Habermas appreciates the progressive value that countercultural movements have had on pushing for "green" reforms. Likewise, he believes that average persons can educate their social sensibilities through the reception and production of art, beyond the narrow compass of specialized, technical art criticism and production. Indeed, he does not gainsay the need for some kind of integrative experience as a countermovement to the one-dimensional, fragmented consciousness encouraged by our modern society of hyperspecialists and distracted producers (consumers). This awareness, as we shall see, partly explains his fascination with religion and art as indispensable complements to formal conceptions of reason.

I shall return to this theme. It suffices to note here that Habermas's conception of rationalization complexes provides a critical measure for evaluating the social pathologies mentioned in the previous chapter. Simply put, social pathologies occur when one of the aforementioned six rationalization complexes are not cultivated to the same degree as the other rationalization complexes or when learning in one rationalization complex is not allowed to interact with learning in another complex (TCA 1 240–42). An example of the former pathology is the colonization of the lifeworld; an example of the latter is the fragmentation of expert discourses. Each of these pathologies is classified by Habermas under the rubric of *selective rationalization*.

10. For a discussion of Habermas's theory of art and aesthetics and its relationship to the aesthetic theories of Adorno, Marcuse, and Benjamin, see D. Ingram, "Habermas on Aesthetics and Rationality: Completing the Project of Enlightenment," *New German Critique* 53 (Spring/Summer 1991): 67–103.

In sum, Habermas's account of social rationalization (or social modernization) provides a corrective to Weber's pessimistic diagnosis. The theory of rationalization complexes presumes that normative learning can be institutionalized in moral and legal discourses and that all major value orientations (or validity claims) can be institutionalized in some rationalization complex. In the final analysis, the discursive reason that is common to all rational learning processes provides a deep foundation for democratic ideals of equality, freedom, solidarity, and inclusion that Weber simply neglected. Selective rationalization, then, is not caused by a dialectic intrinsic to cultural and social rationalization as Weber thought, but is caused by a particular—and by no means universal—capitalist path of modernization (*TCA 2* 303–31).

Secularization and the Rationalization of the Lifeworld

Showing that "social modernization *too* can be guided into *other,* non-capitalist directions" (MUP 354) does not, however, suffice to dispel the dialectic of enlightenment that worried Weber and first-generation critical theorists. These theorists believed that no formal conception of reason could replace the substantive values and meanings implicit in premodern metaphysical/religious worldviews. In their opinion, the rational secularization of religion destroys—without preserving—religion's moral and ethical contents.

Habermas's own account of secularization—which he addresses in discussing the rationalization of the lifeworld—is offered as a response to this charge. According to the account of secularization that he presented in *The Theory of Communicative Action,* the rationalization of the lifeworld is spurred by the evolution of language, and in particular by the linguistification of the sacred. The evolution of language from symbolically mediated gestures (common to all hominids) to propositionally differentiated speech (developed fully in modern human societies)[11] depends, in turn, on two prelinguistic preconditions: the

---

11. Habermas's discussion of this transition largely follows the account given by George Herbert Mead in *Mind, Self, and Society* (1934). Mead endeavored to show how the concept of self emerges in the course of traversing logical phases in the development of social and symbolic interaction. The most primitive phase—"the conversation of gestures"—can be observed in animals, as when a dog growls in order to ward off another dog. For Mead, the gesture's capacity to stimulate behavior depends on its being *significant* to a recipient who still lacks a consciousness of meaning. Meaning and language first emerge when the gesture becomes a "significant symbol." That happens when dogs learn how to use their growling gestures purposefully. The gesture of growling becomes mutually meaningful once each dog "internalizes" the fact that growling calls forth a specific behavior in the other dog. In order for this to happen, each dog must take the attitude of the other dog toward his own behavior. That is, it must imagine itself being the other dog. In imagining itself thus, it learns to respond to its own act, to reflect on it*self.* Mead's account of childhood role playing and game playing extends this interactive account of selfhood further. The game of tag, for example, only works if the child who is "it" simultaneously adopts the attitude of all the other players. Ultimately, it is the mastery of first-, second-, and third-person

instrumental constitution of objective experience and the *communicative for-mation of subjectivity,* neither of which can come into being in the absence of *social solidarity* (*TCA 2* 60–61).

Appealing to Durkheim's sociology of religion,[12] Habermas observes that solidarity is intimately linked to the use of religious symbols and therewith to a distinction between "sacred" and "profane" domains of life. Prelinguistic rituals involving totemic fetishes initiate a break between action oriented toward mun-dane biological survival and the preservation of community. The emergence of a *collective consciousness* that transcends immediate desire presages the transcen-dent universality that is later attached to validity claims of truth and rightness. Initially, however, the distinctions between validity and efficiency, denotation and explanation, and between the distinctive claims associated with proposition-ally differentiated speech remain implicit. The poetic and metaphorical speech acts that correspond to mythic forms of understanding exhibit them weakly if at all. Indeed, the mythic understanding of the world collapses objective, social, and subjective world orientations into a single seamless reality. Magic, for instance, assimilates social meaning and object, so that invoking the name of a thing gives the supplicant causal power over it (*TCA 2* 47–56, 87–92).

Mythic language remains impervious to rational criticism in its conflation of validity claims. According to Habermas, the residual imprint of this conflation in subsequent archaic, traditional, and early modern "forms of understanding" explains why religious and metaphysical justifications of domination survive even after more rational forms of communicative action have evolved (*TCA 2* 189–97). For instance, archaic kinship societies depend on rational forms of communicative action that already exhibit a high degree of propositional dif-ferentiation and that therefore possess a capacity for logical and rational reflec-tion. However, they do not allow this profane "common sense" to seep into sacred contexts of speech action. With the emergence of state-administered civilizations we find class structures whose religious legitimation still requires a conflation of validity claims, although by now the logical and reflective functions implicit in everyday communicative action have partially influenced religious thinking. The extent to which rational thought permeates religious language is evidenced, for example, by the Hebrew separation of transcendent creator from natural creation. Yet, despite this process of secularization, the rationality gap between sacred and profane levels continued to be exploited in the early

---

roles implicit in propositionally differentiated speech (language games) that cements this complex web of self/other relationships. In participating in a social speech community, the child learns to adopt the moral standpoint of the *generalized other.* The capacity to adopt this abstract point of view in turn enables the self to become the unique individual self that it is by critically distancing itself from the multitude of particular roles it has internalized. Individuality is thus the outcome of freely reconstituting and reinterpreting the various habituated social roles within a repertory (*TCA 2* 22–42, 58–62).

12. E. Durkheim, *The Elementary Forms of Religious Life* (1912; repr., London: George Allen and Unwin, 1976).

modern period. Theories of natural law, for example, still confuse man-made norms with divinely preordained metaphysical necessities (*TCA* 2 195).

The relationship between religion and reason is thus dialectical. Just as religion acquires coherence and practical efficacy by incorporating reason, so reason acquires universality by incorporating religious transcendence. As Habermas puts it, modern postconventional morality *metaphorically appropriates* religion in *literal form:* man made in the image of God is translated into the sanctified dignity of the individual as a bearer of inalienable rights (*DS* 43–47).

Notwithstanding its redemptive preservation of transcendent religious ideas, secularization is not without its dangers. Habermas accordingly cautions against a bad form of secularization. Although secularization can promote a demythologizing appropriation of religion that enables religion-descended ideas of justice and solidarity to survive in postconventional morality, it can also lead to their dilution and destruction, as evidenced by a one-sided worship of a state, a party, or a science that seeks to replace God. In any case, secularization cannot heal the wound it has inflicted on the religious worldview. Reason cannot recover the enchantment of mythopoetic unity and fullness of meaning once understanding of the world has become differentiated into subjective (aesthetic), social (normative), and objective (cognitive) aspects. The procedural solidarity and justice of an abstract speech community cannot overcome modern alienation.

The stark opposition between secularization and religious life we have just seen, however, is less evident in Habermas's thinking today than it was twenty-five years ago. As I remarked in chapter 8, Habermas has abandoned the triumphal vision of secularization that he endorsed in *The Theory of Communicative Action*. Indeed, since the late 1980s his views on religion have gradually evolved to the point where he now rejects the strong secularization thesis associated with the linguistification of the sacred (*EFP* 60–64). The "methodological atheism" that he once believed was required of philosophy as a rational discourse as late as "Transcendence from Within, Transcendence in this World" (1988), an essay in which he acknowledged the limits of linguistification, has since given way to a tentative hope that reason and religion can learn from each other. That would imply that at least some religious discourse might be translated into rationally redeemable truth claims after all. In any case, Habermas ventures that religion might just remain an indispensable complement to moral reason (*DS* 51), with the understanding that only it can provide hope for a redeemed, reconciled, and fulfilled life.

If Habermas is right about this, then the primitive "semantic energy" associated with religion would not be reducible, as Durkheim thought, to a collective consciousness that functions exclusively to reinforce social solidarity in some dogmatic way. It would also function, as Marx clearly saw, as a protest against a heartless world that perpetuates avoidable socially imposed suffering and injustice. As such, it must be capable of emerging from the private sphere into the public sphere where it can energize progressive politics by providing citizens with the utopian images by which they can judge the essentially aesthetic (felt) unhappiness of a rational life that is "out of kilter," selectively rationalized and fragmented.

One might object to this defense of religion's indispensability by pointing out that reason is not so dispersed as to foreclose any integral learning. Habermas himself remarks that "radically differentiated" moments of reason aspire to a kind of unity even within highly specialized and differentiated discourses—science is secondarily guided by aesthetic considerations of simplicity in theory formation; morality is secondarily guided by scientific consideration of consequences; and art is secondarily guided by practical considerations of need disclosure. Yet what these examples show is hardly evidence of the kind of integral learning that is needed in order to critically assess modern alienation and offer hope for something better (*TCA 2* 398). If formal reason is inadequate to this task, we will need another kind of reason that is. For Habermas, that kind of reason is aesthetic.

Between Past and Future: Art, Religion, and the Dialectic of Enlightenment Revisited

To test this hypothesis further, we must first examine the limits and possibilities of discursive rationality in greater detail. This formal type of rationality is well suited to discussions aimed at pragmatic problem solving in which the justice of a single norm or the truth of a single description is at stake. In that respect it resonates well with the kind of piecemeal reform that Karl Popper opposed to totalizing revolution. But this form of practical rationality, centered as it is on settling disputes over discrete claims and rectifiable problems, cannot underwrite the substantive reflection by which we judge our entire lives to be alienated—fragmented and truncated by a selective process of rationalization.[13] The tragic suffering and loss of wholeness that humanity has endured in the course of its rational progress, not to mention the cumulative guilt that each generation has borne with respect to the sacrifices made by past generations, is simply not reflected in its one-sided and partial consideration of this or that assertion, prescription, or expression. In its rush to resolve conflict for the sake of progressing inch-by-inch toward a better future, it seems to have forgotten what it has left behind—a religious tradition that projects ultimate value and meaning and a past that memorializes the victims of progress. Indeed, even its vision of a better future is lacking the spark of utopian dreams.

On rare occasions Habermas has acknowledged that first-generation critical theorists might have been partly right when they observed that a concept of rationality other than a formal discursive one might be necessary in order to redeem the archaic traces of human suffering and yearning contained in

---

13. For Habermas, "health" is not a value that can be formally grounded in communication (*TCA 1* 252–53).

myth and religion. For without these memories of happiness betrayed we can scarcely imagine the depths of our present delusion and despair. It is in this messianic Marxist spirit that Habermas raises the most difficult question for his critical theory:

> Is it possible that one day an emancipated human race could encounter itself within an expanded space of discursive formation of will and yet be robbed of the light in which it is capable of interpreting its life as something good? The revenge of a culture exploited over millennia for the legitimation of domination would then take this form: right at the moment of overcoming age-old repressions it would harbor no violence, but it would have no content either. Without the influx of those semantic energies with which Benjamin's rescuing criticism was concerned, the structure of practical discourse—finally well established—would necessarily become obsolete. (*PP* 158)

This passage, drawn from "Walter Benjamin: Consciousness Raising or Rescuing Critique" (1972), revisits once more the apparent inadequacy of a purely formal (procedural) critical theory. Throughout this book I have suggested that the enormous appeal of such a theory—its capacity to provide a universal normative foundation for critique—cannot entirely compensate for its lack of content. Formal distinctions—between ideal procedures and real practices—give us only the barest of ideas for social critique, but judgments based on these ideas and the motivations for making them must draw support from elsewhere. We need, for instance, concrete images—alternative models of democratic society, for instance—and not just theoretical-limit concepts in order to judge the structural unhappiness or injustice of society. Habermas's own applications of his theory in the realms of technology (genetic engineering), religion and politics, multiculturalism, feminism, and immigration—just to name a few—belie his claim that philosophers need only (and can only) justify procedures for critical reasoning, as if these procedures could somehow be understood and applied apart from substantive value commitments.

To put it in Hegelian terms: all thinking is mediation. What functional analysis has sundered and rendered abstract must be reintegrated back into life. As Benjamin himself observed, the dissociation of symbols from their life-giving context (in the mechanical reproduction of art images as commodities, advertisements, and propaganda) robs them of their sacred "aura," their authoritative capacity to capture a seemingly infinite expanse of meaning, value, and purpose. So long as they are not reintegrated back into the lifeworld, they lose their meaning. The distorted communication characteristic of ideology also testifies to the self-deception caused by the substitution of deracinated symbols (e.g., mistaking wealth as an index for happiness and freedom); and so does the fragmentation of consciousness that persists even after ideology has been rationally penetrated and dispelled.

Habermas's appeal to Benjamin is especially instructive because among first-generation critical theorists it was he who urged that we overcome the disintegrity and superficiality of our routine lives by rescuing (redeeming) lost and forgotten meanings. Doing so, he thought, would open up our lives to the possibility of a fully integrated (meaningful and purposeful) future. For Benjamin, those transcendent moments of reconciled life found in history illuminate the fragmentations and superficialities of modern life, even as they project an explosive leap beyond the present to a utopia in which reconciliation embraces even the redemptive remembrance of past suffering. Similar messianic musings are scattered throughout Habermas's writings as well, many of them expressing a deep unease with the "atheism of the masses," who are in thrall to an empty life of excessive consumption and success (*LC* 80).

But what can these musings mean coming from a self-professed atheist?[14] Writing in *Legitimation Crisis*, Habermas ventured a secular replacement for theistic yearnings in which "'God' becomes the name of a communicative structure that forces men, on pain of a loss of their humanity, to go beyond their accidental, empirical nature and to encounter one another indirectly, across an objective something that they themselves are not" (*LC* 121). Although he still associates this moment of divine transcendence with the concept of the unconditionally valid that attaches itself to discursive procedures, he observes that this weak "'founding power' of a linguistically constituted form of life" does not measure up to what existentialists like Kierkegaard think is preliminary to and necessary for rational Socratic discourse and the kind of moral autonomy it engenders, namely, an authentically individuated ethical existence (*EFP* 29). As we saw in chapter 5, the "objective something" Habermas mentions in the passage just cited could also refer to our own common human nature as an ethical idea encompassing both self-realization and self-fulfillment. Or it could refer to the lifeworld ethos itself, the holistic background of meanings, values, and purposes that essentially evades analytic reduction to discrete items susceptible to human manipulation. Here Habermas seems to be gesturing toward Heidegger, whose philosophy of Being once captured his youthful fantasy. For young Habermas, the objectification of nature by modern science and technology—its analytic reduction to discrete quantifiable properties and potencies at the disposal of human will—was also seen as a harbinger for the loss of humanity and the concealment of Being which, as the holistic background against which life and world are foregrounded, makes possible the meaningful and purposeful disclosure of anything whatsoever. This "objective something"—so divinelike in its dispensation of Being—is the essential complement to the human condition. Although Habermas appeals not to Heidegger, but to Heidegger's former student, Hannah Arendt, in elaborating the way in which this communicative condition redeems meaning and Being,

---

14. This profession occurred in a personal conversation he had with me in 2002.

he draws closer to Heidegger by intimating that art, in particular, has a special capacity to found (disclose anew) our understanding of the world. In short, art—and here Habermas has specifically in mind modern nonrepresentational art—functions in a manner that is diametrically opposed to analytic rationality by bringing together a novel synthesis of what are otherwise differentiated cognitive, normative, and expressive values and meanings. In the same way that religious symbolism reveals the unfathomable depths of meaning and value in the condensed form of an image, art

> reaches into our cognitive interpretations and normative expectations and transforms the totality in which these moments are related to one another. In this respect modern art harbors a utopia that becomes a reality to the degree that the mimetic powers sublimated in the work of art find resonance in the mimetic relations of a balanced and undistorted intersubjectivity of everyday life. (QC 237)

Written in 1984, this passage evokes (in a manner not too dissimilar from John Dewey's equation of art and authentic experience) the idea that genuine art articulates life as it is most vividly lived, namely, as an integral and balanced whole that is imbued with emotion. As Hegel noted (and as Dewey would concur) art can be truer than real life by disrupting our routine, fragmented, and distracted mode of living and getting us to see, feel, and evaluate our world more intensely, in a manner that is more focused, more balanced (cognitively, normatively, emotionally) and more integral. In this respect art anticipates the fullness of life as it should be lived—a utopia wherein cognition, evaluation, and feeling inform one another in balanced interplay and our relation to nature, self, and society is restored, not only cognitively and abstractly, but corporeally, in the "mimetic" attunement of the individual organism with its environment.

Habermas proceeds to link this concept of aesthetic experience to cognitive learning, thereby gesturing toward a distinctly aesthetic (and dialectical) concept of rationality of the sort he had hitherto criticized in the work of his predecessors. He even goes so far as to assert that art raises a claim to truth—different from a cognitive claim to truth—whose justification transcends the rational differentiation and abstraction of formal validity claims. As he puts it:

> The aesthetic "validity" or "unity" that we attribute to a work of art refers to its singularly illuminating power to open our eyes to what is seemingly familiar, to disclose anew an apparently familiar reality. This validity claim admittedly stands for a potential for "truth" that can be released only in the whole complexity of life experience; therefore this "truth-potential" may not be connected to (or even identified with) one of the three validity-claims constitutive for communicative action. (QC 237)

Habermas clarifies this thought by appealing to Albrecht Wellmer's insight that "we can explain the way in which truth and truthfulness—and even normative correctness—are metaphorically interlaced in works of art only by appealing to the fact that the work of art, as a symbolic formation with an aesthetic va- lidity claim, is at the same time an object of the lifeworld experience, in which the three validity domains are unmetaphorically intermeshed" (QC 238). Here we are no longer interested in art as an institutionalized rationalization com- plex opposed to other rationalization complexes, a technically specialized do- main of learning that furthers the art of subjective expression with regard to purely aesthetic standards of taste and validity in exclusion of all else. Rather, we are transported back to Friedrich Schiller's idea of art as the vehicle for an aesthetic education in which not specialized experts but lay persons receptively appropriate it to come to terms with problems of alienation. This thought is developed at length in a speech Habermas gave in 1980 when he received the Adorno prize from the city of Frankfurt ("Modernity: An Unfinished Project"): "The layperson should educate himself to the level of the [professional art critic] and, on the other hand, the layperson could act as a connoisseur who relates aesthetic experience to his own life-problems" (MUP 352). Again citing Wellmer, he further adds:

> An aesthetic experience that is not translated primarily into judgments of taste has altered its status. When it is related to life-problems or used in an exploratory basis to illuminate a life-historical situation, it enters into a language game that is no longer that of art criticism. In that case aesthetic experience not only revital- izes the need interpretations in light of which we perceive the world; it also influ- ences cognitive interpretations and normative expectations and alters the way in which these moments refer to one another. (MUP 353)

The reception of works of art for purposes of illuminating life *as it might be lived in its integrity* certainly implicates a language game that incorporates an ideal of communication. But what kind? Not the kind characteristic of ev- eryday language. That game typically highlights only a single dimension of validity (art criticism, e.g., focuses exclusively on the formal merits of a work of art). By contrast, the reception of a work of art illuminates our entire life by putting into play all dimensions of validity. This truth claim is not separated from rational discourse:

> In this context reasons have the peculiar function of bringing us to see a work of art or performance in such a way that it can be perceived as an authentic expres- sion of an exemplary experience. . . . A work validated through aesthetic experi- ence can then in turn take the place of an argument and promote precisely those standards according to which it is an authentic work. (*TCA 1* 20)

Placed within the context of Habermas's later discussion of aesthetic truth claims in *The Philosophical Discourse of Modernity* (PDM 207), the reasons supporting artistic truth relate the three dimensions of validity to one another: *cognitive originality* (regarding the disclosure of a meaningful world), *moral in- tegrity* (regarding the disclosure of freedom and purposiveness), and *expressive authenticity* (regarding the disclosure of authentic needs and feelings) (MUP 347, 351–54).

Here Habermas gestures toward a distinctly *aesthetic conception of rationality* that first originated with Schiller's seminal critique of Kant's philosophy. Schiller aimed at finding a solution to Kant's metaphysical dualism between moral freedom and physical necessity, reason and sensibility, because he believed that it reflected a social schism, reflected in the alienation of individual from state, society, and nature. Schiller found the solution he was looking for in Kant's *Critique of Judgment* (1790), in which Kant appeals to *aesthetic judgments* of taste as mediating reason and sensibility. Specifically, Kant maintained that judgments of taste deploy the *imagination* in bringing about a "free play" and "unforced harmony" between these otherwise opposed faculties.[15] The ground that imagination appeals to in accomplishing this task is nothing other than common sense (*sensus communis*), the very same faculty, Kant notes, that also explains the possibility of *reaching mutual understanding through spoken communication*. For Schiller, it is by means of an *aesthetic education* that our powers of feeling, judgment, and imagination can be cultivated so that we can "enlarge our understanding" (as Kant put it) and communicate better with ourselves, our fellow human beings, and our nature. Without this education, practical judgment and the lifeworld that sustains it cannot but remain uncultivated and irrational. Contrary to his earlier refusal to countenance aesthetic learning in our dealings with society, Habermas here allows that

> an aestheticization of the lifeworld is legitimate only in the sense that art operates as a catalyst, as a form of communication, as a medium within which separated moments are rejoined into an uncoerced totality. The social character of the beautiful and of taste are to be confirmed solely by the fact that art "leads" everything which has been dissociated in modernity—the system of unleashed needs, the bureaucratic state, the abstractions of rational morality and science for experts— "out under the open sky of common sense." (*PDM* 50)[16]

Philosophy, too, can do this, by "rhetorically expanding and enriching"—and thereby *metaphorically mediating*—the various specialized languages of science, morality, and aesthetics that fall within its purview (*PDM* 209). At this point philosophy ceases to be a rigorous exercise in argumentation aimed at reconstructing its own formal conditions of possibility and becomes speculative: a literary exercise in imagining a freer and happier community.

15. Hannah Arendt famously appropriated Kant's account of aesthetic judgment in her posthumously published *Lectures on Kant's Political Philosophy* (1982). For a more recent demonstration of the necessity of aesthetic judgment in political theorizing, see Alessandro Ferrara's *The Force of the Example: Explorations in the Possibility of Judgment* (New York: Columbia University Press, 2008).

16. F. Schiller, *On the Aesthetic Education of Man in a Series of Letters* (New Haven: Yale University Press, 1954), 139.

Appendix A

Explaining Action

Anglo-American action theory analyzes the explanation of an *individual's* action. Two models dominate the field: causal and teleological. A typical example of the former is Carl Hempel's Schema R:

1. A was in situation type C.
2. A was a rational agent.
3. Schema R: In a situation of type C, any rational agent will do X.
4. Therefore, A did X.

Schema R is supposed to express a general causal law. However, it is clear that Schema R fails in this regard. Even if premises 1–3 are true, 4 could be false for any number of reasons (e.g., A's weakness of the will, sudden uncontrolled physiological paralysis, etc.). Of course, one could build into one's description of C qualifications stipulating that none of these reasons obtain, but then C begins to look more like the description of a particular situation than a general law. As William Dray noted, if Schema R is a generalization, it is not causal but normative, asserting that in situation C any rational agent *should* do X. These difficulties speak in favor of the second model, based on Aristotle's teleological (practical) syllogism that explains action as an outcome of intention. An example is Georg von Wright's practical inference scheme (PI):

1. From now on A intends to bring about p at time t.
2. From now on A considers that, unless he does a no later than at t, he cannot bring about p at t.

3. Therefore, no later than when he thinks time t has arrived, A sets himself to do a, unless he forgets about the time or is prevented.

PI, however, fails as an explanation because something else besides A's intentions (a muscle spasm) may have been the real reason (cause) of the action. Unlike action theorists, social theorists focus on actions of individuals only insofar as they are embedded in social action. Although some explanations of social action (notably those based on rational choice and game theory) remain within the Hobbes-inspired framework of methodological individualism, most social theorists (including Habermas) hold that complete explanations refer to "social facts"—social structures and functions—that condition individual intentions. Emile Durkheim (1858–1917), for instance, observed that the strategic choices made by individuals in the market depend on contracts whose binding nature cannot be explained apart from moral convictions that ultimately descend from primordial residues of a "sacred" social solidarity (collective consciousness). This example illustrates another distinguishing feature of social explanations that escapes reduction to an individual actor's intentions: their historicity. Habermas here cites Arthur Danto's notion of "narratives sentences" (such as 'The Thirty Years War began in 1618') that frame the meaning and causality of social actions from the narrator's—not the actor's—historical standpoint (*OLSS* 33–35, 155–60). Weber's famous example of sixteenth-century Protestants inadvertently bringing about a capitalist order by seeking confirmation of their salvation in their amassing of wealth also illustrates this notion. The sociologist's historical narrative establishes an "elective affinity" between an intended action and its unintended effect: the creation of a market economy. See E. Durkheim, *The Rules of Sociological Method* (Glencoe, IL: Free Press, 1950), esp. 95–121; C. Hempel, "The Function of General Laws in History," in *Readings in Philosophical Analysis*, ed. H. Feigl and W. Sellars (New York: Appleton-Century-Crofts, 1949), 459–71; W. Dray, *Laws and Explanation in History* (Oxford: Oxford University Press, 1957); Georg von Wright, *Explanation and Understanding* (Ithaca: Cornell University Press, 1971); and Arthur Danto, *Analytical Philosophy of History* (Cambridge: Cambridge University Press, 1965). For a good synopsis of the debates in action theory, see K.-O. Apel, *Understanding and Explanation: A Transcendental-Pragmatic Perspective* (Cambridge: MIT Press, 1984). For an excellent study of problems linking action theory and systems theory, see J. Bohman, *New Philosophy of Social Science* (Cambridge: MIT Press, 1991). Also, see my summary discussion of these issues in *Reason, History, and Politics: The Communitarian Grounds of Legitimation in the Modern Age* (Albany: SUNY Press, 1995), 84–95. Also see Habermas's *laudatio* for Georg von Wright (*LPS* 56).

Appendix B

Understanding Action

Contextualist approaches hold that the meaning of action is determined by an implicit background understanding that cannot be literally or formally explicated in terms of rational standards. According to contextualism, the only way to make sense of an aboriginal's mythic worldview is to experience it as an aboriginal participant would. The challenge this poses to the ethnographer—who can hardly be expected to bracket out his or her own cultural understanding—gives rise to skepticism about achieving undistorted, objective knowledge of alien cultures. More serious still, it suggests moral relativism or a flat-out denial that there exist cross-cultural standards of rationality by which actions can be critically assessed. These undesirable consequences lead Habermas to reject contextualism. Here Habermas agrees with Weber that an action is meaningful only to the extent that it can be understood as rational (according to some *ideal type* theory of action). Real actions only approximate the ideal type(s). Habermas, however, disagrees with Weber on how the ideal type(s) should be theoretically formulated. According to Weber, an action's rationality must be assessed in light of four variables: (1) The actor must be capable of being understood as having a purpose in mind, or consciously choosing an end, rather than behaving unthinkingly and mechanically; (2) the actor's choice of *ends* must be capable of being understood as reasonable in light of more basic ends, or *values;* (3) the actor's choice of *means* must be capable of being understood as reasonable in light of efficiently realizing those ends; and (4) the actor's rational assessment of all of these must be capable of being understood as reasonable in light of known *consequences*. Weber himself maintained that the most easily understood and rationally explicable type of action involves a rational consideration of all four dimensions: values, ends, means, and consequences. This supremely rational action type—what he called *purposive-rational* action—is *instrumental action* in which the actor tries to achieve some value-informed end by the calculated use of efficient means for achieving determinable consequences. Less rational and less meaningful are actions inspired by moral and religious duty, what Weber called *value-rational* actions. Here the rational choice of efficient means is entirely geared toward performance in accordance with a norm as an end in itself, regardless of consequences and prospects for success. Weber believed that this kind of action, which plays an important role in politics (where, e.g., obviously futile and costly acts of rebellion are undertaken on principle), is more rational than *emotional* (or *affective*) action, in which the actor blindly chooses ends without regard to their relationship to higher-order values, or long-term goals. Least rational (and least meaningful) are *traditional* actions done out of habit, rather than conscious choice, where even the end to be achieved has been lost sight of (*TCA 1* 282).

Habermas agrees with Weber that certain types of action are less rational and meaningful than others. The difficulty that cultural anthropologists encounter in trying to make sense of such practices as witchcraft, in which rational distinctions between means and ends, not to mention between self, nature, and society, appear not to hold, bears witness to this fact (*TCA 1* 63). We can only understand witchcraft as something analogous to a child's fantasy that gives way once rational maturation has been achieved; in the words of Habermas, "we must be able to reconstruct the successful and unsuccessful learning processes which separate 'us' from 'them'" (QC 239). Even a less Eurocentric anthropologist, such as Claude Lévi-Strauss, concedes that in dealing with the "primitive" mind, cultural anthropologists must sometimes relinquish the aim of rational understanding in favor of rational scientific explanations. These explanations appeal, for example, to universal structures embedded in the unconscious pertaining to, for instance, the categorical distinction between nature and culture (the "raw" and the "cooked"). Leaving aside the problem of understanding (or explaining) ritual behavior, Habermas disagrees with Weber that purposive rational action is the most rational and meaningful kind of action. Purposive rational action no doubt provides the model for teleological explanations of individual action. It can even explain *strategic* social action in which an actor views others as objective means or obstacles to the attainment of personal ends. Although this type of social action certainly dominates in certain economic and political contexts, which explains its importance for game theorists, it is of little value in explaining more *cooperative* social endeavors based on *mutual understanding and respect*. In these contexts, actors hold one another rationally accountable for their *knowledge,* their social *rectitude,* and their *sincerity*. Social action of this kind is essentially *communicative,* involving the raising of validity claims to truth, rightness, and sincerity as well as the readiness to justify them. Here, too, we discern levels of communicative rationality and meaningfulness within each subcategory of communicative action, depending on the number of validity dimensions that come into play and the extent to which they are treated critically and reflectively in justificatory dialogue. In *normatively regulated action* (or action that highlights a claim to rectitude or rightness) two or more persons signal their cooperative intention to coordinate their purposive-rational (teleological) actions on the basis of social norms; not only do they relate rationally to an objective world of means and obstacles, they also relate rationally to a social world of norms, in the sense that they may do so with varying degrees of reflection; for example, they may take the rightness of social norms for granted (what Habermas calls norm-conforming action) or they may seek to justify them argumentatively in light of their consequences vis-à-vis the interests of those affected by them (what Habermas calls practical discourse). In *dramaturgical action* (or action that highlights a claim to sincerity) persons relating to one another as actor-to-audience signal their cooperative intention to coordinate their purposive-rational actions on the basis of roles and sincerely represented subjective personality traits. Here they relate rationally to their own subjective world of experience as well as to the objective world of things. Again, this kind of action admits of degrees of rationality (e.g., one can enter therapy in order to gain rational insight into one's inner psychology). Finally, in *conversation* (or action that highlights a claim to truth) persons signal their intention to cooperate in ascertaining the truth of an assertion more or less openly and disinterestedly (*TCA 1* 327).

In sum, purposive actions are typically pursued within communicative and strategic actions (which are parasitic on communicative actions). This means that fully understanding purposive actions requires understanding how actors might rationally justify them to others. However, as I note in chapter 3, Habermas concedes that the communicative rational meaning of action occurs against a holistic preunderstanding, or background context of meanings (the lifeworld) that cannot be rendered rationally transparent. In this respect he can be said to endorse a qualified contextualism. See M. Weber, *The Methodology of the Social Sciences*, trans. E. A. Shils and H. A. Finch (New York: Free Press, 1949); and *Economy and Society*, vol. 1 (Berkeley: University of California Press, 1978), 4, 24, 26.

Appendix C

Habermas and Brandom

Robert Brandom, in *Making It Explicit: Reasoning, Representing, and Discursive Commitment* (Cambridge: Harvard University Press, 1994) (hereafter *MIE*), and Jürgen Habermas present competing theories of meaning and accountability. Habermas accuses Brandom of limiting meaning to cognitive (assertoric) meaning, but Habermas's account of the referential structure of validity claims—normative included—as well as his account of the analogy between truth and rightness should incline him to accept a reduction of normative claims to assertions à la Brandom. Once assertions are accepted as the privileged mechanism for communicating content, then the difference between Brandom and Habermas seems relatively superficial. Brandom's inferential semantics bears a strong resemblance to Habermas's, in that both theories tie the meaning of assertions to validity claims and justifications (or commitments and inferential entitlements, as Brandom puts it) in communicative exchanges between an "I" and a "Thou." Both therefore presuppose that speakers' attitudes, beliefs, and claims about the world alone do not entitle them to these beliefs. Entitlement is a normative concept such that if two speakers contradict each other in their assertions, one of these assertions is not entitled. Entitlement, in other words, implies commitment to a "single right answer." Finally, given their commitment to *internal realism* (see chapter 4 of this book), both hold that the origin of objectivity is explicable in terms of speakers' normative assumptions, without reference to a realm of language-independent facts. But there are important differences between them as well. Brandom frames his pragmatic account of meaning in terms of a weak notion of communication that assumes only that speakers make claims that can be understood and used by others for their own purposes. He explicitly refrains from making assertions about the fundamental telos of communication (be it agreement or mutual understanding). Although he emphasizes (as does Habermas) the reliability of information, which requires that speakers take responsibility for what they say, he does not believe that this requires that they also understand what is said in the same way. All that is required is that they be able to talk about the same things that have been said by others and play the same game of holding one another accountable for what gets said. Furthermore, whereas Brandom describes the act of asserting as an impersonal act of making a claim public "for others to use in making further assertions" (*MIE* 170), so that communication is not specifically targeted toward an addressee who must respond, Habermas describes it as an act that is addressed to a particular addressee who then must respond with a yes or no. Because Brandom does not explain rational accountability in terms of a direct addressor-addressee relationship, he does not develop, as does Habermas, an essential role for rational discourse, or dialogue, with its strong normative idealizations.

These differences underscore the fundamentally different way in which Habermas and Brandom conceive of accountability, autonomy, and objectivity. To begin with, Brandom describes language use from the standpoint of a virtual participant who observes language as a game in which everyone is simultaneously a game player and a scorekeeper. As scorekeeper, we keep track of what people have committed themselves to believing on the basis of what they say (people may be committed to claims that inferentially follow from their assertions without explicitly knowing it or admitting that they do, and this failure can be cause for criticism). We also keep track of our own normative (inferential) commitments. Here, however, we encounter a fundamental tension between Brandom's inferentialist account and Habermas's firmly communicative account. According to Brandom, each of us has our own system of more or less interconnected commitments that need not overlap with others' systems beyond the bare essentials. For instance, what a defender of intelligent design is committed to when she says that a certain single-cell organism exhibits complexity is different from what a defender of evolution is committed to. Because each inserts this claim within her own set of inferential chains and thus "interprets" this claim in terms of her own set of commitments, what they understand (mean) by this claim will be fundamentally different. In short, the *holism* (*contextualism*) of inferentialist accounts of meaning poses the problem encountered earlier with respect to Hegel: language users confront one another with seemingly self-contained, incommensurable systems of meaning. How, then, can they be said to communicate?

Four plausible responses given by the classical semantic tradition are rejected by Brandom as problematic. We cannot assume shared meaning or even partially shared (overlapping) meaning without begging the question. We cannot assume that everyone will hold certain belief commitments simply because such commitments are "true by definition" (or true solely in virtue of the meaning of words), since as W. V. O. Quine and others have shown, what we take to be a defining part of a word's meaning is relative to our other commitments. We cannot assume that people share a common world of objects that precedes the different ways in which their peculiar commitments categorize, select, and describe things linguistically. We cannot assume, finally, that we are all committed to reaching uncoerced agreement about what there is and what we mean. The only way to explain communication, according to Brandom, is to equate score keeping with "double bookkeeping": as scorekeeper, each of us keeps track of how our inferential commitments cross paths with the inferential commitments of others.

Unfortunately, this *perspectivalism* seems to run afoul of Brandom's structural commitment to objectivity: "what is shared by all discursive perspectives is that there is a difference between what is objectively correct in the way of concept and what is merely taken to be so" (*MIE* 600). Brandom allows that in principle everyone might be mistaken about what is objectively correct, nonetheless he grants that certain ways of describing the world and their corresponding commitments about what sorts of things exist in the world are held to be privileged over others as a matter of negotiated social convention. If the need for mutual recognition and conformity to social convention leads one to accept the privileged commitments of science, say, then one should accept those commitments as the objectively right ones. However, this commitment to a preexisting normative consensus appears to conflict with another Enlightenment value that Brandom, along with Habermas, holds dear: the freedom of speakers to withhold assent to any authority (including themselves) based on the possibility that they could be wrong. As Brandom puts it, "there is only the actual practice of sorting out who has the better reason in particular cases" (*MIE* 601).

Here is where Habermas detects a problem with Brandom's "phenomenalist" (or observational) understanding of commitment and entitlement. Brandom makes the critical assessment of validity a monological affair; playing the role of scorekeeper, each of us assesses the inferential coherence and entitlement of the other's assertion from our own monological point of view. We are like jurors overhearing a courtroom conversation, not litigants arguing with one another:

> Certainly, in the courtroom the judges hearing the case and the jurors listening to it are the ones who in a sense are keeping account of the progress of discussion and forming a judgment as to who is scoring what points in order to be able to say in the end, for example, how the statement of the controversial witness is to be assessed. During the dispute, however, a reaction is required not from the listeners but from the parties directly involved who address utterances to one another and who expect each other to take positions. (*TJ* 163)

Because Brandom "identifies the interpreter with a public that assesses the utterance of a speaker—and not with an addressee who is expected to give the speaker and answer" (*TJ* 163), there is no expectation on the part of language users that they must enter into critical dialogue in order to coordinate their actions, no expectation that they must be confronted by addressers whose arguments might compel them to alter their deepest commitments. In Habermas's formal pragmatic account of commitment, the objectivity (or truth) of a claim is decided through mutual dialogical questioning of prejudices (or discourse); in Brandom's, it is largely decided through a process by which each speaker privately makes explicit the same inherited sets of factual presuppositions he or she ostensibly shares with other speakers. Thus it is the largely unquestioned "normal" interpretation of the world that speakers and their fellow speakers have inherited from their common upbringing in a single, unitary tradition that forms the basis for a speaker's judging whether they are entitled to their commitments. Thus, for Brandom it is reason as socially instituted *norm* that *factually obliges* them to think a certain way, not reason as a *counterfactual regulative ideal* that *directs* them to criticize established ways of thinking as such (*TJ* 140). In this respect, as Cristina Lafont argues, it is not always clear in Brandom whether objectivity really is (as he says) a *structural presupposition* of language use that forces speakers to adopt an autonomous standpoint critical of any de facto social consensus or whether it is simply the outcome of deferring to such an "authoritative" consensus as a matter of social necessity. As Brandom himself remarks in his reply to Habermas:

> The acknowledgement of the existence of conceptually structured facts to which our practices (according to us) answer...is not meant to have any explanatory value except what can be cashed out in terms of the deontic and social-perspectival articulation of our discursive practices [and so]...it is not intended to explain so much as the possibility of that articulation—rather the other way around. ("Facts, Norms, and Normative Facts: A Reply to Habermas," *European Journal of Philosophy* 8 [2000]: 360)

Merging rationality, objectivity, normativity, and truth into a factually preexisting social perspective, Brandom abandons his Kantian transcendentalism in favor of Hegelian idealism. His belief that "fact-stating talk is explained in normative terms and normative facts emerge as one kind of fact among others" thus commits him to both conceptual and moral realism, a position that Habermas strongly rejects (*MIE* 625; *TJ* 168). See C. Lafont, "Is Objectivity Perspectival? Reflexions on Brandom's and Habermas's Pragmatist Conceptions of Objectivity," in *Habermas and Pragmatism*, ed. M. Aboulafia, M. Bookman, and C. Kemp (New York: Routledge, 2002), 185–209. For an excellent summary of Brandom's views on communication from which I have freely drawn, see Jeremy Wanderer's *Robert Brandom* (Montreal and Kingston: McGill–Queens University Press, 2008), chap. 7.

Appendix D

Developmental Psychology

Piaget's genetic structuralist approach to cognitive and moral development explains the genesis of adult competences in terms of the developing child's innate capacity to articulate all-encompassing structures (*Gestalts*) or forms of thought in the course of acting on his environment and subsequently reflecting on what he has done. According to Piaget, child development proceeds through four stages: (1) *sensorimotor/symbiotic* (birth to two years), (2) *preoperational* (two to seven years), (3) *concrete-operational* (seven to eleven years), and (4) *formal-operational* (eleven years and beyond). At the sensorimotor/symbiotic stage children react to their environment through a stimulus-response circuit involving little reflection; they are thus not fully able to distinguish themselves as corporeal subjects apart from either the social world of primary reference persons (family) or the objects composing physical reality. At the preoperational stage children are able to distinguish themselves from their environment by intentionally acting on it. However, they are not yet able to differentiate this environment into distinctive social and objective domains. Because they have a tendency to transfer to things responses acquired in their dealings with persons—compare, for instance, an adult's analytic detachment in dealing with a broken hammer with the young child's anger and sense of betrayal—Piaget finds this structure of cognition to be analogous to magical thinking. Furthermore, children at this stage of development continue to perceive and judge situations solely from their body-bound perspective. Only when they begin to engage in concrete operations and logical operations using practical aids that enable them to recognize, for example, the *conservation* of quantities, weights, volumes, and the like across superficial variations do they acquire the ability to fully differentiate subjective, social, and physical domains of reality. With the onset of adolescence and the full acquisition of formal logical operations children are finally able to differentiate abstract universal principles of cognition and morality from more concrete and context-bound systems of rules.

Piaget's developmental scheme is of great importance to Habermas (*TCA 1* 67–69), since it enables him to describe both child development and social evolution in terms of learning processes that articulate progressive stages of cognitive-moral *decentration,* or differentiation combined with formal unification. Drawing on the research of George Herbert Mead, Habermas interprets this process as a process of *self- (ego-) development* that also has a linguistic component (*PT* 171–93; *TCA 2* 96–100). The mastery of speaker and listener roles enables the child to simultaneously adopt two perspectives: a first-person (speaker) perspective and a second-person (listener) perspective. As we saw in chapter 3, this perspectival dualism in turn enables the self (from a first-person perspective) to achieve a reflective relationship to itself (from a second-person perspective). Such a reflective self—what Mead calls "me"—has both theoretical implications for the possibility of sustaining a general sense of selfhood and practical implications for achieving a personal identity. By learning the role of an impartial third-person to whom speaker and listener direct their exchange, the "me" acquires a "we" perspective (what Mead calls the "generalized other"), which represents the conventional perspective of society. Initially, there exists no tension between self and society. However, the perspective of the generalized other can be expanded to designate that *ideal* community about which Peirce spoke in discussing truth and objectivity. Corresponding to this perspective is a critical distancing from conventional social roles (conventional *role identity*) whose crowning achievement is moral autonomy. Acquired, too, is the capacity to imaginatively create one's own sense of self (*ego-identity*). Extending this internal dialogue (self-critique) may even require entering into psychotherapy. Socialization (communicative acquisition of multiple roles) thus drives individuation. Parallel to the *ontogenetic decentration* of the individual in socialization we have the *phylogenetic decentration* of society. Society evolves by growing out of mythopoetic forms of communicative understanding and acquiring more reflective (decentered) forms (see chapter 11). J. Piaget, *The Principles of Genetic Epistemology* (London: Routledge and Kegan Paul, 1972); and L. Kohlberg, "Stage and Sequence: The Cognitive-Developmental Approach to Socialization," in *Handbook of Socialization Theory and Research,* ed. David Goslin (Chicago: Rand McNally, 1969).

Appendix E

Rational Choice Theory

Rational choice theories are variants of an economic theory of democracy that goes back to Joseph Schumpeter's classic *Capitalism, Socialism, and Democracy* (1947), which emphasized the importance of democratic elites in facilitating the top-down aggregation of competing preferences. There is a vast literature (see Jon Elster) on the disjunction between a person's expressed choices and preferences, on one side, and their real interests, on the other, that deliberative democrats focus on when recommending deliberation as a method for critically revealing persons' concealed and adaptive preferences. Citing Elster, Habermas notes that rational choice cannot even explain why people who calculate costs and benefits in pursuing their aims would spend the time and energy necessary to cast a vote that has a miniscule impact on an electoral contest (*BFN* 336–41). The literature on problems of social choice is equally vast. In *A Theory of Justice* Rawls points out that the economic model of maximizing utility cannot be transformed from the individual case to the group, since the group is not a unified subject capable of ranking the diverse preferences of its members in any coherent way. This result—much talked about among theorists of collective choice—was already anticipated by the marquis de Condorcet in his *Essay on the Application of Analysis to the Probability of Decisions Extended to a Plurality of Voices* (1785). Condorcet noted the potential for different majority groupings within a democracy to prefer conflicting preference rankings. This potential exists in cases involving, for instance, the ranking of items A, B, and C on a legislative agenda, where each item is paired off against another (A to B, B to C, and A to C). It is possible that one majority might prefer C to A and another majority might prefer A to

C if they preferred A to B and B to C. Similar "cycling" can occur in cases in which voters are given more than two options in deciding a single issue. More recently, Kenneth Arrow proved in his "impossibility theorem" that if there are more than two alternatives, any democratic decision procedure preserving transitivity in reasoning will, under certain conditions, require the imposition of decision from the outside. Some of these conditions can be represented as follows. Given three individuals (A, B, C), three alternatives (x, y, z) and the following distribution:

A prefers x to y, y to z, and x to z
B prefers y to z, z to x, and y to x
C prefers z to x, x to y, and z to y

no alternative is preferred more than the others (A prefers x, B prefers y, and C prefers z). Given 101 individuals, the following distribution pertains:

1 person prefers x to y and y to z
50 persons prefer z to x, x to y
50 persons prefer y to z, and z to x

This yields the paradoxical result that 51 prefer x to y, 51 prefer y to z, and assuming transitivity of choice, 51 prefer x to z, while 100 prefer the opposite. In this case, the majority of people prefer x to z even though all of them (minus 1) prefer the opposite. Majority rule therefore issues in contradictory results. Abandoning the rule of transitivity eliminates the contradiction but not the problem of choice, since roughly half prefer z and half prefer y. William Riker and other collective-choice theorists have used results like this to argue that democracy cannot express the will of the people (or cannot serve to rank preferences) but can at best serve the simpler function of electing (or recalling) government elites. (As he notes, people can disagree markedly among themselves about what is most urgent yet can easily gather a majority to get rid of incumbents for any number of reasons.) His deflationary reasoning therefore seems plausible, given that cycling occurs more frequently in legislative agenda-setting contests than in elections involving candidates who (unlike agenda preferences) are not transitively ranked. It seems even more plausible when we consider that methods for assigning values to ranked preferences can vary markedly. For example, a Borda count involving a simple ordinal ranking of preferences (where among four preferences the strongest is valued as 4 and the weakest as 1) can yield markedly different results from that obtained by using a Benthamite count that factors in strength of preference. Of course, the mere fact that different methods for weighing preferences are more or less arbitrary does not mean that the results obtained by using any one of them are any less meaningless than, say, a football score based on the arbitrary assignment of 6 points for a touchdown and 3 points for a field goal (see Coleman and Ferejohn). However, a deliberative democratic like Habermas need not be overly troubled by the paradoxes of using voting procedures to rank agenda preferences, since for the deliberative democrat it is public opinion or, more precisely, informed, inclusive, egalitarian, unconstrained—in short, rational—public opinion that should guide legislators in setting their agendas. Furthermore, the consensual nature of rational deliberation, both within and without the legislative chamber, has at least a prima facie advantage in reducing conflicts of opinion and thus managing the proliferation of irrational and antagonistic preferences. See J. Elster, "The Market and the Forum: Three Varieties of Political Theory," in *Foundations in Social Choice Theory,* ed. J. Elster and A. Hylland (Cambridge: Cambridge University Press, 1986), 103–28; K. Arrow, *Social Choice and Individual Values* (New York: Wiley and Sons, 1951); W. Riker, *Liberalism against Populism: A Confrontation between the Theory of Democracy and the Theory of Social Choice* (San Francisco: W. H. Freeman, 1982); and J. Coleman and J. Ferejohn, "Democracy and Social Choice," *Ethics* 97 (1986): 6–25.

Appendix F

Systems Theory

In viewing society as a system, we seek to *causally explain* how specific structures *function* to maintain the system in ways that are unintended by the actors whose actions create these structures. Jon Elster formulates the model of *functional explanation* accordingly: A social structure (pattern or institution) X is said to be causally explained by its function Y for group Z if and only if

1. Y is caused by X,
2. Y is beneficial for Z,
3. Y is unintended by the actors who intentionally produce X,
4. Y or the causal relationship between X and Y is unrecognized by the actors in Z, and
5. Y maintains X by a causal feedback loop passing through Z.

Adam Smith functionally explained the market's "invisible hand" in advancing the public good of self-interested competitors. In a market society actors intentionally compete with one another, which unintentionally causes the flourishing of profit-maximizing firms, which in turn causes (through a feedback loop) more competition and wealth maximization.

Emile Durkheim, Bronislaw Malinowski, and A. R. Radcliffe-Brown compared societies to biological organisms. The functionalist explanations they offered tended to be vacuous and question begging, purporting to show that certain structures came about because they conduced to the harmony, solidarity, or survival of the system. Any structure could be said to contribute in some way to this end, and other structures could be imagined that might have functioned better in this regard. Habermas cites Ernest Nagel's devastating critique of biologically modeled functionalist accounts (*OLSS* 80–84). Nagel observed that a structure could be proven necessary for the maintenance of a system only if the boundaries of the system, the state in which it tends to maintain itself, the functions necessary for its maintenance, and alternative processes by which these functions could be carried out were empirically specified—conditions, he concluded, that could be met in organisms but not in societies.

Habermas insists that societal goal states and boundaries cannot be determined apart from the understanding of social agents who inhabit them. Societies are not spatially bounded like organisms, and their goal states—what is "beneficial" to them—cannot be determined by empirical observation alone, but depends on how the agents acting within the system understand and value their way of life. Hence, contra Talcott Parsons, he opts for a *bilevel*, or *dual perspective* approach, to society as combining both a meaningful *lifeworld*, which can best be understood at the *microlevel of (intentional) action theory*, and a mediated *system*, which can best be understood at the *macrolevel of (unintentional) structural effects*. Following Parsons, he notes that structures that are functional for some ends (groups) may be dysfunctional for others, that structural changes may enhance rather than threaten system performance, and that institutional practices may have both latent (invisible) and manifest functions (*OLSS* 85–88, 187–89).

Critical theories of society show how lifeworld and system dialectically complement and oppose each other. For example, Marx's critique of political economy contained in *Capital* (1867), which Habermas and other critical theorists regard as the prototype of critical social theory, begins by describing how economic agents enter into a contractual exchange of commodities under the mutual understanding that, as free and equal parties, their agreement is just and advances the genuine happiness of all. It then shows, by way of functionalist explanation, how the aggregate effects of these intentional actions, unintended by the actors themselves, produce a market system. This system then reinforces (or sustains) contractual (commodity) exchange relationships in a feedback loop, without the contractors themselves being aware of this causal effect on their conscious (and by their accounts, fully voluntary) behavior. The feedback from the system, however, is nonetheless felt by the contractors as a form of self-alienation (alienation from their own understanding of themselves as free subjects). Furthermore, a more direct consequence of this feedback— the growing inequality in wealth and power between capitalists and workers, the latter's impoverishment, subsumption under the dehumanizing conditions of mechanized production, and decreasing self-esteem—is causally connected to systemic crises of overproduction. Criticizing this injustice depends on workers "internalizing" the contradiction between this crisis and their own identity crisis, experienced as a contradiction between their self-understanding as active, productive "equals" engaged in mutual wealth maximization and their felt helplessness, unproductivity, dehumanization, impoverishment, and lack of self-esteem (*LC* 1–7; *TCA* 2 338). Marx explains the systemic crisis of overproduction in terms of the unequal distribution of society's surplus product and the replacement of workers by competitive labor-saving technologies. The tendential decline in the number of workers and labor hours (the source of profit), and therewith the tendential decline in the rate of profit, combined with the technical organization of workers, generates unemployment, underconsumption, economic stagnation, as well as revolutionary worker solidarity. Critical theory can conceptualize this social crisis as a combined system/identity crisis thanks to its interpretative-(causal) explanatory methodology (see table 9). Ultimately, resolving this dual crisis requires a revolutionary transition to a more *progressive* system with fundamentally more harmonious structures and goal states that are compatible with human, lifeworld aspirations (see chapter 10).

Habermas uses the lifeworld/system distinction in four ways. First, he uses it to distinguish between institutions whose members relate to one another through the normative medium of communicative action and institutions whose members relate to one another through the "norm-free sociality" of strategic action (*TCA* 2 114). Following this reading, family and public sphere fall within the lifeworld, while business and government fall within the system. This way of putting the distinction, however, is misleading, since businesses and government bureaucracies, markets and law-enforcement agencies, also rely on communicative action to coordinate their internal and external transactions (and, conversely, it may be argued that families and mass-mediated publics rely on strategic media of money and power in coordinating their internal and external transactions) (see Honneth, *The Critique of Power;* and McCarthy, *The Critical Theory of Jürgen Habermas*). Second, Habermas uses the distinction to designate distinctive contributions to the reproduction of society, with the lifeworld contributing "symbolic reproduction" (i.e., the education of children, the creation and transmission of cultural meaning and knowledge, the generation of public opinion, and the coordination of action by means of commonly accepted norms) and the system contributing "material reproduction" (the organization of economic production and distribution, the maintenance of security, etc.) (*TCA* 2 140–52, 232) This distinction, too, is misleading, since families directly contribute to the reproduction of labor power (most obviously through child rearing) while economy and state generate publicity and propaganda while reinforcing ideologies (see Fraser, "What's Critical about Critical Theory"). Third, Habermas uses the distinction to designate different perspectives—inner and outer—that any social institution can be said to manifest. We can, for instance, regard law from the inside, from the perspective of those who relate to it as something normatively meaningful. Or we can regard it from the outside, from the perspective of the social scientist who observes law as a self-regulating system possessing its own unique code for interpreting its environments and its own unique power medium for

Table 9
Marx's functionalist explanation of social crisis in capitalist society
Key:
$\downarrow\uparrow$ = Functional (causal) pathways

	Sociological Explication	Coordinating/Integrating Mechanism		Crisis
System	Empirical description	Market structure Law (imperative) of competition, accumulation, supply and demand, technological substitution of labor, economic inequality, and hierarchy		Overproduction Unemployment, declining wages (buying power) relative to productive capacity and investment capital
	Functional explanation	Function $\uparrow\uparrow\uparrow\uparrow$ Unintended action effects	Function Intended feedback loop $\downarrow\downarrow\downarrow\downarrow$	Revolution
Lifeworld	Interpretative description	Contractual relationships Presumed voluntary communicative action between equals; justice as an exchange of equal values for mutual advantage; wealth as happiness		Alienation Poverty, lack of self-esteem, unfreedom, and objectification

influencing events in those environments. Fourth, the distinction designates a methodological distinction between understanding and causal explanation.

In *Between Facts and Norms* Habermas delivers his most trenchant critique of systems theory, with Niklas Luhmann as his chief target. Habermas has been fascinated with and repulsed by Luhmann's *functional structuralist* approach dating back to their debate in the 1970s. Unlike Parson's *structural functionalist* approach, Luhmann's reduces all normative social structures to adaptive ones; namely, he reduces the lifeworld to a subsystem, and meaning, validity, and truth to the functional simplification of environmental complexity, the selection of environmental inputs according to binary codes and the achievement of social stability, respectively. Luhmann's demotion of the political system to an environment of the administrative system (which filters and selectively interprets public opinion according to its planning agenda) reflects his idea that true systems are "autopoetic," or self-contained and self-regulating vis-à-vis their environments. The legal system, too, "interfaces" with many environments—each of which can be described as a system in its own right (the economic system, the political system, the educational system, etc.). The legal system also contains subsystems that relate to one another as environments (e.g., the federal system and the state system, the system of family law and the system of property law, etc.).

But how can a legal system interact with another system that does not share its code? Events in the economic system are coded in terms of money; those in the legal system in terms of government-sanctioned performances. So what appears in the economic system as a transfer of money from father to son appears in the legal system as a will setting up a trust. Each system registers the effects of the other only by processing them according to its own program. This becomes problematic whenever subsystems come into conflict. For example, the legal system can only register acts of civil disobedience as illegal. However, from the perspective of the political system, these acts can be registered as legitimate. In Habermas's opinion, resolving this intersystemic coordination problem requires both experts from within these systems as well as lay persons who speak to one another in common, uncoded language. The lifeworld—not the administration—thus remains the coordination medium of last resort (*BFN* 43–54). Related to the coordination problem is the problem of system overloading (internal complexity complicates the selection of inputs) and the problem of distinguishing structural changes that indicate the emergence of a new system from adaptive changes that do not. See J. Habermas (with N. Luhmann), *Theorie der Gesellschaft oder Sozialtechnologie—Was Leistet die Systemforschung?* (Frankfurt: Suhrkamp, 1971); N. Luhmann, *A Sociology of Law*, ed. M. Albrow, trans. E. King and M. Albrow (London: Routledge, 1985) and Luhmann, "Some Problems with Reflexive Law," in *State, Law, Economy, as Autopoetic Systems: Regulation and Autonomy in a New Perspective*, ed. A. Febbrajo and G. Teubner (Milan: D. A. Giuffre Editore, 1992), 389–416; N. Fraser, "What's Critical about Critical Theory?" in *Critical Theory: The Essential Readings,* ed. D. Ingram and J. Simon (New York: Paragon House, 1991), 357–87; T. McCarthy, "Complexity and Democracy, or the Seducements of Systems Theory," in *Communicative Action: Essays on Jurgen Habermas's The Theory of Communicative Action,* ed. A. Honneth and H. Joas (Cambridge: MIT Press, 1991), 119–39; A. Honneth, *The Critique of Power* (Cambridge: MIT Press, 1991), chap. 9; E. Nagel, *The Structure of Science: Problems in the Logic of Scientific Explanation* (New York: Columbia University Press, 1961, 421–22, 527–28; J. Elster, *Explaining Technical Change* (Cambridge: Cambridge University Press, 1983), 57. For a more detailed discussion of Habermas and his relationship to Parsons and Luhmann, see T. McCarthy, *The Critical Theory of Jürgen Habermas* (Cambridge: MIT Press, 1978), 213–32; and D. Ingram, *Habermas and the Dialectic of Reason* (New Haven: Yale University Press, 1987), esp. chap. 9. For a more detailed discussion of functional explanations in sociology, see J. Bohman, *New Philosophy of Social Science: Problems of Indeterminacy* (Cambridge: MIT Press, 1991).

Index

abortion, 117, 139, 142, 146, 223, 228, 230–31
Ackerman, Bruce, 126, 209, 219–20
action, 23, 26–27, 35, 37–38n5, 39–40, 41n7, 46–50, 52, 57, 63, 67, 69, 70n6, 83, 85–87, 99–101, 115, 119, 121n2, 123–24, 136n21, 138, 151, 154, 163, 167, 189, 194n2, 206–7, 345–46; covering law and teleological theories of, 39, 67, 265, 329–30, 332; types of, 46, 60, 81, 92, 331–32
Adorno, Theodor Wiesengrund, 4–9, 17–18, 24–25, 34–35, 37, 39, 143, 268, 318
aesthetic judgment, 140n24, 319, 326–28
Alcoff, Linda, 58, 101
Alexy, Robert, 133–34
alienation, 6, 30–31, 43, 56, 60, 272, 275–76, 283, 305, 310, 312, 319, 322, 346, 348. *See also* lifeworld: colonization of
anomie, 272
Apel, Karl-Otto, 9, 74, 103, 131, 136–37, 167, 264–65
Aquinas, Thomas. *See* Thomas Aquinas
Arendt, Hannah, 4, 143, 157, 194–95, 325, 328n15
argumentation, 34, 102, 130, 132–34, 147–49, 151, 255, 328; and abductive inference, 136n21; cogency of, 133, 137, 147–50; formal versus informal

(substantive), 133n19, 134–35, 137, 138n23, 147–48; and inductive inference, 147; and logic/rhetoric distinction, 133–34, 147–49; moral, 110, 122n4, 129, 146, 178, 185; rules of, 90, 132–34, 136n21, 154, 167; in science, 133n19, 147; transcendental, 28, 136–37, 153
Aristotle, 133, 148, 157
Arrow, Kenneth, 342
art, 42, 78n16, 85n19, 140n24, 272, 315, 317–19, 323–28
Audi, Robert, 223
Austin, J. L., 72, 79, 85, 92
autonomy, 53, 55, 62, 111–12, 123, 136–37n22, 144, 165, 189, 193, 194–95n3, 198, 232n19, 257–59, 264, 272, 291, 307–8, 310–11, 325, 340; private versus public, 170–71, 190, 201, 212–13, 215, 230
Ayer, A. J., 128

Bangkok Declaration, 184n23
Barry, Brian, 159, 236, 243
Basic Law (German), 10, 236, 244, 245n36
Baudrillard, Jean, 58
Beitz, Charles, 161, 182
Benhabib, Seyla, 117, 121, 133, 182–83, 245–50, 283

Benjamin, Walter, 318, 324–25
Bentham, Jeremy, 287
Bohman, James, 283
Brandom, Robert, 71n7, 78, 96, 112–13, 335–38
Bühler, Karl, 72, 77–78

capitalism, 2, 5–6, 13–14, 17, 26, 29–30, 42, 43–44n15, 54, 56, 57n28, 64, 153, 164, 167, 172, 182–83, 187, 212, 250, 261–63, 291, 303, 305, 308–9, 312, 316, 320, 330; and class stratification, 5, 43, 164; crisis tendencies of, 30, 153, 164, 261–62, 267–86, 346–48; and Great Depression, 269; late (welfare), 14–15, 65, 153, 269–86; and recession of 2008, 284
care ethics, 28, 121, 141–42
Carens, Joseph, 245–46
causality, 19–23, 47–48, 84, 100–101, 123, 309n3, 346, 348
Chambers, Simone, 160
Chomsky, Noam, 74–76, 78
Cicero, 287
civil disobedience, 217, 229n13, 258
civil society, 30, 70, 165, 197–98, 201–3, 204–5n12, 214, 216, 237, 246, 256–58, 301
collective bargaining, 165, 179–81, 196–97, 216, 270
collective consciousness (conscience), 56, 321
communication, 1–4, 8–9, 11, 15, 27–28, 37–38n5, 43, 50–55, 58, 65–66, 71–73, 75–76, 83, 84n19, 87, 89–91, 93, 94n27, 95, 99–100n3, 110, 112, 118, 135n20, 136–37n22, 145, 180, 198, 201n9, 204–5n12, 211n22, 236, 241–43, 248, 254–58, 263, 284, 297, 327–28, 340; distorted, 7, 65–66, 87, 272; three-tiered model of, 98, 148; types of, 52
communicative action, 8–9, 26–28, 30, 46, 48n18, 52–53, 60–61, 63–64, 67, 71n8, 84–86, 93, 118, 131, 136n22, 137–38, 145n29, 154, 167, 173, 190, 214, 243, 261–62, 267, 272–74, 290, 308, 321, 332; and strategic action, 83, 273, 280, 283, 308, 332; weak and strong, 85, 87–88, 228, 336–38
communism, 4–6, 17, 42, 57n28, 312
communitarianism, 117–18, 182n19, 201, 245, 247, 259
complexity. See under system
Comte, Auguste, 34

Condorcet, Marquis de, 341
consensus, 28–29, 46, 49n21, 53–54, 65, 74, 89–90, 93, 103, 110, 126, 130, 132, 138, 148, 150, 151n40, 155, 166, 178, 184, 187n25, 188–89, 204, 209–10, 216, 227n12, 261, 274, 291–92, 300, 303, 338; and compromise, 8, 122, 125n5, 126, 132, 133n19, 140, 143, 146, 150, 167, 190, 195–97, 199, 202, 205, 209, 255, 302–3
Constitution, American, 174–75, 194
Constitution, French, 175, 194
constitutional patriotism, 10, 246
contextualism, 35, 38, 91, 94, 100, 101n4, 111–12, 331–33. See also realism
Cooke, Maeve, 228
cosmopolitan order (tri-level), 29–99, 30–5
crisis, 8, 219–20, 255; economic, 253, 269, 284, 346–48; identity, 16, 267, 271, 346–48; legitimation, 30, 269–70, 284; motivation, 269–72; rationality, 269–70
Critical Legal Studies (CLS), 213n23, 291, 302
critical theory, 5–6, 8, 13–15, 18, 27, 41n7, 43, 56, 67, 91, 94, 111, 115, 147, 151, 324; first-generation, 12–15, 30, 64, 189, 258, 282–83, 305, 310, 316, 320, 323; third generation, 282–83
critique, 15–16, 45, 57n28, 68, 130, 143, 157, 188–89, 203, 215, 324; internal and external, 12–13, 60, 64. See also ideology: critique of
culture, 2, 6, 9–10, 23, 64, 100, 121n2, 125n5, 182, 201, 222–23, 235–43, 246–47, 250, 253, 257; differentiation of, 314; and elite sub-cultures, 2, 277–78; and identity, 52, 180, 182n19, 235–42, 244, 246–47; impoverishment of, 65, 272–73, 275, 277–83, 285; and meaning, 180, 183, 235, 272, 274; preservation of, 238–42, 270; and value spheres, 272, 282, 305, 316–17

Dahl, Robert, 197, 325n31
Danto, Arthur, 330
Davidson, Donald, 36, 57, 99–100, 104
democracy, 1–3, 6, 8, 11, 27n30, 29–30, 54, 58, 138n23, 153, 155–57, 159, 161, 166–70, 174–75, 186, 190–93, 198, 204, 209, 210n19, 212, 214–16, 219, 221, 226, 249n45, 251, 253–54, 267–69, 282, 284, 291, 300–301, 307, 316; deliberative, 29–30, 155–61, 189, 191, 215, 217–18, 255–58, 305, 308–9, 343;

discourse theoretic concept of, 26, 216, 253, 255, 290; economic, 255; formal, 188, 194n3; global, 30, 249n45, 292–94, 298, 301, 304–5; justification of, 156–60, 174; liberal paradigm of, 29, 160, 186, 204, 212, 214–15, 224, 259, 295; and majority rule, 120, 156n6, 158–60, 166, 190, 197–98, 208n16; principle of (PD), 167–68, 195–96, 198, 201, 218; proceduralist paradigm of, 26, 29, 157–61, 189, 191, 212, 214, 224–26, 231, 234, 244, 247, 258–60, 265; and rational choice, 156, 343; republican paradigm of, 157, 201, 204, 209, 214–15, 259, 294–95; sluice model of, 204, 216, 256–57, 259; as two-track procedure, 177, 188, 194n3, 197n5, 204, 255–56; workplace, 29, 191n29, 197n5, 259–63, 310n4. *See also* cosmopolitan order; law; rights

democratization, 276, 281, 301–5
Descartes, René, 1, 18–19, 26, 33, 61, 68, 96
Dewey, John, 155–56, 208, 326
differentiation. *See under* culture; lifeworld
Dilthey, Wilhelm, 27, 35, 37, 47, 50–51, 63, 72
discourse, 3, 28, 61, 67, 78n16, 83, 102–3, 111, 112n23, 115, 117–18, 122n4, 125, 126n8, 130–34, 136–37, 139, 146, 149n36, 154, 166–67, 169, 177–78, 180, 183–84, 187–89, 195, 197, 200, 201n9, 202–4, 204–5n12, 206, 210–11, 216–17, 222, 227n11, 228, 229n13, 241, 243, 327, 333; and ideal speech situation, 9, 90, 103, 130–31, 133n19; practical, 28, 87n22, 110, 116, 130, 132, 135; types of, 28, 81, 168, 200, 202–3; theoretical, 28, 130, 135, 180–82, 208
discourse ethics (DE), 9, 26, 28–29, 115, 118, 120–22, 125–27, 133, 137–38, 142, 144–46, 150, 153, 166–67, 193, 198, 207, 216, 247, 249n45; and counterfactual consent, 110, 130, 144–45; discourse principle (D) of, 131–36, 167, 169, 174, 190, 195–97; and justification/application distinction, 121n3, 140–42, 199–200, 210, 250n47
Donnellan, Keith, 106
Dray, William, 329
Dummett, Michael, 74, 77–78, 91
Durkheim, Emile, 312, 314, 320–22, 330, 345
duties, 33, 122–23, 165, 172, 176, 264–65; to animals, 142n25; to the environment, 142n25; negative and positive, 172–73, 187; and rights, 142, 172–73, 177, 184n23, 185–87, 250. *See also* moral theory

Dutschke, Rudi, 8
Dworkin, Andrea, 232–33
Dworkin, Ronald, 178, 208, 211, 213, 217

education. *See under* system
Elster, Jon, 204, 341, 345
emotivism, 34
Enlightenment, 1–4, 9, 17–18, 24, 26, 65, 177, 179; dialectic of, 4, 9, 12, 17–18, 22, 24–27, 30, 63, 68, 71, 305, 308, 320
eugenics, 117, 143–44, 146, 230, 282
European Union (EU), 11, 30, 245n36, 248, 289, 292, 296–301, 303, 305
evolution, 24, 119, 223; and knowledge, 46, 62, 109; natural, 27, 46, 62, 109. *See also* social evolution
existentialism, 3–4, 68, 325
explanation, 33, 37, 45, 47n16, 76, 83, 91, 95n1, 122n4, 132, 162, 166, 168; functional, 346–49; and understanding, 60, 329–33

family, 65, 70n6, 117–18, 136n22, 139, 180, 184n22, 221, 225n8, 231, 241n33, 249n45, 250, 263, 270, 275–77, 279–80, 314; patriarchal, 179–83, 229, 277, 279–80, 282, 285
federalism, 296
Feenberg, Andrew, 43–44, 58, 263–64, 278–83
feminism, 9, 229, 232–35, 277, 324; and pornography, 232–33
feudalism, 13–14, 164, 269, 275
Fichte, Johann Gottfried, 5, 23, 45
Fishkin, James, 256
formal pragmatics. *See* universal pragmatics
Foucault, Michel, 69, 71, 229, 233
Frankfurt Institute for Social Research. *See* Frankfurt School
Frankfurt School, 4–8, 12, 17, 268, 305
Fraser, Nancy, 205, 229, 236, 277, 283
freedom. *See* autonomy
free will/determinism problem, 309, 328
Frege, Gottlob, 72, 77, 104–5
Freud, Sigmund, 6, 55–57, 63, 318

Gadamer, Hans-Georg, 7, 27, 51–52, 57–58, 64, 72–73, 87, 89, 93–94
Galston, William, 238
game theory, 122, 330–32
Gehlen, Arnold, 49

gender, 121, 151n40, 180–81, 183, 221, 229, 231n18, 233–34, 237, 248, 277, 279–80, 282–83, 285

genetic engineering, 9, 28–29, 117, 143–45, 206, 272, 279, 282, 324

Gettier, Edmund, 95–96

Gilligan, Carol, 120–21, 141–42

global domestic policy, 11, 30, 181, 187n25, 292, 294, 296–97, 299, 302, 304

global economic multilaterals (GEMs), 285, 297, 300, 304–5

globalization, 11, 30, 249n45, 265, 267, 283–86, 296

global warming, 126, 150n37, 270, 285, 296, 299, 301, 304

Goldman, Alvin, 95–96n1

Grice, H. P., 77

Grotius, Hugo, 287

Grünbaum, Adolf, 63

Günther, Klaus, 208, 210

Gutmann, Amy, 155, 160

Habermas, Jürgen, biography of, 1–12

Habermas, Jürgen, works by: *Das Absolute und die Geschichte* (dissertation), 4; *Between Facts and Norms*, 29, 142, 154, 158–65, 167–71, 175–78, 184–85, 193–215, 218–19, 229–34, 247, 253–58, 261; "The Hermeneutical Claim to Universality," 64n33, 89–90; *Knowledge and Human Interests*, 6, 27–28, 37–38, 40–41, 44–49, 51, 53, 55, 57–64, 67–70, 109; *Legitimation Crisis*, 16, 30, 153, 197, 269–72, 325; *The Logic of the Social Sciences*, 27, 39–40, 51, 63, 89; "Modernity," 327; *The Philosophical Discourse of Modernity*, 18, 71, 82, 327; *The Structural Transformation of the Public Sphere*, 8, 27, 153, 204–5, 221, 256, 258; *The Theory of Communicative Action*, 8, 30, 35, 58, 64–68, 72, 75, 86–87, 153, 227, 264, 268, 272–78, 283, 320, 322; "Transcendence from Within," 322; "Wahrheitstheorien" ("Theories of Truth"), 130; "Walter Benjamin," 324; "What Is Universal Pragmatics?" 90

Hare, R. M., 128, 134

Hart, H. L., 162, 165, 207, 211, 288–89

Heath, Joseph, 87, 122

Hegel, Georg Wilhelm Friedrich, 5–6, 22–24, 45, 50, 63, 69–71, 73, 100, 133, 205, 265, 318, 326; *Phenomenology of Spirit*, 23, 50, 60, 68, 69n4, 71, 236, 283;

System of Ethical Philosophy and First Philosophy of Mind, 70n6

Heidegger, Martin, 2–4, 7, 31, 42–44, 68, 72–73, 101, 281, 325–26

Heisenberg Principle of Uncertainty (Indeterminacy), 24, 108

Held, David, 249, 284

Hempel, Carl, 39, 329

Herder, Johann Gottfried von, 72

hermeneutics, 27, 50–52, 58, 72–75, 87, 89–91, 93, 103

Hintikka, Jaakko, 131, 136

historians' debate, 9–10

historicism, 37

Hobbes, Thomas, 122, 194, 287–88, 330

Honneth, Axel, 69–71, 137, 143, 191, 233, 236, 280, 283, 309n3

Horkheimer, Max, 4–5, 7–9, 13, 15, 17–18, 24–25, 41, 43, 53, 143, 268

human nature, 7, 28, 34–35, 57n28, 62, 117, 143, 188, 191, 287

Humboldt, Wilhelm von, 72–73

Hume, David, 19–21, 33, 40, 47–48

Husserl, Edmund, 37, 42, 46, 68, 74, 77

idealism, 24n27, 25, 73, 94, 107, 111, 338; German, 23

ideal observer, 68, 125

ideal speech situation. *See under* discourse

identity, 24n27, 25, 31, 50, 52–53, 63, 69, 70n6, 71, 95n1, 104–5, 116–17, 124, 135n20, 139, 145, 174, 180, 205, 214, 219, 224, 226–27, 233–39, 241–47, 249n45, 297–98, 300, 304, 340

identity politics, 229–30, 234–39, 243; and aboriginals, 121n2, 241n33; and Amish, 237, 239–40, 244; and ethnicity, 235n24; and France, 223–24; and Quebec, 235n24, 240–44, 246; and race, 235n24, 237n27, 238n29, 239

ideology, 6–7, 41n8, 43, 54, 60, 62, 64–65, 271–72, 324; critique of, 7, 12, 16, 27, 34, 44, 56, 58, 63–64, 130, 283

immigration, 118, 183n20, 196, 221, 244–49, 284–85, 296, 299, 305. *See also under* law

individualism, 164, 271; methodological, 330

individuation. *See* socialization

interests, 16n24, 34–35, 38–40, 41n8, 50–51, 58, 94, 111–12, 117–20, 122–26, 130, 132–33, 145, 155, 163, 167, 172, 177, 187–88, 194–97, 201n9, 203–5, 208n16, 210, 214, 216–17, 232, 235n24, 243,

245–46n38, 247n40, 249, 257, 290, 292, 341; generalizable, 54, 109, 111, 112n23, 125, 132, 135, 140–41, 189, 199; knowledge constitutive, 46, 58, 62, 67, 109
International Criminal Court (ICC), 30, 177, 188, 288–89, 293–94, 296, 302
international relations, 286–89. *See also* law: cosmopolitan; law: international
intuitionism, 187

Jakobson, Roman, 77–78, 93n27
Jaspers, Karl, 4
Jonas, Hans, 143
Jones, Peter, 158
judicial review, 29, 162, 190, 200, 206–7, 209–10, 215, 217–20; and discourse, 200, 210; and legal interpretation, 200, 206–7, 209, 211, 291. *See also* law
justice, 12–14, 24n27, 46, 53–55, 112n23, 116–17, 120–21, 124, 135n20, 141–42, 158, 160n10, 161–63, 165, 168, 174, 186, 190–91, 196, 207, 210–11, 217–19, 223, 229, 231n18, 236, 238, 245n38, 250, 253–54, 288, 304, 315, 317–18; distributive, 29, 42, 54, 159, 181, 186, 229, 236–37, 259–62, 285, 291, 296–97; procedural, 158, 174; and solidarity, 110n21, 134, 135n20, 136n22, 142, 172, 322

Kant, Immanuel, 6, 9, 17, 74–75, 100, 118, 165, 172, 199, 309, 317, 328; on cosmopolitan law, 249, 286, 295; on knowledge, 18, 20–22, 24, 33, 44–45, 50, 53, 60, 62, 100; on moral duty, 22–23, 25–26, 63, 69, 110–12, 116, 122–25, 134, 137, 140, 200, 264–65
Kelsen, Hans, 207
Khatami, Mohammad, 12
Kierkegaard, Søren, 4, 228, 325
Kirchheimer, Otto, 275
Kittay, Eva, 232
knowledge, 1–2, 8, 20, 22–23, 25–28, 33–36, 38–40, 43–44, 47–49, 57, 60–62, 68–69, 71, 75–76, 83, 86–87, 92–96, 99–101, 104, 115, 148–49, 153, 157, 163, 207, 209, 211n22, 225, 240n31, 242, 318; and discourse, 61, 67, 80, 87, 98, 109, 111, 137, 140; and early modern philosophy, 63, 68, 96; foundational theory of, 96–97; and Gettier's paradox, 95–96n1; and human interests, 41, 44, 50, 58, 67, 109; and naturalism, 99–101, 109; philosophical, 22, 63; and reflection, 45,

63; subject-object paradigm of, 19, 26, 61, 63, 97, 99; and transcendentalism, 19, 33, 46, 67, 100–101, 338. *See also* science; truth
Kohlberg, Lawrence, 28, 119–21, 138
Koskenniemi, Martti, 291
Kripke, Saul, 106, 108
Kuhn, Thomas, 41, 47n16, 61, 219n26
Kymlicka, Will, 182, 235, 240, 246

labor, 37–38n5, 43, 56–57, 63, 70, 164, 179–82, 196, 203, 204–5n12, 212, 232, 240n31, 245, 261, 269–70, 282; division of, 30, 43, 62, 147, 229, 231n18, 261, 272–73, 275, 277, 279–81, 283–85, 303, 311–14
Lafont, Cristina, 90, 92, 96, 103–4, 109, 112, 122, 145, 187, 227–28, 338
language, 1, 38, 51–53, 55n25, 58n30, 67, 70n6, 71–77, 80n18, 83, 85, 87, 89–93, 95, 97, 99n3, 101, 102n5, 113, 128, 130, 136n21, 136–37n22, 138–39, 143, 176, 189, 224, 227n11, 228, 238–41, 243, 246, 248, 320n11, 327–28; evolution of, 65n34, 320–23; functions of, 72–73, 77, 84; theories of, 39, 72, 100–101, 104, 111. *See also* linguistics; meaning; speech
Larmore, Charles, 126
Lasch, Christopher, 276
Latour, Bruno, 58, 282
law, 1, 14, 25, 34, 70, 119–20, 122, 139, 146, 153–56, 161–70, 174–75, 177–79, 190, 193–94, 196–97, 200, 204–5, 207–12, 216–19, 222, 223n4, 224, 231, 234–36, 241, 248, 250n47, 272, 315, 317–18; civil, 225n8, 275; constitutional, 11, 159, 161, 165, 170, 175, 178–79, 206, 219, 274; cosmopolitan, 30, 175, 179, 185, 188, 286, 289, 302–3; cosmopolitan order of, 188, 286–305; evolution of, 163, 315–16; and gender, 221, 229, 231–34, 240; immigration, 199, 221, 245–48, 250, 260, 299; international, 175, 179, 286–97, 301–4; and juridification, 275–76, 316; labor, 179, 231–32, 276, 279–80; liberal paradigm of, 29, 207, 212–15, 220, 231, 233, 237, 245, 259, 291, 303; modern, 119, 164, 168–70, 178–79; proceduralist paradigm of, 26, 29, 213–14, 220–21, 233, 237, 248, 251, 259, 267; regulatory, 205, 269; religious, 163, 225n8; rule of, 123, 159, 165, 167, 168, 175, 178n17, 200, 211,

law, *(continued)*
    276, 286–87, 289–94, 301–2; social, 231,
    276; sociological genesis of, 161, 163,
    287–88; tribal, 163, 240n32; welfare
    paradigm of, 29, 205, 212–15, 220, 231,
    233, 236–37, 245, 259, 291, 303. *See
    also* civil disobedience; collective bargain-
    ing; democracy; judicial review; natural
    law theory; positivism; rights
League of Nations, 286, 288
learning, 60, 69, 73, 76n12, 98, 101, 102n5,
    103–4, 108–10, 119, 166, 175, 188,
    219, 239, 242, 298, 312, 318, 320n11,
    323, 339–40
legal form (LF), 167–69, 173, 190, 207
legality, 165, 197, 200, 287–89; and legitimacy,
    165, 174–75, 178, 193, 195, 197, 199,
    207, 209, 211
legitimation, 5, 11, 54, 151, 164, 167–68,
    184n23, 247n40
legitimation crisis. *See under* crisis
Lévi-Strauss, Claude, 332
liberalism, 4, 8, 117, 165–66, 239; political,
    5, 124–25n5, 189, 222–23, 245n38; and
    republicanism, 166, 168, 294–96
lifeworld, 9, 26, 31, 69, 73, 95, 112–13, 118,
    136n22, 204–5n12, 310–16, 324–25,
    327, 347–48; colonization of, 65,
    271–77, 319; differentiation of, 31, 274,
    314–16, 326, 340; as implicit back-
    ground, 73–74, 81, 93; rationalization
    of, 267–68, 274, 278, 314–16, 319–23;
    technicization of, 278–83. *See also under*
    system
linguistics (structural), 55n25, 73–76
linguistification of the sacred, 314, 320–23
literary criticism, 78n16, 85n19
literature, 84n19, 227n11
Locke, John, 165, 185, 194, 205
Lorenzer, Alfred, 55n25
Luhmann, Niklas, 255, 278, 348–49
Lukács, Georg, 6, 18, 143, 278
Lyotard, Jean-François, 2, 24, 201

MacIntyre, Alasdair, 104
MacKinnon, Catharine, 232, 233n21
Marcuse, Herbert, 5–6, 8, 42–44, 57, 263,
    318–19
market economies, 14, 17, 54, 122, 179,
    184n23, 214, 253, 258, 261–62, 268–69,
    273–77, 282, 297, 300, 307, 330
Marshall, T. H., 171

Marx, Karl, 4–7, 12–14, 23–24, 37–38, 44,
    56–57, 62–64, 69–70, 205, 268–70, 275,
    278, 282–83, 310–12, 316, 322, 346–48
Marxism, 4–6, 261–62, 324
mass media, 153, 256–58, 270, 284
McCarthy, Thomas, 62–63, 120, 137, 283
McCormick, John, 304n29, 305, 316n8
Mead, George Herbert, 28, 309n3, 320n11, 340
meaning, 14, 26–28, 30, 35–39, 41–42,
    43–44n15, 48, 50–52, 55, 58, 60, 65n34,
    67, 70n6, 71–73, 75, 77–79, 81, 83, 87,
    89–94, 99, 101, 104–7, 112–13, 115,
    120n2, 137–38, 146–47, 149, 151, 156,
    160, 164, 166, 176, 178–79, 188, 211–12,
    213n23, 217, 226, 227n11, 230, 232,
    235, 280, 305, 316, 322, 325–26, 320n11,
    336–38; illocutionary, 79–81, 84n19,
    85–87, 90–93; literal, 91–93; locutionary,
    79, 81, 90–91, 93; perlocutionary, 30, 81,
    85–86, 93; and reference/sense distinction,
    52, 104; verificationist theory of, 36–37,
    50, 78, 99. *See also under* culture
Meinong, Alexius, 105
metaphor, 84–85n19, 216, 321–22, 326–28
Mill, James, 156
Mill, John Stuart, 121, 130, 155–56, 204,
    230, 245
Minow, Martha, 229, 231
modernity, 9, 18, 40, 167, 227n9, 261, 267,
    274, 281, 305, 307–10, 316, 328; theory
    of, 75, 281–82, 307–10
modernization, 65, 263, 268, 272, 274–75,
    282, 307, 316, 320. *See also* rationaliza-
    tion; social evolution
Moore, G. E., 127
moral development, 8, 28, 55, 76, 119–20,
    121n2, 138n23, 315–16; stages of, 55,
    119, 340
morality, 9, 20, 22–23, 25, 28, 34–35, 41–42,
    46, 71, 109, 119, 121, 123–24, 125n5,
    138, 153, 164, 196, 225–27, 265, 274,
    287, 312, 316, 323, 328; and ethics, 26,
    85n19, 118, 139, 146; and law, 94, 120,
    139, 146, 154, 162–63, 165, 168, 178,
    185, 188, 211
moral relativism, 13, 92, 331
moral skepticism, 28, 33, 44–45, 92, 115,
    127–29, 316, 331
moral theory, 120–24, 132, 142; deontologi-
    cal, 120–23, 171; discourse ethical, 28,
    115, 118, 120–22, 132; duties, 115, 122,
    172, 264–65; emotivism, 128–29; ideal

observer, 127; intuitionism, 127, 187; Kantian, 22–23, 118, 123–24, 171–72, 317; prescriptivism, 128–29, 190; social contract theory, 120–22, 124, 126; utilitarian, 120–22, 124, 318. *See also* care ethics

multiculturalism, 2, 221, 234–36, 238–39, 243, 263–64, 294, 298, 303, 324. *See also* identity politics

myth, 97, 321, 324, 332

Nagel, Ernest, 346
nationalism, 10, 295, 298
natural law theory, 162, 165, 170, 287, 318, 322
Neblo, Michael, 256
neo-Aristotelianism, 138, 191
neo-liberalism, 183–84, 285, 297, 300, 303
Nietzsche, Friedrich, 9, 24–25, 41–42, 319
nominalism, 96–97, 108
nongovernmental organizations (NGOs), 257, 296, 301, 303, 305
Nussbaum, Martha, 188–91, 231, 234, 240

objectivism, 33–34, 37, 40–41, 44, 78, 87
Ohmann, Richard, 84
Okin, Susan Moller, 231, 234

Parsons, Talcott, 273, 346, 348
patriotism, 298
Peirce, Charles Sanders, 27, 47–49, 63, 99, 103, 130n14, 136n21, 148, 340
performative contradiction, 131, 136–37
perlocutionary effect. *See under* meaning
Peters, Bernhard, 197, 204, 256–57
philosophy, 3, 6, 11, 17–18, 22, 24n27, 25–26, 33, 35–36, 38–42, 44, 53, 63, 68–69, 72–73, 75, 78, 84n19, 95–96, 99, 118, 123, 128, 136n22, 137, 161, 175, 227–28, 328; of consciousness (subject-centered), 63–64, 68, 70, 96, 166; of history, 27, 64; Jewish, 4; transcendental, 9, 45, 60, 63, 75
Piaget, Jean, 28, 119–20, 339–40
Pippin, Robert, 71
Plato, 3, 15, 42, 72, 95–96, 218, 228
pluralism, 164, 198, 204, 214, 223, 225n8, 228, 254, 305
Pogge, Thomas, 182–83, 186, 246
politics, 34, 146, 153–54, 187n25, 230, 243–44, 255–59, 263; and privatism, 271
Popper, Karl, 27, 34–35, 37–39, 46–47, 63–64, 134, 323

positivism, 34, 41, 45, 48n17, 57, 67, 87, 128; legal, 162, 170, 207
positivist debate, 27, 35
postmodernism, 2, 9, 22n26, 24
power, 24, 29, 41–43, 54, 58, 65n34, 66, 122, 126, 136–37n22, 145–47, 149, 151, 158n8, 161, 163–65, 167, 194, 196–97, 200, 212, 217, 254, 271, 305; administrative, 29, 149, 161, 163, 194–95, 197–98, 201–3, 216, 253, 268, 273; communicative, 29, 85–86, 194–95, 197–98, 201–5, 253–54, 294; constitutional flow of, 197, 202–3, 215–16, 253–55, 257, 259, 285; constitutional separation of, 197, 200–201, 206, 295, 297; social, 27, 29, 149, 163, 197–98, 201–3, 209, 216, 253, 255–58, 267; as steering medium, 263–64, 273, 275, 280–81, 296
practical reason, 6, 22, 26, 116–17, 311n5; types of, 317
pragmatism, 47, 101, 208n16, 290
Pratt, Mary, 84
preimplantation genetic diagnosis, 117, 144, 145n31
prescriptivism, 128–29, 159–60, 190
Protestant work ethic, 17, 164, 271, 330
psychoanalytic theory, 7, 27, 39–40, 54–58, 60, 63, 67, 318
psychology, 35–36, 147–48, 318
public opinion, 29–30, 153, 156n2, 178–79, 194–95, 198, 200–201, 203–4, 204–5n12, 210, 216, 248, 254, 256–59, 295, 297, 301
public sphere, 29, 65, 153, 168, 178, 194–95n3, 197–98, 201, 204–5, 210, 214, 216, 221–22, 226, 254–59, 261, 264, 270, 276, 282, 292, 294, 303–5, 322; structural transformation of, 153
Pufendorf, Samuel, 287
Putnam, Hilary, 101–4, 107–8, 110

Quine, W. V. O., 99–100

rational choice theory, 258, 330, 341–43. *See also* game theory
rationality. *See* reason
rationalization, selective, 319–20, 323. *See also* lifeworld
rationalization complexes, 30, 315, 317–20, 327
rational reconstruction, 76
Ratzinger, Joseph (Cardinal, later Pope Benedict XVI), 1

Rawls, John, 28, 124–27, 159, 178, 181–84, 186, 188–91, 217, 222–24, 227–28, 229–31, 238, 245–46, 251, 291, 307, 341

realism, 28, 94, 108, 111–12, 208n16, 213n23; internal, 101, 112, 335; moral, 28, 109–12, 127–28, 187, 189, 338

reason, 2, 4, 8, 12, 20–25, 28, 31, 33, 38, 41, 44, 46, 94, 109, 118, 123, 129, 165, 214, 221–28, 318, 331; aesthetic, 18, 31, 84, 319, 323–28; analytic, 18, 68, 325–26; communicative, 18, 26, 31, 61–62, 83–84, 168, 172, 268, 270, 332–33; dialectical, 69, 311, 326; discursive, 61, 83–84, 113, 268, 323; formal, 323; functional, 9, 84, 268; instrumental, 18, 25, 61–62, 116, 122, 268–69, 283, 308, 311, 331; in Kant's philosophy, 9, 20, 22–23, 33, 118, 123, 165, 309; roots of, 84; transcendental, 16, 21, 33. See also knowledge; practical reason; science; technology

recognition, 40, 50, 70, 71n7, 86, 117, 134–35, 137, 156, 162, 180, 229, 233, 235–37, 241–44, 246, 280, 283. See also identity politics; justice: distributive

Rehg, William, 130n14, 132–33, 136n21, 148–51

reification, 94n27, 143n27. See also alienation

religion, 36, 62, 126, 164, 180, 221–22, 224n5, 225, 227, 230, 237, 305; and reason, 118–19, 126, 136–37n22, 222, 226–28, 248, 310, 319; and secularization, 259, 300, 305, 320–23; as source of ethical motivation, 126, 139; and state, 126, 208, 221–22, 259, 302, 324

religious fundamentalism, 2, 65, 222, 317

republicanism. See under liberalism

revolution, 36–37, 49, 259; American, 295; French, 295; scientific, 41n8, 103

Rhodes, Deborah, 234

rights, 2, 5, 11–12, 29, 70, 116–18, 120, 124, 135n20, 136n21, 142–43, 145–46, 158n8, 159–62, 164–75, 178–79, 187, 190–94, 200, 206–9, 211–16, 218, 222, 224n6, 225n8, 229–34, 237–38, 240–41, 244–45, 247, 249, 255, 259–60, 287–89, 314, 316, 318, 322; aspirational versus claim, 176–79; civil, 29, 171, 174, 184n23, 185–87, 188n26, 209n17, 217n24, 238, 240n31, 249n45; to citizenship, 169, 185, 241n33, 245, 249n44; classical (liberal), 166, 176–79, 182n19, 183–87, 188n26, 190, 215, 220, 237, 245–46n38, 302; constitutional, 142, 168, 170, 174,

185, 202, 214, 219, 274, 295; cultural, 182n19, 184–85, 234–35, 237, 243; to due process, 169, 185; group-based, 29, 182n19, 234–35, 237–39, 241–42, 244, 260; human, 2, 11, 30, 65, 110, 146, 160–61, 166, 167n13, 169–71, 173, 175–89, 201n9, 237–38, 245n38, 246–47, 249n45, 251, 265, 286, 291–96, 299, 301–4; institutional versus interactional, 180–83; juridicial conception of, 169–70, 175, 177, 179, 181, 185–86; political, 29, 160, 168–71, 174, 176, 182n19, 184–87, 188n26, 201n9, 207, 209n17, 214, 217n24, 249n45, 302; positive and negative, 169, 171–73, 177, 207, 214–15; property, 70n6, 122, 171, 173, 177, 184n23, 185–87, 190, 194, 208n16, 213n23; social, 168–71, 184–86, 207, 214, 249n45; subjective, 169–70, 198, 212; subsistence, 29, 170, 172–73, 176–77, 179–80, 181n19, 183–87, 188n26, 189–90, 196; system of, 169–70, 174, 190, 207, 219; welfare, 29, 170–71, 190, 208, 220, 230, 237, 300; women's, 139, 179–83, 223, 229–34, 282. See also duties; Universal Declaration of Human Rights

Riker, William, 342

Rorty, Richard, 2, 58, 102, 156

Rousseau, Jean-Jacques, 8, 156, 166, 194, 198–201

Russell, Bertrand, 72, 105–7

Sartre, Jean-Paul, 3–4

Saussure, Ferdinand, 74–75

Scanlon, Thomas, 125

Schelling, Friedrich Wilhelm Joseph von, 4–5, 23, 31

Schiller, Friedrich, 327–28

Schmitt, Carl, 8, 178, 199–200

Schopenhauer, Arthur, 24

Schroeder, Gerhard (Chancellor), 1

Schumpeter, Joseph, 255, 341

Schweickart, David, 182, 262

science, 1–2, 6, 14, 20, 22–23, 27, 33–35, 37, 41–44, 46, 50–51, 54, 57–58, 60–61, 70, 73, 75, 84n19, 107–8, 133n19, 136n22, 143n27, 145–48, 150, 208n16, 219n26, 222–23, 225–26, 227n11, 311, 315, 317–18, 322–23, 325, 328; empirical-analytic, 33, 45, 60; hermeneutical-historical, 35, 45–46, 50, 52, 54, 60; natural, 22n26, 27, 35–36, 38, 43,

45–47, 58, 61–62; paradigm shifts in, 28, 61, 109; social, 6, 27, 34–40, 44, 46, 54, 57–58, 269

scientism, 33–34, 37, 41, 45

Searle, John, 79–80, 91–92

secularization. *See* realism

Shue, Henry, 181–82, 186

Singer, Peter, 156

Smith, Adam, 17, 125, 345

social complexity, 253–56, 305, 307, 348–49

social contract theory, 120, 166, 185, 194, 245–46n38, 287, 290–91, 294–95

social evolution, 2, 15, 24, 26–27, 34, 37, 46, 56–57, 62, 109, 138, 163, 263, 310–16, 340; and principles of organization, 14–16

social integration, 154, 161, 270, 279, 299–300

socialism, 5–6, 14, 29, 43, 182n20, 261–62, 281–82, 312. *See also* communism

socialization, 28, 52, 54, 65n34, 70n7, 71, 73, 76, 123, 136–37n22, 145, 244, 270, 272, 274, 280, 320n11, 340

social movements, 8, 257–58, 263–64, 285

social pathologies, 7, 26, 30, 258, 267–85, 319. *See also* crisis; lifeworld: colonization of

social roles, 119–20, 271, 274, 314, 320n11, 340

society, 23–24, 26–27, 36, 38–39, 42, 45, 53, 56–57, 60, 64, 71n7, 74–75, 83, 90, 94, 111, 119–20, 121n2, 123–24, 138, 151n40, 164, 172–73, 176, 178, 183, 185, 187–88, 197–98, 201, 204–5n12, 211–12, 213n23, 214–15, 218, 220n29, 221–22, 223n2, 226, 228n13, 229–30, 231n18, 234, 236–37, 240n31, 244, 245n38, 246, 250, 271; bi-level model of, 188n26, 273, 283; modern, 25, 65, 83, 119, 136n22, 138, 146, 154, 163, 165–66, 211, 261, 307–10, 312; premodern, 65, 118, 136n22, 138, 163, 310, 312, 321, 332; post-secular, 31, 228, 310, 322–25

solidarity, 24, 29, 40, 56, 71n7, 110n21, 121n3, 134–35, 136n22, 162–63, 173, 180–81, 184n23, 187, 195, 214, 246, 258, 285, 296, 298, 300, 303–4, 307, 320–21, 330

speech (acts), 30, 38–39, 60, 64, 70, 72, 75–83, 84n19, 86, 90–93, 99, 113, 130, 138, 146, 157, 174, 177, 185, 194–5n3, 201, 208, 227n11, 228, 233, 320–22; literary, 78n16, 227n11; structure of, 47n16, 73, 75, 105, 110, 324, 355; types

of, 78, 82, 91; and validity claims, 28, 80–82, 85–86, 87n22, 90, 102, 109, 138, 314, 317–18, 326–27, 332

state, 29, 54, 70–71, 164, 177, 180, 185, 193–94, 197–98, 200–201, 204–5n12, 215, 221–22, 224–25, 229, 239n31, 241, 246; global, 292, 294–96, 299; liberal, 214, 240n33, 271; nation, 30, 176n16, 246, 284–85, 287–89, 296–98, 302; sectoral, 303–4; socialist, 271; welfare, 30, 42, 54, 153, 215, 255, 269–85, 298, 301, 303, 316

Stevenson, Charles, 128

Strawson, Peter, 106–7, 128

Stump, D. J., 281

system, 14–16, 24n27, 43, 136n22, 154, 156–57, 162–63, 187, 216–17, 232, 236, 303; administrative, 161, 163, 202–3, 255, 267, 274–77, 282, 349; complexity of, 119, 212, 310, 348–49; counter-steering of, 257; economic, 5, 14, 54, 57n28, 119, 153, 161, 163, 180, 202–3, 212, 229, 253–54, 258, 261–63, 273, 305, 346–47; educational, 254, 263, 270–71, 275–76, 282, 348; legal, 119, 154, 180, 187, 208n16, 210, 217–18, 224n6, 229, 240n33, 241, 253–54, 273–74, 302, 305, 311; and lifeworld, 26, 30, 262–64, 268n1, 273–83, 315, 346–47; political, 54, 153, 349; steering media of, 54, 254, 262–63, 273, 280–81

systems theory, 216, 282, 345–49

Tarski, Alfred, 97–98

Taylor, Charles, 140, 182, 236, 241–42, 307

technocracy, 253–55, 259, 262–64, 304–5

technology, 1, 17, 34, 42–43, 43n15, 50, 57–58, 69, 144, 259, 262–64, 272–73, 278–84, 300, 308, 311, 318, 324–25

terrorism, 66, 173, 284; war on, 31

theory/practice problem, 40, 44, 67

Thomas Aquinas, 287

Thompson, Dennis, 155, 160

Thompson, Paul, 278

Toulmin, Stephen, 129

truth, 26, 28, 36–37, 41, 46–47, 52–53, 61, 63, 67, 73, 79n17, 80–81, 83, 84n19, 85–87, 92, 96–98, 101–3, 106, 109–10, 127–28, 134, 137–39, 141, 147, 150, 172, 216, 223, 227n10, 229n14, 318, 322, 326–27; consensus theory of, 28, 48–49, 94, 103n7, 148; semantic theory of, 74, 78, 97–98, 104–6

Unger, Roberto, 291
United Nations (UN), 11, 30, 176, 188–89,
    249n45, 286, 288–89, 296; Assembly,
    288, 292–94; Charter of, 187n25, 292–95;
    Security Council, 177, 288, 292–95
Universal Declaration of Human Rights
    (UDHR), 176–77, 184, 288, 290
universalizability, 22, 122n4, 124–25, 127,
    129, 131–32, 134, 140; principle of (U),
    111, 123, 125n7, 130–39, 167–68, 317
universal pragmatics, 28, 72, 74–78; cri-
    tique of, 87n22; and transcendental
    philosophy, 74

validity claims. See under speech
Vattel, Emmerich de, 287

Walzer, Michael, 245, 249
Weber, Max, 6, 17, 27, 35–36, 46,
    119, 194, 205, 207, 227n9, 268,
    316–17, 320, 330
Weizsäcker, Carl Friedrich von, 8,
    292
Wellmer, Albrecht, 103, 137,
    326–27
Willke, Helmut, 255
Winch, Peter, 39
Wittgenstein, Ludwig, 27, 36, 38–39, 50–51,
    72–73, 79, 94, 100
Wood, Allen, 86
Wright, Georg von, 309n3, 329–30

Young, Iris Marion, 183, 229–30